Two Hearts in
TANZANIA

DICK AND MARY CABELA'S
HUNTING CHRONICLES II
with David Cabela

Mary Cabela

Dick Cabela

David Cabela

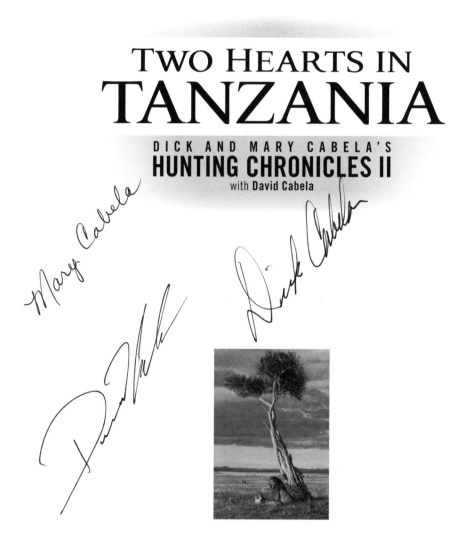

CABELA PUBLISHING, LLC. | 3020 11TH AVENUE, SIDNEY, NE 69162

Cabela Publishing, LLC.

3020 11th Avenue

Sidney, NE 69162

ISBN Number: 978-0-9755544-2-5   Regular Edition

ISBN Number: 978-0-9755544-3-3   Limited Edition

Library of Congress Control Number: 2010927608

Cabela, Dick, Mary & David

  Two Hearts in Tanzania

  Dick and Mary Cabela's Hunting Chronicles II

  with David Cabela

1. Hunting—Africa

2. Hunters—Big Game—Africa

3. Adventure and adventurers—Africa

Writer: David Cabela

Editor: David Draper, Draper Communications

Artwork: John Banovich

Management: Rickard Bailey, P.C.

Book Design: Mark Schuler, ProDesign

Printing: Toppan Printing in China

First Edition

10 9 8 7 6 5 4 3 2 1

ACKNOWLEDGMENTS

Like all worthwhile projects, this book was a team effort. I would like to express my gratitude to all those who helped take this from an idea to a finished product. Rickard Bailey was the glue—he held the entire process together and kept us on a focused track. Mark Schuler took a jumble of pieces and designed them into a perfect fit. John Banovich's sketches added breath to every story. As always, David Draper, like a riverbank, steered the flow of words to their final destination. With her fire for life and her never-quit work ethic, Stacey Peretz held nothing back in her efforts to ensure our success—we are lucky to have her in our corner. Whenever I contacted her with a request, Cari Wamsley worked hard to get me what I needed expeditiously. My sisters, Cari Harvey and Teri Wolff, generously allowed me to scour their journals and helped fill in many details. I am ever thankful to my dear wife, Shari, for believing in me and, by her dedicated love, allowing me to retain perspective.

DAVID CABELA
2010

Dedicated to the memory of our friend.
We miss you, Cotton.

CONTENTS

FOREWORD

When a boy glances across the Nebraska prairie and dreams about the adventure that lies beyond, what does he see? When a girl envisions a world past the skyline of her Wyoming home, what does it look like? Dick and Mary Cabela never quit looking forward and their hearts have taken them to places that far surpassed every image from their young minds.

When they began their journey together, they were still kids with mountains to climb and stars to touch. As they grew, their love deepened until they knew one another so intimately their two hearts became indistinguishable. They shared an innate hunger for adventure; a passion for hunting and animals and untouched land. It allowed them to follow their hearts to places they never even knew existed.

When they founded the "World's Foremost Outfitter" at their kitchen table, they could not have imagined how far the discipline of hard work and determination would allow them to go. Dick and Mary have hunted all over the globe, pursuing creatures that pushed them to the edge of their limits. They have shared camps with people who live the same way their ancestors did hundreds of years ago. They have followed the tracks of buffalo and eland and lions to places few people are lucky enough to see. These things changed the way they would view the world and molded who they would become.

Tanzania took hold of them in ways they never expected. It wrapped around them and held them in a warm embrace as if they had come home after a lifelong absence. What they found in Tanzania were golden sunsets, remarkable people, plants and animals perfected by God, and new friendships that would span generations. Tanzania allowed them to rediscover that part of themselves which lies deep within us all—the part waiting for us to open our hearts and allow ourselves to reconnect. That alone made Tanzania an endless gift.

Not really knowing why, Dick and Mary Cabela began keeping journals to capture moments that would be special far into the future. They never considered these events might later be chronicled in a book. When they finally made that decision—with considerable prodding from family and friends—I was humbled they asked for my assistance. They are two of the most remarkable people I know. The best parts of me come from the sum of these two people. It was my honor to help them put their Tanzania adventures into words.

Their story is about more than adventure. It's a story about two people who love the outdoors, who love being a part of it, and who love exploring it together.

DAVID CABELA
2010

INTRODUCTION

Someone once said that fame and celebrity are fascinating. We are drawn to people who are famous and we want to know about them. I've known Dick and Mary Cabela for more than two decades and am not sure they realize how famous they are. They are two of the most down-to-earth people you would ever want to meet.

My late husband, Cotton, and I have had many wonderful hunting clients during the last forty years. A hunting trip often reveals a person's true character. It wasn't hard to get to know Dick and Mary. And I quickly realized why they are so successful. After they started hunting with Cotton, we formed a strong friendship. It was our good luck. Some of my fondest memories are of our numerous hunts together.

Dick and Mary's success is a tribute to their entire family. Raising nine children and starting a business from their home while Dick was working for his parents are extraordinary accomplishments. Aside from their business achievements, they have hunted on six continents, experiencing what few people have in the hunting world. However, you would never know about their hunting successes unless you asked them. They are truly humble people.

Tanzania is among the finest big-game hunting destinations in the world. Cotton had the privilege of hosting Dick and Mary four times and I had the pleasure of being on three of those safaris. They never pressured Cotton on what to hunt or when. They would simply say, "You're the expert; you tell us," and that's how they started the day. Professional hunters always hunt hard for clients like the Cabelas.

I was in Tanzania when Mary shot her first lion. She was a nervous wreck. Fearful she might not get a clean kill, she told Cotton, "I'm not going to shoot a lion."

Dick was standing behind her and shaking his head up and down, thinking to himself, *yes she will.*

The lion was feeding on a freshly killed gazelle when we spotted him.

"Mary, would you just get your gun out so we can go have a look at him," Cotton said. "He's not going anywhere. We haven't spooked him and he's just lying there resting."

We used a thin brush line to sneak closer.

"Can you see him well?" Cotton asked.

The lion had moved back and was lying down a few feet from his prey. Cotton had seen Mary shoot a number of other animals earlier in the hunt and knew she was ready.

"Do you mind if I take my gun and look at him, too?"

"No, that's fine. He sure is big!" Mary said.

"He's a dandy."

I realized then that Cotton was going to walk her through the shot. Dick stepped back and I sat down with the trackers.

"Now, Mary, I want you to do me a favor. Keep your eye on the lion, but gently push the safety off just as if you were going to shoot."

Mary did what he said. Cotton signaled the tracker to whistle. The lion stood up broadside.

"He's up," Mary said.

"That's fine; he just wants to know what the noise was."

Mary kept the gun steady.

"The lion isn't moving and you've had a good look at him."

"He's bigger than I thought."

"Now very gently squeeze the trigger," Cotton said.

She did everything perfectly and the lion dropped where it stood. It was one of the sweetest scenes I have ever seen. Dick ran over, grabbed her, and kissed her. The trackers started singing and clapping their hands. Mary had the biggest smile on her face.

The driver brought the truck up and we took pictures for the next forty minutes. Then everyone joined in to load the lion and we headed back. As we were approaching camp, everyone including waiters, skinners, and trackers could hear us. They ran down the road to join us in singing and clapping. When Mary stepped out of the truck, one man put her in an armchair and several other men lifted her high above their heads, carrying her into camp. Dick, with a smile all over his face, was snapping pictures. Mary ended that safari by taking three of the Big Five. She went on to hunt all over the world and eventually won the prestigious Diana Award given by Safari Club International. Dick has received the equally prestigious C.J. McElroy Award, named for SCI's founder.

In all of our years hunting, few have impressed us as much as the Cabelas. They are kind and hard-working and courteous to a fault. They have been a great joy in my life and I am honored to call them friends.

JOAN GORDON

2010

ix

PART I
NEW FRIENDS
1992

MAMA'S LION: MARY

"I can't believe it's been two years."

I am not sure if Dick heard me.

Two years. In some ways, it did not seem so long—in others, longer. Two years since we had stood on African soil. It had been Ethiopia then. Now we were on our way to Tanzania.

We thumbed paperbacks and watched an in-flight movie during a restless flight from London to Arusha. Waiting by the carousel after touching down, it became apparent some of our luggage had not made it. Twenty minutes after the last suitcase came through, we were still missing one large bag and four ammunition boxes.

"I am sorry, madam. We will try to find them. Then we will get them to you," a customer representative said from behind a tall counter. She looked past us to the next customer. She hadn't even asked our names.

"Excuse me," Dick said. "In London, they specifically pulled the four missing ammo boxes and asked to go through them. They promised to load the boxes on the plane. Here is the name of the man who helped us. Can you please call him to see what happened?"

"We will contact you when we find your bags, sir." She slid the paper Dick put on the counter out of her way. "Next, please."

"Don't you need our names and contact information?"

The young woman sighed before handing Dick a pad.

We would be lucky if we ever saw our luggage again.

Cotton Gordon and his wife, Joan, picked us up at the airport and whisked us off to a hotel for the night. We had one more hour-long flight first thing in the morning and then a half-hour drive to camp. We would hunt in the afternoon. I slept in short, fitful minutes, dreaming of piercing fangs and razor claws. I couldn't believe I let Dick purchase lion and leopard licenses for me. He reminded me I had done fine with buffalo; that I had done even better with elephant. Didn't

I want to hunt the Big Five? I told myself he talked me into it. I hadn't fought it all that much.

What if I wounded one?

We were in camp for lunch the next day.

"What's the plan?" Dick asked Cotton from across the table.

"You two should rest. We'll go out this afternoon, see what we can find. Let's meet here at three. We'll sight in the rifles first to make sure they didn't get knocked out of whack during travel."

We were in Africa. Golden grass danced in the swirling breeze. Miombo trees congregated at the edges of fields. Giant baobabs, some many miles apart, with bases as big as houses, stretched gnarly, leafless fingers high into an endless blue sky. A tsetse fly stung through my long-sleeve shirt. I slapped it hard; it flew away unharmed. As much as I hated the tsetse fly and its unquenchable, pestering way, I didn't mind that first sting. The pain was proof I was not dreaming. I was in Africa—in Tanzania. If there was such a thing as having a home where you have never lived, never even been to, this was it. I felt as if this place was a part of me—as if it always had been.

"What do you say we shoot some leopard bait?" Cotton asked. "Let's you and I go get an impala."

I grabbed my 7mm, eager for the challenge. We found the ram with a small harem of ewes. He wasn't huge, but respectable. They knew we were there, nervously milling about as we closed the distance. Their eyes darting, necks cocking back and forth, feeling an urge to run. The ram prevented it. Holding them in a tight group, he seemed to think we were a rival ram attempting to steal his harem.

"This is as close as we're going to get," Cotton said.

Cotton Gordon was not a tall man, but he was solid, like a bulldog. He was patient, deliberate, and kind. We fell in love with Cotton and Joan from the start. When not hunting, they lived in Colorado Springs, just a few hours drive from our home in Sidney, Nebraska. Having much in common, conversation flowed easily. But on this stalk, we kept it to a minimum.

"Can you use that tree for a rest?"

"I think so," I said.

"Next time he gets clear of the females, take him."

Pushing the rifle butt snuggly into my shoulder, I found the ram through the scope and centered the crosshairs on his shoulder. A ewe stood behind him.

I stayed on his shoulder, waiting. She wouldn't move. He stared at us. *Move. Come on. Move.*

Not a step.

The gun's weight grew heavy and strained my muscles. I had to lower it.

"Take him now."

Yanking the rifle back up, I found the herd again. The ram had moved to the outside edge, quartering away, but looking back. Trembling, I took the shot.

I missed.

The herd ran a few yards in jumbled confusion. The ram stopped broadside, away from the females.

"He's clear, Mary. Do you have a shot?"

I worked a new bullet into the chamber and squeezed off another shot.

I hit him, but not well.

I wanted to cry. The shaking intensified and the wounded ram was limping away. I fired the final bullet.

Another miss.

Tears welled up while I reloaded. Now we had to move back into range. It didn't take long.

"Take your time. Line up on him and squeeze when you're ready." Cotton was unflappable.

I was nearly frantic.

Calming myself the best I could, I rested the gun inside the crook of a tree, held my breath and fired.

"He's down. Good shot."

"That was horrible," I said.

"No, you did fine, Mary. Just first-day jitters. The next animal will go right down. I know it."

"I'm not sure if I should try for something else."

"I saw you shoot the target. And that last shot, when you were nervous and angry, was a great shot. I'm not worried."

A wounded animal is like a needle in your heart. At least we got him down quickly.

Cotton found a way to take my mind off it. As we drove around spotting, he made a game out of how many different species we could find.

"What's the count up to, Mary?" he asked on our way to check a leopard bait and refresh it with my impala, if need be.

"What's that down there in the ravine?" I asked. I had just seen Peter, the lead tracker, pointing it out to Hillary, Cotton's apprentice hunter.

Cotton told the driver, Durani, to stop. Peering through his binos, Cotton said, "Eastern Bohor reedbuck."

"That makes twenty, then."

We hadn't seen anything great yet.

"We want this one," Cotton said, the binoculars still tight to his eyes. He glanced over his shoulder as I followed him from the vehicle. "Remember, one shot, like I said." Smiling, he turned back toward the goal—reedbuck.

We snuck to the edge of the ravine where we could see the reedbuck feeding on a small patch of short, green grass. He had no idea we were within one hundred yards. It should be an easy shot.

It was.

I had a good rest, plenty of time to get comfortable and the reedbuck had not moved. Just what I needed to boost my confidence.

By the time we loaded the reedbuck and glassed a few more animals, it was time to head back to camp. A sunset in the African bush is a beautiful sight. It had been some time since we had seen one. Dick and I were looking forward to it. The sun had just begun to fade behind a line of miombo trees when we stopped.

"It's not often things fall into your lap on the first day like this," Cotton said. "But that's a good lion there." He pointed.

A lion already? It was a pair: a female and a thick-maned male. The lioness walked a short distance. The lion plopped down on his belly. Before long, the lioness decided she needed a rest as well. How fortunate. Dick might just get a lion on the first day.

"Grab your .375, Mary."

Me?

Cotton and Dick looked at me, waiting.

"I think Dick should try for this one. I don't want to be responsible for a wounded lion."

"This one's yours," Dick said.

"We can use that line of thorn bushes to get closer," Cotton said.

Closer? I didn't know if that was a good idea either.

"How about you and Dick get closer? I'll stay in the truck and watch with the binos."

Dick nudged me. "You said you wanted to try for one. This is your chance."

He had a point. I wanted my own lion. Now that it was time, I didn't think I was ready.

"How about this?" Cotton said. "Let's just sneak over there and get into position. You can put the crosshairs on him and get used to the idea of hunting a lion. You don't have to shoot if you don't want to. What do you say?"

"I guess I can do that," I said. Dick has always believed in taking baby steps. I suppose this was a step toward taking my first lion. "I'm not going to shoot. I can tell you that right now."

"That's fine," Cotton said. "You don't have to."

"But if it's a good lion, maybe Dick should take him."

Cotton smiled at me. "Let's go."

That was it. He seemed to be going with or without me. So, I followed.

"I don't know why you don't have Dick shoot him," I whispered once I had caught up. "I'm not going to."

"Let's set up under that tree." Cotton pointed. "You'll have a good shot from there."

"But I'm not going to shoot," I said softly, following him to the tree.

"Find a steady rest."

"I'm not going to shoot," I whispered through my teeth.

"I know, I know. Just set up on him as if you *were* going to shoot."

It seemed an awful waste not to let Dick take the lion. How often do you get a chance at a good lion?

Their piercing stares shot fear to my bones. Without moving, they made part of me want to run away. But another part of me, primal and ready, wanted to try. It wouldn't be a good idea to let that part take over. Partly hidden in the grass, the lioness turned her eyes away momentarily. The male's stare never wavered. A breeze rippled his mane; it floated as if suspended in water. He was beautiful.

"Okay," Cotton whispered. "Find him in your scope."

The lioness stood up, acting as if she might wander off. This seemed to agitate the male. Standing up, he glanced her way, and then turned back to us with a look that said *you'd better be on your way if you know what's good for you.*

"Do you see that spot of dark hair in the middle of his chest?"

"Yes, I can see that spot."

"Are you steady?"

"Yes."

Faintly, I could hear Cotton. "Mary, I'd like you to click your safety off as if you were going to shoot."

Almost without thinking about it, I did as he instructed.

"Now all you have to do is hold on that spot and, very slowly, squeeze the trigger."

I was no longer scared. Just squeeze the trigger and I would have a lion. *Yeah right. My luck I'll wound him and we'll have to go into the bush after him.*

Shoving my doubts to the side, I began squeezing. Was I mad? I squeezed more, a tiny voice in my head whispering. *Don't you wound him. You're going to wound him. Cotton will have to go after him. You'll be sorry.*

"Just squeeze nice and easy, Mary. Whenever you're ready. There's nothing to it." Cotton's gentle, soothing voice pushed that irritating worrywart into the shadows.

The rifle kicked me. Losing sight of the lion in the recoil, I let that nervous voice jump back into the picture. *Did you wound him? Did you wound him? Oh no. You did, didn't you?*

"Great shot, Mary." Cotton was on his feet, aiming his big-bore rifle at the downed male while we watched the female scoot into a nearby bush.

I was shaking. How had I kept steady?

"Let's go have a look," Cotton said, lowering his rifle only slightly as he started toward the lion.

My right leg was beside itself with adrenaline. Cotton's unwavering focus made the walk intense. This was no impala. This was a 500-pound predator with razor-sharp claws able to disembowel a person with one swipe. Other than his thick mane blowing in the wind, he was not moving. I was still afraid.

Cotton touched the lion's rump with his barrel. He motioned for me to wait before he slipped around to face the lion head-on. He edged closer, his big-bore rifle ready for anything.

Please be dead.

He finally touched his barrel to the lion's eye. Nothing.

Thank You, Lord.

Dick, Joan, Hillary, and Peter caught up to us just as I knelt to slip my fingers through the full mane of a creature so self-confident that it had earned the nickname king of the beasts. And Tanzania, itself enchanting and unpredictable, would be wanting indeed, if not for the lion's majesty. His arrogance, his fiery stare, they are so much an integral part of this simple place and time. A place that has the ability to snatch a part of your soul and send it with the twirling wind. It changes you forever. I was now a lion hunter. I would never be the same.

With my eyes welling, a touch of pride lifted my chin and sent a brief taste of confidence to my otherwise trembling voice.

"Bring on the buffalo."

I wanted to take it back immediately.

Laughing, Cotton touched my shoulder. "That's the spirit," he said. "Don't forget the leopard."

"I was only kidding about the buffalo. I'm not ready for either. I don't think they will give me the same kind of opportunity my lion did. It's Dick's turn." My leg was still shaking.

The African sunset, so important not too long before, passed without notice. What a day. What a lion.

As we approached camp, the trembling in my leg tapered. I heard something. Too faint to hear above the humming engine, too faint to be certain. The soft, but growing sound soon became melodious. Singing—many voices creating a happy, celebratory tune.

Cotton smiled. Hillary, Peter, Durani, and Kafia began clapping as they joined mid-chorus with the rising voices.

Cooks, skinners, water-bearers—the entire camp staff—greeted us. They were waving branches and lanterns, clapping, and singing.

Hillary leaned down over my shoulder, pointing. "For you, Mama," he said.

My eyes welled up.

A few of the men carried a chair to the truck. One of them took my hand and led me to the chair. I sat down and four men hoisted me into the air. The singing, clapping, and dancing never paused.

They carried me through camp, bouncing, singing, and smiling until finally placing me gently beside the fire. Many gathered around to congratulate me. A few said, "very good, very good." One small, young man in a blue jacket brought me a Coke and shook my hand. He was smiling. So was I.

Laughter filled the night. Cotton toasted me. We toasted Africa. We toasted the lion. Though we gave and took most of the credit, the lion deserved the evening's tribute. Without the lion, our campfire wouldn't have been the same. Because of the lion, our evening focused on memories so new and clear it seemed as if they would stay that way forever.

As the fire died to glowing coals, tiny sparks intermittently popping into the black night, rising and fading until engulfed by the never-ending sky, I looked to the smiling faces in that dying light once more. Friends. The lion connected us forever, fusing bonds between us that would have taken too long to mold other-wise. Before I wandered to bed, weary but happy, I thanked Cotton. I thanked Joan, Hillary, Peter, and the staff. I thanked Dick with a kiss. I looked up to millions of stars and silently thanked the lion. And I thanked God for all he had blessed me with.

SOMETHING
ABOUT BUFFALO: DICK

"Leopard hunting is usually a tedious affair," Cotton said as we approached the vehicle. "Miles and hours checking and placing bait, followed by hours sitting in a blind waiting for a ghost that may or may not appear. All for a few of the most intense moments of hunting you may ever experience."

Cotton scooted into his seat. "Today we'll check and refresh baits. We'll hunt along the way, but the baits are far apart. It will be a lot of driving."

"Whatever it takes," I said.

"If we see a good trophy, we won't pass it up without good reason."

Throughout the morning we glassed herds of antelope—cows and ewes with young rams and young bulls, but nothing great.

One bait had been hit.

Pugmarks surrounding the bait tree suggested a leopard worth a closer look.

"Chances are slim that something bigger than this boy has hit one of the other baits. What do you say we drive around for a bit, see what we can see while the boys build us a blind for this afternoon?"

Before long, we spotted a Roberts gazelle. Cotton said it looked good. A few steps into the stalk, a jackal scampered into the open fifty yards ahead of us. The gazelle trotted away.

Cotton leaned over without taking his eyes from the darting scavenger. "Want a jackal?"

I answered by raising my rifle. By the time I found him in my scope, he was on the move. Cotton whistled. The jackal stopped for a quick glance. It ran as soon as it discovered the source. I fired at that moment. The last we saw of the jackal was his back legs kicking up a tiny dust cloud.

"We'll get another chance. It might not last that long though. They never hold still."

"I gathered."

Cotton made it difficult not to have a good time. He gave a tremendous effort and kept an upbeat attitude that made even the monotonous days checking bait fly by.

"How is it you became a professional hunter in Africa?" Mary asked on our way to pick up Peter and the others for lunch.

"After Joan and I married, we bought a dude ranch near Colorado Springs. We had a good location and it only seemed natural to start guiding hunts. We were doing well. Our clients were taking beautiful trophies every year. Then, in the mid-1970s, trophy quality began declining for a number of reasons. We took a safari in Africa and, like most hunters, were hooked. I served ten years as the President of the International Professional Hunters Association. During that time, I met Mike Rowbotham, who was managing Zambia Safaris. He talked me into coming to hunt for him. We never looked back. Life sometimes knows which way to lead you. Some people never see the directions as clearly as I did, or are just unwilling to follow them. Not me. I haven't been steered wrong yet. At least, I don't think I have."

Cotton and Joan were a lot like us. Fate gave us a nudge and we ran with it. Next thing we knew, we were so far from where we started, our past was almost unrecognizable. Like Cotton and Joan, it wasn't all fate or luck or providence or whatever you want to call it. We worked hard, sometimes so hard it didn't seem worth it. We rarely knew if we were heading in the right direction, but pushed forward, looking to the future as best we could, changing direction when necessary. Often it felt as if Cabela's guided us as much as we nurtured it. We had no idea what the rest of our lives had in store for us, but it had already led us to nine wonderful children, an international company, and even to a small safari camp in Tanzania.

"It seems the location and size of the blind the boys have built is not big enough for all three of us," Cotton said. "I guess it'll just be you and me tonight, Dick. I hope you don't mind spending the afternoon in camp with Joan, Mary. It'll give you two a chance to get to know one another better. Besides, a leopard blind isn't much of a social place. For the most part it's pretty darn boring." Cotton briefly looked to Mary and me, then back to the trail road. "That is, until a leopard shows up."

Questions raced through my thoughts as we bounced down the jarring trail road in silence.

Do you wait for the leopard to feed? Do you take him on the ground, or in the tree? If he hears or smells us, will he come investigate or scamper away? What if I wound him? Do we go after him right away or wait?

"You know, Dick," Cotton said without severing his stare from the path ahead. "If I've learned one thing in all my years hunting leopards, it's that they are unpredictable. Sometimes leopards do things they are not supposed to do. Just when you think you have them figured out, they do something you've never seen before. Sometimes it's something unbelievably crafty and sometimes it's something so foolish that you wonder if you're giving the species too much credit. Most of the time you're not, of course."

My questions had found an answer. Leopards are unpredictable. Our inability to know what wild animals will do in any given situation makes the hunt that much more alluring. Chances for success are never guaranteed. If they were, what would be the point? The most difficult hunts are the most memorable. Sure, I enjoy a more relaxed hunt now and again, even an easy one, but hunts that involve special situations or that push me to the edge of my physical or mental limits are the ones I return to most in my memories.

My first leopard hunt introduced me to the common challenges of leopard hunting. The professional hunter and trackers do most of the physical work. Few hunting endeavors, however, are more mentally exhaustive. Sometimes everything falls into place perfectly, giving you an opportunity the first night in the blind. Other times, you sit for hours every day, for days on end, with nothing but bad luck paying you a visit. Your mind can lead you in all kinds of directions during those intensely quiet hours—paths you know you should not follow.

Approaching my first leopard blind, I felt more of an excited curiosity of what we might encounter. That, and a bit of apprehension of what might happen once we encountered it.

"When we get into the blind, it's important to be quiet and still. The leopard will not feed if it senses anything is wrong."

We had just stepped from the vehicle and already Cotton's voice was a whisper. The others drove away as we moved toward the blind. They would go about a mile, returning only after they heard a shot or after it became too dark to shoot.

I stared at the bait tree as we passed by. The hind leg of some small antelope hung crimson and black, its haunch gnawed on the night before by our quarry, its rotting stench drifting across the plain, attracting flies and other small scavengers and, hopefully, a big, male leopard.

I soon discovered that a leopard blind was a lonely place. Less than two feet away, Cotton sat relaxed, reading a paperback. I kept peering through the shooting hole, expecting, nearly trying to will, a cat to appear. Nothing.

What was that?

My head twitched toward the barely audible sound. I glanced to Cotton, still reading. Maybe he hadn't heard. Maybe I had imagined it. Maybe the sound was irrelevant. For the next fifteen minutes, I listened with an intensity I didn't know I was capable of. I heard nothing. As dusk approached, the dark, silent walls of grass seemed to close in around us.

Peering through the shooting hole again, staring at bait wanting only to be devoured, my thoughts drifted from leopard hunting altogether. Jumping from one subject to another without any reason or, sometimes, even coherency. I should have brought a book. At least I could concentrate on something. I only had so much focus for a leopard that, seemingly, cared little about eating that evening.

Pain jabbed at my lower back with rising persistence. As shadows crept in on us, I began hearing sounds again. A snapped twig, a single cry from a distant bird, but the rustling was the worst. Sometimes it was a soft rustle, not too close. Other times, it sounded like something trying to dig into the blind. Cotton periodically looked up from his book to stare out the shooting hole. He never seemed concerned or excited.

Before long, the half-light made reading too difficult. Cotton's concentration intensified on the bait. Maybe he heard something. I hoped so. It would prove I was not crazy. Then again, part of me just wanted to head for camp. You can only sit perfectly still and quiet for so long.

With shooting light fading, our opportunity disappeared with it. I found myself wishing for darkness to hold off a while longer. I wanted to see a leopard.

The night would not be pushed away so easily. Not tonight. It came at an accelerated creep, tightening its grip around our hopes for the evening. Finally, when I could no longer see the bait, just the outline of the tree, Cotton looked away from the shooting hole.

Shrugging, he whispered, "You just can't predict what they will do. The way he only gnawed on it last night, I thought he'd come in for a real meal tonight. All we can do is keep trying."

You would think I'd start jabbering after so long in silence. Instead, I merely nodded, even though it was too dark in the blind for Cotton to see. As hard as it had been to stay quiet and still, there really wasn't much to say. So, sitting in silence, we waited for Peter to bring the vehicle.

I ambled toward the flames of the campfire after returning to camp. I felt exhausted. It had only been a few hours of sitting, but I was pooped.

"We didn't hear any singing on the way in," Mary said. She and Joan were sitting by the fire like they had been awaiting our return for some time.

I shook my head as I slumped into one of the empty chairs beside my wife. "How was your afternoon?" I asked.

"Joan and I got to know each other better. Just before you pulled in a bunch of hyenas were making all kinds of racket. They must've heard the truck. I don't hear them anymore."

"I better go see how dinner's coming," Joan said before disappearing into the dining tent.

"Did you and Cotton have a good time today?"

"You have to be really quiet in the blind. We didn't talk or anything."

"Joan is a remarkable person. They both are. I couldn't imagine spending so much time away from home."

"We spend a lot of time away from home," I said.

"They come over here to stay and work for months at a time. That takes a certain kind of person. They must be perfect for each other. They've been through a lot; enduring more than most people should ever have to. Their strength and devotion to one another is impressive." Mary looked into the sky. "Did you know they lost a son?"

"No."

"Joan pointed out the first star of the night. She called it Ben's Star. That was their son's name. I couldn't imagine that."

"Neither could I."

Few people can earn the respect we had for the Gordons in the few days we had spent with them. Mary was right; it took a certain kind of person. They were the kind of people you felt comfortable sharing personal details with and the kind of people you would socialize with. It was safe to say that we liked the Gordons from the beginning.

During dinner, lions roared above the crackling fire, piercing the night sky with sounds of triumph. Leaning back slightly, stretching below the dull light of a lantern, I grinned.

"We'll get that leopard," I said to Cotton. "But later. I'm too tired now."

We thanked everyone for a fine meal and headed for bed. On our way, the lion roared again. Mary reached for my hand. Without hurry, we strolled to our tent underneath a shower of stars. It was perfect.

"What's on the agenda for today?" I asked Cotton during toast and tea.

He raised his eyes to mine, serious as the day. "Buffalo," he said, nodding slightly.

Buffalo. It had been a while—too long. There is something about buffalo. Unlike any of the other Big Five, buffalo gets under your skin. Lion, leopard, elephant, rhinoceros—all of them provoke at least some thoughts of glamour. Not the buffalo. He is the blue-collar beast. Strong, steady, always ready for battle. Though he may run, he does not fear you the way you fear him. His eyes show defiance, obstinacy, even rage. The look of the buffalo is impossible to forget.

When he is facing you with no intention of running and you have determined he is the bull you want—that is when you find out what you are made of. Sometimes slinking away, even running, is the proper course of action, but not when your bull is before you, waiting for a showdown. And certainly not after he has taken a dose of your lead as if you had done nothing more than thrown a stick at him.

Mary had an uneasy look in her eyes, but it was a willing trepidation. There is just something about buffalo.

"Are you ready?" I asked her as I loaded our rifles into the vehicle.

"I don't know."

"You've shot buffalo before."

"And every time my stomach boils. It does with all dangerous game. I guess I'm as ready as I'll ever be."

Her stomach does boil, of that I am certain. So does mine. She would deny it, but I think she enjoys the boiling more than she lets on.

"According to Peter, several large groups of buffalo moved onto the plains last night."

Mary glanced at Peter, then back at Cotton. "How would he know that? He was still in camp when we went to bed. It was dark."

"News travels fast in the African bush. Almost as if it floats in the wind. I've learned not to question."

Sure enough, less than fifteen minutes later, we spotted a herd nearly five hundred strong.

"Are you ready to shoot your buffalo, Mary?" Cotton said, lowering his binoculars.

"Do you think it's wise to go after one in such a large herd?"

Cotton chuckled. "Let's go. There's a good bull there."

"Should I wait here?" I asked.

"No, come on. It'll be fun."

Mary raised her eyebrows at me. Fun?

Some of the buffalo formed a wall, stuck their noses in the air and attempted to stare us down. They knew we were coming and intended to hold their ground.

We followed closely behind Cotton and Peter in a semi-crouch, moving in slowly at an angle. Mary leaned back, her eyes wide. "There are a lot of them."

At one hundred yards, a few buffalo on the outer edges shifted. The group in the middle never allowed their stares to waver—a street gang ready to rumble.

"Shoot that big bull there," Cotton whispered as Peter opened the shooting sticks.

"Which one? They all look big to me."

"See the one straight in front of us? The one between two much smaller buffalo? He just turned his head to the left."

"Okay, I see him."

Resting her .375 in the shooting sticks, Mary took several deep breaths. Her legs were shaking when she looked over the scope, her eyes darting through the herd.

"Focus on the bull we want," Cotton said. "Concentrate on one small spot and squeeze. Just like you've done thousands of times before."

The bull turned with many of the others.

"Take him right in the shoulder," Cotton whispered. "Just concentrate and squeeze."

Mary's rifle popped on her shoulder. The herd scattered.

"Reload."

Jacking another shell in, Mary glanced my way briefly. "Did I get him?"

"Looked good, but he's not down."

"Where is he?" Looking through her scope, Mary's rifle barrel darted back and forth. "I don't see him."

"I've got him marked, Mary. It's fine."

Buffalo were scattering. Dust and grass rose into a light cloud. The distance between us widened. It would be tough to keep on him if they went much further.

"Let's go," Cotton said. He started to jog after them.

Peter snatched up the shooting sticks and fell into step behind Mary and Cotton. I brought up the rear.

"It was a good shot," Cotton said, his breathing catching up to his stride. "Sometimes buffalo just don't know when they're dead. I haven't seen many one-shot buffalo kills. I'd say four shots are about average." He never took his eyes from the herd.

They had broken into two main groups, with smaller sub-groups trying to rejoin the rest of the herd. Our bull was in a small bunch. He kept up with the other buffalo at first. Then he began to slow. When he stopped, the others only ran a few more yards before halting their stampede. They looked back at him. He turned to face his attackers, blood staining his nose.

"Shoot him again."

Mary couldn't get steady.

"Put another one in him, Mary."

She finally fired, slammed another bullet into the chamber, and fired again. The bull staggered toward us.

"What about the others?" Mary asked, while she re-chambered a fresh load. They had drifted to our right, closing the distance between us.

"Don't worry about them. Keep on him. Shoot him again if you can."

Mary anchored the rifle butt to her shoulder. Her finger found the trigger. The buffalo stumbled, his face slamming into the hard ground before she could squeeze. His brief struggle ended with a somber death bellow deflating his lungs.

Mary's head jerked to her right. There was nothing there, just open plain dotted with a few acacias.

Peter started shaking her hand. Cotton smiled. So did I.

"I'm sending one of the boys back to retrieve some help. That way they can get your buffalo skinned and cleaned while we keep hunting. Not like back home, where we'd spend the rest of the day cleaning and packing out our elk."

Africa's good outfitters and professional hunters know how to take care of their clients. I don't mind getting my hands dirty and working hard on a carcass, but if I don't have to—I don't mind that either.

Trackers, skinners and all the others employed on a safari leave more of your limited time for hunting. If you book a hunting trip to Africa, then, for goodness sake, you are going to hunt. Caping, quartering, and packing are all part of the hunt, but they don't always have to be your part. Within minutes after Mary shot her buffalo, we were hunting again.

"We'll make the rounds, check our leopard baits and maybe find something worth shooting along the way." Staring through his binoculars, Cotton's mouth crinkled on one side, as if deep in thought. He was watching an impala. "I think it might be best if you'd shoot this ram. He's not great, but he's good. I'd like to have some fresh leopard bait either way. If one of the baits has been hit, it would be good to replenish the meat. If nothing's been hit, I want to place a new bait in a spot where Peter said his cousin saw a leopard yesterday."

I was nearly out of the vehicle before he finished. He was the professional. If he thought we should try something, it was in our best interest to listen. He knew the area. He had hunted many leopards. We paid him for his expertise. If we disagreed or questioned something, we would let him know. For the most part, Cotton knew what we wanted and we rarely found reason to disagree or question his actions.

During the short stalk, Cotton's mouth curled up on one side, thinking again. "That ram's not as good as I thought," he whispered. "Let's take one of the females and let the boy grow another year."

Ten minutes later, we were dragging a ewe impala by the hind legs. We only had to drag her a few yards. Durani met us with the truck right away.

Checking baits is not a fun part of leopard hunting. It is important, necessary, even interesting the first few times, but it is not very enjoyable, especially if, during your rounds, game is scarce.

Driving through beautiful country, we began by leaning forward, searching the fields and under the trees for game. After a while, we stopped looking so intensely.

Eventually, we only stared at the moving landscape. No matter how monotonous it might seem, a zebra or eland or wildebeest or warthog might appear at any moment. Wild animals can be predictable to a certain extent, but it is their unpredictability that draws us to the challenge. It boils down to you and your quarry trying to outsmart each other. If we kept a scorecard, the bucks, bulls, rams, and toms would be so far ahead it would be embarrassing. Occasionally, we do things just right; making fewer mistakes than the buck we are after and luck sways in our direction. It is then, when our patience and persistence pay off, that we know what it means to be hunters. We couldn't give it up if we wanted.

"This one hasn't been hit either," Cotton said. "There's only one left. It's been a honey hole this year. I'll be surprised if it hasn't seen any action."

Thirty minutes later, we pulled up under an umbrella acacia tree. Two hundred yards further into a shallow depression, the bait hung on a limb, undisturbed. Cotton should have been discouraged. Instead, we loaded back into the truck and sped off to hang the new bait.

Finding a good spot for a leopard bait is harder than it sounds. You don't simply throw it in any productive-looking tree you come across. It needs to be placed in a tree that will allow for optimum wafting of scent. There needs to be adequate cover to build a blind that will not interfere with the cat's approach. It also has to be a tree that would be easy for a leopard to scale but difficult for a lion to reach.

We drove slowly through the area where Peter's cousin had seen the leopard. Cotton studied every tree, every bush, each shadow. Finally, we stopped. Cotton stepped from the vehicle, his gaze fixed on one tall tree, his hand at his forehead blocking the sun's glare. He glanced at the surrounding shrubbery and kicked the dirt to see which way it floated in the breeze. Hillary grabbed a coiled length of rope from the back and tied it to the hitch. Peter and the other tracker, Kafia, began dragging the carcass all around the area.

"That's good," Cotton said after ten minutes.

Peter took the rope and zipped up the tree with such agility a ladder would have been a hindrance. How he shinnied up those first twelve feet without aid of any kind is beyond me. I looked for a knob or something he could grab for leverage. I found nothing. Once out on a long limb, he dropped the rope, which was quickly tied to the carcass. Durani inched the Land Cruiser forward until the impala reached Peter. Hillary had already attached two smaller lengths of rope to the carcass, which Peter used to tie our bait to the tree. When he finished, he shinnied back down, tore some leaves from a nearby bush and zipped right back up the tree with his new load to make the bait look more natural and hide it from vultures. The entire process took less than twenty minutes. Efficiency at its best.

On our way back for lunch, Peter spotted a Defassa waterbuck on a ridge slinking in and out of the trees. Green leaves sprouting from every bush gave it maximum cover. The bull stopped in the open, but could be gone in a step. Facing away from us, he stood motionless, his head held high, tall horns jutting into the sky as if the ridge was the castle of his small kingdom.

"Grab your rifle, Mary," Cotton said. "If we can get to that small tree, I think you'd have a good quartering-away shot."

"I'm not too fond of uphill shots," Mary said, grabbing her rifle anyway.

"Just aim where you want to hit him."

She glanced at me, her eyes asking whether I would join them or not. I waved. This was her chance. A light breeze blew from the waterbuck toward us. Even from this distance, I thought I could smell him. I hadn't smelled a waterbuck for two years, but their stench is hard to forget. The sun beat down on us, turning our boot leather to lead. Another fine reason to wait in the truck. The breeze, though increasing, offered little respite.

The truck, parked under a shade tree, offered Hillary, Durani, and I a grand view of the waterbuck five hundred yards away. We lost Mary, Peter, and Cotton intermittently as they weaved in and out of nearby brush. The bull never moved. Not once. Watching him through my binoculars, I didn't believe any living creature could hold so still for so long. I briefly questioned if it was a waterbuck at all.

We lost Mary and the others when they slipped into a dry creek bed. The tree they wanted sat alone downhill from the bull. Waiting for them to show up, I kept lowering my binoculars. What was taking so long?

Then they were there.

Cotton pointed to the bull. Mary's rifle moved to her shoulder. Unable to watch both through the binoculars, I chose to keep an eye on the waterbuck. He had moved. Now looking down toward the hunters, his arrogance became concern. Soon survival instinct would trigger full-blown alarm and he would disappear.

I waited for the shot. When it came, the bull ducked, stiffening for a brief moment. Long enough for another blast. Then he was gone. Both shots missed clean.

After lunch, Mary and I took a stroll around camp.

"I'm sure Cotton, Hillary, and all the trackers and skinners think I'm a terrible shot. I shouldn't try uphill shots."

I didn't say anything.

"I know you think it's all in my head, but I always miss uphill."

"You want to practice some angled shots?"

"I don't want to shoot at angles—up or down."

"Not every situation can be perfect."

Two members of the camp staff we hadn't met walked by. They both waved and smiled. We waved and smiled back.

"I guess I should try to practice some."

"I'll tell Cotton. We'll go find a good spot this afternoon."

Nailing a couple of bulls-eyes would boost her confidence.

On our way to target practice, Peter pointed out a small herd of buffalo under a large acacia. They were some distance away, a few small specks in the landscape.

"Let's have a closer look, Dick," Cotton said, snatching his binoculars.

Any buffalo herd is worth a closer look. Throughout the entire approach, you are psyching yourself up, telling yourself you are ready, willing courage to rise. Just when you have garnered enough nerve to face a buffalo head-on, your professional hunter turns to inform you the bull you want is not in the herd. I hate that. Then you have to muster up another dose of courage later.

Looking at the herd, only seventy-five yards distant now, I didn't see a big bull.

At least my heart could slow down as we backed away.

"There's a good bull," Cotton said, peering through his binoculars.

What?

"Where?"

I thought I had looked them over carefully. With the herd bunched up under the shade, I guess I could have missed him. They had no idea we were nearby. The way they lolled about, I wondered if they would care.

"He's behind the tree. I can only see one horn, but it's a good one. If the other side is good, we should try to take a shot."

We needed a plan. Sneaking around was out of the question; there were too many buffalo surrounding him. We could try to wait them out, but who knows how long they planned to laze in the shade. We could try to make them move, but they might bolt at the first sign of danger. The bull we wanted could stay mixed in the middle of the herd. Or, they might just stand their ground right where they were; you just never know with buffalo. Peter said he would circle around undetected then strategically expose himself to try to get the herd to move away from the tree. It was worth a try.

Peter disappeared. We waited.

The buffalo soon focused their attention on Peter. He had appeared more quickly than we anticipated on the southern edge of the field. He started toward them. The few buffalo lying down stood to face him. They formed a half circle around the base of the tree.

"Is Peter a little crazy?" I asked. Who would walk toward a herd of buffalo—unarmed?

Cotton laughed and shrugged his shoulders. "I guess so."

Peter strolled toward them as if he was on his way to greet a friend. He appeared unconcerned. From our position, he appeared close. He kept moving forward.

"Let's move to that tree over there. It will give us a better angle if they move away from Peter."

By the time we scooted over there, Peter had stopped. When he did this, the one buffalo still lying down, sprang to its feet. With that one movement, it demonstrated the fluid agility these massive beasts harbor. For all of their power, stamina, and ability to take bullet after bullet, it is their smooth quickness that is most overlooked.

Peter had to be crazy.

Before he stopped, a few buffalo had shown some concern. Now, more of them moved about nervously. An edgy buffalo does not pose a tranquil situation. I felt it in my stomach. I could see it in Cotton's focus. We were at that point when anything could happen. A momentary lapse in concentration could hold negative consequences. I felt alert, alive.

We had reached a stalemate—the kind that takes a wrench to your heart and twists it tight. Peter, finally unwilling to venture closer, contemplated his next move. The buffalo, unsure just what kind of threat he posed, contemplated their own. We needed one buffalo to make a decision to move, hopefully away from Peter. A few of the smaller buffalo behind the front wall were ready to flee. Their heads swung tautly from Peter back to the safety of distance. If one of them moved, the rest would follow. Of course, there was always the slight chance they would stampede over us, but that only seemed to concern me.

"Keep your eye on our bull when they move. If he gives you a chance, take it."

When Peter took a step to his right, one of the buffalo bucked. That was it. The herd galloped off, kicking up dust, heading right for us. Their run lacked resolve. After only fifty yards, they turned back toward Peter. He was gone.

I have no idea how he vanished so quickly or where he disappeared to, but the bull held my focus, so I will forgive myself for losing Peter. The buffalo wandered about in a cluster, searching the field for the vanished intruder. A few of them took cautious steps back toward the tree and exposed our bull's shoulder.

"There. It's clear. Take him."

The rifle bucked. The bull lunged forward.

Dust rose as hooves stampeded across the plain. I lost the bull in the hazy storm.

"Let's go." Cotton tugged at my sleeve.

Hurrying into the field, I stepped into a hole, nearly losing my balance. Cotton, a few steps ahead of me now, began slowing. The settling cloud revealed a dark form, undistinguishable at the moment, but defining in detail by the second.

Buffalo.

Our buffalo. Alone and quartered away from us not more than fifty yards distant.

"Shoot him again," Cotton said, his gun shouldered.

At the shot, the bull lunged forward again, running a few yards before stopping. He turned, rage in his eyes, blood spraying from his nose and mouth like dragon's fire.

"Again."

This time he didn't lunge. The only indication the bullet struck him at all was the solid *thwump* as it slammed through his thick skin. He moved to face us head on, staggering. Somehow, the distance between us had closed to thirty yards.

Keeping my eyes on the bull, I reached into my pocket for the extra .375 bullets I wouldn't dream of going after a buffalo without. I knew they were there, but the reassuring feel of brass in my fingers kept my actions deliberate. *Get it loaded. He's about to charge. Get it loaded.*

One bullet slipped from my grasp. Ignoring it, I snapped one into the magazine and shoved another into the chamber. I slammed the bolt down.

The bull's legs buckled at the next shot. His chin slammed into the dirt, his eyes fixed on us, full of murderous intent to the end. One finishing round and he was done.

Peter was suddenly next to me, his hand extended. I took it.

"Good shot, Bwana Dick," he said smiling, his accent heavy. "Very good."

"Good job, honey."

I turned to see a wide-eyed Mary coming toward me with a smiling Hillary. They were following at a safe distance the entire time. Hillary's rifle rested loosely on his shoulder.

"Not many animals can bleed from their mouth and nose like that and appear unhurt. Any one of your shots would have put any other species down instantly.

Buffalo just don't know when they're dead."

I tried to absorb it all. It is rare when there is enough time in one day for two buffalo.

"He's about the same size as Mary's. A fine, fine buffalo." Cotton stood over the bull with his hands on his hips. He raised his hand to his forehead, looking toward the descending sun. "By the time we finish skinning, cleaning, and loading this old boy it'll be close to dark. If we hurry, we might still get in some hunting on the way back to camp."

My blood was still pumping, but how much more hunting do you need during a day like that? Few days afield can truly compare for a big-game hunter who had allowed buffalo hunting to wriggle its way under his skin.

Hunting, however, is an opportunistic endeavor. So, when two silver-backed jackals zipped onto the gut pile as we drove away, I fell back into hunting mode.

We drove until the truck would be out of view, then hopped out. Using brush for cover, we ended up right back where we had begun glassing the buffalo when they were lazing under the tree. Both jackals appeared to be the same size. I shot the closer one. Peter ran out to grab it. Halfway there, he turned and ducked into the nearest cover.

Perplexed, I glanced at Cotton.

He shrugged. "Let's just wait. He must've seen something."

A moment later, Peter appeared beside Cotton. At the same time, two hyenas slipped into the open. Their long jaws were open, revealing a set of dark teeth. Their massive heads swayed with each awkward step. Their hair was mangy and bald in spots. When these two brutes rambled in, it was easy to see why they are often depicted as vile, ugly creatures.

I picked one out and dropped him less than twenty yards from the jackal. His companion chose not to stick around.

"Okay, Dick. I think that's enough for now," Cotton said with a half-grin. "We're out of room in the truck, and we only have about fifteen minutes before dark. What do you say we just head back now?"

It had been a good day.

Before long, we were in the vehicle speeding back to camp. It wasn't quite dark yet, but it was close enough that we had stopped looking for game. Sometimes, it just happens.

"Stop, Bwana," Peter said pointing.

A serval cat slipped into a patch of long grass. It's slender, tawny form, painted with black spots, blended with the grass as well as any camouflage pattern on the market. Knowing he was hidden, he remained motionless. We had coasted past him fifty yards. I couldn't see him at all. Peter insisted he was still there in the grass. I had already learned to trust Peter.

The three of us, Peter, Cotton, and I, slid from the vehicle. Peter led the way, his keen eyes leveled on the quarry that I could not locate. A few more steps and he crouched to one knee. We did the same. Without pulling his gaze from the cat, Peter slowly raised his arm and pointed.

"He's just inside the grass there, Dick, watching us," Cotton said.

He disappeared at the blast. Did the cat drop or run off? Springing to his feet, Peter sprinted to the grass.

"Good shot, Dick. You nailed him."

Peter grabbed a stick and jabbed the limp body. It didn't move.

Darkness hit so fast, it was as if a light switch flicked off. If we had seen the cat thirty seconds later, it would have been too late. Not possible on that kind of day. A day when everything seemed to go my way.

SILENCE: MARY

"Now all you have to do is shoot a leopard."

"I'm not going to shoot a leopard," I said.

"It's not any different than lion or buffalo."

"Leopards are the worst. You wound them and then they hide in the grass waiting to maul you. I'll be too nervous to shoot straight. I'm not going to shoot a leopard."

"We'll talk about it later," Cotton said.

"You won't talk me into it."

Cotton smiled. "After you finish your breakfast, we'll check leopard baits and hunt for plains game."

"I'm not going to shoot a leopard," I said to Dick.

"You'll do fine."

"No, I won't. I can't take the chance. What if I wound it and someone gets hurt? I couldn't handle that."

"Cotton knows what he's getting into."

"I don't care. I'm not going to shoot a leopard."

"Okay," Dick said. "Whatever you say."

Nothing had fed on the first bait, but the second one had been hit.

"Would you look at those tracks?"

The claw marks on the tree were massive.

"We'll come back tonight." Cotton gave Dick a thumbs up.

I noticed more of a spring in Cotton's step the rest of the day.

Leopards didn't have that affect on me.

"Let's go see if we can find a Chanler's mountain reedbuck."

On the way, Dick shot at a warthog, but missed. The darn thing kept scampering around. That is what warthogs do. They scamper, they run, they roll around in the mud. Rarely do they hold still. If one gives you the slip, however, it is best not to worry. Another will be along shortly. Most wild hogs come out at night. Warthogs love the day. Their relative abundance and fondness for sunlight put them on the list of critters to watch for at all times. One can zip into the open at any moment. Because of this, and their tendency to scurry with tails raised like flags, warthogs are a constant source of entertainment. We were laughing even after Dick's miss.

To find the reedbuck, we headed for the hill country. Trees dotted the rolling landscape with pockets of lush, green undergrowth. In areas with direct sunlight, the grass was like that of the plains: dry, scorched, and dying.

We spotted a heavy-horned reedbuck resting under a small acacia atop a nearby hill. With one well-placed bullet, Dick had his Chanler reedbuck. While taking pictures, Peter pointed out another reedbuck on the next hill. We stalked to within three hundred yards. I told Cotton I could try.

I didn't like long shots. I didn't like shooting uphill. It made me nervous. So what did I try to do? I tried a long, uphill shot while I was a nervous wreck. I missed horribly.

It could have been worse. I could have wounded him. Still, a miss like that does little for confidence. Mine was already thin.

"We're close enough to camp for an early lunch. Peter and the boys can build a blind for the leopard hunt tonight."

Cotton did a fine job of changing gears to pull my mind away from my bad shooting. I never thought about it during lunch. How could I? Joan was telling us about the time Cotton jumped into the water and grabbed a wounded crocodile by the tail.

"It was a big croc," Cotton said. "I didn't want to lose it."

"Smells like the wind might've shifted," Dick said.

"Or the Maasai have started a field to our east on fire."

Maasai tribesmen had set the whole mountain ablaze. Two of Cotton's leopard baits and blinds were burned the week before.

"There's still plenty of game around. Not like it was a week ago, but better than before the green grass started sprouting outside our hunting concession."

Fire is essential to the health of the savannah, burning the old, dry grass to make way for new green growth, giving nourishment to the large herds of buffalo and plains game. The black earth surrounding us would sprout green within a few weeks. Still, the fires had drawbacks for visiting hunters.

"I wish they wouldn't burn my leopard baits. Especially after a cat has hit and we've gone to all the trouble to build a blind. Then again, sometimes fires just go where they want."

Cotton glanced at his watch. "Let's meet at the truck at four fifteen."

"I don't think I'm going to go tonight," Joan said. "I want to get a few things finished up."

"Mary, you're still welcome to sit in the truck with Hillary."

"If I can't sit in the blind, I think I'll stay with Joan again tonight."

After the boys left for the blind, I tried to help Joan make an angel food cake.

It took five of us to beat the batter with a hand mixer, continuously turning the bowls until the egg whites stiffened. Once mixed, we poured it into a tube pan. To heat it, we placed it on a bed of hot coals and covered it with a half drum. Then we covered the drum, sealing it all around with more hot coals. I thought it would never work.

Throughout the afternoon, I kept one eye on four male lions resting across the creek and the other on approaching flames from the opposite direction. I wanted them both to go away. The lions lazing about on the opposite bank of a shallow creek stared at me as if I were on the menu. They pretended they didn't care what I did—as if trying to lull me into a false sense of security. Their eyes told me a different story. They said, *Mmm, lunch.*

On the other side of camp, a fire was trying to push me toward the creek. Fingers of flame stretched into the air, creeping closer to camp with every passing minute. Their words were, *gonna getcha, gonna getcha.*

Joan and some of the boys glanced at the fire every now and again—unconcerned. However unwarranted it may have been, it felt like impending doom closing in on us from both sides. Dick would probably laugh at me.

If there were any real danger, Joan and the camp staff would let me know. Still, it was my nature to fear lions. I did not care if they didn't pose a threat. I wanted them not to pose a threat elsewhere. Was that too much to ask? Apparently so. They hung around all day. At sunset, they were there. After dark, I pointed my flashlight across the creek. Three sets of glowing eyes stared back at me. Wait. Weren't there four lions? Oh dear. Now I would never calm down.

Lions sizing me up from the right, fire taunting me from the left, darkness hiding every shriek, roar, and yip. I wished Dick and Cotton would return. I hoped he shot his leopard. That way, I wouldn't have to endure the madness another night.

By the time they returned, the flames had altered their course and the fourth set of eyes had returned. At least I knew where the lion was.

"Vultures did a number on the bait. The leopard never showed," Cotton said.

"Four lions set up stakes across the creek tonight," I said.

"Was there a good male?"

That wasn't the reaction I thought I would get.

"They all look big to me. They've been looking over here all night like they want to come into camp."

Cotton laughed.

I found little humor in the situation.

"Don't worry, Mary. They won't come into camp."

"Are you sure? They seem like they might."

"They won't cross the river here."

"They don't seem afraid at all."

"I guess they don't think we will cross the river either," Cotton said before excusing himself to check on supper.

"They look at me like they know I'm afraid," I whispered to Dick.

He laughed. I knew he would.

While we enjoyed a supper of enchiladas and Joan's delicious frosted angel food cake for dessert, I didn't think about the lions. During drinks and conversation by the campfire, I only shined the light over there once. I was moments into a decent sleep when they reminded me of their presence.

"Dick. Wake up. Did you hear that?"

He rolled over.

"I think the lions are in camp."

"They're not in camp." He rolled back.

"I think they might be. They were roaring across the creek. Now they sound like they're on this side. I think some hyenas might've pushed them over here."

No answer.

"Dick. Did you hear me?"

I woke up again around two in the morning having to use the restroom. I heard a growl. A lion was definitely in camp.

The small grassy fence around camp couldn't keep out a warthog let alone a lion. I shook Dick's shoulder.

"Dick. Wake up," I whispered. "Dick."

"What is it?"

"The lion is right outside our tent."

"They always sound closer than they are."

"They are right here. They're close. I know it."

He started snoring.

The bathroom was thirty yards from our tent. I could hold it. I crawled back into bed, my heart beating in my throat until five. The lion roamed around outside our tent, snarling every now and again. When he finally started moving away, Dick's snoring grew so loud the tent shook. A sound like that could bring the lion back to investigate. I couldn't hear anything over Dick's snorting wheeze. All night I tried unsuccessfully to wake my husband. At least when I heard the lion, I knew where it was.

The sun rose without a lion attack.

"Did you sleep well," Joan asked at breakfast.

"I would have, but Mary kept waking me up," Dick said.

"At least you got some sleep. I couldn't sleep at all with the lions in camp."

"There were no lions in camp last night," Cotton said.

"There was one right behind our tent."

Cotton's eyes showed skepticism. "I'll have Peter take a look, see if he can find any sign over there. I think you probably heard the lions across the river fighting with hyenas. They always sound closer than they are."

"That's what Dick said. This one was much closer, growling and sneaking about."

Cotton stretched his neck and then stood. Walking toward the creek, he motioned me to join him. "All four lions are still across the creek." He pointed.

About that time, Peter returned with his report.

"There are no tracks anywhere inside the fence," Cotton relayed. "The lions won't bother us. And if there is ever a problem, my tent is only a few yards away."

I am sure they all thought I was a worrywart, or a fraidy-cat, or whatever. I did not care.

Lions are beautiful. But that beauty disguises massive fangs, flesh-gripping claws, and a powerful body capable of killing with one swat or bite. I like lions. I certainly respect lions. Most of all, I fear lions. I would sleep better if they found a different place to hang out at night. I said as much to Dick. He told me not to worry about it. Typical.

The midnight blaze had charred the area to a crisp, smoldering landscape of ash and smoking coals. How could such destruction be beneficial? Long-term it was. Short-term, the flames pushed critters to greener pastures or, at least, pastures that wouldn't melt their hooves and feet. Thousands of buffalo roamed just a day before on fields we passed through. The next day—nothing. Impalas, wildebeest, gazelle, hartebeest—all gone. The lions would follow.

"Our area is big," Cotton said. "We'll drive through this in no time. In a way, these fires may be good for us."

Was that hope?

"We may have to travel further," Cotton continued. "But game shouldn't be hard to find in a field where new grass is sprouting. This is just a small hurdle."

We did our morning routine, checking every leopard bait for signs of action. One had been devoured by a cat with big tracks.

"Let's refresh the bait," Cotton said.

It didn't take long to find an impala. As Cotton had predicted, the unburned fields were teeming with game.

I took the shot.

Miss.

"Can I see your rifle?"

Cotton slid another bullet into the chamber and we stalked another impala. He fired.

Miss.

The dust cloud where the bullet struck the ground puffed up two feet from its mark. Roughly the same place mine had missed. Cotton took aim on a nearby tree.

Low and to the right.

After a few adjustments, we had the scope dead-on.

"That still doesn't mean I can hit anything," I said.

"Nonsense. We just need to restore your confidence. We also need camp meat. I think a topi will do the trick."

Topi are interesting creatures. Their high shoulders and long legs allow for a top speed and lasting endurance most animals would envy. They are one of only three antelope species known to form a breeding *lek*. Males do not chase down females to mate. Instead, when the female is in estrus, she will visit the *lek* and mate with the dominant male.

"Whenever you're ready. Take your time. Just squeeze."

Everything felt right. I was steady. But my confidence wavered. A tremble slithered up from my stomach. I needed to fire before it hit my arms. The crosshairs were perfect; the topi standing still. If I missed this shot, my nerves would be shattered beyond repair. Those thoughts intensified the tremble that had reached my chest. I fired.

"Great shot," Dick and Cotton said together.

The topi ran a few steps before tipping over. Confidence extinguished the trepidation. How could I miss now? My emotions took me on a roller coaster. I guess it kept me from complacency.

After replenishing bait, Cotton decided to test my rediscovered self-assurance.

"Now that you're scope is on and you're shooting like yourself, what do you say we find a big male topi?"

We glassed three bulls before finding one Cotton thought was worth pursuing.

"He'll make the record book for sure."

"Record book?"

"The Safari Club International Record Book of Trophy Animals."

We had never heard of it. The organization sounded vaguely familiar, but we didn't know what they did or what they stood for.

Cotton took the time to educate us on the important role SCI played in the conservation and management of big-game animals. He explained the scientific importance of record keeping and tracking both the quantity and quality of animals in any given area. For professional hunters and their clients, the record book served as a guide to what areas and what outfitters consistently produce.

We had been walking during the entire conversation. It was hard to imagine we were on a stalk. Peter had led us through a line of brush that brought us to the edge of the field where the topi was grazing.

"Looks like just under two hundred yards. Get comfortable right here and take him whenever you're ready." Cotton was talking softly, not quite whispering.

Peter and Dick waited behind the brush-line.

Doubt never entered my thoughts. The shot dropped him. Yes.

Hearing the shot, Durani found a traversable path through the brush and entered the field as we started taking photos. He saw me posing when he stepped from the truck and hurried over.

"Mama is very good shot," he said.

Hillary, Kafia, and Young Peter piled from the truck to congratulate me as well. Cotton's entire staff knew English. A few spoke it quite well. They all seemed to enjoy practicing. Kafia and Young Peter were both trackers. Old Peter was the head tracker. Hillary had put in the time and hard work to become an apprentice professional hunter.

I stood on a pedestal so high it seemed nothing could bring me down. Cotton must have thought I was higher.

"Mary, you and I will go for leopard tonight," he said during lunch.

"What? I don't think so."

"It's a perfect setup. It will be an easy shot. I think the leopard will come."

"I'm not going to shoot a leopard, Cotton."

"You weren't going to shoot a lion or a buffalo either," Dick said.

"This is different. Leopards maul professional hunters all the time. I don't shoot well enough to try a leopard. I can't do it. I won't."

"I'm not going to make you do something you don't want to do. How about this? Tonight, you and I will go to the blind so you can get used to what it feels like to have a leopard come in. It's quite an experience."

"I'm not going to shoot one."

"I know, I know." Cotton smirked. "Meet me at the truck in an hour." He started walking away. "Don't forget your rifle."

"I told you I'm not shooting."

"I didn't say you had to shoot. If it's a big enough leopard, I might want to shoot it. You only get so many chances at leopard." When Cotton walked away, I was sure his smirk lingered.

We met Cotton at the Land Cruiser an hour later. Dick brought my .375, even though I told him not to bother. He would wait in the vehicle with Hillary while Cotton and I sat in a dark, dusty blind made out of grass. Grass? Great protection, I was sure. Cotton said it was safer than it sounded. I had a hard time believing him.

Dick and Hillary dropped us off and drove away. The heavy rope in my stomach started knotting, turning upon itself, twisting my guts. I felt like running away.

"What if the leopard tries to get into the blind?"

"He won't," Cotton whispered.

"What if he does?"

"That's why I've got this." Cotton raised his shotgun.

For some reason it failed to give me the comfort I wanted.

Just before we entered the blind, Cotton turned to me.

"If the leopard looks into the shooting hole, try not to look him in the eye."

He ducked into the blind. I couldn't see a smirk, but I was sure it was there. I inched in. It seemed cold, dark, almost menacing. Three cantaloupe-sized holes faced the bait. I could see it hanging there on the tree, a piece of rotting meat. I shivered. What kind of beast would find that appetizing? At least it was downwind.

I couldn't see anything to either side of us. Only forward. Only a putrid slab of animal flesh. I heard nothing. My own breath was all that was audible. From the way Cotton talked about silence in the blind, I was probably breathing too loudly. I tried to tone it down. Cotton stared out his shooting hole. I peered out periodically as well. The bait stared back at me, unmoving and unpleasant.

Spend enough time in a leopard blind and you are liable to go mad trying to combat the quiet. You can't move. You can't talk. You can't breathe. It is enough to push you to sanity's edge. A stealthy, quick, powerful leopard can pounce on you and tear you apart in a snap. I must have been crazy.

I didn't even hear birds. Nothing. I tried to decide what was worse—a leopard approaching loudly or not knowing if a leopard was approaching.

When the day faded gray at the edges, I thought I might lose it. During all that time, I had only heard a single sound. The snap of a small twig. Cotton had stiffened. He was focused. Was it a leopard? Where was it? I stared out the hole, afraid of what I might find moving in the shadows, terrified of what might be lurking in the shadows that I couldn't see to my left, right, and rear. I held my breath and listened. Nothing.

It was faint at first, almost inaudible. Maybe it was just my imagination. No, it was there, nearly imperceptible, but there. What was it? Clicking. *Tictictictictictictic.* Maybe it was a woodpecker in the distance. No, closer. Maybe just outside the blind. My God. What was it?

My eyes darted from the shooting hole to Cotton. Waiting for him to give some indication that he heard it, that he knew what it was. *Tictictictictictictic.* I couldn't take it anymore.

Willing Cotton to look my way was not working. Slowly, so very slowly, silently, I reached my hand toward him, my fingers blurred by incessant trembling. Wait. I peered down. My leg was doing an interpretation of the jitterbug. A button on a lower pocket was tapping the butt of my rifle. I pulled it away—the clicking stopped.

I didn't know if I should laugh or cry. Cotton looked my way and put a finger to his lips. He pointed to his ear and then toward the bait.

A troop of baboons shattered the silence. Barking, screeching, hissing, screaming, almost to a deafening volume. Their sudden outburst might mean a leopard was prowling through their territory. Baboons hate leopards.

I breathed a sigh of relief. Hard to believe, but the ticking was more intense.

Now I had something to focus on. Baboons. They quieted down just before dark. Just after dark, when the air was black and I couldn't see one foot beyond the shooting hole, I heard a rustle. My eyes snapped toward Cotton. If he was looking at me, or out the shooting hole, or sleeping, I couldn't tell.

There it was again, closer. This was insane, idiotic even. Why were we still sitting in the blind when a hungry leopard was stalking around outside? He could be looking at me through the shooting hole and I wouldn't know it. I wanted to scream.

Dark. Silent. Alone.

A growl.

Not loud, but close. I almost jumped into Cotton's lap, wherever that may have been.

What was happening? Where was the leopard? What if it attacked?

Cotton's hand wrapped firmly around my arm, reassuringly. I was trembling. He was not. I knew the leopard lurked just outside the blind. I knew it could sense my fear. I could feel it coming closer. I heard something else, something so sweet and comforting I could have cried. The steady hum of an approaching vehicle.

"Ready to go?" Cotton asked.

I wondered if I could stand up. I nodded even though I knew he couldn't see me. At least he wasn't whispering anymore. I heard him stand up. He flipped on a small flashlight. I was on my feet and behind him in an instant. Wait. My rifle was leaning beside the shooting hole. I wanted to tell Cotton to wait for me to grab it. Looking back, I realized I couldn't see it.

"Cotton," I said meekly.

He didn't turn.

Clearing my throat, I called for him again, more forcefully, but still weak. When he turned the light, I snatched up the rifle.

"Okay," I said.

The Land Cruiser arrived shortly, every passenger wearing a smile. Not me.

"He didn't come until after dark," Cotton said.

"Did you get to see him?" Dick asked.

"No, but he was there."

"Could you hear him?" Dick said.

I nodded. "He was right next to the blind."

"Oh, no, Mary," Cotton said. "He never came near the blind. He never made it past the bait tree. He walked around under it for a few minutes until he heard the Cruiser. Then he just slipped away."

"He sounded closer than that."

"They always do. So, what did you think? Think you can shoot a leopard?" Cotton was smiling like the rest of them.

I felt strange as we sat down to dinner. Tired, exhausted even, but too wired from adrenaline to think about sleep.

John, the cook, and Kidago, his assistant, proudly placed the evening's meal before us. We each had a slab of meat, garnished with scalloped potatoes and green beans. Cotton's meat was noticeably different in size, shape, and texture.

"You're not having buffalo tongue?"

"He has this thing about eating parts most people throw away," Joan said.

"He obviously has no problem letting us eat it," I said. "Not that I'm complaining, I love buffalo tongue."

"Give the client what they want." Cotton lifted a piece of his buffalo T-bone, pierced with a fork. "That's what I always say."

"What if a client wants you to eat a part that most people throw away?"

"What?"

"I said what if a client wants you to eat buffalo tongue?"

"I'm sorry; I don't think I heard you correctly."

"Okay," I said. "I see how it is."

Cotton popped another bite into his mouth, held up his fork and winked.

Strolling back to our tent with the sky full of stars, I reached for Dick's hand. He pulled me close.

"I'm beat," I said.

"Maybe you'll sleep better tonight."

"As long as the lions don't roar too much—or too close."

Lying in bed, we listened to hyenas in the distance. Strangely soothing, I fell asleep before Dick started snoring. That hardly ever happened.

As usual, Dominique brought us morning tea promptly at seven. We sipped it while we finished getting ready. Ahead of schedule, we stepped outside the tent to watch one of God's simplest and most overlooked gifts—the sunrise.

The early morning chill would soon be replaced by a blistering sun in a cloudless sky. We would peel layers before the first stalk.

"I think we'll take it easy this morning. Maybe glass the rocks for a klipspring-er," Cotton said as we loaded into the truck.

Cotton always rode in the high backseat with Joan, Dick, and I. Durani drove, and Hillary, Old Peter, Young Peter, and Kafia, who wore a stocking cap, even on the hottest of days, stood in the back, always on the lookout for game. Cotton and the boys always spotted everything before we did. As we approached the *kopje*, they all pointed simultaneously. Durani even saw them from his lower position behind the wheel. I saw a mountain of rocks.

"See that dead tree at the edge of the large overhanging rock." Cotton pointed.

"I got it," Dick said.

I still didn't see it.

"He's standing just behind the tree, staring at us."

Then it moved. Hopped right over the rock face and out of sight. I spotted it just in time to watch it spring away.

"Let's walk up there. See if he didn't just go over the top and stop."

"I thought you said we were going to take it easy today? That doesn't exactly look like a leisurely stroll to me."

Durani, Young Peter, and Kafia stayed at the truck. The rest of us started hik-ing behind Old Peter. It seemed he had been up that *kopje* hundreds of times, slipping around rocks and finding a path through brush that looked impenetrable from the outside. The steep incline was scattered with rocks from baseball-size ankle-twisting stones to giant house-sized boulders. They made keeping up with Old Peter all but impossible. He seemed to be taking it easy on us.

We reached the top without collapsing. Another small victory. Conquering he-roes, we poked our heads over the last hippo-shaped stone. The dainty klipspring-er and one of his buddies that we hadn't seen before gave us a quick confirming glance before darting away, their hooves clacking as they crossed over another rock face that would take us the rest of the day to defeat. We no longer felt heroic.

Staring up at the obstacle, Cotton shook his head and laughed.

"We could go after them. Or, we could hunt hartebeest. It's up to you."

"I wait here," Old Peter said.

"I think I'll stay with him," Joan said.

"You know," Cotton said. "That's not a bad idea. You two go ahead. We'll wait for you here."

"Truck's this way isn't it?" Dick started down the *kopje*.

"There you have it," Cotton said. "One more example of how I always give the clients what they want."

Hiking down was more difficult than you would think. Dick's bad knees threat-ened to buckle. All of us, save Old Peter, had difficulty finding secure footholds. Just when you thought a rock was safe to put your weight on, it shifted. We finally made it, not feeling quite as proud as we had at the top.

Still, we laughed much of the way down. That is the measure of a quality ad-venture. If you can look back on it, knowing you gave everything, knowing it was not all laughs, knowing the people you shared it with will also remember it fondly, then you have taken more with you than just an adventure. I watched them all joking and carrying on—happy. I smiled. New friends—good friends—tend to do that to you.

We checked baits and glassed hartebeest for the rest of the day. The stiff-gaited antelope were in a jumpy mood. Finding a mature bull was always a problem. That day, we found more than one and couldn't get a shot at any of them. We would just start to set up for a shot when a sentry would start jerking around and make the entire herd nervous. With little cover available, they usually knew we were there.

"There's the bull we want," Cotton said, staring through his binoculars.

"He's big," Dick said.

The five cows with him were fidgety and tense.

"How're we going to get close enough to shoot?"

Cotton thought on it for a moment. "This sneaking around hasn't done us much good today. How about we walk right at them?"

"You think it will work?"

"I guess we'll find out."

For a moment, Cotton's plan seemed as if it might work. The hartebeest turned to face us, the bull in back. They stared at us as we closed in on two hundred yards. Cotton slowed, not wanting to push our luck. It seemed far to me.

"Doubt they'll let us get closer." Cotton placed the shooting sticks. "If he steps into the clear, take him."

The moment we stopped, they dashed. With shoulders high above their hind-quarters, their awkward gait was faster than it appeared. They were five hundred yards away before Cotton picked up the shooting sticks. He took off his hat and ran his fingers over his scalp.

"Let's try it once more," he said. "This time we'll use that tree-line for cover."

We backtracked to where we could sneak into the trees. After a few yards, Old Peter appeared beside Cotton.

"How does he do that?" I whispered.

"He won't admit it, but I think he's half ghost."

Old Peter took the lead, directing us in a zigzag route with no apparent reason. Half the time, it felt as if we were moving straight away from where I thought the hartebeest should be. When it comes to tracking and finding game, however, I learned not to question trackers like Old Peter. His ability put most to shame. If he wanted to lead us away from the game, he had a reason. As sure as the sun would set, when Peter faded into the landscape, the hartebeest would be close by.

After a ten-minute hike, we slowed to a creep. I didn't even notice Cotton slip ahead of Peter, or maybe Peter slipped behind us—so hard to tell with a ghost. Cotton bent to one knee. Squinting my eyes, I crouched next to him.

Our bull stood less than fifty yards away watching over his harem. One female's eyes darted from spot to spot, but the rest milled about lazily. Standing tall and proud, the bull seemed to size them up.

This was it. The opportunity. Fleeting and momentary. That's hunting. Lots of ups and downs, full of determination, trying to outsmart your quarry, being outsmarted so many times it is almost embarrassing. Then, after many mistakes, many failures, everything falls into place and your chance presents itself, perfectly broadside, completely unaware of your presence. You cannot miss. Finding the spot on the shoulder, your finger touches the trigger. Shoot now or maybe not at all. Every stalk, every missed opportunity, rises to that moment. Your heartbeat reminds you of what it feels like to be alive, warning you of the emotional influx you are about to experience. Then, in an instant, it is over.

The beast was dead. I dropped him in his tracks. Cotton and Old Peter congratulated me. I smiled sheepishly and said thank you.

It was a moment I have experienced many times. After every kill. Though I know it well and can remember it, I cannot explain it. It was part of me now. It always would be.

I was tired that evening. Everyone was.

"I hope the lions keep their distance tonight," I said to Dick as I crawled into bed.

Half asleep, he grunted and rolled over. I stared at the darkness. It was quiet. I thought about the kids, wondered how they were doing. I wanted them to experience Africa, to feel what we felt there. It would be like giving them a piece of ourselves.

Drifting in and out of sleep, in that moment before dreams take over, I heard a lion roar.

I fell asleep anyway.

WITHIN THE FIRE: DICK

"Been a while since we've seen a buffalo," I said to Cotton over breakfast. The fires had pushed them from the area.

"Think we'll go across the river today. We'll find them sooner or later."

"Will they be over there with the lions and hyenas?" Mary asked.

"Something's keeping the lions and hyenas around. They've been fighting almost every night. I think the lions might be killing buffalo. It can't hurt to look. Besides, I saw one hell of a lion come for a drink yesterday. Wouldn't mind getting a crack at him."

"Me neither."

The fields across the creek hadn't been spared from flames. Many looked like blackened deserts. Pockets of long grass and char-free woods remained. A chill breeze swayed golden waves of grass in a peaceful flow of land and air. A lioness glided into the thick mass of moving blades, fading to an apparition as if she were never there.

"Think our boy's in there?"

"Wouldn't surprise me."

Hillary tapped Cotton's shoulder.

"Stop."

Durani slowed to a stop. Cotton glanced back to Hillary expectantly, then turned his head so his eyes could follow his apprentice's pointing finger.

"That's him. Get your rifle, Dick. He's in the open."

The lion loafed at the edge of the seven-foot-high grass, indifferent to the world around him. A long mane, colored black around the neck, encircled his massive head. The hair waved in the breeze like an extension of the grass.

Sneaking along the grass line, I remembered the lioness that had disappeared moments before. She, or one of her pride, could be mere steps from us. I kept watching the shadows stirring in the dry weeds.

As we rounded the edge of the grass, the lion turned his head to face us, his stare full of disdain. I moved into position. The lion rose to his feet. His quick and fluid movements left me with no misconceptions of how easily he could close the distance between us. The look in his eyes changed. Still indifferent, but now laced with irritation. I looked for the fear you often see in antelope. It was not there.

The lion turned to face the grass. I had a perfect angle. He flopped one paw forward and stepped toward the cover. His walk was more of a swagger, as if annoyed at having been bothered from his morning rest.

I centered the crosshairs on his shoulder, following along as he strolled to cover. I had him.

He spun at the bullet's impact, crashing down in mid-turn. He was on his side, unmoving. We kept our aim steady. He didn't stir, not a muscle twitched. We moved toward him cautiously.

I killed my lion less than a mile from camp.

Singing rose from the good men behind us. They were perfectly in tune, their voices following timeless rhythms celebrating a successful lion hunt. Mary clapped to the beat. The entire camp staff met us as we rolled in. Singing and dancing, clapping and laughing. The trackers led me to a chair, had me sit, and then hoisted me onto their shoulders. They paraded me through camp and then lowered the chair beside Mary. One by one, every person in camp congratulated me with a handshake, many of them still singing and dancing—all of us smiling.

When we pulled away from camp for the second time that day, the mood had mellowed, but it was still buoyant. Many of the boys waved and cheered until we were out of sight.

We had four zebras on license and soon found a herd with a good stallion. The zebras slipped in and out of a heavy brush line, bobbing heads following the tail ahead of it. Cotton picked out the lone stallion in the back and told Mary to shoot. She put it down with one bullet.

Once again, we were less than a mile from camp. After loading the zebra,. we drove it back, had a cup of tea and went hunting for buffalo. It wasn't even noon yet.

"Sure wish we could find a buffalo track today."

"We'll find them. With all the grass burned, there are only so many places they can go. Just a few days ago, the fields were full of them. Huge herds. You saw them. They couldn't have gone far."

We had both taken buffalo already, but there's just something about buffalo. If I could choose only one beast, one creature, to hunt only once, it would be buffalo. There are many fine animals more difficult to hunt; many I have hunted, many I have not. But it is the buffalo that allows for the most complete hunting experience, one many hunters can undertake. Buffalo hunting takes hold of you, pulls you in, and refuses to release its grasp.

Sometimes though, the fields are burned, the buffalo pushed from the heat until new grass grows, and their tracks are covered by ash. So what is there to do? Continue to hunt and seize opportunities as they arise.

"Now that's a Tommy," Cotton said.

Bigger than any Thomson's gazelle we had seen, he had horns thick at the base with points much higher than double his ears. For the moment, I forgot about buffalo and seized my rifle. We needed to close the distance.

In a large, nervous herd, it should have been more difficult. They pronked away once, but not far. Both sexes carry horns. Losing an ordinary ram in the bouncing crowd of identical antelope jumbled together would have been a foregone certainty. Not this ram. Not with horns like his.

We crawled within range. The ram stepped clear of the group. I put the crosshairs on his shoulder and fired. He dropped, his back legs flailing a moment before settling alone in a vast, open savannah. Satisfied he was not going to move, I peered over the scope. The herd had disappeared.

A whoop sprang up from Peter behind me. He and Hillary charged ahead of us, reaching the Tommy before Cotton finished congratulating me.

"I tried not to let on too much, Dick. But that's the biggest Tommy I've ever killed. It's the biggest I've ever seen."

Hillary and Peter were running their fingers along the horns, chattering away like excited boys who had found a buried treasure. Hillary stood as we approached. He reached for my hand, his eyes wide. "It is very good. It is very big."

"Good. Good. Good." Peter said, pumping my hand with both of his as soon as Hillary released it.

The others appeared with the truck a few moments later. Durani beat Mary and Joan off the truck. He ran over and joined the others in their chattering.

"Oh my," Joan said.

"Something, isn't it," Cotton said as Joan moved in close to him. "I'd say he's seventeen inches. Don't you think, Hillary?"

"Yes. Seventeen." Spreading his thumb and pinky finger as far as he could, Hillary rough-measured the right horn. "Yes, he is seventeen."

The scent of hot ash drifted on a nearly undetectable breeze. A single vulture circled high above, clinging to hope that the two-legged creatures below would not steal away with the tiny carcass. A scavenger senses death. After hefting the Tommy into the back of the vehicle, I glanced up. The vulture was no longer there.

Cotton was late for lunch. "We were wrong about your Tommy gazelle, Dick. It wasn't seventeen inches."

"How big was it?" Joan asked.

"I've measured it three times just to be sure I wasn't misreading the tape or adding the numbers incorrectly."

A Master Measurer with Safari Club International for many years, it was doubtful Cotton had misread the measurements three times.

"Each horn measured seventeen and three-fourths inches long with five and one-fourth inch bases."

During the conversation, Joan slipped away from the dining tent, returning a moment later with a large book.

"What total did you come up with?"

"It doesn't seem right, but it is what it is. Forty-seven."

Joan flipped through a few pages before stopping. She ran her finger up the paper then looked at Cotton. "Are you sure?"

"It's right."

"If it is, then Dick just shot the new number one."

"Really? That's wonderful." Mary's eyes beamed.

"What about the drying out time? How much will it lose?" I asked.

"Not enough to change anything. It's huge."

"It beats the record by a lot," Joan said. "Nearly three inches."

A world record. Something I never expected. Something few honest hunters should ever expect. Mine was ninety percent luck. Nonetheless, it was the new number one. I could pretend I did not care, that it did not matter at all, but I am not one for pretending. I will just say that it felt good. And that is enough.

Cotton talked about it all through lunch. It was as much his as mine. His name would accompany the listing. It could only help his reputation, and his area would be coveted more than it already was.

"Well, Mary. Since the Bwana here shot a lion, your hunt is now a true two-by-two. You know what that means?"

"What?"

"You're going to have to shoot the other leopard."

"What do you mean I have to?"

"You have a license and since you each shot a lion, you're paying for the two-by-two hunt anyway. You have to shoot one."

Mary thought on this for a moment before further protest. She shook her head the entire time. "I'm not going to shoot one unless there's plenty of light left. And you have to back me up, Cotton."

Cotton winked. I smiled. We both nodded.

"I'm serious," Mary said. "My stomach hurts just thinking about it."

Most of the fields were covered black in ash and hot coals. Some of the fallen branches had been smoldering for days. In fields where fire had raged days ago, small green shoots of grass desperately tried to sprout through a layer of scorched earth. Escaping the soot was impossible. Our faces, stained with dark streaks of ash and sweat, looked tired. Our lungs fought to filter clean air, but the smoke attacked them and caused them to clench with every breath.

We drove from bait-tree to bait-tree, through scalded earth and smoke, to hang rotting meat from their branches. We escaped the smoke while suspending meat from un-charred trees in the few areas untouched by fire's hand. The sun cooked the bait just enough for a stench to ooze. It stuck like a thin slime to our nasal walls. We were ready to rid the truck of bait.

"That's five down. Only five left to go." Cotton said.

Mary held her hand over her mouth and nose for most of the afternoon.

The Land Cruiser convulsed as we pulled away from a tree. Durani drove one hundred yards before turning to Cotton and shrugging his shoulders. Cotton hopped from the truck. Durani, apparently able to read the Bwana's mind, scooted from the driver's seat. Restarting the engine, Cotton drove only a few yards. He shifted into park, left the engine running and popped the hood. Hillary and Peter sprung from the back. After a few moments, Cotton slammed the hood down and they climbed back in. Durani slid back into the driver's seat and we were off again.

"Going to head back now. Gotta figure out what's wrong with the Cruiser before it gets worse. Have to finish hanging the baits tomorrow. Who knows? Maybe we'll find a buffalo on the way to camp."

We hadn't driven more than fifteen minutes when Hillary and Peter tapped Cotton's shoulder almost simultaneously.

A small herd of Thomson's gazelle scattered. A female leopard sprung from the bush and tackled a young antelope. With the darting quickness of a mamba, the leopard found the poor Tommy's neck. The little thing kicked with all four legs, but the spotted cat glided from their reach. Her teeth clamped tight around the gazelle's fragile neck, waiting for it to suffocate.

A safe distance away, the rest of the herd regrouped. They turned, witnesses to the fate of one of their own. A sacrifice the herd has known before. One final glance and they trotted away.

The leopard, now aware of our presence, gave us a yellow stare. She lifted the young Tommy's lifeless body and trotted into the brush. Such killing power. Speed, stealth, quickness, and beauty. All of it, down to the final clench of her teeth around the throat, was graceful, almost elegant. God's finest predatory creation, the leopard, though not as powerful as the lion or as speedy as the cheetah, possesses an impressive combination of the two. Like a ghost, the leopard kills in the shadows, only allowing itself to be seen in rare instances. And, like a ghost, it leaves doubt hanging in the air as if it were never there, as if it hadn't just stole off with a baby in the night.

I couldn't wait for a leopard to feed on a bait.

The next morning, we checked every bait—no hits. We spent the remainder of the morning hanging the last five carcasses. Baiting for big cats takes time. It is hard work, with no guarantee of success and little in the way of action. Baiting with recently harvested game meat has been the most common and effective way to manage the leopard population throughout most of Africa. A population that is healthy, even booming in many areas. Cotton's area was full of leopards. We would get one to hit sooner or later.

With the baits set, we were in a waiting and checking game. Wait for tomorrow morning, check every bait-tree again. A leopard hadn't even inspected one yet. Not a single track.

Since no leopard fed the night before, a renewed quest for buffalo commenced. Determination etched itself on every face. Durani slowed in any buffalo-looking areas. Peter scouted the landscape for buffalo and the ground for tracks. Cotton's focus was intense. Hillary kept his hand over his eyes to block out the sun. With wind in our faces, Mary and I tried to watch under the trees for sign of game we knew someone else would probably see before we did.

Like the day before, and the day before that, we sped through the large smoldering fields, ash and smoke finding ways to absorb itself into our bodies. At the edge of one of the more massive of these fields, Peter told Durani to stop. We coasted well beyond the spot that interested Peter. He slipped off the back and ran down the trail road. Durani backed up after him.

"What is it?"

"*Mbogo.*"

Cotton's head perked up as he turned to see what his lead tracker was doing.

Running a few more yards, Peter finally stopped where the black desolate field met a perfect line of un-torched earth, amber blades of grass struggling to live under a hammering afternoon sun. Once there, his eyes searched the ground, following it into a thicket of short grass and thorn bushes. We could barely make out his tall, thin form bending over before Durani brought the Cruiser to a halt.

Mary and I knew *mbogo*, but for all our neck-straining and peering through our binoculars couldn't see a single buffalo.

"Where are they?" Mary asked Cotton as he stepped away from the vehicle.

"These tracks lead the way." Waving us forward, he disappeared into the grass like Peter had a moment before.

I snatched my rifle and we hurried to follow Hillary into the thicket. A few yards into the thorns, Hillary pointed to the ground. It was impossible to miss. Layer upon layer of massive hoof prints, a river of tracks leading to an unknown destination. We intended to follow.

Your gut tells you what it thinks about tracking buffalo. It starts as a tickle, like a feather tip wriggling in your hollow stomach. When you catch the scent, that unmistakable buffalo odor hanging faintly in the air, the feather becomes a sharpened pencil, jabbing at your stomach's walls, prodding you to investigate further, or possibly begging you to abandon the trail—so hard to tell. When you close the distance, sweat gathering like a storm cloud on your forehead, the pencil transforms once more into a spiked medieval mace, churning throughout the insides of your torso. The bull turns with his nose high in the air, arrogant fire in his eyes. Which of you is more afraid? Trying to will your nerves into submission, you squeeze the trigger, knowing you will have to squeeze again. The hunt is at its height. What happens after that can go either way, but a different part of you takes over then, a part ruled by instinct and resolution, and the tickle fades.

Fear and desire, excitement and trepidation, sanity and passion, grapple like monsters. In the end, buffalo hunting is an obsession. The bull you are after may take days and miles of hiking and tracking or he may offer a quick opportunity during the first hour of the first day. Regardless, it exhausts you, physically and mentally. Sometimes to the point of sickness, as if he had put you under his horns and rolled you along the plains. It is a good sickness. You have hunted buffalo and, even if you failed to realize it at the time, it will stay with you—it will change you in ways you will never notice. I could never get enough.

When Peter pushed his finger into a steaming pile of buffalo dung, we knew the hunt was on.

"Want rifle?" Peter said, wiping his finger on his pants.

Cotton nodded.

Peter ran off, returning a moment later with Cotton's .458 side-by-side.

Peter and Hillary took the lead. They glided through the thicket, one eye on the tracks, one focused ahead. Following the trail, stomped low from hundreds of heavy hoofs, did not take a seasoned bushman. But Hillary and Peter were not just following the mass to the middle of the herd. Somehow, they distinguished two big bull tracks buried in the jumble of interlaying marks. By the time we found the herd, the bulls could be mixed in anywhere, but if Peter or Hillary could find an advantage against a herd this large, we would take it.

We resisted quick movements. Not because we saw our quarry, but because we did not see them.

Less than ten feet ahead, Peter crouched, his visible form barely distinguishable from a tangled mess of thorns. We inched beside him. He had just removed his finger from another dung pile. It had been so soft that he motioned for Cotton and his big-bore to take the lead.

Hillary leaned forward to whisper. "*Mbogo.*"

Cotton stood motionless beside Peter. My palms sweat.

Where was it?

A snort, followed by the snapping of wood finally gave them away. Deep silence crept in, holding us at bay. As we listened to the quiet, an odor emanated toward us. My body seemed to absorb it as if it seeped into my pores. The scent was an unforgettable mix of dried manure and a three-day-old, sweat-soaked t-shirt. After a few encounters, you come to anticipate that smell, even to crave it.

Cotton waved me forward.

"We think they moved into a big open field just through here. There might be a straggler, so we'll take it slow." Cotton's whisper was difficult to hear. We were both on one knee. "Peter saw a good bull. When we see them, be ready."

For fifty yards through thorns scratching and slicing at my arms and legs, I shadowed Cotton. The smell, distinct as ever, grew to an invisible cloud so thick you could almost touch it.

A few more steps and the thicket thinned. Just enough to see a mass of black, moving, nearly undulating, as the herd positioned itself in defense.

They all looked huge. Hard muscled, thick-necked, and not afraid to defend themselves. When a buffalo knows he is dead, his every intention is to take someone with him. With fifty of them staring you down, chests out, noses in the air, steady nerves must dictate actions. Focusing in on one bull while, at the same time, not forgetting about the others is like trying to read a novel and absorb an opera at the same time. It's impossible to give both the attention they demand.

"He's the third from the left."

He stood as defiant as the others did, his chin gray as dusk, his head drooping from the constant weight of his horns. With a full, heavy boss, they swooped down, pushing his ears against his neck. Their upward curve lasted forever, reaching out so far they looked as if he could wrap them around a large sausage tree, pierce it with the tips and uproot it with a sweep of his solid neck.

He had, no doubt, fought off many attackers, both predator and competitor. His furrowed brow and hardened stare suggested he had seen his fair share of battles. A few puny bipeds were cause for caution, but he would fight if need be.

He was about to find out how serious we were.

I had two possible shots—the brain or, my preference at this range, the chest just below the neck where his soccer ball-sized heart should take the full effect of lead. My finger went firm around the trigger. I hardly felt the .375's mule kick.

The herd, so bold a moment ago, rumbled off, our bull disappearing into the crowd. I kept on him until a cloud of dust blurred our view.

"Give them a moment," Cotton said.

"Good shot." Peter and Hillary appeared next to Cotton; Mary and Joan were just behind them.

"How'd it feel?" Cotton asked.

"Perfect."

I have had perfect-feeling shots turn into all-day affairs after wounded game.

"He should have a hard time keeping up with the herd."

If I hit him as well as I thought, he probably wouldn't even try. Wounded buffalo often turn to face their attackers.

A lone, dark figure appeared through the settling dust. His eyes, more rage than before, seemed to say, *Is that all you got?* He did not intend to go peacefully. He caught sight of us and lunged forward.

My rifle snapped to my shoulder. I knew Cotton's did as well. The bull's initial burst carried him only a few feet. His legs gave out. He staggered sideways and crashed to the ground. The somber death bellow sounded a moment later.

Silent and awestruck, we did not move.

Hillary and Peter shook my hand. "Good," they said. "Very good."

"Congratulations, Dick. He is a fine bull. One of the best I've taken this season," Cotton said.

Mary, my sweet wife, kissed me.

After making sure he was done for, we all chipped in to help Hillary, Peter, and Kafia skin and quarter the old bull. Their precise, quick knife-work equaled that of any butcher I had ever seen.

"What is that?" Mary asked. "It sounds like frogs."

"Must mean it's going to rain," Cotton said. "We're still a month away from the rainy season, but that doesn't matter. The frogs are better rain forecasters than any meteorologist."

"Don't see any clouds," I said.

"I don't question the frogs."

Hillary, Peter, and Kafia picked up the pace. When they started the skinning process, they joked and laughed. Now they sliced and cut without as much as a word or glance at each other. Their hands and clothes bloody, they seemed not to notice the stench rising from the entrails, cooking in the heat. We all moved upwind.

"Peter, why don't you go get Durani and have him bring the truck."

"Must finish first." He pointed to the sky. "*Mvua*."

"Peter says he needs to finish before the rain comes," Cotton said. "I'll run back for Durani and the truck."

By the time Cotton and Durani returned, Hillary, Peter, and Kafia were nearly finished and a storm cloud had rumbled in to block the sun. As we loaded the skin and meat, it started. Not as a trickle, but as a torrent, a violent gush.

The Land Cruiser had an open top.

Durani huddled over the steering wheel, raindrops pelting his face. The rest of us hunkered, risking only brief glimpses at the trail ahead. Peter and Hillary faced the back, crouched over, trying to make themselves small.

Moments earlier, we complained of the heat. Now, dripping wet, shivering, we desired it. Mary scooted close, pressing against me. If we wanted to talk, we had to yell above the rain and engine. Remaining quiet seemed the order of the moment. Realizing the fire pit had no cover, making it back to camp didn't seem nearly as imperative. Drying out would be interesting.

Halfway back, the rain stopped as abruptly as it had started.

Camp had been untouched. The sun set as we pulled in. Hurrying to the fire, Cotton had the boys throw a few more logs on before he headed to the dining tent to check on dinner.

We crowded the flames until it was time to eat, trying to get rid of the wet chills clinging to our skin under a change of dry clothes. Mary shivered again. I do not think it was from the cold. It was the shiver of a woman who had found happiness in a single moment.

The fire's snapping almost seemed to have a rhythm, like the hyena laughing in the distance. All of Africa, in fact, was rhythmic, harmonious and discordant at the same time. Full of energy, yet surrounded by death on so many sides. Everyone, everything, thirsting for life, while evading the fangs of death in all its forms.

Staring into the fire, I saw more than dancing flames of yellow and orange and every shade of each. Deep within, where spots of black charged like a buffalo stampede, I saw the stories of past hunts and the untold stories of hunts yet to unfold.

I was no longer cold.

SEEING SPOTS: MARY

"I told you, I'm not going to shoot a leopard unless it's posing for me. It has to be less than fifty yards, in good light, perfectly broadside, and you have to back me up. I couldn't live with myself if you were attacked again."

"All I said was that I think you should join me in the blind the next time a leopard feeds. If you decide not to shoot one..." Cotton shrugged as he ambled away from the Cruiser.

The only creatures that visited the first bait were flies and other insects. It was the same with the second bait and each bait after that.

"Leopards are being finicky."

"That's fine with me."

"There are less than two weeks left and two leopards to go. That doesn't leave much time."

"That's why Dick should sit in the blind."

"We'll see."

"What does that mean?"

"It means, we'll see. If it looks like a situation for Dick, then it'll be him. But I think it will be your turn next."

"Oh yeah? Well, we'll see."

Cotton chuckled.

I'm not sure it was funny.

Hillary spotted a small impala herd shortly after we left the last bait.

"We should be able to get a shot from that tree over there," Cotton said.

The impalas trotted in circles. They snapped their eyes and noses back and forth, but they never ran off. Dick shot a female for bait and camp meat.

We drove to the thickest, darkest looking mess of trees, thorns, and vines in the area. The sun was bright, but peering into the shadows from the outside, you'd swear you were about to enter a cave. It had to be more than a thousand acres of thicket.

"If there's no leopard here, we may never find one," Cotton half-joked.

"How come we didn't try here before?" I asked.

"You'll see." Cotton winked at me. One side of his lip curled up. The thicket seemed to darken.

Hillary, Peter, and Kafia pulled three long *pangas* from behind the driver's seat. Durani hefted the impala to his shoulders. The boys whacked away, hacking a narrow trail through a mess of razor thorns. Just before Cotton fell in step behind them, he glanced back at me with that same half-cocked smirk. The shadows swallowed him. The thicket seemed to close in behind him. I took a deep breath and ducked in. A branch snagged my shirt as if trying to warn me. The boys moved fast. I was already lagging. Behind me, Durani waited patiently with his heavy burden. Thorns or no thorns, I hurried to catch up.

The shadows wrapped over us. Tiny spots of light penetrated the dense canopy and painted the trail like diamonds shining under a thin layer of dust. The sound of snapping branches and steel blades meeting wood signaled every turn. We zigged and we zagged. We stepped over so many logs and exposed roots and pushed away so many vines, it was hard to know the direction. We could have been going straight or walking in circles. I followed Dick, his arms covered in thin scratches. In front of him, I saw only shadows and thorns. They seemed to move with us, pushing us into the unknown.

Hillary, Peter, and Kafia kept chopping away. You would have thought their trail would have been wider. It was as if they would sever one branch and another would grow back instantly in its place. Sweat soaked our clothes. How Kafia kept that stocking cap on his head, I will never know. I had never seen him without it.

We ducked, crouched, stepped high and low, twisted around tangles, and were slapped by more branches than I care to remember. At one point, a strange thorn bush grabbed Dick and pulled him back violently. He grunted and glanced at his arm. He gave a tug. It did not budge. Reaching down with his free hand, he clasped the end thorn and pulled. One-by-one they popped out, leaving instant bruises around every small puncture. Wincing and rubbing his arm under the area, he looked back at me.

"Careful of the wait-a-bit thorns," he said.

I managed to squeeze through without suffering Dick's fate. I glanced back at Durani, wondering if he would be smiling. He was. His smile was always there, always genuine. Whether driving, hauling an impala, or eating lunch, he wore a grin. I had walked by once while he napped under a shade tree—he even smiled in his sleep. That simple, honest contentment made me forget about vines, slapping branches, and even wait-a-bit thorns.

One by one, we stepped into a clearing. My lower back creaked like a slowly opened door in a haunted house.

"I hope there's another way out," I said.

Cotton put his index finger to his lips. "Hillary saw a fresh track as we came through," he whispered. "It'll be better going out. The boys will find an easier trail—or cut one. We need to get in and out of here quickly and quietly."

They picked a short, thick tree. Peter scaled it with the speed and confidence of Spiderman zipping up the side of a skyscraper. Hillary threw a rope up to him, while Kafia tied the other end to the impala carcass. Before Peter hoisted it up, Hillary sliced the ewe up the belly and had Kafia drag the entrails around the immediate area. After securing the carcass, Peter snapped some nearby leafy branches to cover it. The three of them stood for a moment with their hands on their hips, admiring their work.

All we needed was a hungry tom.

We strolled from the forest with little more than a few bushes or wide-trunked trees encumbering the trail. Peter led as if he had hiked the same path hundreds of times. We could have driven the Land Cruiser most of the way to the bait if we cut down a few more thorns.

"Why didn't we come in this way?"

"You didn't find our stroll enjoyable?"

"We could've driven to the tree."

"What fun would that have been?"

Neither Cotton nor the others had known about our newfound path. From outside, the forest wall appeared denser where Peter found the trail out. They would use it in the future.

"We'd hunted leopard there many times, but had never found an easy way in and out." Cotton's eyes gleamed. "Has anyone ever told you that you're good luck?"

Cotton was able to pull off a tease and a compliment in the same sentence. He and Joan were gracious hosts. Whether we realized it or not, a friendship was forming that would last our lifetimes.

"Let's see how lucky you really are. Hillary says we drove over a line of fresh buffalo tracks."

I smiled meekly. Dangerous game makes my lungs feel like I am inhaling frozen air and leaves my fingers trembling. I am afraid of elephants, lions, leopards, rhinos, and buffalo. So why put myself in such situations? I told myself Dick and Cotton talked me into it. Yet, they never had to try too hard. Part of me wanted to see if I could do it. Part of me needed to do it. I cannot explain it better than that. Some people know what I mean. Some folks never will. A hunter lives inside me. She needs to get out, to explore, to feel wonder and awe. Each expedition, each hunt, she takes over a greater portion of who I am and leaves me in what I can only describe as withdrawals once a hunt ends. At the same time, I was scared out of my wits. I needed somebody to talk me into doing something I was addicted to.

Speeding across an open field, charcoaled from a week-old fire, I watched the horizon and wondered what was beyond that line where the sky met a row of trees. Would I find my buffalo there? Or would it be something else? The most I could know, the most I cared to know, was that it held the future. I took Dick's hand. He and Cotton were laughing and joking about something. I wasn't listening. I didn't have to. He was smiling; I was smiling. What else did I need to know?

"Stop," Peter said shortly after we entered an amber field free of ash.

Acacias dotted the landscape. Under one of them, a single, dark mass moved. Buffalo.

"Are you ready?"

Dick handed me my .375. "Here you go."

The rifle fostered confidence. Maybe just one more nudge from somebody would do it. I do not sweat much, but I could feel a bead itching through my forehead. I waited.

Cotton stared through his binos, evaluating the herd. Everyone was quiet.

The silence, the uncertainty, allowed reservations to rise in my stomach.

"Is there a good bull?" I said, trying to sound enthusiastic.

Cotton studied them through his binoculars, sizing them up. He could have grunted or nodded—anything. Couldn't he see I needed something? Yes or no; it didn't matter. Any answer would do.

"There he is."

"Bwana." Peter tapped Cotton's shoulder and pointed past him.

What was that marching across the *pan?* Eland. We'd never successfully hunted eland before. As tempting as buffalo were, our focus changed without hesitation.

The largest antelope in the world, an eland bull can weigh up to two thousand pounds—heavier than its antlered counterpart, the moose. Eland move with a fluid grace. An old male's smooth, tan skin almost hangs from its body, most conspicuously on its thick, black-tufted dewlap waggling from its neck. Its skin undulates as it walks, each step an effortless glide across the savannah on a never-ending nomadic journey. I've rarely seen an eland stand still for more than a few moments. With a top speed around twenty-five miles-per-hour, it is unlikely an eland will win any sprint, but their endurance is legendary.

We had hunted eland during our inaugural trip to Africa in 1987. We had seen a few, but with their uncanny ability to trek and trek, they gave us the slip every time. With at least one hundred in this herd, and many bulls, it was a prime opportunity. Cotton instructed Durani to drive in a big circle ahead of them where we could attempt an ambush. Predicting an eland's destination is a guessing game, but their current course seemed honest. We drove in a route parallel with the herd at first, then turned along a line of fever trees.

With luck, their course would hold true. Though slow by antelope standards, twenty-five miles-per-hour was faster than we could sprint. With the herd in the open, our best bet was to try cutting them off.

We skipped the usual ritual of stepping from the vehicle, hem-hawing around with our rifles, and trying to be quiet before beginning a stalk. Instead, we took off on a jog through bushes laden with thorns. Our arms and legs and faces were bleeding after a few yards. Branches snatched our clothes as we passed, holding just long enough to snap back at the unfortunate follower. After one or two slaps from a thorn-covered branch, we spaced out at a safer distance. It didn't protect us completely, but helped prevent a thorn in an eye. Our pace slowed to a hasty walk, fast enough to make good time, slow enough to avoid most of the thorns. Each pierce, each deep scratch, burned, but there was no time to lick our wounds. Our quest—eland—pushed us through the midday heat.

Eland are hard to come by. You can track them for weeks, suffering only missed opportunities, setbacks, and physical exhaustion. If we were to have a shooting opportunity, we would have to hurry. We would find them soon, or not at all.

"There." Cotton went to one knee.

Trying to catch our breath, we crouched beside him.

Unaware of our presence, the eland marched on, moving from our right to left.

"Shoot the bull in front," Cotton said without looking away from the herd.

The eland didn't stop to pose. They meandered along, apparently with somewhere to go. Dick fired.

"He's down. Good shot. Mary, shoot the third one from the left." Cotton's voice was calm, confident, firm. "You don't have much time."

They started running, though without conviction. Where had the shot come from? They paused. I started squeezing the trigger. A few of the others decided they didn't care where the danger was, they wanted to run. My bull joined them. I followed, sweeping the gun with him like on a rising pheasant. His momentum built with each step. Mostly on instinct, I squeezed, following through the way wingshooting had taught me. The bull crumpled to the ground, sliding a few feet before coming to a final rest.

Peter whooped.

Hillary laughed.

Dick smiled.

I beamed.

"That was a fine display of shooting," Cotton said. He shook Dick's hand and gave me a hug.

Hillary and Peter both congratulated us with handshakes and "good shot, good shot." Peter then ran back through the thorns. He reappeared a few minutes later with Durani and Kafia in the Land Cruiser. Laughing and carrying on, they went to work on the carcasses.

"The boys can skin an eland fast, but two eland?" Cotton raised his eyebrows. He smiled that half-open, one-sided grin we had come to expect. "Might be late for lunch."

"It's worth it," I said.

Cotton's half-smile formed again. "At least she's got her priorities straight."

Peter and Durani worked on Dick's bull; Hillary and Kafia on mine. Slicing and cutting, skinning and carving, the task seemed daunting, almost impossible. They plugged away, chattering and laughing all the while. We helped when we could, stayed out of the way when we needed to. Within half-an-hour, they had made enough progress that an end felt attainable. They carved all the humanly edible meat from those two eland, taking the heart, liver and most of the other organs as well as every small piece of fat they could find. The back end of the Cruiser sagged and the bumper scraped the ground whenever we rolled over a rise on the trail.

Another rain shower surprised us as we drove to camp.

I held my hands near my face to shield it from the heavy drops. My hair, flat as an elephant-stomped field, hung in my eyes when the rain stopped. Our clothes gained a few pounds.

After changing, we scarfed down a bowl of buffalo tail soup and hit the trail again. We checked all six baits, keeping our eyes open for prey. None of the baits had been touched. You bait and bait, hoping for a leopard to feed. When one finally claims the bait as his own, there is no guarantee he will show up the following night. Even if he does, it might be dark. Though always hunting, traveling from bait to bait usually takes the better part of a morning or afternoon. Maybe we were not meant to get a leopard.

"We couldn't keep them off the baits two weeks ago," Cotton said. "One morning we had three baits hit by three different cats. And we'd only hung four."

"Just finicky I guess."

"Kind of like a woman," Cotton smirked. He winked at Dick.

"Now, Cotton," Joan said. "We don't need to go there do we?"

Cotton wrapped his arm around his wife. "No? I guess it was me who needed all that time to fix my hair before hunting."

"Who's the one who needs the best camp in Tanzania?"

"Clients need to be comfortable."

"Your sleeping quarters are always just as nice."

"But dear. I just want you to be comfortable."

"Maybe we should call the battle of the sexes a draw for now," I said.

"Why sure, Mary. That sounds fair." Cotton winked at me before leaning over to Dick's ear, speaking loud enough to make sure everyone heard. "Darn women always get their way."

I shook my finger at him and gave him my best motherly *you had better be good* look. I received a hoarse guffaw in return.

With less than two hours before dark, we hunted back to camp. Dick shot a Coke's hartebeest after a short stalk and while we were field dressing it, Peter spied two hyenas skulking in the shadows.

"Grab your rifle, Mary," Cotton said as he hefted his own from the vehicle. "Let's see if we can get them both. Probably be gone before we get a chance, but it'll take a few minutes to get the hartebeest loaded anyway."

Peter was on their trail instantly. He bent over to touch the dirt, examining both tracks like a detective sorting out clues, trying to determine where they would go.

"No hunting. They go just to go," he said shrugging. "No much. Two only." He held up two fingers.

"Think they'll go far?"

"No, just there," He pointed past a narrow line of brush fifty yards distant. "Come. Mama shoot good." Nodding his head, he smiled and led us forward.

Cotton and I followed almost at a jog. We stopped at the edge of the brush to catch our breath and survey the situation.

"There." Cotton raised his rifle. "You take the one on the left. I'll shoot the other one. On three. Ready?"

I snapped the rifle to my shoulder. "Wait," I said.

With the scope turned up to a higher power, I couldn't find them. Lowering the barrel, I twisted the scope to its lowest level. Jerking it back up, I found both predators.

"Okay. The one on the left."

"One, two, three."

Cotton's rifle barked an instant after mine.

Then silence. The kind of silence that only exists after a hunter fires a weapon. Everything pauses, wind seems to calm, birds do not flutter, leaves forget to rustle. It lasts only a moment. A moment of utter stillness. A moment so frozen in briefness it almost does not exist. More sensed than known, it is a moment the hunter cannot turn away from. The bullet has been fired. The result determined.

Peter spoke first. "Good shot."

"Great job," Cotton said, grabbing my shoulder.

"Did you get yours?" I had watched mine run twenty yards before it tumbled.

"I got him. He ran the opposite way from yours and disappeared in to the trees. I hit him well. He won't go far."

"Congratulations."

"You too. Now let's go get them." Cotton turned to our trusty tracker. "Why don't you run back to the truck and bring the others."

"Yes. Soon sun gone." He glanced at the horizon.

"I'll find him. I don't think he went far."

"Yes, good shot."

Twilight began and ended at the snap of a finger. Lions began to roar, hyenas laughed and yipped, many smaller predators were prowling. Darkness in the African bush, sometimes so black that visibility cannot be measured, made me feel alone. I couldn't get to camp, to the fire, soon enough.

We'd had a good day, productive and engaging. The kind of day you didn't want to end, but one your body couldn't fight off long. I fell asleep so fast I thought nothing could wake me. I thought wrong.

A lion's roar rattled my eardrums. I pulled the covers tight to my chin.

I heard footsteps—soft footsteps. I tried to tell myself it would be all right, that I should go back to sleep, but between the memory of that lion's voice, the footsteps sneaking closer, and Dick's snores, I did not stand a chance.

When I finally fell asleep, it was in short, almost immeasurable, moments. But I dreamed and my dreams were of a creature without fangs and claws. Eland—sleek, elegant, and huge with tight-spiraled horns and a creamy coat, forever roaming Tanzania's plains—allowed the sleep I stole to be tranquil. It never lasted.

Rain began spattering camp. Millions of tiny splashes collectively bombarded us with machine-gun attacks. What else could keep me awake?

When the hyenas showed up, that just made the lions angry and a raucous melee ensued. The night air echoed with growls, yips, and occasional roars for an hour, alternately fading to a rustle and then rising to a deafening crescendo. It finally stopped with the abruptness of a judge's gavel, but their shrieks and bellows echoed through my head for the rest of the night.

"Ready to do the rounds?" Cotton asked the following morning.

We had settled into a routine of checking leopard baits first thing each morning, always with reserved hope that dwindled after each untouched slab of meat. At the sixth tree, we found leopard tracks. The cat had patrolled back and forth beneath the tree and climbed it once. It never touched the bait. The paw prints were big enough to suggest a tom.

"I've told the boys to build a blind that Mama will be comfortable in."

"I think they should build one Dick will be comfortable in."

"I thought you said you wanted to get this leopard hunting over with. Tonight could be your chance."

It felt like a thousand electric eels slithered in my belly. Cotton was right about one thing: I wanted it to be over. I watched Peter, Kafia, and Durani construct the blind. They gave special care to every detail. They built it thirty yards downwind and covered it with leafy tree branches, all using nothing more than *pangas* and the natural resources around us.

Part of me was ready to duck into the dark shadows and listen for an approaching leopard, hoping for the leopard to step onto the branch, silhouetted perfectly against the fading twilight. I couldn't wait.

After testing the blind's sturdiness, we decided to check one other bait. It had been hit as well. This time the leopard had fed, devouring nearly half of the carcass.

"This leopard doesn't appear to be as big. I think we'll stick with the other blind tonight. He's probably hungrier anyway since he didn't gorge himself last night the way this one did."

"Seems to be more cautious too," Dick said.

"The big ones usually are."

Driving away from the bait, I noticed that Joan seemed nearly as jumpy as I was. Cotton didn't seem worried at all. After being mauled by a leopard in the past, you would think he would be reluctant to get back in the blind with someone like me. I know I would. Not Cotton. Throughout the rest of the morning, he almost had a glow to him. He didn't say much, but when he did, it was usually something like "those tracks sure looked big," or "I hope he comes back tonight."

Joan didn't say anything directly to Cotton, but when he and Dick left to stalk an oribi, it seemed she had to talk to somebody.

"I sure get nervous whenever Cotton hunts leopards. After that time he was mauled, it's never been the same. He was in such bad shape. Can you believe he went back after that leopard the very same night? Said he had to get it sorted out or something before his wounds stiffened. I know he's a great PH, but leopards are sneaky and when wounded they are darn aggressive. I know you probably don't want to hear this. I just get anxious before a leopard hunt, that's all."

"How many close calls has he had?"

"Not many. He's killed more than two hundred leopards with clients and only had one or two accidents. You'll be fine. It's just difficult for me to forget the close calls. Cotton is very careful. I don't think his mauling affected him as much as me. I'm sorry to make you nervous. I just needed to get that off my chest."

"It's okay. I guess I'm better off knowing the risks. I will not take a shot unless I'm sure of it."

Dick and Cotton seemed extra jovial. My head swirled with images of leopards flying through the air, teeth bared, claws curled, streaking toward me. How was I going to do it? Was I ready? Sure, I *could* do it. I wanted to. Maybe I should try to talk Dick into taking my place. But it would be something to take a leopard.

Do you want to get Cotton mauled again? My mind played ping-pong with these questions throughout the remainder of the day. There were brief moments when I forgot them, like when Cotton and I stalked a Thomson's gazelle. Somehow, I focused enough to put it down with one shot.

At lunch, Joan offered me a soft drink. I declined. Once seated in a leopard blind, it is important not to move or talk or make a sound until after a shot has been made. Under those circumstances, the discomfort of a full bladder would be too much. I would rather be thirsty. I could take a bottle of water and drink after I shot the leopard or after it became too dark to shoot. I could wait that long.

That afternoon, when Cotton, Hillary, and I stepped from the truck, I briefly thought about jumping back in. Then Dick hopped out to wish me good luck with a kiss before he and the others drove away. He was smiling. I was not.

At first, we sat reading. My legs stiffened. Occasionally, I peered through the shooting hole to look at the bait. Cotton also looked up from his book, but with less regularity than I did. He had been there many times. The leopard would come when it wanted to—most likely not for another hour.

Silence ruled the afternoon. Sometimes a bird called overhead, but mostly— nothing. If there was a breeze, I couldn't hear it. I thought I heard a soft crunch, but when I looked to Cotton and Hillary, they seemed oblivious. It sounded as if it came from behind us. What if the leopard was sneaking toward us? A shiver inched into my leg. I couldn't tell if it was from fear or adrenaline. I couldn't tell if I liked it or not.

Thirty minutes later, I could no longer read. The sun's movement cast long, dark shadows over the beams of light that penetrated through the tiny open spaces of the blind. I felt the world closing in. Daylight faded and all that existed were a stuffy blind, three hopeful hunters, and a leopard bait eager for a cat.

I almost felt alone. If a tom showed, my world would condense even further to the conflict inside my head and a beautiful beast standing atop a branch thirty yards away.

Stiffness in my right leg turned from a tingle to a pain. Stabbing and throbbing at first, it twisted into a constant ache. I moved just enough for my muscles to tense, but not enough for any relief. I think I made it worse. I pushed myself up with my arms. Grunting, I slid my leg and stretched it. My foot scraped across the ground and kicked a small pack I had brought along.

Cotton turned to me, his eyes wide, his features stern. He raised a finger to his lips and then pointed toward the bait tree.

Was there a leopard in the tree? I had to see.

I was still looking at Cotton and he at me. "Don't move," he mouthed.

I sucked in a deep breath, my rapid heart knocking my lungs. Where was it? Something rustled. It sounded close. Too close. Oh my goodness. What if it tried to get in the blind? There was a coughing growl. He was right there. I wanted to scream. I needed to look. I didn't dare move. Another cough. This one closer. He was almost on top of us. What was Cotton doing? My leg, my right leg, so painful just a moment ago, was going to give us away. I couldn't stop it from shaking. It thumped the ground. It didn't hurt anymore, but it convulsed as if having a seizure. I reached down with my hand and tried to pressure it into submission. My arm started shaking. The leopard would surely hear. What if he came to investigate? I had to look. What if he ran away and I never saw him? What if he charged? Cotton wouldn't put me in danger. But what if Cotton couldn't see him charge? I swear I heard the leopard breathing. I had to look.

I heard the quick scrape of claws on a tree. He was climbing. Too close to be the bait tree. Much too loud. Could it be the tree beside me? It sounded like it could.

Without taking his eyes from the shooting hole, Cotton eased his hand over and tapped my knee. I stared at him for instruction. I wanted to claw out of the blind and yell at the leopard. I watched Cotton. What should I do?

Cotton signed that the leopard was in the tree and that it was safe to look.

In the bait tree? He sounded closer.

I leaned forward and squinted into the fading evening. I saw the tree. I saw the bait. I did not see the leopard. Where was he? Maybe I had read Cotton's sign wrong. Maybe the leopard was in a different tree. It could be right above us. Staring at the bait, I tried to listen. Nothing. Other than the thumping of my leg—silence. Where was the leopard? I prayed it wasn't ready to pounce. I glanced at Cotton. He was staring toward the bait tree. The leopard had to be there. I looked again. Still nothing. I stared until my eyes went blurry. I didn't see any spots. It had to be somewhere else.

Claws hit bark again, rapidly scraping. The bushes rustled behind the tree then silence.

Cotton shrugged.

"I never saw him," I whispered as softly as I could.

"He was in the fork staring at us for nearly ten minutes," Cotton whispered just as inaudibly. He put his finger back to his lips. "He might come back. Be ready."

Evening withered to twilight. My leg was as jumpy as ever. Maybe it was trying to keep up with my heartbeat. I couldn't slow either.

A branch snapped in the distance. The shakes grew more pronounced. Was he coming back? Would it be too late? I peered through the shooting hole. Deep shadows darkened my view. Some of them seemed to move, to sneak like a cat prowling for dinner. Each shadow cast lifelike silhouettes. Shadows on top of shadows, interacting, coalescing into forms both real and imagined.

The bait grew fainter each moment. Maybe next time. I would have liked to see him, but if he failed to return, there was no chance for me to wound him.

The leopard coughed. Close.

My entire body started shaking. Where was he? Too close. Maybe at the tree, maybe closer. Every shadow became a possible tom slipping closer, inching its way toward food. I wished I could see it.

Scrap-scrap-scrap.

In the tree again.

Concentrating on the limb where the bait hung, I expected the leopard to ease out. I waited. Nothing.

"Take him whenever you're ready," Cotton whispered.

Where was he?

"You better take him."

I couldn't find him through the scope. I found the bait again and searched around it. Why couldn't I find him?

"Shoot him now. He's going to jump."

There. The leopard was standing broadside, staring at the blind. I stole a brief glance into his eyes before lining up on his shoulder. They glowed. His eyes did not hold fear. They were calculating. He knew something was out of place.

I told myself I would only shoot a leopard under perfect conditions. None of those self-promises entered my thoughts. My concentration centered through the scope to the leopard's shoulder. The focus managed to stay my unruly nerves. I picked out a single rosette on his coat and squeezed when the cross-hairs settled.

The impact from the bullet knocked the tom off his perch. He hit the ground with a hollow thud. Silence lasted only a moment before a rustle and a scampering of paws faded into the shadows. Then, a lasting quiet.

What happened? I thought I hit him perfect. Why did I let them talk me into hunting leopard?

"I thought you hit him well," Cotton finally whispered.

"It felt good," I said. I was shaking worse than I had all night.

"I'm sure he didn't go far. We will wait until the others arrive. They heard the shot and should be on their way. We'll just sit here and listen."

I nodded. By then darkness had overwhelmed the blind to the point that Cotton's form was less than an outline. I could still see he was there, but the line where he began and where the air started had no distinction.

We listened to nothing for so long I thought the leopard must still be alive. Only a leopard stalking through the forest can be that quiet.

Where was the truck?

Blackness engulfed the night. No outlines. Nothing. I could no longer see the peephole. I couldn't see my hand two inches from my face. I tried anyway.

I heard a baboon bark and then one or two baboon screams—just as they would do if a leopard were nearby. Great. The rattled drone of the approaching vehicle cut off their voices.

Feeling for the peephole with my hand, I stuck my eye up to it, wishing I could see something. Anything would be nice.

The glow from approaching headlights pierced the darkness. The shaking abated.

"Hand me the torch, Hillary."

I felt Hillary reach past me, then heard a click, followed by light. I could see again. Cotton pushed away the grass door. A rush of cool air alleviated the stuffi-ness. How comforting to see again.

Dick walked up with Peter and Kafia. Dick and Kafia were smiling. Peter resisted.

"Did you get him?" Dick asked.

I started to shrug, but Cotton interjected.

"She drilled him in the shoulder. He went down, but got right up. Most likely we'll find him dead in the scrub brush."

"What's the plan?" Dick asked, slipping over to my side.

"I think it'd be best if you stayed here with Mary while the boys and I go have a look."

"Whatever you think is best," I said. Inside, razors were tearing me apart.

Cotton was about to head into the darkness with a shotgun—to face down a potentially wounded leopard waiting for the opportunity to attack. I shot the leopard. If Cotton or one of the others got mauled, or worse, it would be my fault. What had I been thinking? I shouldn't have shot. I had allowed myself to get sucked into the moment. I should have been out there with Cotton. My nerves could never handle it. Cotton was the professional. He had been in this situation before—but I hadn't put him in his earlier situations, had I?

"Did you hear that? Was that a leopard growl?"

"I didn't hear anything," Dick said.

"Shine the flashlight over there."

"Where?"

"Over there. That way."

"What're we looking for?"

"Shh. Just a minute."

I stared into shadows cast by the flashlight knowing Mr. Tom lurked there somewhere, alive, ready for vengeance. I listened. I stared. I waited. We heard Cotton and the others inching their way through the darkness for the first ten minutes. Then silence. They had gone past earshot, past any probability my leopard ran a few yards and died, past the chance that the bullet hit him in the vitals. I felt nauseous.

For another twenty minutes, Dick and I stood beside the blind, listening to quiet darkness, periodically chasing shadows with our beam of light. I expected to hear gunfire, followed by screams and more gunfire. The longer I didn't hear it the more I expected to. The waiting, the silence, the shadows. It was too much. I couldn't imagine what Cotton and the boys must have been going through.

"Did you hear that?"

"What?" Dick said "Where?"

"Over there. There's something out there."

Dick shined the light toward the source of the sound. He heard it too. Rustling. Unmistakable and coming toward us.

Dick pushed the flashlight into my hands. We stared into the brush. Dick reached his left hand to his right shoulder, to his rifle's sling. A form came through the brush. I stepped back, my palms sweating as my grip tightened around the flashlight. Preparing myself to run, I kept the beam locked on the shape moving into full light.

Peter.

Thank God.

He waved us forward. When we didn't follow right away, he took another step forward.

"Come," he said, pointing into the darkness.

He was smiling. My muscles relaxed. Peter's demeanor suggested everything was fine, in fact, better than fine. Could I believe they had found the leopard without incident.

"Peter?"

"Yes, Mama." Peter turned his head to answer without breaking stride. He had traveled back to the blind without a light and was now leading in only the half-light of our flashlight's beam.

"Did you find the leopard?"

His grin widened. "Come, we go."

Peter quickened his pace. Without turning back, he knew when to slow down so we could stay within a few yards of his lead. We continued at this sporadic stride for ten minutes before I spied a flicker through the foliage, and then the sound of rising voices. Cotton's hoarse laugh prodded us forward. All three of us lengthened our strides.

Peter touched my arm. "Good shot, Mama. Good shot."

"Thank you, Peter. *Asante sana.*"

Cotton, Hillary, and Kafia had a fire blazing. I hadn't thought about what might be lurking in the shadows since Peter confirmed the leopard's death.

"Congratulations." Cotton rumbled over and almost lifted me in a bear hug. "He is a beautiful cat."

"I'm just glad nobody got hurt."

"Never a chance of that. You hit him perfect. We would've found him sooner, but most of his bleeding was internal. We had some difficulty tracking him. But here he is, dead as he's ever going to be."

I knelt beside the great cat, the ultimate predator of the dark. His coat was soft, his rosettes almost moving in the dancing glow of the fire. I had killed a leopard. Me, the mother of nine from Sidney, Nebraska. Cotton had been right. It was a beautiful creature. I held back the tears. They almost came anyway.

Cotton sent Peter and Kafia to retrieve Durani and the truck. While we waited, I stared into the shadows and wondered what else might be lurking out there. Cotton told Dick about the hunt, exaggerating my courage and role throughout most of his monologue. I listened in sporadic moments. Every crunch of leaves, every baboon bark, every scampering rodent, shocked my attention into the dark. Cotton, Hillary, and Dick never glanced into the bush. They carried on, laughing and warming up beside the fire. Smiling uneasily, I joined in the conversation occasionally, but mostly prayed Peter and Kafia would hurry back with the truck.

Hillary, Peter, Kafia, and Durani began singing as we rounded the last corner on the final stretch to camp. Voices rose from different locations in camp as the staff congregated at the main entrance. They greeted us with the usual energized ceremony celebrated each time a hunter kills one of the big cats. As they carried me around camp on their shoulders, singing, clapping, and laughing, I wondered if they were happy for me or if they were grateful to have a competitor and potentially dangerous predator gone. When you have to live among Africa's unforgiving, opportunistic reality, where everything is either food or rival, you look upon creatures with different perspectives than some Westerner whose utopian idea of

Africa comes from television or drive-through photography parks. However the staff looked at it, their exuberance was genuine.

"This Nile perch is delicious, but I'm ready for bed. I'm so tired I actually think I might be able to sleep tonight."

"Even if the lions roar?"

"I don't mind if they want to roar. Just as long as they do it away from camp."

"But then you wouldn't know how enjoyable a lion's roar can be. They're just letting us know they're satisfied with themselves."

"I think I'd enjoy it more if they'd express their enthusiasm during the day."

Joan laughed. "That would be more enjoyable I should think."

"I'd love to stay up all night, but I'm pooped," I said.

Before we crawled under the covers, the lions started in. They seemed closer than usual. Close enough that when one of their deep guttural reverberations boomed, the ground seemed to shake.

I pulled the blanket over my shoulders, turned on my side, and listened to them. There was a lot of growling and a few uncommitted roars, but every once in a while, one would rear its massive head back and bellow into the air with such force it felt as if the stars would stir.

After one of the loudest and closest roars, I curled up in a ball and thought to myself that I should be more afraid. Then I fell into a deep, peaceful sleep.

CHUI: DICK

A scheduled camp change took us across the Serengeti in search of different hunting grounds. We would miss our current camp and staff, but the allure of a new adventure had us stuffing our bags. We jammed bullets into empty pockets of bags too full to zip shut; forced rolled up t-shirts into bulging luggage; and filled our daypacks with every other loose item. We had given away a ton of candy and some of our clothing, but it still seemed as if we had more gear than when we first arrived.

Safari buses filled with wide-eyed passengers, their faces bonded to the glass or their heads popped above the roof, hands clutching tightly to cameras and binoculars, were ubiquitous as we drove through the Serengeti. Around every termite mound, behind every baobab, and scattered across every field, buses and wildlife watchers crowded any living creature. The animals had adapted their lives to the invasive metal beasts of the plains.

We were not above it. Like the other visitors, we stopped to ogle. Some animals have forever piqued the darker side of human curiosity. A pride of lions or a rough-looking pack of hyenas has qualities we cannot ignore. We appreciate their beauty and the freedom they represent, but deep down, our fascination clings to the hope that they may do something extraordinary, like run down a wildebeest to strangle it to death or gang up on a cape buffalo, clawing and biting on its flesh in a fight to the death. The struggle to survive is a bloodthirsty affair. People travel from around the world for the chance to see it unfold. After waiting twenty-five minutes for a pride of lions to stand up and do something, we continued on our way. We had our own hunting to do.

"This is Raphael, the resident PH here at Fort Ikoma," Cotton introduced us as the camp staff crowded around the vehicle to help unload our gear. Hillary and Peter had come with us to the new area.

"Hello," Raphael said, extending his hand. "Very pleased to meet you." Like Hillary, Raphael spoke nearly perfect English. His accent was heavy, but he had a firm grasp of the language. "Let me show you to your tent. Do not worry about the luggage. We will bring it along shortly."

"It seems hotter here," Mary said. "I hope it cools down at night."

So did I. I might drown in my own sweat otherwise.

Along with the intense heat, Mary fought a hopeless battle against tsetse flies. Slapping and itching, flinching and cursing. The flying menaces showed her no mercy. Welts the size of half dollars, big, red, and irritating, swelled all over her body. Repellant seemed to intensify their hunger. There must have been something about the way Mary's blood tasted. Forsaking the rest of us, they devoured her skin to a war zone. I would blame it on the repellant, but they had assaulted her before she applied it.

"What do you say we sit in a leopard blind tonight?" Cotton said. "Rafael has a bait that was hit last night."

"Yes," Rafael said. "We have been seeing much action. Many leopards live here. Too many."

"Hillary will come with us. Mary, you and Joan will go with Rafael this afternoon. Be more fun than sitting in the car waiting for us to shoot a leopard." Cotton winked at her.

"I'll be glad when this leopard hunting is over," Mary said as we slipped into our tents.

"What's wrong with leopard hunting?"

"I'll just be glad after you shoot yours. I won't have to worry as much."

"There's nothing to worry about."

"I'll still be happy when it's over."

Cotton, Hillary, and I slipped into the blind an hour later. The sun burned down on the plains with a fury. It felt as if the grass could burst into flames. Placed in the shade, the blind offered some respite, but sweat managed to soak through our shirts. If the leopard approached from downwind, the hunt would be over. A leopard could smell three sweaty, stinking men from miles away. The wind was perfect. Our tom had approached and left the prior evening from upwind. All we had left to do was wait.

Another quiet night in the leopard blind. For the pursuit of game, we put ourselves through many things. What hardship could possibly come from sitting in a relatively comfortable leopard blind waiting for a tom to slip in and steal a bite of meat? Physically, not much. Your muscles stiffen and your limbs sometimes fall asleep and it is more energy draining than it sounds, but relative to other species, leopard hunting is not physically demanding. Mentally, that's another matter. Leopard hunting toys with your mind, sometimes twisting your thoughts into a gnarled mass, representing traces of what might once have been sanity.

You hunt for and hang meat day after day, sometimes for weeks, wondering if the leopard will strike. Full of more hope than you know what to do with, you brush away the first few days of nothing like a fly on your arm. A few more days and you begin to wonder if any leopards exist in the area. Your professional hunter will try to boost your spirits by telling you about the big toms taken on previous safaris. That lasts a day or two before you start wondering if previous hunters took the last leopards around or, worse, if your guide is stretching the truth. You tighten your grip around what optimism remains. Maybe, just maybe, a leopard will feed tonight. Maybe.

Then, one morning, after checking four bait trees, your professional hunter indifferently announces, "Looks like a big tom."

You nearly jump. Finally, the chance you've been waiting for. You envision the leopard silhouetting himself on the perfect branch, you making the perfect shot, the boys cheering. That afternoon, you can hardly understand what your guide is waiting for. There is a leopard out there. Come on. Let's get to the blind. Eventually, you slip into the blind, almost ready to burst. You stare out the shooting hole, inhaling deeply, almost enjoying the rotting scent sure to attract a great cat. You stare at every bush, every shadow, knowing he will appear soon. No one else even glances to the tree. You don't care. He'll be there. You do not want to miss it. The others just don't have your diligence.

Two hours later, you give up on the possibility that a leopard even knows there is a free meal. Then the others peer out. This bolsters your waning confidence. He'll be here soon. Yes, very soon.

When darkness hits, your guide says it is time to go. Maybe tomorrow. You take one last glance, thinking you can still make out the carcass, thinking if you give it one more minute he might show. Not a chance.

You're asleep when your head hits the pillow, beaten again. The next day the process starts over. The next time you find yourself in a blind, your optimism abates at a greater rate. Each time after that, pessimism's ugly smell stinks up the blind. After spending enough nights in a blind, your mind wanders, taking you places you specifically try to avoid. Talking, laughing, or any kind of companionship are absent from a blind. You are alone. You try to steer your thoughts in certain directions. It works—for a while. You try to guide them toward the task before you. They drift with the wind. They always seem to cross trails with mortality. Then you wonder what kind of spice was in the eggs six days ago. Has the air gone out of the bike tires you haven't ridden in years? What does it feel like to be a ghost? Is hell really hot? Wonder how the girls are doing? Where should we hide the Easter eggs for the kids next year? It sure would be strange if that tree exploded.

This can go on for seconds or hours. The longer you sit, the darker your thoughts become. Sometimes it is coherent but unnerving. A saint would question his or her life if they spent enough time in a leopard blind. Questions about yourself that never surfaced hit you like sucker punches. Trying to answer is futile, even dangerous. Some questions you do not want answered.

If you are lucky, something amazing will happen. A leopard will cough as he approaches the tree. You forget everything but him. You can see clearly, hear better, smell the leaves. The unfocused grayness of life sharpens to one purpose and every second, every bad thought, and every stiffened muscle are almost forgotten. You remember because they were all worth it. When that leopard claws up the tree, sleek and graceful and stares into your blind with those penetrating eyes, you feel alive.

Waiting in the dark for a fully capable predator requires some control over fear. Eventually, experience takes over, but before then, every rustle, every squeak, and every breaking twig has you questioning your resolve.

Was that a growl? I glanced toward Cotton, barely able to see him through the darkening air. What I could see of his features were expressionless. Had he even heard? I couldn't ask him. If it were a leopard, it would be there soon.

It started pouring. Nearly too dark to hunt anyway, we pulled our jackets up over our ears and high-tailed it back to camp. Hillary and Peter rode in the back and were drenched by the time we reached the skinning shed.

"Dick?" Cotton asked as we stepped from the vehicle.

"Yeah."

"I've seen Mary saying her Rosary. Would you like to go to Mass tomorrow morning?"

"Mass? Where?"

"Mugumu. It's about an hour away."

"If we can go to Mass, we'd like to. I'll tell Mary."

"We'll need to leave around eight to get there for nine o'clock services."

I found Mary in the tent unpacking.

"How was your day?"

"It was fine. No leopard, huh?"

"Maybe next time."

"We didn't see much either."

"Cotton says we can go to Mass tomorrow."

"That would be great. How far is it?"

"About an hour." It would cut into hunting, but some things are more important. Always have been. Always will be.

"I'm not sure about this tent," Mary said while fluffing an unfluffable pillow.

"What do you mean?"

"There's no straw enclosure around here for one."

"That wouldn't stop anything from coming into camp anyway."

"But the back zipper is broken."

"So."

"So what if a baboon or a snake wandered in? We couldn't stop them and then they'd feel threatened. It's not safe."

"I'm sure it's fine."

"I don't like it."

"What do you want me to do about it?"

"Nothing I guess. I just don't feel very safe."

"I'll take a look at the zipper. See if I can do anything."

"The zipper's not even there."

"I'll see if I can't rig something up."

I poked a few holes on either side of the opening and tied it together with a length of string. Critters could still slip in, but Mary felt better about it. At least a bigger animal wouldn't be able to waltz in without some effort.

I fell asleep to the sound of rain pattering the roof.

The truck slipped and slid on the sloppy road. Our tires sunk occasionally, almost to the point of sticking. It was a miracle we made it to church only two minutes late. The congregation's collective voices carried into the street. Without a piano, without a guitar, without an organ, without accompaniment of any kind, their voices rose into the morning air in perfect harmony. Understanding the meaning of their words was unnecessary to feel the uplifting spiritual power of their song. The morning held us in a captive trance. It was as if God's finger had touched their tongues with a drop of the divine.

After Mass, Father Bryan welcomed us, both in English and Swahili, and asked that we stay for a few minutes. We waited toward the back of the church. Many parishioners filed by to shake our hands.

"*Karibu*," they said. Welcome.

"*Karibu*." One by one, most of the parishioners wanted to greet us. "*Karibu*." We said, "*Asante sana.*" Thank you very much.

"It's not often we see Americans here," Father Bryan said after the last parishioner had pumped my hand with both of his. Originally from Michigan, Father Bryan had been in Africa demonstrating, by example, the power of charity and Christianity. Such devotion is commendable. His faith was strong and his compassion for his fellow people ran deep.

"We'd love to have you for dinner tomorrow evening," Joan said.

"I'd be honored to join you."

"We'll meet you at the main road around six," Cotton said.

"Perfect."

"We'd love to stay and chat, but Dick's got a leopard he needs to sort out." Cotton winked at Mary.

"I'll be glad when it's over," she said.

"Good luck." Father Bryan shook our hands one more time, then waved before slipping back into the church.

"What do you think, Dick? You feeling as lucky as I am?"

I shrugged. "Maybe I'm jaded."

"Don't believe it. There's no room here for false pessimism. You're feeling lucky too. I can tell."

"I guess your confidence is rubbing off on me."

"I wouldn't get carried away. What do you think, Peter? Will we get the *chui* tonight?"

Peter stared at Cotton. He put his hand on his head, rubbed it slowly. "Leopard is tricky. He show up when you not expect. Stay hidden when you sure he come. We must have tricky thoughts to bring him."

"Will it work if you don't believe it?"

"That is what we find. Leopard can see if you not think truth."

"*Mkichaa*," Hillary said.

"No, no. He jealous he no think of first."

"*Mkichaa.*"

Durani's shoulders shook as he giggled in the driver's seat.

"What did he say?" I asked.

"It means crazy person."

"Only crazy to believe leopard no see your mind. He see your fear. Eyes see in your soul."

Durani nodded seriously to this.

"If luck is for us, he cannot see a lie."

Hillary seemed to consider this for a moment. Then he nodded again. After a long pause, he said "*Mkichaa.*"

Our laughter continued until after we had left camp well behind us.

Raphael, Hillary, and Durani stayed in the truck with Mary and Joan while Cotton and I followed Peter to the blind. We parked a mile away so as not to disturb the leopard with the rumbling engine. We slipped into the blind without speaking, careful not to step on anything that might give us away.

After a quick glance at the hanging meat, Cotton settled into a paperback. Peter stared out his shooting hole for a few minutes before his head started bobbing. He drifted off within the first half-hour. I watched for movement around the tree. Maybe the tom would come early. Nothing moved. I reached in my bag for my own paperback. For the next two hours, I intermittently lost myself in an adventure novel and stared at a dangling carcass filled with the promise of imminent action. With each passing minute, my focus reverted less to the book and more to shadows around the tree.

Deepening shadows pushed the afternoon to evening. Cotton and I put our books away. Peter perked up. In the distance, a leopard growled. Yes.

When you know the leopard is near, yet cannot see him, you enter some of hunting's most indescribable moments.

Will he commit? Or will he stay in the shadows? Did something move? No, just my imagination. What was that? Probably just a rodent. Breathe.

I reached for the rifle without looking and knocked it against a post. It seemed to echo toward the mountains. I glanced at Cotton and Peter. It seemed so loud. To be so close and screw it up because of carelessness. What kind of hunter did that make me? I needed to calm down. Needed to be in control. Only confident shots are acceptable with dangerous game.

It growled and sawed loudly. So close.

Cotton tapped my leg. When I looked at him, he motioned for me to slide the barrel through the shooting hole. It took me nearly a minute to move it into position. It obstructed much of my view. I looked through the low-power scope. It blocked out most of the peripheral. No cat.

I concentrated on a particular shadow shading the gray earth beneath a thorn bush. I heard a crunch. I listened. Nothing. Nothing at all. Not a tweet from a bird. Not a peep from a baboon. Not even a snake rustling the leaves. The leopard was coming. When a predator like a leopard prowls through the forest, the other creatures give plenty of room—if they know he is there. A leopard can strike with such sudden force and speed that it is not worth the risk. He had announced his arrival. The other animals took heed. So did three human hunters crouched in a dark, suffocating blind.

There.

Crunch. Crunch. Crunch.

Closer now.

My eyes scanned the underbrush. He was close. Where?

Paws scraped up the tree. I couldn't see him, but the sound of his speedy ascent up the opposite facing side of our bait tree was unmistakable.

I peered through the scope and focused on the branch where the bait hung. At any moment, he would enter my line of sight. Any second he would be inside the field of view. Wait. Anytime.

I peered over the scope and found the bait. No leopard. I followed the branch to the trunk, then down to the bushes. Had he scampered away? I didn't think so. I followed the trunk back up, searching the edges for a claw or whisker or even a full leopard. They blend with Africa's landscape like ghosts. I scrutinized every inch. I would find him. Damn right, I would.

From the trunk back to the branch, I didn't see him. But I heard him again. This time it was the sound of scratching.

The carcass.

My eyes shot across the branch. There he sat, pawing down at the meat, his body quartered toward us.

"Let him start feeding before you shoot," Cotton whispered so softly that I might have only imagined it. Cotton had mentioned that before, hadn't he?

The leopard's gaze lifted from his task. He focused on us. His eyes glowed in the darkening air. They bored into mine. We had not made a noise, had not moved an inch. It felt as if he could hear my thoughts. *We're not here for you. Just keep eating.*

His stare was piercing, his big, round eyes unwavering. I told myself not to make eye contact. I couldn't help it.

Then, with an air of indifference only a cat can exhibit, he turned back to the meat, pulled it up to the branch and bit into it. The sound of ripping muscle shot into the blind.

He shifted just enough. I centered the crosshairs for a vital shot. I wouldn't miss. I couldn't. My hands should have been trembling. They were rock steady. I squeezed.

The tom leapt at the blast. He hit the ground running. Everything went quiet.

I searched the brush through the scope and found only shadows. We listened for any sign of life. Silence.

"We'll wait for the others, then go have a look. What took you so long to shoot?"

"What do you mean?"

"I kept telling you to take him."

"I'm not sure I heard you."

"I was hardly whispering. He's huge, Dick. Huge."

"I thought we were busted when he stared in here."

"I not let him see truth," Peter said. "He search for truth. I not give to him."

Cotton nodded. "I've learned not to question things beyond logic."

"To be honest, I may've twisted the facts in my thoughts when he was staring in here."

Cotton laughed without opening his lips. He mouthed the words "me too". He cocked his head toward Peter and put his forefinger to his lips. "Don't want him getting a big head."

Peter smiled. Just before ducking out of the blind, he said, "It no work unless we all not tell truth."

This time Cotton and I both laughed, subduing the volume as best we could.

By the time the others arrived, twilight had given way to darkness. Not optimal conditions for following up a potentially wounded leopard. We flipped on our flashlights and made our way to the tree. Plenty of blood splattered the ground, but we did not see our cat.

I held my .375 ready. Cotton had his twelve-gauge on his shoulder. Peter and Hillary carried flashlights. After a few yards, Cotton looked to Peter.

"Hit good," Peter said softly. "Maybe no dead."

We looked back to the girls waiting by the blind. Their eyes were wide. Joan was fidgety.

"Peter found lung blood. It looks as if your bullet did a good amount of damage. My guess is we'll find him dead here in a few yards."

We moved at a snails pace, one step every thirty seconds. When a wounded leopard attacks, it waits for the last possible moment and springs with such speed that a shot isn't always possible.

I thought I heard a rustle. Nobody's flashlight pointed in that direction. The lights created a layer of shadows that seemed to move through one another. The tight canopy above us blocked out the stars and the moon. Without the flashlights, we wouldn't be able to see each other. Rarely do we encounter that kind of darkness. When you are in Africa, where most predators use the cloak of night to hunt, that darkness closes in on you. I didn't know which was worse, the occasional rustling or the utter silence. When the leopard had finally come, he brought the quiet with him. Sometimes, happy medians do not exist.

What if the shot hadn't been true? I was sure of it at the time. But now?

No. I had been steady. Damn steady.

Peter pointed out another splotch of blood.

Every shadow moved at the edge of the light. A chill air seemed to follow us toward a heavy thorn bush. The spoor led into the bush's heart. We stopped five yards from it and listened. Quiet. We stared into the tangle and prepared ourselves. The night held its breath.

On Cotton's cue, we moved forward as one. My focus centered on a low dark spot. I pressed the rifle butt against my shoulder. Another step forward. I heard each foot crunch the ground beside me. Sweat dripped from my nose.

Cotton crouched as the boys probed the bush with their lights. I waited.

Peter pointed to the ground. The cat's tracks went into a dark opening too tight for us to follow. We began to circle the bush slowly aware that the leopard could be hiding in another bush, waiting for us to turn our backs. Peter stopped. He pointed into the bush. Cotton directed his shotgun to the spot. I tilted my head. Spots. Yellow and black. Unmistakable. Nobody moved.

I estimated we were looking at an eight-inch circle of the leopard's back. I watched for the slow rise of breathing. I couldn't be sure. My finger moved the last inch to the trigger.

Without pulling his eyes or flashlight away from the cat, Peter bent to the ground and found a stone. He tossed it in. Cotton leaned forward, bracing himself for the charge. Nothing.

Turning away for a moment, Peter found a long branch and poked the leopard. When it didn't move, we dragged it out and admired it in silence.

Then Hillary took hold of my hand, enclosing it with both of his.

"Good shot, Bwana. Good shot."

Peter pushed in to give his congratulations.

"You do well, Bwana," Peter said, shaking his head.

"Thank you. *Asante sana*."

"Very good, Bwana," Raphael said. "It is a big *chui*." He pulled me to the ground and lifted the cat's paw.

"It's a fine leopard," Cotton said.

If allowed, the celebration could've lasted throughout the late hours of the night. Heavy eyes sparred with jubilant hearts. We couldn't fight it. Our wake-up call would come at five thirty in the morning. The hunt dictated our schedule. With such a constraint, our festivities would be subdued—but hopefully only postponed.

Arusa, the skinner, met me on the path to our tent. He handed me two small bones—the floating bones from the leopard's shoulder. He shook my hand. He smiled.

DEATH BELLOW: MARY

I set up on the shooting sticks beside the thorny bush. Staring through the scope at a big-game animal, finding something inside you, is a powerful moment in hunting. It is okay, or it isn't. It is rarely conscious, almost never recognizable. In a fleeting moment, too brief to describe, too intense to dismiss, either you pull the trigger or you let the animal fade into the brush.

It is not the same as deciding to hold the shot because an animal is too young or too small. Those deliberate choices are thought out, predetermined. This is deeper. More connected to the part of you that makes you a human hunter.

When the trigger finger applies gentle pressure, you have reached the apex of the hunt. In a fleeting, almost unnoticeable moment, your heart spins just to remind you there are memories in our fallible minds we should never forget.

My finger tightened around the trigger until the rifle kicked my shoulder. The Grant's gazelle bucked and ran less than fifty yards before collapsing.

I didn't know how I felt. Satisfied—yes. Elated—not necessarily. Sad—a little. Regretful—not really. It was a combination of many emotions. After a hard stalk on dangerous game or a certain trophy you have been after for so long that success seems impossible, elation is most often the first, and most pronounced, reaction. Sometimes you hardly feel it at all. In rare instances, your sadness almost turns to regret. You have killed something. Something beautiful and full of life, wanting only to escape you, the predator. In the end, that is what we are—predators. Different from any other predator on earth in our ability to feel remorse, to see the beauty in that which we pursue, to understand the finality of our actions. And to know the hunt itself has a meaningful place. To know it is also beautiful.

"That was fun," Cotton said.

I nodded. "It was."

"That's the kind of day we need. Relaxed. No worries about leopards or lions or buffalo or kudu. We'll just wander around the rest of the day and see what happens."

"Sounds good to me. No pressure, less stress."

Though a comparatively relaxed day of hunting, it held our share of difficult stalks. Like one that Dick and Cotton put on an "easy" impala ram.

We spotted him with a group of eight ewes. His horns curved back, up, back in, and flared out at the tips. A magnificent ram. We were five hundred yards away glassing them. The ram gave us a glance. The ewes stared at us for a few moments. Before long, they lowered their heads to graze, only lifting them in periodic intervals to make sure we hadn't narrowed the safety gap.

"Back under that tree," Cotton said to Durani. He pointed to an umbrella tree thirty yards off the trail. "You can stay under the shade while Dick and I sneak over and pop that ram. After Dick shoots him, come pick us up."

They walked in and out of sight during a stalk that seemed to take hours. Watching the impalas through the binos, I noticed one ewe that seemed jittery. Her head popped in our direction every few moments.

"She sure is nervous," I said mostly to myself, but hoped for an answer to confirm I wasn't just seeing things.

Peter said, "Yes."

He whispered something to Durani, who nodded and sprung up to sit on the back of his seat. They both stared toward the impalas. I exchanged my glances between the nervous ewe and the boys in the truck and tried to figure out why they seemed so interested in this group of impalas. We had seen so many.

"Yes," Durani said. "Eeh, *simba*."

"*Ashiria*, Bwana," Peter said, hopping from the vehicle and trotting toward the brush-line where we had last seen Dick and Cotton.

"Where is he going?" I asked.

Durani pointed toward the impalas. "*Simba, simba.*"

Simba? I knew that word. What did it mean? I gave him my best questioning look and shrugged my shoulders.

"*Simba*. Um." Durani bared his teeth and clawed his fingers. "*Simba.*"

"Lion?"

"Yes, yes. Lion."

I looked to the right and left of the impalas, then ahead of and behind them. I only saw grass, some brush, and a few trees. Snapping the binoculars to my eyes, I scanned under the trees and bushes. Still nothing.

"Where?" I asked.

Durani popped into the seat beside me and scooted close. He stuck his arm directly in front of my face and pointed again. This time it was apparent he wasn't pointing at the impalas. He was pointing toward the brush-line where Cotton and Dick would emerge for a shot.

I flipped the binoculars back up. Where were they?

I caught movement to the right. A lioness had stood up. I saw four more lying in the grass, nearly invisible. If you didn't know they were there, you might walk right into them.

Wait a minute.

The lioness was not looking at the impalas. She was staring through the thicket.

I scanned into the mess of thorns, looking for movement. Dick and Cotton were there. Just on the other side. Seventy-five yards from the lions and moving closer. They had no idea. We had to warn them. Where was Peter?

In the best scenario, the lions would move away, spooking the impala in the process. Worst case? I didn't want to think about that.

It was like watching one of those stupid horror movies. You want to reach into the screen, grab the idiot walking into danger, and smack him. I wanted to scream at them. They were too far away to hear. I watched them look through their binoculars at the impala, then move forward in a crouch. Right for the lions.

A second female stood, then another. Then one I hadn't seen before. They all looked poised for action, as if a fight was just what they were waiting for. One of them took a few steps forward and cocked her head.

Shifting my glance to Cotton and Dick, I saw that Peter was finally catching up. They didn't see Peter. They continued toward a confrontation they wanted no part of. What could I do? I prayed. I prayed Peter would catch them in time or the lions would move off.

God must have been listening. At nearly the same moment Peter caught them, the lions trotted away. Dick and Cotton never saw them.

The impalas dashed off. They stopped after one hundred yards and turned to see that the lions were not on their trail. Their higher state of agitation would make a stalk more difficult. It appeared as if the boys were going to try anyway.

The herd moved further into the open. Dick, Cotton, and Peter emerged from the brush sneaking in a crouched cluster, trying not to look like humans. Every eye from the herd was on them. The boys would take a few slow steps, then stop and glass without standing straight. This went on for two hundred yards before Dick raised his rifle. The impalas seemed on the verge of running.

I kept my eye on the ram, waiting for the shot, watching for the impact. *Okay, he's in the clear. Take him. What're you waiting for? He's standing broadside. It's the perfect opportunity. Maybe I should see what they're doing.*

I fought the urge. Dick was usually a quick shot. Maybe the ram was not as big as they had thought. It had to be something.

I'll just take a quick look. Just to make sure they're not walking back to the truck. I'll keep the binos pointed at the impalas. It will only take a second.

I glanced over the binoculars to see them still clustered in a tight group, but standing up straight.

Was that the echo from a rifle?

My eyes shot back to the impalas, kicking up dust from their hooves as they charged away, the ram unable to stay with the group. He staggered to the side and fell. I would have seen it all had I not been so impatient.

Durani fired up the ignition and we drove out to meet them.

"What took you so long to shoot?" I asked Dick after the round of congratulations.

"We forgot the shooting sticks," Cotton said.

"I couldn't get steady."

"What did you do?"

"Cotton loaned me his shoulder."

"You be careful with that. You'll lose your hearing."

"What?" Cotton said.

"I said..."

Boys are boys and men are boys. Is there any happy medium? I have never seen it. "Very funny. If you're not careful, I'll sick Joan on you, Cotton."

"I am sorry, Mary. It will never happen again. Please forgive our imprudence." Cotton tried to keep a straight face as Dick chuckled in the background.

Boys.

"We best be heading back to camp."

I glanced at my watch. "It's only eleven."

"I need to use the radio before lunch. I'd like to get the rest of your ammunition here before we run out of bullets. Last I talked to them, they said it was in Arusha. If true, we should be able to get it here with the next shipment of supplies."

"I'll believe it when I see it," I said.

"Remember, Mary, positive thinking is half the battle."

"Oh, goody. The ammo will be here before we know it."

"Now who's teasing?"

"Thought you could use some of your own medicine."

"Okay. I deserve it. But be careful. I've been known to escalate things beyond any resemblance of civilized behavior." Cotton winked at me.

"I'll be sure to watch my back."

I needed a reprieve from the tsetse flies. The unbearable heat and my sweating only added to the itching. Tsetse flies did not occupy a warm spot in my heart. They benefited the wildlife by keeping cattle farms away, but the tradeoff was nearly more than I could take. They chewed every inch of my skin, biting through layers of clothing I thought would protect me from their menacing ways. I am not tolerant of whining and hate to bellyache, but when it comes to tsetse flies, I cannot help myself. The bites swell to the size of half dollars. I looked like I had a terrible skin disease. I could live with that—could deal with such uncomely blemishes—could even tolerate the initial sharp sting when they attacked. But I couldn't endure the endless and painful itching. I tried every over-the-counter/homemade/witch doctor remedy known to humans and some only the gods were privy to. Nothing brought reprieve. And nothing quelled their hunger for my skin. Super-strong bug spray with ingredients banned in over fifty countries only intensified their fervor for my blood. It is hard to believe an insect can be evil, but they always attack me with greater resolve than they do anybody else. They hate me. What did I ever do to them?

Back at camp by five thirty, we took quick showers and prepared for dinner. Joan drove to the main road to show Father Bryan the way to camp. They were back by six. We had been visiting around the fire for half an hour when Kidago politely slipped over.

"Dinner is served," he said. Though heavily accented, he spoke English well.

Cotton believed in customer service. He taught his staff to speak English so they could communicate better with clients. Most of the staff spoke in broken English, but their English was far superior to our Swahili.

Eland steaks cooked medium rare over an open fire pit were the center of dinner. Sweet potatoes, salad, strawberry crepes, cabbage, and green beans accompanied the main dish. The tender meat slid off our forks and nearly melted in our mouths. It was milder than any game meat I had ever tasted. We barely said a word through dinner. If I had to choose my last meal, it would be eland steaks, cooked medium rare over an open fire pit. The setting would be under African stars with hyenas and lions calling in the distance.

Father Bryan cared deeply for the people in Africa. He wanted to be in Tanzania, not only preaching the Word, but also helping in any way he could. He had trained teachers, had started charities, and had worked his hands to shreds helping to build and rebuild homes, schools, and churches. His courage, devotion, and genuine love of the human spirit were admirable. We were better for having met him.

"Grab your rifle, Mary," Cotton said. "Let's take a walk around this waterhole. See if we can't start the morning off with a bang."

A pair of oribi zipped past us and into the open grass.

"That's a good buck. Take him when he stops." Cotton opened the shooting sticks in front of me.

I worked a shell in and set up. I lost sight of him in the recoil.

"Miss. Again, before they run."

Jacking another round into the chamber, I peered back through the scope. How did I miss? This time I had him for sure. I fired.

"Miss. Reload."

Oribi are a dainty antelope, but that was ridiculous. When I found them through the scope again, they were running.

"He's going to stop. When he does, take him."

"Okay."

"Now. Take him now."

My body trembled. Determined, my finger found the trigger.

"You hit him. Let's go. Reload. We've got to hurry."

I flipped the rifle to safety and ran behind Cotton and Peter. What a nightmare. I caught a glimpse of the ewe outrunning a limping buck. I had broken his leg. I wished I had missed.

By the time we closed enough distance for another shot, the ewe had long left the area. The buck just didn't have the stamina. My next shot hit him in the heart. What a mess. He deserved better than that. I didn't deserve the honor of hunting him if I couldn't put him down quickly.

I was shaking. Tears threatened to fall. "That's it. If I'm going to wound them I'm not going to shoot."

"It's okay," Cotton said. "With the way you've been shooting you just got overconfident. You needed this to get your focus back."

"If this is what it takes, I don't want my focus back."

Cotton gave me his best sympathetic smile. "You'll do better next time, I promise."

"I'm not sure there should be a next time."

"You don't stop riding a bike when you fall, do you?"

I tried not to roll my eyes at him. "That's not the same."

"Sure it is. We've all had bad days. It's *those* days, not the good ones, which make us better hunters."

"I think Dick should hunt next."

"Sure. Then it's your turn."

Dick shot a reedbuck later that morning. I think Cotton had Dick shoot the first decent buck just to make me hunt again.

Cotton was right. I felt like giving up. I even told myself I was going to. I never really meant it. Hunting was a part of me. It always would be.

Another chance never presented itself that morning. Instead, we ran into a band of poachers. When they saw us, they dropped their booty and bolted—all in different directions. There were at least five of them. Peter said he saw seven. In the dense bush, they disappeared within seconds.

"I'll send a couple of the boys here to track them later and then let the authorities know where their village is. Someone will give them up. The punishment for poaching is harsh."

We gathered the animals they had been carrying—nine dik-diks, one impala, and one Thomson's gazelle, all with snare marks on their legs or necks.

Elephant, rhino, and other *glamorous* animals get the press, but there had been a shift in poaching. As authorities cracked down on ivory poaching, criminals set their sights elsewhere. They found meat poaching could be nearly as profitable. They could place as many snares across as many trails as they liked, catching anything unlucky enough to walk, crawl, or slither through. If it could be cut up and eaten, they could sell it as meat. Whether an endangered species or something as plentiful as impala made no difference. Meat was meat. It all brought a good price at the market.

In some countries, elephants are numerous to the point of overpopulation. Through education and the direct benefits that the local population receives from big game hunting, elephants now hold more value than just the price of their tusks. One hunter who hunts a single elephant brings in more revenue than a whole herd slaughtered for their ivory. Once a local population realizes this, the internal pressure alone is sometimes enough to thwart poaching. Sometimes, however, poachers are not swayed by the locals. They travel from place to place, following game, stealing what they can and disappearing into the veldt.

The single hunter killing an impala or bushbuck to feed his family was of little concern. Wouldn't we all do the same if put in such a situation? It is the bands of poachers, after only money, which needed to be dealt with.

For the most part, poaching across Africa has declined. Will it ever be wiped out completely? Not likely. Progress, however, continues and, as long as it does, the hope that our children's grandchildren can someday hunt the same ground we have been fortunate enough to explore will endure.

By the time we had loaded the snared animals and marked the spot, it was time for lunch. We ate, showered, wrote in our journals, and rested until it was time to head back out. Was I ready to shoot yet?

Cotton didn't even ask.

"That's an outstanding waterbuck."

"Very big," Peter said.

I'd only seen a glimpse of him before he disappeared into the trees.

I snatched my 7mm from the truck and fell in step behind Peter and Cotton. I made sure the magazine was full and that I had extra bullets in my pocket.

I turned back to Dick and Joan. "Aren't you coming?"

"We'll catch up."

I hadn't realized how quickly I jumped out of the vehicle.

I couldn't explain it in a thousand words. But that excitement when you begin a stalk—the mouse tickling your stomach—pulls you forward. Will you catch up to the buck? Will he be what you expect? Will you shoot well? Will you shoot at all? It rarely happens the way you see it in your mind. You want to find him just around the next corner. You need to see him standing behind the next tree.

He was close. I felt it. I knew he was there. Our steps softened and slowed. We crouched. We studied every branch, every bush, every dark spot. We listened. Peter moved like the grass, swaying almost imperceptibly. Compared to him, I was a clod, stomping through the woods like a buffalo. I tried to mimic Peter's movements. Impossible.

Peter read the sign as if there were neon lights flashing. *This way. Turn here. Just a little further.* He never seemed to break stride, never stopped to study the ground or verify what he saw. He knew where the waterbuck had been as well as the waterbuck itself knew it.

Sometimes, everything is perfect. You know you will find your quarry. Know, with certainty, that once you do, you will shoot well.

I couldn't miss. Doubts often pulled at my thoughts during a stalk. Not that time. Overconfidence be damned. If Peter put us in position—and I knew he would—I would make a good shot.

Peter slowed as we approached a wide thorn bush, just starting to green. When he knelt on one knee, we did the same, knowing the waterbuck was close. We didn't see it, but we knew.

Glancing back, I saw Dick, Joan, and Raphael standing beside a termite mound fifty yards behind us.

I concentrated on a small opening in the bush. I saw open space but no waterbuck.

"Do you have one in the chamber, Mary?" Cotton whispered.

As gently and quietly as I could, I slid the bolt back and forward again until it clicked into place. My heart trembled. A good tremble. The kind that prepares you for what's to come.

Peter pointed just before fading from view. Almost as if he was never there. Our tracker simply melded with the land.

Cotton and I scooted around the bush in tiny scratching advancements. There. Less than fifty yards. Regal and alert. Standing with his shoulders high and his nose in the air. Our waterbuck.

He surveyed a small waterhole, a king in his court. He advanced a few steps. To shoot, I would have to scoot further around the bush. I would have to expose myself.

"Take him when you can," Cotton whispered, nudging me into position.

I pushed myself across the dusty ground. If the waterbuck looked our way, he would see me. I shifted into the prone position. Cotton unsnapped a fanny pack and slid it beneath the stock. The waterbuck's head jerked in our direction.

Be a rock. Be a bush. Be anything inanimate. Just don't be a bumbling human.

I tried to control the shakes. I failed. Instead of looking away, like I hoped he would do, he turned his entire rigid body to face us.

"Whenever you're ready," Cotton whispered without moving his lips.

I didn't like the angle. Head-on shots always make me nervous. My soaring confidence from a few moments earlier wavered. Could I make that shot cleanly? I had done so before on smaller game. Could I do it again? I had to concentrate.

Thinking only about the small target between the waterbuck's legs and below his neck, I centered the crosshairs. It took all my will power to steady them. I forgot about the waterbuck and the fact he may run off at any moment. I forgot about everything but the center of the crosshairs and a small patch of gray fur.

When I squeezed, I knew. I couldn't have been steadier. I expected to see the waterbuck tipping over. It disappeared into the brush. Not again.

"Good shot."

I thought I hit him well. "Are you sure?"

"You nailed him."

"Good shot, Mama." Peter appeared just as magically as he had disappeared before.

I shook his hand. "Thank you. *Asante.*"

"Come, we find."

"Let's wait for Dick and Joan," Cotton said.

"I find. You come, yes?"

Cotton nodded and Peter hurried toward the brush.

I think Cotton saw doubt rising in my eyes. "Not to worry, Mary. You hit him well."

I responded with the most genuine smile I could muster. It wasn't much. A few bad experiences had tempered my optimism.

We found Peter moving around beside a wide acacia bush. When he noticed us coming, he waved. His huge smile put my fears to rest.

"This is one fine waterbuck," Cotton said.

"Thank you." I held my head high and allowed my smile to mirror Peter's. "What's next?"

Cotton laughed. "Would you look at her now? She makes a perfect shot and her head swells. Since you're feeling so good about yourself, how about we give bushbuck a try."

"You had to pick one of the hardest animals, didn't you?"

"It's the perfect time of day for bushbuck."

"They never stand still." Every time we saw a good buck, it high-tailed it to the next country before I could set up. We usually saw them sneaking through grass and brush, keeping out of sight until just before dark. By the time we saw one, it was usually dusk when the shadows, especially in the thick bush, had become deep caverns.

The confidence acquired from the waterbuck demanded I push intimidation to the side. Bushbuck were difficult antelope, but they were fun to hunt.

On the way to Cotton's secret bushbuck hotspot, a dik-dik darted into the grass. "Ready, Dick?"

Dick answered by grabbing his rifle and following Peter and Cotton. They had walked twenty steps when the dik-dik dashed into the open. The buck made the fatal mistake of stopping to look back. Dick put one in his boiler room. There were a few handshakes at the fine shooting. Then, after quick photos, we loaded up and were back to bushbuck business.

As we neared the area, Cotton had Durani slow the vehicle to a crawl.

"Be ready to go, Mary. If we see a good buck, Durani will stop and we'll try a quick stalk before dark."

The sun began its descent. Would we find a buck? Would I, with my lengthy shot preparation, have time to shoot? No sense worrying about that yet.

If not for the rumble of the vehicle's engine, you could have heard a mosquito buzzing ten feet away. Our focus was glued to the shadows, our concentration at peak intensity. So many shapes, mostly false, had me doing double-takes. Eventually, Durani pulled over. Did he see something? Was there a bushbuck?

"Let's walk for a bit. There's a small clearing through these trees where they like to hang out."

Peter took the lead again. He and Cotton worked well as a team. Cotton trusted Peter's tracking abilities without question. Most of the time, they seemed more friends than employer and employee. Sneaking through the green brush, I concentrated on trying to be as quiet as Peter. I didn't have a chance. He was so natural. He slid through the bush, his steps hardly rustling a leaf, his shoulder or hip instinctively knowing when to dodge a branch or thorn. I hit them all. My feet bumbled along, snapping every twig within ten feet. My arms tangled in every thorny branch. Nobody turned to *shh* me. Maybe I was doing okay. It didn't seem like it.

We stopped every twenty yards to survey the area. At one point, we nearly stepped on an old warthog with a single, massive tusk. The other was broken off at the base. The pig spun and dug his hooves into the ground. His ruckus could've caused an elephant stampede. Every bushbuck within a mile would be alert. We continued anyway.

A snail could have overtaken our pace. It was effective. Two female kudu wandered by without giving us a look. Maybe we had a chance. Maybe I was better at stalking than I thought. Probably just lucky.

We snuck to the edge of the clearing, careful not to expose ourselves. We scanned the area. Nothing. Cotton and Peter sat down. We were going to try waiting them out.

In much of Africa, the sun sets quickly. Twilight speeds into darkness before you realize you missed it. The sun had fallen behind the trees. The perfect time for game to be on the move.

Peter tapped Cotton's shoulder. Pointing with his eyes, he directed Cotton's gaze to our left. Trying to hold still, I prepared myself mentally. I stared. If I could just see through the shadows. The far edge of the clearing had become hazy. Darkness only moments away.

Cotton touched my knee.

Where could it be? Wait. Was that movement?

Just another shadow reaching into the night.

How could I shoot if I couldn't see? This could be our best chance, but I couldn't see the buck.

"Get ready."

For what?

I raised the rifle anyway.

"Take him when you're ready," Cotton whispered.

"I can't see him."

"He's beside that tall tree."

I might never find him in the shadows.

I stared so long that Cotton turned toward me.

"Do you see him yet?"

Wait a minute. That looks like something. Maybe.

I peered through the scope. There he was, feeding beside the tree. Little more than an outline in the dying light. I would have to be quick. I tightened the rifle into my shoulder and slid my finger onto the trigger. I could just make out the muscle lines of his shoulder, but visibility was fading. Concentrate.

The bushbuck appeared to drop at the shot. I reloaded and found the base of the tree through the scope. No sign of the buck.

"I hit him, didn't I?"

"I think so," Cotton said. "Let's go look before it's too dark."

We walked at a quickened, cautious pace. Ready.

Peter spotted the buck first. He stopped and pointed. A brown hump on the ground. We could have walked right past if we hadn't been looking for it. The bullet penetrated the heart and one lung. Perfect.

"Nothing to it." Cotton slapped my shoulder.

"They usually never hold still for me."

"You did great."

Darkness closed in. Peter hoisted the bushbuck onto his shoulders and we hiked to the trail road. Peter hardly broke a sweat. I was breathing heavily.

At one in the morning, a ruckus arose from behind the tent. It sounded like the neighbor kids having a party. As the screaming and jabbering rose, I came out of my groggy state. Those weren't kids. Those were screaming baboons and a sawing leopard. The baboons shrieked. Then the leopard growled. It sounded as if they were fifty feet from the tent, moving closer.

"Dick."

Nothing but a snore.

"Dick. Wake up." It was a loud, anxious whisper. "Dick. Don't you hear that? Quit snoring for goodness sake. The leopard will hear you."

"Wha—what is it?"

"The leopard's outside the tent."

"No. He's a long way off. Go back to sleep."

"You're not even listening. I can hear his footsteps."

"It's probably just a snake or something."

Was that supposed to make me feel better? "It's not a snake. He's growling and sawing. He's fighting with baboons."

Dick rolled over. "Good. He won't bother us then."

"That's not funny."

My eyes were wide for the next half hour. Staring into darkness, I listened until the brawl simmered to a distant rustle. At two thirty, just after I had fallen asleep, they woke me again with more squabbling. The baboon screeches sounded like something from a horror movie. I almost fell out of bed. Dick kept snoring. After fifteen minutes, they quieted down. I do not know if they got bored or if the lion pride that moved in scared them away. The lions roared often, each time closer. Then, I heard them traipse by the tent growling and scratching. I could feel them coming closer. It felt as if they were circling the tent. How could Dick sleep through that? They wandered to the other side of camp where the scent of hanging meat emanated from the skinning shed. When I had not heard them for thirty minutes, I fell asleep.

We hunted at a leisurely pace the following day. Dick shot a topi for camp meat and a nice Grant's gazelle. For lunch, we had dik-dik roast. It was tender and succulent. After eating, we took a nap and then hit the trail again.

We followed the tracks of a waterbuck most of the afternoon, catching only two glimpses of his backside. His long, sweeping horns prodded us to give chase. Waterbuck usually stay close to water, but this old buck kept giving us the slip by taking long treks away from anything resembling a puddle.

"He not seem much like *kuro*," Peter said.

"Does that mean waterbuck, *kuro*?" I asked him.

He nodded.

"Is the *kuro* smarter than you?" Cotton said to Peter.

"No, no. *Kuro* very smart. More smart than many man," he smiled at Cotton. "I know well. We find soon."

After another hundred yards, Peter stopped.

Did he see the buck? Where? I stared into the grass and listened to silence. The waterbuck was out there somewhere. Master of concealment. Adept at eluding predators. Its skill born of instinct, honed by experience.

It was hot. We were tired and thirsty. Nobody moved. Peter stared forward. We stared at Peter. The silence surrounded us like humidity. The world held still. I almost felt alone.

In Africa, you are never alone. You are surrounded by life where life began. You are home. Few places make you feel so close to heaven. It is nothing you see, nothing you smell, nothing you taste. You feel it in a deep place where the soul meets the body and reminds you of what it means to feel alive. You are more aware, more in touch with the world. You notice the way the earth feels beneath your feet, the air passing through your lungs, the way the loudest sound can be absorbed and how the buzz of a fly can be deafening. You notice it and you cannot get enough—ever. You may forget for a while, but Africa will call you back again and again.

We had to keep ourselves from charging forward, from streaking past Peter in some primal scream in an attempt to force the waterbuck into giving away its position. Like lions waiting in the grass, we fought the urge.

I did not see the waterbuck. Peter stared ahead, though his gaze did not seem fixed. It was more of an analytical stare as if he was deep in thought. Cotton had his binoculars to his eyes and Dick watched ahead, his rifle ready. Just as I was about to look through my own binos, Peter spoke.

"He go drink now."

"Do you want to stay on his trail?" Cotton asked.

Peter shook his head. "We catch at water."

Cotton stared at Peter. Peter nodded.

We jogged through the brush, dodging trees, ducking under branches and tearing through thorns. Peter glanced back to wave us forward as we tried to keep up with his pace. We were sweating and panting. Peter wasn't winded. I tried not to whip myself on too many thorns. Where was the waterhole? It seemed we would never make it. I couldn't make it. I would have to stop. Somehow, my legs kept churning. I told myself I was going to stop. I told myself that they would wait for me if I did stop. I told myself that Dick was shooting, not me. I kept going. My legs began to question Peter's judgment.

We slowed to a fast walk, then to a normal pace and, finally, to a crawl. We caught our breath and each drank a bottle of water. The sun was dragging to the horizon. The air cooling. My sweat caused me to shiver. If the bull failed to show at the waterhole soon, it would be too dark.

We approached the waterhole with stealth, as if we knew the bull were already there. At that time of the afternoon, any number of critters might be slipping in for a drink. Spooking any one of them could blow our cover and end our hunt.

I stretched my neck every time we paused, hoping to catch a glimpse of tall horns or gray fur. It felt like game was close. Peter's body language suggested he thought so. That only intensified my own premonition.

Cotton motioned for Dick to kneel beside him. My heart sputtered. The hunt's climax is the moment right before you squeeze the trigger. When you know you have made the right moves. You have to ignore the speed of your heart, the tremor of you breath. At that moment, the predator's instinct within you emerges. Many of our human characteristics separate us from animals. This one re-connects us. Both primal and modern, it is impossible for some of us to suppress.

My body tensed as I braced for the blast. I still jumped. Dick worked another shell into the chamber and prepared for another shot.

Peter stood, barely able to contain himself. He was a hunter's hunter. For him, both a fact of life and a passion. Peter understood why we were there. He was a man of courage, who had never heard of political correctness and wouldn't understand it if he had. Peter was a hunter, because that's what he was. I liked Peter.

Dick looked poised to fire again. I lifted my neck to see around the boys. Was the buck down? Was he wounded?

Peter ran forward when Dick and Cotton stood.

The bull was dead.

"By the time we get back to camp with this old boy, we'll only have a few minutes of daylight left. There's an East African duiker that's been hanging out in a thick area just south of the tents. Joan has been trying to get one for three years. If you don't mind, I'd like to give her another shot tonight."

"I think it would be great if she got one," I said.

"That's the spirit, Mary. You're turning into one heck of a hunting partner."

"I thought we were supposed to be clients."

"Being pals is more fun."

Nobody said professional hunters couldn't have fun, and Cotton loved fun. He also believed in hard work. Effort was more important than outcome. Nobody wants to go home empty-handed, but the client who doesn't recognize genuine effort doesn't deserve positive results. Cotton worked as hard as the rest and knew how to have fun doing it.

We didn't find Joan's duiker that evening, but anything resembling the client/ guide relationship had been shattered by laughter. We would call them friends for the rest of our lives.

"Happy birthday, Dick," Joan said the following morning as she placed a muffin on the table. It had a lit match protruding from the top.

"How'd you know?"

"Lucky guess." She winked at me.

"What do you say we go find Mary a buffalo?"

"I thought it was my birthday."

"Yes, but Mary still needs a buffalo. Besides, isn't everyday like your birthday here?"

"You've got a point."

"I thought we were going back to Loliondo today," I said.

"We are. But we should be there in time to hunt this afternoon."

We took photos of everyone in camp and said our goodbyes.

We arrived at Loliondo in time to eat lunch and take a nap before hunting. Sometimes, when you change camps, you lose the staff, including trackers. Peter traveled with us. His natural abilities on the trail of any animal were the kind legends were born from. It would have been nearly tragic to leave him behind.

We found buffalo tracks from a bachelor group of bulls right away. Tracking buffalo is not as difficult as tracking a leopard or one of the smaller antelope like bushbuck, but the way Peter anticipated their moves kept us constantly impressed. Most of the time, I knew which tracks we were following, but occasionally, we moved away from anything resembling hoof prints for long periods. If I hadn't already experienced that kind of tracking with Peter, I might have thought we were wandering, hoping to stumble into something. Not with Peter. He was trying to outmaneuver them.

We approached a heavily brushed waterhole and I was sure that was where we would find our quarry. Our steps did not slow, but I tried to walk softer.

The ground shook. Dust flew. A stampede? I jumped back and must have let out a squeal. The others chuckled as a company of warthogs dashed away.

As we continued past the waterhole, I never saw a buffalo track. But when we tiptoed into miombo woodland, the dark form of a huddled horde of Cape buffalo appeared.

Peter had managed to place us directly in their path. How he did that with such consistency in a place so wide open with wilderness was beyond my understanding. Who was I to question such ability? It should be appreciated, respected, admired, and even awed. Peter was one of the best.

If not for twelve old buffalo bulls rumbling toward us, I might have let it sink in. An advance of beasts like that demands attention. They had ours—my own laced with a heavy icing of fear. Cotton studied for a good set of horns, Peter slipped out of the way and Dick had one of those, *Isn't this awesome,* smiles on his face. It was awesome, but somehow I don't think I got the same adrenaline charge from it that my husband did. I loved hunting, but dangerous game always had me shaking. Dick lived for it. I may have been the one with the rifle, but it was still partly Dick's hunt. We could have walked away right then and it would have been worth it to him. I wouldn't have minded putting some distance between us and those unpredictable buffalo either.

Cotton kept the glass to his eye, studying the horns of each individual bull as they advanced. I don't know why he needed those binos. They were already too close. They looked big, mean, and ready for trouble—almost as if they wanted it.

My knee shuddered. Half my body urged me to run; half said hold steady. Cotton turned and shook his head. Peter nodded, then motioned with a twitch of his head that we should skedaddle. I saw it. Even if they would never admit it, the boys were concerned over how close those bulls had come. We could jump up, wave our arms and shout. We might turn them or we might infuriate them. We could hold tight and hope they rumbled by without notice. It had happened before. We *could* get trampled either way. Everything inside me screamed to run.

Peter jumped and exposed himself. He whistled, clapped, and stomped his feet. Cotton stood beside him, his big bore steadied on the lead bull twenty yards away. Dick and I rose. *Please let them run away. Please.*

The buffalo formed a half-circle. Dust swirled around them. Their noses raised and their muscles tightened. Their eyes turned to fire.

We were in a standoff. I knew Dick was beside me. I could feel him there—could see his outline from the corner of my eye. I didn't dare look away from the buffalo. The next few seconds were key; our fate decided within them.

Just run away.

They mocked my fear with defiant stares.

Peter lunged toward them. They did not move.

He picked up a stone and threw it. They shuffled their feet slightly.

Peter found a two-foot branch and tossed it their way. They rumbled thirty yards before turning back the way buffalo often do.

"Okay," Cotton said. "Let's move away. There's no good bull in this group. These fellas can be unpredictable. They think they rule the *veldt*. I'd rather not get tangled in a scuffle."

We backed out the first few yards, then turned to walk at a brisk pace, periodically glancing over our shoulders. They were not following us. Thank God.

Once we gained a safe distance, we hiked back to the waterhole to check for zebra tracks.

A zebra can keep the staff full for days. We hunted them for the adventure as well. Zebras are not horses. Not even close. They are as wild and wary as whitetail—a fine challenge for any hunter. They are as tough as any plains game. We have hammered stallions before, hitting them perfectly, smashing mushroomed bullets through their vitals, only to track them long distances before finishing them off with another round. I always tear up. Their power and stamina, even after hit, are admirable.

Dick's zebra proved more cooperative and the shot placement, shock value, and expanding bullet had the desired effect. The zebra went down hard and died quickly.

"It's getting late," Cotton said. "How about we hunt our way to camp? We'll drive through some good areas, maybe glass something, get back early enough to drive to Lobo Lodge and go to dinner for Dick's birthday."

"How far is it?" I asked.

"Not far. An hour or so."

"Sounds good. What do you think, Dick?"

"I'm fine either way."

"Good," Cotton said. "It's settled then, we'll go to dinner to celebrate your birthday, since that's exactly what you want." He winked at me.

We left the truck once on the way to camp, following another zebra, but turned back when he gave us the slip. With more time, we might have tracked him further.

More time. That would be something. Two, three, or even four weeks in Africa seems like a long time. It is never enough. One minute you are arriving in camp, the next you are wiping away tears of goodbye, without having experienced a grain of what you could have. It is not about the numbers or the size or anything else you become involved in. It is about the experience—the hunt. Sometimes, that includes numbers or size, but they are encompassed by a bigger experience, one that stays with you far beyond mere memories. In the end, the accumulation of significant as well as seemingly unimportant events makes us who we are. Dick and I are hunters.

Built into the rocks of a mountain, Lobo Lodge had six levels enclosed entirely by glass. Wherever you were in the complex, you could see wildlife. Management pumped water into a manmade lake in an open valley where animals sauntered in to drink. The game-watching was fabulous. The Lodge was on the park/ hunting line and some of the animals hadn't completely lost their natural fear of humans. Many parks throughout Africa border hunting concessions, which provide buffer zones between agricultural fields and wildlife areas. Nothing can destroy a year's crop faster than unbridled grazing. The system has worked well for many years in a number of countries. The buffer zones not only keep a check on the number of field-marauding beasts, but also help keep the park's animal population in balance.

Dinner left a lot to be desired, but the company and conversation made it an enjoyable evening. Cotton and Joan were easy to fall in love with. They adored each other, enjoyed their lives, and had a way of making you feel as if you had been friends forever.

"Happy birthday, Dick," Joan said before we headed for our tent later that evening.

"Couldn't think of a better way to spend it," he said.

A lion roared.

"Even the lions want in on the celebration," Cotton said. "They're on the prowl tonight. Probably like to get their hands on some of that zebra meat." He winked at me.

When the generator powered down, the lions started moving closer, roaring and growling all the way. They were headed right for the skinning shed. I just knew it. Were we in their path? I was certain of it.

Our wall tent held two single cots. If I were not so afraid of what might have been outside, I would have walked over and elbowed my husband out of his stupor. Instead, I lay there wide-eyed staring into the dark, occasionally urging Dick to wake up—but not too loud. I didn't want to give the lions any more reason to come have a look.

The tent shook from a roar so loud and so close that it hurt my ears. It had to be right outside. I held my breath. Dick's snore abated, but he didn't wake up. Soft footsteps padded the grass outside, claws scraping on the dirt like fingernails on a chalkboard.

What was I going to do? I couldn't move. So I prayed. *Please God, don't let the lions eat us. Please God, keep Dick's snores to a minimum.*

I heard only Dick's heavy breathing for the next thirty minutes. Then a horrible scream pierced the night, followed shortly by a whining cry. This cry went on for a full minute until stopped by the sound of crunching bones. Not snapping, but crunching as if a vise were squeezing them into mush. I heard struggling, kicking feet slowing with each beat of my heart. What a horrible way to die. Suffocated by the jaws of a lion while being gnawed on by its cohorts. I shivered. Another roar shook the tent. The beast was pleased with itself.

I pulled the blanket up to my neck and prayed myself to sleep.

"I can't believe you slept through that last night."

"I'm sure it wasn't as close as you thought."

"I heard the life being squeezed out of some poor animal while the lions roared and growled. It was so loud my ears rang."

"If they killed something, then you didn't have anything to worry about."

"It felt like I was on the dessert menu."

Dick smiled at me. Inside, I bet he was rolling his eyes.

We found Hillary and Cotton in the mess tent tinkering with the radio.

"Why don't you two relax a bit," Cotton said. "It's important that we get this working before we go. Grab yourselves some French toast and tea. We'll come get you when we're done."

An hour and a half later, Cotton appeared, his shirt drenched with sweat. "You two ready yet?" He smiled. "I think it's time for Mary to get her buffalo."

I wished he hadn't said that. If we had just found the buffalo while hunting for something else, I wouldn't have had to be nervous for so long. My stomach was in a double surgeon's knot.

We found tracks within fifteen minutes of leaving camp and caught up to the herd half an hour later. It was a massive herd, nearing one thousand animals. That many buffalo are used to being given quarter. A big bull ambled along the edge of the herd—we didn't intend to give way.

We tried to sneak into position. One strange movement, one strange sound, one strange smell. Whatever it was, our gig was up. With military-like precision, the buffalo formed a wall. We were staring at hundreds of buffalo. Hundreds of buffalo were staring at us. Fear must have illuminated from my wide eyes like brightness shining from the stars on a clear African night.

"You see the bull on the left?"

It took me a moment to realize Cotton was talking to me. A herd of Cape buffalo, all of them staring directly into your fear, is an awesome sight.

"Where?"

"Fourth from the left. His horns are massive. You can't miss him."

One, two, three, four. I had the crosshairs on him, but never touched the trigger. I couldn't see much difference between him and the others.

"Whenever you're ready."

I held my finger. "I'm not sure I'm looking at the right bull."

"He's the fourth from the left. When you see him, you'll know. Are you sure you're looking at the fourth one? There's a small group before the main herd."

Further left. The bull I had the crosshairs on wasn't the one. I peered over the scope to find the small group. Back to the scope, I counted again. *One. Two. Three. Holy four.* No question. Nothing in the herd had that kind of headgear—at least nothing I could see. Confidence and inadequacy melded into something like fear. It wasn't fear, but the feeling was just as intense. It affected me in an eerily similar way.

"Have you got him, Mary?"

"I got him," I whispered.

A Cape buffalo never has the look of fear. It will run as if afraid, but when it turns to stare you down, when it fights off a pack of lions, when it peers from the bottom of its eyes, with no strength remaining as a lion's jaws clamp around its neck, rage and fire burn in its pupils. The buffalo is intent on destroying its attacker. Even in the last seconds of life, it has no time to contemplate fear.

If you look into a buffalo's eyes, it is difficult not to hesitate and that can be fatal. The buffalo may or may not feel fear, but it does not show it as the antelope does. His stare is designed to instill fear.

I looked into his eyes.

"Take him when you're ready."

My hesitation—the hesitation I knew would come if I looked into his eyes—gave the herd time to crash away.

They didn't go far, but their run revealed some nervousness. Hundreds of anxious buffalo do not create a *Kumbaya* situation.

Cotton grabbed my arm, to pull me after a black mass of destruction.

I kept the big bull in my sight. We ran after him, Cotton carrying the shooting sticks, me with my rifle, and Peter close behind with Cotton's rifle. At one hundred yards, I felt we were close enough. I could make that shot. And I wasn't a track star.

Cotton finally slowed to a sneaky walk. We ducked into position. While I caught my breath, Cotton opened the shooting sticks and took his rifle from Peter. It was time.

My chest heaved. The sun beat down on the back of my neck. With the rifle stock on the sticks, I found the bull through the scope. Same shot as before—frontal chest. Not ideal on any game. With buffalo, the first bullet needs to hit vitals. Things can get messy in a hurry if it doesn't.

Sweat beaded at my hairline. Resisting the urge to scratch, I concentrated low on the bull's chest. *Take a deep breath. Calm down.* The recent jog and the adrenaline from facing down a beast that could gore me to death had my hands quaking. I had to get it under control. The buffalo were not going to wait.

I took a deep breath and eased it out.

There. Now hold and squeeze.

At the shot, the herd stampeded, kicking up a cloud of dust that a whirlwind could only imagine. Their hooves shook the ground. It sounded like thunder. I couldn't tell if they were approaching or moving away. Cotton and Peter held steady. As the dust settled, the thunderous rush subsided. Thank goodness.

It took a few moments for the dust to clear. Did I see something through the haze? It started as a shadowy figure, dark through the dirty air. It took on a fuzzy outline and finally a distinct shape. A lone buffalo bull standing broadside. I couldn't believe he was still there. I wished he had been off his feet.

He didn't move. We didn't move. Maybe his appearance from the ashes had us all speechless. Without another living being in sight, he would locate us soon enough. Either choice he made from there wouldn't be good for us. The last thing we wanted was a charge. Ten hours of tracking a wounded animal didn't sound like fun either.

"Put another one in him."

I fired. The bull bucked, hunched his shoulders, and thundered into a nearby wall of long grass. He disappeared before I could slide another bullet into the chamber.

"Good shot." Peter hunched his shoulders, mimicking the buffalo's response to the bullet impact.

Though the buffalo was hit twice, I was not confident. I would rather see him piled up on the dry, hard ground.

Cotton pointed at his ear. "Listen for the death bellow."

Walking toward the tall grass, I heard nothing but our footsteps. They slowed as we closed the distance. Blood splattered the ground ahead of us. Anyone could read this trail. Peter led the way, holding only the shooting sticks. I held tight to the freckle of comfort my rifle gave me. Every step closer to the grass became more cautious. Cotton half-shouldered his rifle. Any second now, an enraged buffalo could explode from the grass with fire shooting from his nostrils.

The blood trail petered out just before the grass. I had not heard a bellow. We planned to follow him into the natural labyrinth. Had we lost our minds? I had a responsibility to finish what I started, but the grass stood three feet above our heads and was as thick as a wheat field. I wouldn't want to go in there without a wounded buffalo waiting to gore me to death. Yet, when the grass closed in behind Peter, Cotton followed him. I stayed right with them, finding courage from their quiet determination.

We moved in inches, trying to confirm the breath we heard was our own. It felt stuffy. The world closed around me in the form of grass blades. I wanted to claw something. I just knew that bull was waiting for us to get so close that he could take all three of us out with one massive swipe of his horns.

When Peter stopped, my heart fell to my ankles. We crouched slowly. I couldn't see anything. I only heard my trembling breath. Where was the bull? I could smell him, the faint scent of manure gone stale after three days in the sun. If we were close enough to smell him, he could smell us. He probably had us pinpointed by scent alone. We depended too much on our eyesight for that kind of encounter. I prepared myself to run. I couldn't help it.

Nobody moved.

It wasn't that far to go back—to leave the grass. All we had to do was back out, walk away. Easy as that.

Nobody moved.

The bull was waiting for us to make a wrong turn. I could feel it. Every direction felt wrong. What in God's name made me put myself in those kinds of situations?

Nobody moved.

At least a charge only lasts a moment. This waiting for a charge by an animal you cannot locate takes a toll on your sanity. It plays with your conviction, causes you to second-guess yourself.

At the same time, it shoots your body full of adrenaline. The senses we rarely find use for fire into hyper-drive. You smell things you normally wouldn't notice, like the distinct scent of buffalo. You hear sounds you would normally ignore, like the sound of your own breathing or the slight whisper of tall grass swaying in a light breeze. Everything but the moment fades away. You don't think about tax forms or birthdays or what to have for dinner. You are focused. We experience that far less than we should.

The bull could rumble over us without any kind of warning, leaving us as vulture fodder.

A heavy thump. A rush of hooves. I stumbled backwards with a shriek. We were dead for sure.

Cotton snapped his eyes back at me and raised his finger to shush me.

Shouldn't he be getting ready to fend off the buffalo?

He tried to give me a stern look, but had to contain a laugh.

What the heck?

The rush of hooves was actually more of a scamper fading away. Damn warthogs. I might have a heart attack before the buffalo had a chance to kill me.

Peter had noticed the warthogs and didn't want them alerting the buffalo that we were on his trail. Somebody could have told me that.

What had I smelled? It had to be the buffalo. It had to be close. I wanted to tell Cotton, but silence was more important.

We stepped through an area of matted and bloody grass where the buffalo had recently lain. The stench stronger than ever. I had smelled him. Had he been watching his back trail? Why did he get up and move? Maybe the warthogs pushed him. I didn't know.

The buffalo had enough strength to get up and walk away. Not good.

When we stopped, Peter and Cotton studied the grass all around us, not just along the trail ahead of us. Every scenario running through my thoughts turned out a bloody mess.

The buffalo led us into an open field. The second we pushed through the grass, he turned to face us.

"He's going to charge. Shoot him." Cotton's rifle was ready to back me up.

The bullet's impact seemed to have no effect. The bull staggered forward, the fire in his eyes aimed at us. His body language said, *I'm taking you with me*. His legs gave out. His nose slammed to the ground.

A somber death bellow from a noble warrior gave me shivers.

PART OF US: DICK

"Do you want the good news or the bad news first?" Cotton asked.

"Give me the good news."

"Your bullets have finally arrived."

"I already know the bad news."

"What's that?" Cotton asked, one eyebrow rising.

"Too late to use them."

"We've still got klipspringer and Chanler's mountain reedbuck."

"You want the good news or the bad news first?" I said.

Cotton laughed. "The good news."

"We have enough ammo to shoot a truckload of klipspringer and reedbuck."

"Okay, what's the bad news?"

"It's all for the .375."

Cotton rubbed the back of his neck. "I see your point. Heavy load for small game. You still have some 7mm bullets?"

"Just what we have on the stock sleeves."

Cotton followed me to the tent where I counted the bullets on Mary's rifle and then mine.

"What's the verdict?"

"Nine."

"Nine's five more than we need."

"I'm glad you're confident in our ability."

"Mary should have no problem. You, I can't be sure."

"There's one good thing about it," I said.

"What's that?"

"At least it's not you who has to do the shooting."

"You'd better not miss now."

I would never hear the end of it if I did.

That evening the fire cast an orange glow around camp. A campfire can make an evening almost perfect. Conversation usually revolves around the hunt, but it doesn't matter what you talk about or if you talk at all. You can sit quietly around a campfire and know it was a good day and that tomorrow holds possibilities worth a lifetime of memories.

Fading flames and thousands of flickering stars lit our way to the tent. Walking hand-in-hand, we felt young again, without a care in the world, with adventure before us. We breathed in pure, cool air and gazed at the stars. A lion roared.

"Let's get in the tent, Dick," Mary said. "That one sounded close."

I smiled and slipped into the tent behind her. There's nothing like the lion's voice in darkness.

"I can't believe you slept through the lions again last night," Mary said.

"They came into camp again, huh?"

"They kept their distance for a couple of hours, growling, roaring, and having a grand old time. I don't know why they didn't just stay where they were if they were having so much fun."

"It's nothing to worry about."

"You read about tourists getting killed by lions and elephants all the time. I over-heard Cotton talking about some woman in the national park across the river who walked back to her tent to use the restroom. When she didn't return, they went look-ing for her. The next day they found what was left of her one hundred yards from camp with a jackal picking at her skin. Does that sound like nothing to worry about?"

"I think you're overreacting."

"I'd rather be too cautious than kitty chow."

I walked over and kissed my wife on the forehead. "Everything will be fine."

"That doesn't mean I'm going to get any sleep. The lions didn't leave until four this morning."

After toast and oatmeal under the grass dinner canopy, Cotton excused himself. "We'll meet you at the car in ten minutes. Don't forget your bullets."

"All nine of them?" Dick said.

"I told you, we only need four. But you better bring the other five. You know, just in case." Cotton winked.

"Yes. Just in case."

We piled into the Land Cruiser like a high-school basketball team heading for the conference championship game. We had two days to hunt four animals. Klipspringers are compact antelope that blend with their surroundings. They live in rocky hills and *kopjes*, hopping from rock to rock with acrobatic ability.

"Get comfortable," Cotton said. "It's an hour drive to the best klipspringer hangouts. Not much to see along the way. Try to take a nap."

"On these bumpy roads?" Mary said.

"It's never a problem for Dick."

When Cotton said over an hour, it probably meant closer to two.

An hour later, we hit a rock. The vehicle jolted and shot me three inches into the air.

"At least that got him to quit snoring," Mary said.

"Very good, Mama," Peter said from behind us. Everyone was laughing.

"We only have nine bullets," Mary said. "Maybe you should shoot first, and then, if I have to use more bullets it won't matter as much."

"It wouldn't be the end of the world if we had to use the .375."

"I thought it was too big for klipspringer and reedbuck."

"It is too heavy, but it's better than throwing rocks."

Mary rolled her eyes.

A *kopje* jutted from the flat plain like a whale's back on a calm day. Dozens of klipspringer could hide in its crags, brush, and back-shadows. A hunter could spend all day exploring that one *kopje* and still not see half of it.

"I don't see any water around. A few miles seem like a long way for a small antelope to travel."

"Klipspringer can survive a long time from the water in plants. They're a hardy creature. We'll just mosey around the rocks and see if we run into one or two. They blend in well. Sometimes you'll swear you're looking at a rock until they bounce away. Peter has a knack for spotting them, though." Cotton slapped Peter's shoulder.

Peter focused on the minute intricacies of every cliff.

We took it slow, peeking around each corner with the binoculars before exposing ourselves.

Peter crouched. Cotton leaned around the boulder we were hiding behind.

"Female," he whispered back.

I wanted to pop my neck out and have a look. I'm sure Mary and Joan wanted to as well.

"Come on up, Mary. There might be a male close by."

Joan and I stayed back.

"There he is. Get ready."

"I don't see him." Mary said.

"Off to the right a bit and one hundred fifty yards up the hill."

I leaned out to look over Peter's shoulder. I saw boulders and steep rock faces. We waited.

Mary finally said, "I still don't see him."

"They're both standing on that small boulder." Cotton pointed. His voice, though calm, had a quiver to it as if it could burst from tension. He would be whispering through his teeth before long. "Do you see that big cliff with the rusty color in the center?"

Mary nodded.

Straining my neck again, I found it as well.

"Go straight up from there to where it flattens out. There's a light-colored boulder to the right. Do you see it?"

"I see it," Mary said. She was looking through her scope.

"Ten yards below that boulder—toward us—is a smaller rock. They're on that rock. Do you see them?"

I saw the big boulder and thought I saw the small one.

"The rock with the rounded top?"

"That's it. Do you see them?"

"No—oh wait. Yes, I see them. Two of them."

"The one on the left is the male. Take him when you're ready."

We waited.

I stared up the *kopje*, still trying to locate the klipspringers, waiting for the shot. Mary struggled to get steady. She didn't want to put the rifle directly on the rock. Peter whipped off his jacket and handed it to Cotton.

"Try this." Cotton lifted her barrel and placed the jacket under the stock.

You never realize how quiet hunting is until a rifle goes off. The sound of the blast seemed to echo off ten cliffs before fading into the huge silence of the calm day.

I scanned the hills, hoping to see a single klipspringer bounding away. I was not disappointed. It bounced up a vertical cliff with the ease of a spider crawling up the wall. Then, it was gone.

I knew the answer, but I asked anyway. "Did you get him?"

Mary shrugged. "I think so."

She thought so? Not very definitive. I had been there. All hunters have. The pre-shot routine feels good. You feel steady as a tightrope walker. The squeeze is going perfect. Then, a momentary lapse in concentration, a barely noticeable twitch in your finger and, right at the blast, you flinch. Not bad. Just enough to make you lose sight of the animal and question whether you were dead-on. You think you were, but an inkling of doubt tinkers with your conviction and makes you shrug your shoulders and say, "I think so."

Cotton lowered his binos and gave me a tentative thumb up. "I'm sure she hit him," Cotton said. "I'm just not sure where."

Peter looked as if he wanted to clap. My doubt lifted. During the short time we had hunted with Peter, I had learned to trust his observations. If Peter said an animal went right when the rest of us thought it ran left, Peter was right. If Peter said Mary hit an animal well, he would lead us right to it. And that is what happened.

What took a klipspringer less than three seconds to spring up, took us over thirty minutes to climb. If Peter had gone by himself he might have done it in ten minutes or less, but my creaky legs demanded a subdued advance. Peter led us up the *kopje* with a refined patience that wasn't pushy or hurried in any way.

We found Mary's klipspringer humped on the very rock where it had been standing. The rock's shape had hid it from us as we scanned from our lower vantage point.

"See Mary," I said. "You hit him perfect."

"One shot, one kill. That's the way these gals like to do it." Cotton smiled at Mary and Joan.

"Probably just lucky," Mary said.

The look in her eyes said *I'm trying to be modest, but I am pleased with myself.* Some hunters might have bragged. Mary felt no need. She knew things could go downhill in a hurry. Braggarts often turned out looking like horses-asses.

As I soon found out.

Mary checked the chamber, emptied the magazine, and handed me all the 7mm bullets. "It's your turn."

I only took one from her and made sure Cotton saw.

Cotton snatched up the rest. "Your wife might be able to shoot like a pro, but you better have these." He stuffed them in my pocket.

"You don't trust my abilities?"

"If we had time, I'd hand-load a case for you."

"After all we've been through, this is the kind of confidence you have in me?"

"I like to hedge my bets."

"No, no," Peter said. He looked concerned. "Bwana Dick shoot very good."

"You'd think after all this time with a rascal like Cotton, Peter would know to *rarely* take him seriously," Joan said.

"It's okay," I said. "Bwana Cotton is just crazy." I pointed at my head and spun my finger while crossing my eyes.

Peter tried to hide a smile as he looked away from Cotton.

"Okay, okay. Let's get this ram back to the truck."

I heard Peter chuckling during our descent.

"He probably can't wait to tell everyone what you said about the boss, right in front of the boss," Cotton said. "You'll have the whole lot of them making fun of me behind my back."

"At least there's one good thing about it."

"What's that?"

"You don't know any of my employees."

Cotton had a deep, booming laugh. "I'll just have to get to know some then, won't I?"

"Not if I can help it."

He laughed again. "You should hunt with us again. This has been more fun than hard work should be."

"We'll check our schedule when we get back to camp. See when we can make it work."

"We'll figure it out before you leave. Deal?"

"Deal."

"For now, let's find a klipspringer."

"Deal."

"And I don't care how many shots it takes you."

"I do. We're running out of bullets."

Kopjes dotted the plains. The big ones usually held klipspringers. We found a nice male at the next outcropping.

"When he quits jumping around, take him."

With a solid rest, leaning over a table-sized boulder, my rifle stock resting on a large bag full of sand, I couldn't miss. But that klipspringer refused to slow down.

"He's going around the corner. Let's move."

We grabbed the sandbag and raced as fast as the rocky terrain allowed. I tried to keep my footing. A twisted ankle could put a downer on a good day faster than a hailstorm.

We rounded the corner too quickly. Had we slowed and peered around more carefully, we might have spotted the ram standing on a big rock less than one hundred yards away. We expected to come around and see him jumping around like a rock-climbing kangaroo.

When we clanked into view, it took him a few seconds to realize we posed a threat. Just enough time for me to squeeze off a round. His mistake should have cost him a trip to the taxidermist. The bullet ricocheted off the rock below him. He took a few quick hops and disappeared over the other side of the *kopje*.

Cotton kept his mouth shut as we stared up the brush-sprinkled rocks in disbelief. He even held his tongue as we began our hike down to the vehicle. I waited for so long that I almost thought he would let it slide. I should have known better.

We took a break halfway down the slope. He made sure I saw him counting the bullets in the band affixed to my rifle's buttstock.

"I have plenty left."

"Plenty?"

"Enough."

"I hope so. It would be a shame to put a .375 hole in one of these antelope." It was only a half-joke.

I deserved it. I had been giving it out all morning as the over-confident hunter. After that last shot, my self-assurance may have waned. But I couldn't let Cotton know that.

"Maybe if you found one we didn't have to chase all over hell's rock I'd have a better chance."

"Just trying to keep you on your toes. Be prepared—you know, like the scouts."

"Even an old Eagle Scout's knees go bad."

At the next *kopje*, there were no excuses. I had a good rest. The klipspringer was oblivious to our presence and within two hundred yards. I missed. This time high. If low, I might have wondered about the scope's zero. One low and the next high had to be my mistake.

"We're pushing the envelope, aren't we?" Cotton said.

I have been around hunters who would throw childlike fits after two misses. That ruins the mood for everybody. Many people would grasp for excuses. Their scope was off. Their rest was bad. Anything to deflect blame. Sometimes there are merits to malfunctioning equipment, sometimes not. It is better to pinpoint the problem before hanging blame. I had been guilty of these things. I probably would be again, but it is better for everyone involved to keep the mood from getting too dark. It exacerbates your own misery and makes those around you uncomfortable. Cotton understood this and had learned enough about me to know I wouldn't take much offense to his mild ribbing. I also trusted him not to take it too far. Underneath Cotton's gruff, wild exterior was a tactful man.

I considered myself a competent shot with a rifle. Maybe not great, but pretty good. I had been shooting since I could hold a gun. When you learn to shoot as a kid, becoming proficient is as easy as learning to read or throw a baseball. A child's ability to absorb knowledge is beyond impressive. If you continue to practice into the later stages of your life, it becomes natural.

I had been hunting and shooting for as long as I could remember. I had shot everything from a darting cottontail to a charging elephant. Klipspringer, though small and always on the move, shouldn't have given me such problems. Some days were good and some days were—humbling.

We didn't have to leave the large *kopje* to find another klipspringer. We found one five hundred yards around the northeast side of the outcropping, apparently oblivious that bullets were ricocheting off rocks. He was bedded down, his vitals partially covered by a dark, oval-shaped rock.

"We can wait; see if he decides to stand," Cotton said. "Or we can try to make something happen."

"How far?"

"Two hundred yards."

"You want to climb up there?"

"Hell no. Not if we don't have to. We'll have Durani drive over there below it in full view. If he gets out and starts up the hill, it should get the klipspringer's attention. When it stands up, you blast it."

The klipspringer watched the vehicle as if it were a UFO. When Durani stopped, its head perked up. When he stepped from the vehicle, it was as if a troop of armed aliens were advancing upon it. The klipspringer sprung to its feet, its body the definition of tense.

I had the crosshairs on his shoulder and began squeezing the trigger. He jumped just as I fired; the bullet hit behind him.

A long period of silence. Not a word from anybody. I think they expected one teed-off hunter to go into a rampage and smash his rifle on the rocks.

I didn't want to disappoint them with nothing.

"That couldn't have gone any better."

"What?"

"I'm three for three."

"I'm not sure that's a stat worth bragging about."

"I don't have to tell anybody three for three of what."

Cotton shook his head. "Wouldn't that be misleading?"

"There's no reason to get technical. It makes you look good too. Cotton put me on three nice klipspringers. We went three for three."

"Didn't I put you on the klipspringers regardless?"

"There you go with the technicalities again."

Cotton laughed. "How many does that leave us?"

"Five."

"We still have one klipspringer and two mountain reedbuck."

"That's only three."

"That kind of thinking put us here in the first place. What do you say we drop the next one?"

I shrugged. "I tried to drop the last three."

"Good point," Cotton said. "You don't think the scope got knocked out of whack do you?"

"It's just bad shooting and bad luck. That last bullet hit right where I aimed. It's not the gun."

We usually drove around a *kopje*, stopping periodically to glass the rocks and brush. Most of us would scour the cliffs, ledges, and shadows with our binoculars, thinking we had studied a spot so well that an animal couldn't possibly be in the vicinity when Peter would point.

"There," he would say and we would follow his extended finger to parts of the hillside we had already glassed. He never used binoculars.

He must have thought we were blind.

The next ram was jumpy. He had probably heard rifle blasts echoing all over the neighboring *kopjes*. He needn't have worried. If the hunter firing all those bullets hadn't already bagged his prey, he probably couldn't hit an elephant at twenty yards. That jittery ram could have stood there flat-footed while I moved into position. When he finally held, I blew it.

He sprang up two or three rock faces at the shot.

I worked another bullet into the chamber and followed him with the crosshairs. I didn't think about distance or wind. All I wanted was to get one more shot at that klipspringer before he crested the hill. Who cared how many bullets I had left? I shot better than that. I had to get the crosshairs on the ram's shoulder.

I had shot my share of moving game—maybe not small antelope bounding up a cliff. How much different could it be than a tottering bushpig feeding at dusk?

Keeping up with his next upward leap was like trying to anticipate where the next head would pop up in *Whack-A-Mole*. I was always behind. How his rubbery hooves gripped to those vertical rocks was beyond me.

The next time he landed, I squeezed off a round and worked the bolt.

I didn't see the impact, but I knew I hammered him because of the cheers behind me. Typically, hunting isn't a sport where participants have a gallery. It's not a sport where fans purchase tickets to root for their favorite players. It's intimate. We don't hunt for glory or money. We hunt because we love it. Hunter and prey share a bond. The act of killing an animal might seem contradictory to those who have never picked up a weapon in pursuit of game, but that final act seals the bond forever.

Cotton gave me one of those *I'm impressed* nods. Mary had her hands balled into fists shaking them.

My lucky shot on a klipspringer ram had made everybody's day. They had all been rooting for me as if I were an underdog in a championship game. Our morning klipspringer hunt had slid into afternoon without much notice. The tension, which had hovered above us through four missed shots, floated away when the ram's legs buckled.

As we climbed the *kopje*, a thorn bush snagged my sleeve and jerked me back. Cotton stared at me and scratched his chin.

"Go ahead," I said. "Let's hear it."

"Hear what?"

"Nothing. I guess we'll forget about it." I tore my shirt from the thorns and continued the climb. I wasn't getting off that easy.

"That was a great shot, Dick."

"But?" I said without turning around.

"It was a great shot, that's all."

Just above the acacia bush, we scaled an SUV-sized boulder. I had to find firm grips with my hands and feet and use every muscle to pull myself up. It was then, in the grunt of the strain, when Cotton gave me the *but*.

"You hit that ram perfectly, just before he would've disappeared forever. And you saved us three whole bullets for mountain reedbuck."

I didn't answer him until I had pushed, pulled, and grunted my way up the last few feet, where Peter was waiting. Always eager to run to downed game, Peter showed great restraint. I half-expected him to leave us to our lumbering. Instead, he reached down to give me a hand on my final push.

"You know how I like to make things more challenging than they need to be."

Cotton talked between breaths. "The key word in our next prey is mountain. We don't need to make it more challenging." At the top, he caught his breath. "They don't call them Chanler's *mountain* reedbuck because it sounds nice."

After a late lunch, Cotton approached me with a scheduling book. He flipped it open. "I didn't realize how booked I was. My first opening isn't until ninety-four. It's clear after that. You want my best spot in ninety-four?"

"We'll take it. Tell you what—we'll take one in ninety-five as well."

"What do you say we try for a few select specimens on that hunt? Go after some big, unique trophies?"

"We'll iron out the details later. For now, pencil us in."

"Done. We can spend some time looking over what we did on this hunt and talk about what we want to concentrate on next time. But we'll save that business for the off-season. You're still on vacation."

"Reedbuck this afternoon and tomorrow?"

"That's all that's left on license. You've done well. I hope you're as pleased with the safari as I am."

"More so," Mary said.

"No matter what happens in the next day, this has been a fine hunt."

Cotton looked at his watch and spoke without lifting his eyes. "It's already three. Let's meet at the truck at a quarter to five. That should give you enough time for a catnap. I have paperwork to finish and I want to check on the skins and horns. Make sure the boys are taking care of everything properly."

"Mind if I tag along?" I said.

"Not at all."

"You want to go?" I asked Mary.

"You go ahead. Joan and I have to sort some clothes she brought for the staff. I'd like to give some of our extra things as well."

"Is there anyone big enough to fit into our stuff?" I asked.

"I haven't seen one overweight person," Mary said.

"It's not a diet you want to try," Cotton said.

"Somebody could write a book about it and start a fad in the U.S."

Overweight or not, Americans have a life expectancy over twice that of Tanzanians. The average life expectancy was only around thirty-seven. I would rather carry a few extra pounds and be told I was unhealthy than be thin and have died years ago.

"It makes you think about how lucky we are, doesn't it?"

"I'd say we're blessed," Mary corrected me.

The skinning shed appeared to be the same as any other hut in camp. Made of grass, a few sticks, mud, and homemade twine stripped from long-stemmed plants. It was simple, like every hut in every nearby village. Simplicity came from necessity. The grass huts were authentic. They said something about the local people. When an elephant decided to demolish a dwelling, the family could have a new one built within a few hours.

As we rounded the corner of the skinning shed, we stepped into a scene familiar to hunters the world over. Two or three skilled men spent most of every day at the skinning shed. When visiting hunters enjoyed the success we had, skinners often worked into the dark hours. They are rarely alone in their work. After the hunt, the skinning shed becomes a gathering place, where people congregate to help with the work or merely hang out.

An expert skinner could make short work of the two klipspringers we brought in. Two men worked with their knives, while two others, including Durani, helped hold and move the carcasses. Kafia, Peter, Hillary, and three other chaps stood around chattering, laughing, and smoking hand-rolled cigarettes.

The boys stopped talking briefly as we approached and then carried on as if we were part of their gang. I wished I understood Swahili. I wished I spoke it. Then I could laugh at their jokes; tell a few of my own. I might even get my hands bloody. Part of Africa's charm was that you weren't required to do much of the work. Sometimes you dread the work after a long day of hunting. I missed it at that moment. Sitting around with buddies, skinning a deer or elk, worrying about little else but the task at hand, sometimes talking about "important" matters, sometimes joking, sometimes not talking at all—lifelong bonds formed in those moments.

Cotton checked their work, making sure all skins were dried and salted properly and all meat divided amongst the staff's families. I tried to blend in without being too comical. I couldn't understand many words, but it didn't take long to figure out what was going on. The skinners and the two fellows helping them were working hard, concentrating on each cut. Five of the remaining six onlookers were there more to smoke and discuss those "important" topics than to help with any of the real work. The last man was that guy who stands over the top of you while you are cleaning game, making sure to inform you of your mistakes. He never offered to help. One of the skinners tried to give him the knife. He backed away shaking his head and hands. He slid over to join the other onlookers, but kept peeking over to the klipspringers. It didn't take long for him to tire of the conversation. He was back over the skinner's shoulder to point out mistakes before Cotton finished checking the operations. Some guys just can't help it.

Mary and I found Cotton, Hillary, Peter, and Joan waiting at the Land Cruiser. Peter and Hillary, who were leaning on the bumper, rose as we approached.

"Where's Durani?" Mary asked.

"He better be here soon, or we're going to leave without him. Then Hillary will have to drive." Cotton winked.

"No," Hillary said, taking a small step forward. "I must spot game." Hillary spoke English better than anyone else on the staff. "You need me to spot the reedbuck."

Cotton turned his head to hide a smirk he couldn't control.

"I need to go find Durani," Hillary said.

"We're already too late. You're driving. Let's go."

"I do not drive as good as you, Bwana Cotton."

"You drive fine." Cotton said. "Oh, I see. You don't think I can spot the reedbuck as well as you."

"No. You just drive better than I do. You are a very good driver. Okay. I will drive. You are a good spotter."

Cotton started laughing.

"Now, Cotton. That's just plain ornery," Joan said. "Hillary, you spot much better than Cotton."

Durani ran up carrying two jackets. He handed them to Cotton before jumping behind the wheel with a big smile and a look that said *Let's go*.

Joan leaned over to Mary. "I love my Cotton, but sometimes I wonder what I've gotten myself into." She said this loud enough for him to hear. "He thinks it's funny to harass the staff."

"He doesn't keep it only to the help," I said—again loud enough for everyone's benefit. "He's been on me about my poor shooting for so long it's giving me a complex."

Cotton pointed his thumb at me. "As if he needs any help with that."

Peter and Hillary were standing in the back as we approached the mountain. Cotton turned to Hillary. "I better not spot a reedbuck before you do."

We had only just started glassing a rocky slope when Hillary began tapping Cotton's shoulder. "Reedbuck. There. Reedbuck." He pointed and tapped, pointed and tapped.

"*Jike*," Peter said. Female.

Cotton found it through his binoculars. "Females don't count. Only males. Only *ndume*."

"No," Hillary said. "It is a reedbuck."

"*Ndume*," Cotton said. He stared at Hillary for a moment. His second PH looked as if he might protest again. Cotton shot his binoculars up to his eyes and back to the crags of the *kopje*. Hillary began scouring every shadow with single-minded intensity. At least we were getting their best effort.

"Normally, we would've moved on by now," Cotton said. "But with that female hanging around, I thought we might get lucky and find a male. She's moved far enough that if there were a male with her, we'd have seen him by now. We'll give it a few more minutes." He raised his binos back up, but didn't peer through them. He looked at us from the corner of his eye. "There's a ram. *Ndume, ndume*." He motioned with a nod of his head for us to look back at Hillary.

The budding PH had his binoculars to his eyes and leaned forward, looking back and forth across the *kopje*. "*Pi? Pi?*"

"There." Cotton pointed.

Hillary tried to follow the aim of Cotton's finger, obviously frustrated he failed to spot the animal before. This was the first we had seen Hillary anywhere near the point of losing composure. He had always been in control, calm as an African morning.

"Now, Cotton," Joan said. "Don't you think that's enough?"

"He knows I'm just having fun with him."

Hillary shook his head and pointed with his fist. "You know I will get you back."

"I hope you do," Joan said.

"When you two finish conspiring to *get* me, I think we'll move over to the other side. There has to be a male around here somewhere."

Thirty minutes later, Cotton's prediction came to fruition.

"*Ndume*. Yes. Male." Hillary was pointing and tapping again. His shoulders rose. He beamed as if the sun's reflection came from beneath him.

"Good spotting," Joan said, then nudged her husband.

"Not bad, Hillary. Not too bad. But I was looking down so that one doesn't count."

"Ahh." Hillary waved his hand forward and blew air from closed lips.

Everybody laughed.

Cotton glanced over his shoulder. "Where's he at?"

Hillary crossed his arms and shrugged.

"Do you see him?" Cotton asked Peter.

Peter closed his eyes and put his hands out in front of himself as if he were blind.

"What if he gets away?" Mary asked.

"They know better than that. They're just giving me a taste of my own medicine."

"What's that way up there?"

Cotton searched through his binoculars. "That's a pretty good Chanler's reedbuck."

"Everyone spots better than the Bwana."

Laughter erupted.

"I deserved that," Cotton said. Then he was all business. "It's a bit of a climb, but I think we can get to him if we use that ridge for cover."

The reedbuck was bedded in the shade of a small thorn-tree and should stay put as long as we didn't spook him.

"This one's yours, Mary," I said. "I'll just tag along."

The slope rose gradually at first, growing steeper every few yards. We stayed below a ridgeline separating us from our quarry. Few physical endeavors test your limits the way following native guides up a steep mountain face does. I tried to keep in shape at home—jogging, hiking, running up and down steps, even traveling to Colorado and doing those things at 10,000 feet. Still, next to Peter and Hillary, I was like a sloth trying to keep pace with mountain goats. They waited patiently for the slow American to climb what they must have deemed a little hill. I was grateful for that, even if I was too short of breath to express it.

The problem with keeping the ridge between the reedbuck and us was that we couldn't see the animal. We might spend the next hour climbing that mountain, sweating in cooling air, tripping over dying grass, and snagging ourselves on thorn-bushes only to peek over the ridge and see that our reedbuck had moved to a tree on the other side of the mountain.

"He should be just on the other side," Cotton said after thirty minutes.

My knee couldn't take anymore.

"I'll wait here while you sneak over the top. We'll spook him if too many of us go."

"Good idea. It's probably best if just Mary, Hillary, and I go."

At the top, they hurried Mary into shooting position. My wife didn't take quick shots. Even when the rush was near a panic, she took her time. Everything needed to be perfect. She lowered her barrel and they pushed themselves from the ground to hurry forward. They were going to find her a better setup or they were rushing to get one last possible shot. Whichever it was, half of me expected to hear a blast and the other half expected them to appear over the ridge empty-handed.

We only stood there a few minutes, but I had to slug it out with my impatience. I felt like jogging to the top of the ridge.

A cold chill slipped down my back. I held my hand over my eyes and squinted. What harm could come from crawling up the ridge and peering over? Maybe just a few steps up, then I could see something. Mary was probably trying to find the perfect shot. I didn't move.

Peter smiled at me. Did he know something I didn't? No, Peter just smiled a lot.

I told myself not to look at my watch. Hold out. Give two minutes a chance to pass. I could go every day without looking at the time and wonder what happened to the week. Now the seconds ticked by so slowly I began convincing myself they didn't matter.

I started up the ridge.

"Wait, Bwana. They no shoot. Mama shoot, we go. Yes?"

Maybe I was hasty. I could give it another five minutes. I glanced down at my watch in time to see the final seconds tick away from the last five minutes.

I didn't claw up the hill and rumble over to see how my hunting partner was doing. I didn't because Peter stopped me. That kind of stunt would have only spooked the game into the next concession. Peter had to think I was out of my mind—or at least naïve.

Twenty minutes later, Mary followed her two professional hunters over to our side of the ridge. I hadn't heard a shot so I watched their faces for hints. They were all smiling. They were not the smiles of a bagged buck or meat in the pot or a one-shot kill. They were of three hunters who had been bested by a wary old buck—more rewarding than it deserves to be. It isn't shameful for your quarry to put you in your place. Shame lies in failing to take something positive from your quest. A healthy respect for the animal and the rocky hills and crags he calls home at the least.

"Well?" I said once they descended the slope.

Cotton and Hillary both looked at Mary, giving her the opportunity to tell it.

"I was on him twice, but couldn't get steady before he ran off."

"They weren't great situations," Cotton said. "He knew we were after him and was jumpy."

"He means that literally," Mary said. "He bounced up and down those hills like a kangaroo. I should've been able to get on him."

"Don't beat yourself up," Cotton said. "Not many hunters would've had time to get off a clean shot. Some guys might fling bullets and hope for the best. Believe me, your approach is better."

Last days are full of urgency. Our safari had been successful by any definition. We had hunted many fine animals and, more importantly, forged lasting friendships. We had already planned future hunts with Cotton and promised to get together back in the states. We would miss the camp staff, especially Hillary, Peter, Kafia, and Durani. Returning within a few years increased our chances of seeing them again, but the harsh realities of African life made these men elders. They were in their late twenties and early thirties. With luck, we would meet them again.

"Today, we will find your reedbuck," Hillary said to Mary after breakfast

"I hope so."

"Not hope. We will find your reedbuck." He held up his thumb.

"Okay," Mary said, returning the thumbs-up.

Hillary assisted Mary and then sprung into the truck.

I noticed Peter and Durani smiling and nodding.

"Everybody seems optimistic this morning," I said to Cotton and Joan as they climbed in next to us. "Our last morning."

"Peter doesn't get this confident very often. When he does, something usually gets shot."

"You don't believe he's psychic?"

"Let's just say I've seen things in Africa and little would surprise me."

Cotton practiced two main methods for hunting mountain reedbuck. One was to work around the base of the mountain, glass the hills and cliffs, spot a buck, and then stalk it. The other, and one I preferred though my aging bones and joints disagreed, was to hike to the top of the mountain and hunt down.

"How do you feel about a hike?" Cotton asked.

"I think I'd enjoy that," Mary said.

"What kind of hike?" I asked.

"What difference does it make?" Mary said. "I need to work off all that food we ate last night."

"I just want to know if Peter needs to bring me a litter or if it's going to be steep enough to slide down." I smiled. "Looks almost steep enough to slide down to me." I guess most worthwhile endeavors hurt a little. "What are we waiting for? We have mountains to climb. The reedbuck isn't going to sit around and wait on us."

"I thought I was the PH?"

"By all means Mr. PH, Bwana, lead us up the mountain." I offered him the lead with an open palm.

"Remind me again why we want to book you another hunt?" Cotton said as he walked by. He winked at Mary.

We took our time climbing up the slope, peeking under every tree and into every shadow. We tried to blend in with the habitat. Tried to move like we belonged. The most difficult part of blending in is moving like you belong, something our disconnected existence in cities had caused us to forget.

Peter and Hillary belonged.

A lifetime of city-life had not tainted their instincts. Years of careful practice had honed them. The harsh realities in the African bush dictate that you adapt to your surroundings or you do not survive. We tried to emulate our native hosts.

They moved with silent grace—without effort. They stepped around thornbushes like a whisper of wind. We snagged and bumbled on everything.

With years of practice, we might gain a sliver of their stealth. Without that kind of time, we walked in their footsteps and tried not to blow the stalk.

After an hour, Peter slowed. He saw something. Reedbuck? Where?

Peter and Hillary stopped under the shadows of a small acacia. The rest of us were mostly in the open. Cotton ducked. Hillary smiled at us and stuck his thumb up at Mary. We stretched our necks out. The others obviously saw something. It had to be a reedbuck. I knew the reedbuck was there. I knew it. If Peter and Hillary said it was there, then it was there. I had to see it.

There. I ducked. Not slow and deliberate like Cotton, but quick and jerky. Those kinds of movements could end a hunt. If I popped my head back up, the reedbuck would probably be gone. He was within one hundred yards looking right at us.

Cotton scooted beside Hillary and Peter and motioned for Mary to join him. I didn't move. Rifle in hand, Mary shuffled the few yards to Cotton.

I had only caught a quick glimpse of the reedbuck. It was enough. He was the best we had seen. Fighting the urge to look, I watched Mary follow Cotton's instructions. Hillary arched his shoulders back and held his chin high.

Somehow, Peter appeared next to her with the shooting sticks. Mary rested her rifle into the cradle. It was padded by a leather strap that held the three sticks together.

Mary focused. I thought I saw her trembling. I usually watched the animal to help determine the point of impact and follow the escape route. Unable to see the reedbuck, I studied my wife.

I almost flinched waiting for her to squeeze. Maybe she couldn't find the reedbuck through the scope. Maybe the reedbuck stepped behind a rock. I almost talked myself into standing to look. I convinced myself to give her a little more time before running over and slapping the trigger for her.

Peter put his fingers in his ears. Cotton's grip was tight around his binoculars. Mary fidgeted, readjusted, and settled back behind the scope. Then, when her finger seemed ripe to squeeze, she fidgeted, readjusted, and settled back behind the scope again. The reedbuck had to be gone. My leg was aching, my foot falling asleep. I almost fell back at the blast.

I heard a whoop. Peter shook Mary's hand, Cotton gave her a hug, and Hillary was saying, "I told you. Did I not tell you? I said you would get your reedbuck. Did I not say it?"

"Yes, thank you," Mary said softly.

Hillary stopped me during our climb. "Did I not say it? I told you before. This was going to be a good day. I told you."

Mary had earned that shy look of pride—her head tucked into her shoulders, her chin low, and her eyes glowing. She had that smile that said *I know I shouldn't enjoy this praise, but I can't help it.*

There was something about a last-minute buck or bird or fish, which put you in a hand-slapping mood. You had worked hard—pushed yourself past limits you thought unsurpassable. Often it was a group effort, everyone nudging those same limits. Each of us knew how the others felt. We would have built a fire, cut off a sliver of backstrap, and celebrated right then if there hadn't been more work to do before we flew out the following day. The long hike down, including a couple of steep rock faces, would take an hour.

As we started down the first cliff, all but a dash of our earlier adrenaline had trickled away like the sweat dripping from my nose.

"Make sure you get a firm foothold with each step," Cotton said.

Peter led. Carrying the reedbuck's horns and cape, he climbed down like a spider on a wall. With a load of his own, Cotton followed. Mary and I, hauling mostly our own gear, were directly behind him. And loaded with the remainder of the meat, Hillary brought up the rear. He was still smiling. Whenever I looked back at him, he pointed at the reedbuck, looked at Mary and thrust his thumb into the air. He stopped short of saying, *I told you.* I know he wanted to.

Halfway down, I started feeling more comfortable with my footing. Complacency, maybe cockiness, found their way into my footsteps. I paid the price. My bad knee buckled and sent me face first toward a cliff too high for a mountain goat to jump off. I reached out to grab something—anything. Cotton happened to be the closest solid object.

He had turned just before my legs went out. It gave him enough time to absorb most of the blow. Peter zipped back up to help.

I'd had a bum knee for so long it was hard to remember when it was strong. When it did give out, it gave out angrily. It swelled to the size of a softball within seconds. I felt it turning purple. It hurt, but it had been worse. I could make it down the mountain. It would just take longer than planned. We hadn't expected to see the truck when we finally reached the bottom.

Our descent had taken us far from where we had left Joan and Durani with the vehicle. I was sure we would have to hike back to the vehicle after limping to the bottom. They must have seen us hiking down.

"Are you okay, Dick?" Joan asked as I limped to the truck and collapsed in the seat.

"I'm fine. Mary put a great shot on him." I pointed to the reedbuck on Peter's back.

"Are you sure you're okay?"

I nodded. My knee was throbbing.

"Ahmed is here," Cotton said as we rolled into camp.

A slender man in a tailored, button-up shirt and brown slacks was standing beside a clean truck that had an official looking insignia on the doors.

"Who's Ahmed?" Mary asked.

"He's the head of the game department in Arusha," Joan said. "He's a very pleasant man."

When he sauntered over to greet Cotton, he held his head high and walked with a swagger. Not a flaunting arrogance. A quiet confidence. He knew he was important, but didn't let it get to his head—a rare quality among most people who are given even an inkling of power.

"This is Dick and Mary Cabela," Cotton said as we shook hands with Ahmed.

"Like the catalog, yes?" He pointed to the dining tent where Cotton had centered a few of our catalogs on the table.

"Yes."

"I am very pleased to meet you. I would very much like to order some cots. Do you ship to Tanzania?"

"They ship gear to us all the time," Cotton said.

"Very good. You will ship to me?"

"I'm sure we can handle it," I said.

"Very good. I would also very much like to order some knives."

"Shouldn't be a problem."

"Yes, but I must have them with the Prince of Dubai's name or initials written in gold on them."

"Inlaid with real gold?"

"Yes, that is very much what I need. Can you do this?"

"I think we can arrange something."

"Yes, very good. I must now speak with Cotton. Then I will get details to you."

"Are you going to take his order here?" Mary said after they had stepped away.

"I'll have him call Teri—she'll be able to take care of it." Teri, our daughter, took care of everything we needed. We would be in trouble without her.

Cotton's view of game management was, in many instances, unique in Tanzania. He worked closely with the game department and told us Ahmed was one who could get things done. Cotton's suggestions were rarely fully implemented. Often they used portions of his ideas and merged them with the status quo. Although results were sometimes mixed, Tanzania seemed headed in the right direction.

Cotton's meeting with Ahmed lasted through dinner. When he left, everybody was beat. A slow walk to the tent and a collapse into the cots we called beds should have been the only sensible option. Not that night. The campfire beckoned.

Laced within tales told to new friends were silent goodbyes we did not dare utter until the following day. We would remember them far longer than the tearful hugs yet to come. We would remember the crackling fire beating a wild rhythm to our last night in camp. As the lions congratulated each other on another fine kill, we stared into the fire, knowing we would never be the same. Maybe we didn't understand it. Maybe we never would. But we didn't have to. Tanzania was part of us now. Nothing could change that.

Joan and Cotton Gordon. Good people. Good friends.

One rock has a giant cross. Another seems to worship below.

Checking a waterhole for fresh tracks.

The king at his throne.

Building a lion machan.

A successful lion hunt.

The buffalo's stare is menacing.

Hanging a leopard bait.

Building a leopard blind.

The leopard hunter returns.

A buffalo came this way.

Who will blink first?

Skinning a buffalo is a team effort.

The skinning shed.

Dick and Cotton with a chui.

Mary and her first Tanzanian buffalo.

Lion Loop finally pays off for Dick, Cotton, and Hillary.

Standing over a fresh kill.

The Cat Lady takes her lion.

Klipspringers often hop to high points to survey the landscape.

Old Peter.

This snared zebra suffered a slow, painful death.

PART II
OLD FRIENDS
1994

COTTON: MARY

"Cotton wanted me to apologize about the hotel," Mike Taylor said as we pulled away from the curb at the Arusha airport. Mike had taken us on a photo safari in 1987 and seeing a familiar face in a crowded third-world airport relaxed us. "The government scheduled a last-minute political meeting and anyone not on the council has been rejected. There was only one hotel with a vacancy and they do not have the best accommodations. Please accept my apologies. I am sorry for you."

The road to the hotel felt like a dark alley in a dangerous neighborhood. We drove the last few hundred yards on something that once resembled a paved road. Full of holes, broken asphalt, and trash, it took us ten minutes to zigzag to a building that would look at home in a war-torn city. Desperate-looking people lined both sides of the street. Women carried huge baskets or bundles of clothing on their heads. Men huddled in small groups, smoking cigarettes and staring at us as we rolled by. Most stares were curious, but some had a hint of malice. I resisted eye contact and focused on the children. Smiling and buoyant, their innocence shielded them from their harsh situation.

A small crowd gathered outside the hotel as we unloaded our gear. They watched from beyond the open door as we checked in. The stench in the muggy lobby was a pungent mix of body odor and dust. Half the tiles on the floor were missing; the other half were cracked and broken. Mike helped us haul our luggage to our first-floor room before apologizing one more time. Then he was gone.

We found a typewritten note under the door:
STORE YOUR VALUABLES IN THE ROOM SAFE AND LOCK YOUR DOORS AND WINDOWS.

"The window doesn't lock," Dick said. "It doesn't even close all the way." The view from the window was another room across a narrow, unlit outdoor corridor.

"The chain bolt is useless as well." I flipped the chain dangling from a single, loose screw.

I worried through a quick dinner. The safe for our valuables was the size of a tissue box. We took all our cash and anything we could carry with us to dinner.

Nothing was missing—I checked twice. When the sun set, the streets erupted in a raucous party. Dancing, screaming, singing, honking, crashing, screeching, and many other loud noises kept me wide-eyed until four in the morning. Desperate *and* intoxicated—not a soothing combination.

"Dick, did you hear that? Is somebody outside the window? I think I heard somebody trying to open the door." My husband thought I was crazy. Maybe so, but I woke him throughout the night to check. He never found anything. I still didn't sleep.

We left the room fifteen minutes late to join our old friends for breakfast. Joan looked great. Cotton was sick with another bout of malaria. Hillary looked emaciated. He was fit the last time we saw him, now he seemed to be withering away. His eyes receded into deep sockets and the skin on his face drooped.

I gave him a hug. "It's good to see you, Hillary. How have you been?"

"I am good. Thank you."

"Hillary has been battling a bad case of malaria," Cotton said. "It was touch and go for a while, but he is on the upswing now."

"Yes, I am very good. You do not have to worry about Hillary Dafi. I am strong. Ready to hunt."

We arrived at Cotton's Longido camp in time for lunch. Only thirty miles from Kenya's border, the camp consisted of big wall tents surrounded by a fence made from six-foot sticks. It gave the allusion of protection. Each tent had a small out-house with a flush toilet. They had to refill two fifty-gallon water drums daily.

That afternoon, we drove around to get a feel for the area. Dust hung in the air like a dirty mist. A hazy cloud rose from the horizon. Was it game? Not likely. Every dust cloud that first afternoon turned out to be Maasai tribesmen herding cattle.

For Maasai, cattle and children constituted wealth. By the looks of it, bovines were making up for a lack of kids. To be fair, we hadn't seen a village yet. If children numbered half the cattle, the village was sure to be a playful place.

Back at camp, tired, dirty, thirsty, and hungry, I scarfed down a bowl of spaghetti, some canned tuna, and a vegetable pie. Without the energy for a campfire nightcap, I brushed my teeth, grabbed a paperback and glasses, and planned to read myself to sleep. After one sentence, they shut down the generator. The lights went out. Groping around, I finally found my bookmark and glasses case. I tossed and turned in the black heat, wishing for a breeze, hoping for sleep. It came in short, sweaty spurts.

"Look at that rock over there on the hill," Joan said during breakfast.

"It almost looks like someone stamped it on."

"It's perfect," I said. Anywhere else, a huge cross like that formed naturally would become a religious icon. But there, hidden in the open vastness of northern Tanzania, few Christians had seen it. It seemed lonely.

"I think it will bring us good luck," Cotton said.

It already had. We were among friends in a land that felt closer to God than any structure built by human hands. A heavenly image reflected from the rising sun reinvigorated our hopes. Each morning I could look up to the cross on the rock and remember how blessed we were.

On the first day of a hunt, just about any animal on license will do. It helps break the ice and relax everyone when the skinners have work to do. Around mid-morning, Hillary spotted a gerenuk under an umbrella acacia tree. We had driven for four hours before spotting a good male. Closing the last few hundred yards in an open field might be tricky. The bull already had that nervous look in its eyes.

Cotton, Hillary, and I marched in single file straight toward the bull. The gerenuk shifted position and gave us a broadside look.

We stayed in a tight formation, only inches of air between us. Bending over, we hoped to portray the illusion that we were a line of ungulates making our way across the field. The bull lifted his front hoof twice, turned his head to the side and then forward to study us from each perspective. Two more slow steps. We stopped.

"We're not going to get closer," Cotton whispered.

"How far?"

Hillary set up the shooting sticks.

"Two hundred fifty yards. You can make this shot."

I cradled my 7mm solidly on the shooting sticks, took two deep breaths, and squeezed. The gerenuk spun and dropped.

"Good shot." Hillary turned to shake my hand.

Cotton never took his eyes from the fallen beast until we confirmed it was dead. Only then did he hug me. "It's a fine gerenuk. Congratulations. Great shot by the way."

"I'm sure it was a fluke."

"I'm sure it wasn't."

With the body of a gazelle and a giraffe-like neck, the gerenuk is a distinctive antelope. Its slender legs and long, thin neck cause both sexes to appear dainty. Like all animals, their physical attributes serve necessary survival functions. Gerenuks stand on their back legs and stretch out those long necks to browse in the thorny tangle of acacias.

Was it possible to feel joy and sorrow at the same time from the same act? Since the beginning of human existence, a predatory instinct has driven us to wild places to find sustenance for the clan. The meat from my gerenuk provided protein for the staff, but I would be lying if I said that is why I killed the bull. My need to hunt rose from an understanding that the instinct driving that need was natural. Hunting is an inherent part of being human. My pride stemmed from a real connection to the hunter who kept his family alive by making a kill. My sorrow overflowed from what drives us to explore the human condition. Because of me, that gerenuk died. I didn't cry that day, but part of me wanted to.

An hour later, Dick had a chance at a gerenuk. A longer shot than mine, he hit his just as well. It ran only a few yards before crumpling. I know Dick's emotions collided just as mine did, but I am sure the swings were not as perceptible.

"I know I packed three tubes of shampoo," I said to Dick. "I need to have shampoo." I had already taken almost everything out of my hair bag and placed it on the cot.

"We can get by with soap."

"Maybe you can." I rummaged through our bags. Do you think I found shampoo? Do you think Dick cared that we didn't have shampoo?

I was running my hands through my hair, feeling the damage the soap had caused, when the Land Cruiser jerked to a stop.

"Get your rifle, Mary. That was a fine lesser kudu."

"Where?"

"Back in the brush. I only saw his head, but that's all I needed to see. He's a good bull. Worth tracking." Cotton hopped from the truck and reached for the shooting sticks. "The wind is good. You up for a little walk?"

We moved like cats stalking prey. A few light steps here, a few there, focused on where we expected to see the kudu. There. We all went to one knee. It was browsing through thorn brush. We waited for it to move into a shooting lane. The lane was only a few feet wide, but it was our only option.

"When he steps in the open, don't hesitate," Cotton said

I would have liked to take my time, to make sure I was steady and that everything was perfect. I could trace most animals I had wounded or missed back to a hurried shot. Some people, like Dick, shot well from instinct. I was not one of those people. I looked through the scope. I peered over it. I rubbed the safety with my finger. I checked the kudu. How close was it? I looked at its horns. Were they big enough? Cotton wouldn't let me shoot a small one. Maybe I should just let it pass. I could make that shot. Couldn't I?

He was close. Get ready. I clicked off the safety. Staring through the crosshairs, I waited. When the bull stepped into the shooting lane, I fired. The kudu jerked stiff and held steady. I had missed.

"Reload." Cotton's whisper could have been a scream.

By the time my hand reached the bolt, it was too late. The bull was gone.

The heavy hike back to the vehicle was silent.

Dick had waited in the Land Cruiser. "What happened?" he asked.

"I missed." Handing him my unloaded rifle, I climbed in.

Dick knew how I felt. Cotton understood as well. He also knew that sometimes the best medicine was another stalk. It focused you on a task and allowed you to leave mistakes in the past. Instead of sitting around trying to figure out why I missed or making excuses, he concentrated on finding another kudu.

We rumbled down a rough trail in the high, back seat of the Land Cruiser until Hillary and Cotton pointed up a distant hill. Three lesser kudu bulls stared down at us, their spiraled horns piercing a cloud-filled sky.

Cotton studied them through his binoculars. "The one on the far right is exceptional." He pulled the binoculars down. "It's a long climb through thick brush. We will have to get close before we can even see them. By the time we do, they will be gone. Our other option is to hike to that rock and shoot from there." He pointed to a boulder at the base of the hill.

"How far do you think it is from there?" I asked.

"At least three hundred yards. Probably more."

"Let Dick do it.".

We ambled to the boulder as if we were heading for a picnic. The kudu could see us no matter what we did, so acting as non-threatening as possible seemed the only option. They would stick around or they would disappear.

"Don't look at them," Cotton said. "If they're gone when we reach the rock, we'll just walk back."

From the rock, we still saw three kudu staring down on us.

"I would say three-hundred twenty yards," Cotton said. "Whenever you're ready."

The impact sounded hollow. Too far back? The quiet could almost be touched. The air seemed to thicken as we began our approach.

"We have to hurry," Cotton said, motioning us to follow. "We're running out of daylight."

The hike included lots of ducking and dodging and climbing. Heavy brush grew thick under a canopy of thinly leafed trees. From below, the brush had appeared to be waist high. Up close, it grew over our heads in many places. I could not see where we had been or where the kudu had been. If not for the capable men leading us, I might have felt lost. I never worried about getting lost with them. I had enough to worry about, like my shooting and tsetse flies and heat.

We found the bull lying under a low-limbed thorn tree. It jumped to its feet. Dick anchored him with a quick shot to the heart.

Then it started pouring. We hunkered under an acacia thick with leaves while Isaac gutted the kudu. The leaves dripped on us like a hundred leaky faucets.

"If it had started raining like this any earlier, we might have had a tough go of it." Cotton had to speak above the rain. "Any blood or tracks would have washed away."

"How did you sleep?" Joan asked at breakfast.

"I slept fine," Dick said.

"And you, Mary? I trust you had a good rest."

"I was up a couple of times. No big deal." A half-truth.

"Are you feeling okay," Joan asked. "You look a bit pale."

"I'm fine, really." More like a half untruth.

"You can get some rest in the truck," Cotton said. "It's a long drive to the oryx spot."

"Is it a smooth drive?"

Cotton winked. "Compared to the Grand Canyon, yes it is."

"That's what I thought."

Fringe-eared oryx have distinctive black and white markings on their faces, legs, and bellies. Mostly found grazing in open fields, both males and females carry long straight horns. They can go days without water—longer than any other antelope species. Their compact, stocky bodies foster speed and endurance. A successful hunt usually involves a long shot.

The area, where oryx supposedly lived, seemed devoid of life. So did the Alaska tundra at first glance. A patient, dedicated search turned up life in the most barren of places. Tsetse flies and ticks did not count. It was hard for me to tell if they were alive or if they were soulless beings sent from the underworld to pester the living.

We drove and glassed until noon before we found an oryx. One moment nothing, then, as if sprouted from the dry ground, two females and a male trudged across the weary horizon, a heat mirage rising behind them.

"The bull is good," Cotton said.

"We're going to have to get closer than this," I said.

The short grass scratched our boots; the oryx never stopped moving. Just as I began to tire, Hillary placed the shooting sticks.

"Is this as close as we can get?"

"I don't want to push them too hard. You can make this shot."

"How far is it?" My head pounded like war drums. An irritation in my throat made me cough as I set up.

"Two-hundred fifty yards."

It looked farther.

Finding the bull through my scope, I tried to filter out the headache. The oryx looked small, the crease behind the shoulder disappearing in the crosshairs. Maybe I should aim high. I moved up the bull's shoulder to the top of his back. That scratch in my throat warned me of an impending cough. I tried to repress it.

"I can't get steady. I don't want to take this shot."

Cotton looked me in the eyes. "Okay. Dick, can you shoot Mary's rifle?"

"It's a little short, but everything else is identical to mine." He looked at me. "You sure?"

"I don't feel right."

"They're moving off," Cotton said.

I thrust the rifle into Dick's hands and he positioned it on the shooting sticks. The oryx trotted from right to left, the bull bringing up the rear. Dick fired. The bull spun, tripped, and then struggled to catch up with the females. They disappeared into a line of acacia bushes.

"Looks like you hit him a little far back. Hillary's going to run to the truck and get your gun, then we'll go find the track and put it down."

Dick stared into the brush. I prayed we would find the bull soon. When Hillary returned, he traded Dick's rifle for mine.

Marching to the first sign of blood seemed to take forever. I counted two hundred steps before giving up. We never broke stride until a few yards from the first thorn bush. From a distance, it looked thick. Up close, the bushes and trees were spaced far enough apart that we never had to duck under a branch or pull one out of the way. So much crimson splashed the ground that I thought we would find the bull right away. I started watching for movement ahead.

We stopped. Hillary and Cotton saw something. What? Where? I followed the path of their gaze. The bull was standing under a shade tree—alive. It turned to stare in our direction.

"That's him. Shoot him. Quickly."

Dick fired off hand.

"Again."

The bull scrambled for deeper cover.

"You hit him both times," Cotton said.

"Yes. It was a good shot. He will not go far." Hillary smiled, his face glistening with perspiration.

"Be ready. If he runs, put another one in him."

We broke into a jog—Hillary, Cotton, Dick, and then me. It wasn't a fast run, but by the end of it, we would be short of breath. Shooting straight under those conditions was never easy. I wouldn't have been able to do it. I wouldn't have wanted to try. Dick had a steady hand. I am glad it was him. We ran past a termite mound and stopped under another umbrella tree. Hillary and Cotton pointed. Twenty yards further the oryx was heaped under a heavy bush. Dick had his rifle up, ready. The oryx never moved.

During the stalk, I forgot about my creeping headache. It returned as a trot up the back of my neck as we hiked toward the vehicle. Then an annoying tickle in my throat interrupted my pace.

By the time we trudged into camp, I had cold chills and massive aches all over my body to go with an incessant cough and a sandpaper headache. "I don't think I'm going to make it for dinner," I told Joan.

"Can I bring you some soup later?"

"I'm just going to rest. If I get hungry, I'll come down."

"Please do, dear."

As I stumbled down the dirt path toward our tent, I glanced at the cross on the rock. It appeared almost white in the afternoon light. It didn't look like part of the rock at all. Cotton said he had been up there and assured us it was a natural formation on the outcropping. I don't know if it meant good luck or if it meant anything at all. I do know I felt peaceful every time I saw it. I looked at it every day.

Tall green weeds and yellow grass lined the path to our tent on one side. They acted as a buffer between camp and a heavy wooded area with long-branched trees thick with leaves. The branches spread to give it a terraced look. They were the kind of trees you expected clouds and mystery to surround. The other side of the path had been trampled free of vegetation. Every few yards grass chalets built over canvas wall tents served as sleeping quarters for guests and staff. The breeze carried the heavy scent from the skinning shed where they dried slabs of meat on long poles and blankets of grass. They kept it surrounded by a wall of sticks. I don't know how that kept the scavengers out. I heard hyenas almost every night. They always seemed close and often kept me up late.

I curled up on the bed without removing my shoes.

The coughing and chills made sleep seem difficult, but I awoke two hours later, sweating. It felt like someone was turning a potato peeler in my head. I started coughing before I opened my eyes. My teeth chattered. I rolled out of bed and managed to work my way to the attached bathroom, where I popped a couple of aspirin. I had to try something.

Dick was standing at the doorway when I returned from the bathroom. "Do you want to come down for dinner?"

"No, you go ahead. I'm going to rest."

"Can I get you anything?"

"I'm fine." I stretched out on the cot, pulled my shoes and socks off and changed into pajamas. The way my head felt, I thought I would have a hard time sleeping so I settled in with a book. I fell asleep before finishing the first paragraph.

I awoke briefly in the middle of the night to a ringing headache and a lion roaring in the distance.

The next morning, the war drums in my head were so loud that I couldn't feel anything else. I convinced myself that if I could relinquish the headache, I would be fine. I popped more aspirin and went for breakfast.

The dining chalet was always colorful. More a result of Joan's touch than Cotton's. I had a hard time believing Cotton would pick out a bright pink tablecloth. The pattern on the cloth was authentic African. Joan always had fresh red, pink, and white flowers as a table centerpiece and surrounding accents. I'm sure the men hardly noticed, but for me it made the gathering area more inviting and homey.

Vincent, the cook, brought us each a plate of fresh fruit, toast, and apple juice. I wasn't hungry, but if we planned to hunt all day, I needed to eat. "I know you said there weren't any lions around, but I heard one last night."

"I heard it too," Joan said.

"Are you sure it was a lion?" Cotton took a bite of toast and gave us a skeptical look.

"It sounded like a lion to me," I said.

"It was a lion." Joan looked Cotton in the eyes.

"If you say so. I've just never seen one around here—or any sign of one. What about you, Hillary, have you ever seen any lion sign around here?"

"No lion. Hyena, yes. Leopard, yes. Lion, no."

"It wasn't a hyena," Joan said.

"Maybe it was a lion," Cotton said. "I'll ask Isaac. Maybe a young male has moved in. You never know."

"What's on the agenda today?" Dick asked.

"We're going to find Mary an oryx."

"I don't want to take a long shot," I said.

"You'll do fine."

"As long as we can get close."

Cotton's crooked smirk made me question if he was listening.

An hour later, the Land Cruiser stopped. Isaac pointed.

"There are four of them," Cotton said. "One looks good."

"How are we going to get close enough? They're already looking at us," I said.

"You worry too much."

"I'm a mother of nine. It's my job to worry."

"This is one thing you shouldn't worry about," Cotton said. "We need to see if it's a male first. Sometimes, big females have longer horns than males do. Telling them apart can be difficult."

"Can you shoot a female?" Dick asked.

"Sure. Some hunters have a bias toward males though. We'll take a big bull if we can find it, but you shouldn't rule out a female. Nobody could tell the difference without checking underneath."

Walking in single file, the oryx kept there noses toward the ground unless they stopped to look at us. I wanted to cut the distance in half. I doubted it was possible.

"We might be able to sneak along that line of high grass."

"Where?"

"Just over there. It's taller than it looks." Cotton pointed to what looked like short clumps of dry grass one hundred yards to our right.

Our cover turned out to be a combination of five-foot-high grass and brush. We had to duck, but the grass proved thick enough to conceal our advance. Wriggling through a few yards of thorny brush, I positioned myself for a shot while Cotton resumed glassing.

"It's the one on the far right. Put your crosshairs on the shoulder."

"How far is it?" Maybe I had psyched myself out. You know, crazy grandmother can't see, can't hear, can't remember how far two hundred yards was.

"Just put it right on the shoulder."

Concentrating on the shoulder, I focused away from doubt.

"It's a female."

"What does that mean?" I asked without looking away from the oryx's shoulder.

"She's got great horns, but I think we'll look for a big male first. We should be able to find this group again."

I wondered if I would be disappointed with a female. I didn't think so. The hunt was no different—that's what mattered. I looked through the scope one last time. Its horns were the tallest and thickest in the herd.

"Do you think we can find a bull bigger than that one?" I asked once we were back in the Land Cruiser.

"I don't know; that was a big oryx. I don't think they will move too far. We didn't spook them. How would you feel about taking that female?"

I shrugged. "As long as it's legal and you think it's worth it, I wouldn't have any objections."

"Male or female, it was a nice oryx."

"What do you think, Dick?"

"It might be nice to have a pair."

"*Choroa. Choroa.*" Isaac pointed. Durani stopped the Land Cruiser.

"Where is it?" Cotton asked.

"Gone. In trees. Big *choroa*. Good male.

Cotton tilted his head and raised an eyebrow. "I didn't see it, but Isaac has a good eye. If he says it was a big oryx, we should go after it."

Ten minutes later, I wished I had protested. My head continued to pound and I couldn't get a full breath in. My vision blurred and I felt nauseous. We trekked on.

Watching the honed craft of a skilled tracker testing his abilities against the just as finely tuned instincts of a wild creature is something every hunter should experience. To see Isaac read oryx tracks as if he were reading the animal's mind left little doubt we would find the bull. Unlike the open plain where the four females gathered, this bull meandered through thicket. It gave us better cover for a stalk while allowing the bull greater chance at concealment.

The pain in my head intensified and my lungs tightened. Sweat dripped from my nose and pulled my shirt toward the ground. Maybe if I weren't so proud I would have said something. I no longer cared if we caught up to the bull. I wanted to rest.

When the toe of my shoe caught the ground, I almost fell on my face. Hillary ran up to see if I was okay. He took one look at me and said, "We must stop now."

Cotton and Isaac turned around.

"You are very sick, Mama," Hillary said. "Your face is like the color of a Maasai *kanga*. You do not look well." He glanced at Cotton. "Bwana. We must go back."

"Do you need to rest, Mary?" Cotton said.

"Just for a minute. Then I think I'll be okay." I wasn't kidding anyone.

"You catch your breath, then we'll head back to find that female."

By the time we reached the Land Cruiser, I could barely take a step. Sweat clung to my clothes like heavy dew on a tree. I remembered it being one hundred degrees before we started tracking, but now it felt like zero. I climbed into the high, back seat of the Cruiser and wrapped myself in Dick's jacket. I shivered for the next twenty minutes, my teeth chattering and my head feeling as if someone worked a saw back and forth in it.

I don't think I fell asleep. I know I closed my eyes and I know I was drowsy and I know I was tired when I arrived at the open field, but did I sleep? Hard to say. Probably not.

I do know I had my eyes closed when Cotton asked if I was ready.

"Did you find them already?" I asked.

He smirked in Dick's direction. "It might not be as easy as before."

"Why's that?"

"Look through your binos. They've joined with a group of eland. We can wait to see if they separate, but if they don't who knows where they'll wander off. Our other option is to take our chances now and hope to get lucky. How are you feeling?"

"Let's give it a try."

"You sure?"

"I'm okay." I felt guilty for stretching the truth—just a little. But I could stalk an oryx.

As we closed in, the eland began to trot. An eland trot is a high speed for almost anything else. For us, it was an impossible pace. The oryx followed them a few yards before breaking into the open. The eland headed for the safety of the trees. Oryx preferred the vision of the open plain. That was fine with us. Those eland could have led them into Kenya. As the oryx distanced themselves from the eland, they calmed down enough for us to move into a more comfortable range.

"How far?" I said. My headache had gone missing.

"Close enough for you to shoot," Cotton said.

"That's not what I asked."

"We don't have time to argue and we're not getting closer. Aim for the shoulder and you will hit it perfect."

I picked my spot.

"Take a breath and squeeze the trigger. Just squeeze the trigger." Cotton's soft voice helped steady the rifle. When it felt right, I did just what he said.

The oryx dropped. The others kicked up dust on their way out of the country.

"What did I tell you? I know how well you shoot."

The oryx sprung to her feet.

"Shoot. Shoot."

Sometimes, instinct takes over. I hardly remember shooting, but I made an off-hand shot and took out the oryx's lungs. It collapsed again, this time finished.

Isaac shook my hand. "Good. Very good. No hunter take so much animal in three day—it take seven day always. You do very good. Yes." He released my hand and pulled out a long-bladed *panga* to field dress the oryx.

As I watched, my headache returned. Before Isaac finished, I was huddled in the vehicle trying to stay warm. Everyone else wore shorts and short-sleeved shirts.

"That's it for this camp," Cotton said on our way to the skinning shed. "It gives us more time in Rungwa. We'll leave in the morning."

After a quick shower, the heat wrapped around me like a flannel blanket. There was no happy medium between chills and sweats. Though weak, I felt I should eat something. We had lesser kudu steaks. They were tender and sweet. The fried potatoes were greasy and the vegetable salad was the same we had twice a day everyday. They complemented the kudu steaks well.

"I believe the safari is going well so far," Cotton said. "Like Isaac said, it is extraordinary that we are moving to a new camp already."

"It doesn't feel rushed," Dick said.

"Nothing in Africa ever feels rushed."

"Not even for you?" I asked.

"You always feel as if your camp will never be built on time—sometimes it isn't, but nobody can tell. Sometimes, staff you've hired fail to show up and you have to scramble to find new help before clients arrive. But there is a pace here that you cannot escape. You just accept it."

"I like it," I said. "I like being able to come down for dinner at any time and spend a few moments at the campfire. There are no lines or signs telling you to wait to be seated. There is just Africa and you. Things happen when it's time for them to happen."

The men spoke mostly of guns and politics and sports. I enjoyed discussing those things, but sometimes I liked to talk about family and clothing and recipes. Thank goodness for Joan. Her presence in camp allowed for a balance between femininity and the testosterone usually overflowing from hunting camps.

I wrapped my sweater over my arms and Dick's over my legs, crawled into bed, and read until they turned off the generator. After that, I tossed and turned trying to find comfort beyond the chills and the headache. I had been at it for over an hour when I heard a lion roar. It sounded close. But maybe it wasn't even a lion. I listened into the blackness. I heard it again. Its voice swept through the night air like a lonely challenge as if it wasn't a lion at all, but the violent retribution of an African curse. What had I done? How had I instigated that wrath? I pulled the blanket tight over my shoulder. My headache felt like something gnawing on my brain.

We packed our bags, watched the staff load them into the vehicle, and settled around the campfire to wait. My chin bobbed to my chest a few times before I wandered back to the tent to lie down. I had just dozed off when Dick came to tell me it was time to go. My headache had let up some, but continued to linger throughout the day.

Quiet unrest often builds during a long flight. In the small plane, the vibrating blare of the engine discouraged conversation. It allowed for quiet thought. Staring out the window, I noticed few signs of human habitation—so unlike a flight across much of the developed world, where the lines humans have mapped for themselves form an unnatural grid. I saw the lines of earth—God's lines. For a time, we followed the Rungwa River. We were not unlike a river ourselves. Finding our way through the world, changing paths, splitting into sloughs and different branches, slowing down, racing onward, testing the banks of conformity, leaving our mark on a world that often doesn't care, crossing paths with new rivers and new streams. A river not only follows the earth's contours. It is relentless in its pursuit to re-carve them—to leave a record of its existence—to say, *I was here*.

We landed on what the pilot called a proper African bush runway. Basically, a mowed-down field ripe with holes from rooting warthogs. We slammed and bumped and skidded along until reaching the end where a group of villagers had gathered to welcome their new guests. Many of the people laughed and waved and clapped. Some of the children danced. A few men stood stoically, waiting as if they had seen this flying metal contraption spit out silly white hunters thousands of times.

We stepped into a pressing heat. I didn't see a vehicle. "How far to camp?" I asked.

"Just there. We are close enough to walk." Cotton pointed and then looked around. "Where's the car. Go for the car. We have too much luggage to carry," he said to a tall, young man standing in front of the crowd. The young man nodded almost to a bow, before racing toward a nearby row of tall trees.

Looking closely, we saw thatched structures and movement through the few openings in the vegetation. "Is that the camp?" I asked.

Cotton nodded.

"Few roads lead here and the ones that do are unmaintained trail roads. The nearest town is at least a twenty-hour drive. You will enjoy this camp. It is comfortable, game is plentiful, and trophy quality is high."

A heavy tiredness weighed on my muscles as if sleep had eluded me for days. The sleep I had managed was restless and brief. I looked forward to a shower, a bite to eat, and a bed.

"I'm going out to sit under Ben's star," Joan said to Cotton after dinner.

He slowly nodded. "I'll be out in a minute."

"I'll join you," I said. Joan eased into a chair beside the flickering campfire. She gazed up.

"There it is there." She pointed.

We stared into the darkening sky for a few minutes.

"You never fully recover after you lose a child." Her voice cracked.

Lying in bed, I thanked God for our children and prayed that they would enjoy long, happy lives. I prayed for them to outlive us. I prayed for Joan and Cotton. I prayed for Ben.

"Are you awake, Dick?"

"Yes."

"Did you hear the baboons screaming?"

"Probably a leopard chasing them."

"They sound like they're just outside of camp."

"I don't think they're that close."

Of course he didn't. He never worried about anything. The screaming and rustling continued for a few minutes. Then a deep, raspy growl, a horrifying, painful scream, and silence.

"I guess the leopard's eating fresh meat tonight." Dick's voice was slow with sleep.

When he started snoring again, the hyenas started whooping, closing in on the leopard to get a piece of his kill. An hour later, the entire sequence replayed—screaming baboons, leopard kills, the sounds of crunching and gnawing, hyenas and jackals moving in. Those sounds were the fertilizer to nightmares.

We spent the morning spotting and stalking. We spotted a small herd of buffalo with no big bulls, two dik-diks, two common duikers, and six kudu cows with two young bulls. On the first day, when you see game like that, hiding behind acacias, darting across the trail, and ducking into the shadows, optimism soars like a bateleur eagle. You brush aside any first-day disappointment as if it were a sweat bee.

A lone kudu bull, standing stiff with its horns in some low-hanging branches of a burkea tree, required a closer look. Working our way from tree to tree, we closed the distance to fifty yards. I could make that shot. Cotton leaned against the tree to focus his binoculars.

"I don't think this is the one. I cannot see the tops of his horns, but he probably does not go fifty inches."

I let out a breath and allowed my shoulders to slump. Nothing rumbles the heart like a close stalk on an animal you intend to shoot. We decided to pass, but my sputtering nerves refused to take a straight-down path.

Though Cotton had deemed the bull not worth taking, he continued to glass until the bull galloped away.

"Take this bull."

I fumbled to get the rifle barrel into the shooting sticks and tried to find the bull through the scope. It was running through a tangle of trees and bushes. I moved the crosshairs forward on its chest and swung with it. I touched the trigger. A branch exploded and the kudu did its best impression of a scared cheetah. Gone. Regardless of the situation or the reason or the justification, the miss chipped away at my confidence. I think my headache returned just to prod my frustration with a dose of pain.

On our way back to the vehicle, hanging my head in self-pity, I almost ran into Cotton.

"Shoot that kudu," he whispered, sliding back to my shoulder. "It's a good bull."

Hillary quietly spread the shooting sticks and stepped out of the way. The kudu could have been the first one's twin. He hid the tips of his horns in another thorn tree and concealed half of his shoulder behind a limb. He was close—just what I needed.

The bullet ricocheted off the limb.

I understood how Charlie Brown must have felt after Lucy routinely convinced him to try to kick the football only to pull it away at the last second. AAUGH!

Game went into hiding the next couple of days. But the animals were out there. I heard predators every night. That many predators wouldn't hang around unless prey was plentiful.

One morning I went with Isaac while Dick, Cotton, and Hillary sat in a *machan*, or tree blind, for lion. We stalked a sable through thick thorn bush, but it gave us the slip before offering a shot. On our way back to the Land Cruiser, we found it sneaking past a termite mound. It walked behind another acacia and stopped. I didn't have a shot.

"Shoot," Isaac whispered.

"I can't see his shoulder."

"Good shot. Shoot. You good shot. You shoot."

I could make out a dark form through the brush. I cranked up my scope and found a crease in the black fur. Was it the shoulder? Where was the face? There— white markings. I repositioned the rifle back to the crease, confident it was the shoulder muscle. I had a branch-free opening to shoot through.

"Shoot. Good bull. Shoot."

I did. The sable ran. It was quiet.

"You hit here." Isaac pointed to the lower half of his ribs.

 Great.

"Good shot."

I don't know if Isaac thought I was shooting poison-tipped bullets or if he was trying to make me feel better, but it was not a good shot. I wanted to bury myself in the termite mound.

"Not go far. Come we find." Isaac motioned for me to follow with a wave of his hand. We found the sable standing sickly underneath a mangled acacia.

Isaac pointed and pulled an invisible trigger with his finger.

Unwilling to risk losing a wounded animal, I fired. The sable ran again. Isaac pulled me forward and we raced after the bull.

It had fallen, fifty yards further—dead.

Isaac pumped my hand. "You shoot very good," he said, his smile more sincere than my uncertain trust in his words.

The sable was beautiful even in death, even humped into the back of the truck. One of the most striking antelope on earth, sable are worthy of a hunter's admiration. They had mine. That sable also gave me something I had been lacking lately—a new foundation on which to build my crumbled confidence.

Dick, Cotton, and Hillary met us at the skinning shed. They had not seen a lion.

"That is a fine sable," Cotton said.

"Hopefully, the curse is lifted."

"What curse?"

"The curse of the bad-shooting Mama," I said.

"It's a curse now, is it? You'll fit right in with all the superstitious tribes of the area. What kind of ritual did you perform to lift this curse? Sacrifice a goat to the gods?"

"The next best thing. Sable steaks for the table."

"That's a ritual we all can benefit from."

The cook added too much garlic sauce, but the tender meat's mild flavor saved the meal.

"Rest until five today," Cotton said. "Nothing will be moving in this heat."

I spent the time writing in my journal, while Dick read one of the few paperbacks we had brought along.

"You won't have any books left for the plane ride home. What are you going to do then?"

Dick shrugged. "Start over, I guess."

By five, a stiff wind bent the trees. It blew my hair to a bird's nest, snapped the tent flaps, and pelted us with dust. My hair was gritty, my nose was caked with dirt, my mouth tasted like sand, and I couldn't stop rubbing my eyes.

"At least we're not getting attacked by tsetse flies anymore." Dick yelled over the wind on our way to the vehicle.

I hunkered close to my husband to shield myself from the wind. It didn't work.

"We're going to drive to an open *pan* this afternoon," Cotton said. "It's always good for hartebeest. Plus, some of the boys say there's been a lion hanging around. I'm not sure if we can pick up a track in this wind, but it's worth a look."

A herd of elephants had taken over the small waterhole. Even with more than one hundred yards between us and the pachyderms, I began to tremble. Ever since our first trip to Ethiopia, when Dick and Nassos Russos had to shoot a charging bull at less than ten steps, I got the shakes when those massive beasts were nearby. Was I afraid? Heck yeah. You know how easily an elephant can kill you? I thought I was dead that day. I thought we all were. It had been too close. Justified or not, my fear never abated. Elephants are one of the most remarkable creatures on earth. We admire them for their strength, their social structure, their unpredictability—we fear them for many of the same reasons.

The herd of twenty cows and calves milled about for fifteen minutes before gathering into a layered formation with the biggest cows out front. Dust blew away from their steps like a hoard of fleeing insects. A moment later, they were gone. I stopped shaking. The shakes were not only from fear. They never threatened us. I trembled from awe as well. I missed the elephants as soon as they were gone.

The wind saved us one day of tsetse fly attacks, but it also drove game into cover. Other than the elephants, we spotted only a single warthog that we spooked from its slumber near the road.

That evening a gust rushed through our tent. It flipped the mirror from the pole and shattered it. Just what we needed—bad luck. I almost forgot I didn't believe in those superstitions.

In my experience, good luck followed hard work and positivity. Bad luck followed laziness and negativity. There may be exceptions, but I had seen it too often to categorize much as dumb luck. Who has a better chance to bag an opening day buck—the hunter who sleeps until ten and then sits by the road or the hunter who wakes an hour before dawn and sets up two miles from the road on a food plot he has been seeing deer at for six months? One hunter needs a little luck and the other needs to hit a royal flush with one card coming. I will take my chances with the well-played two of a kind.

We hired Cotton for a reason. He was a good PH, in a good area, with a reputation for putting his clients on quality animals. He would put us on game; I just had to dig out of my shooting funk and find the confidence to do my part. I would get another chance. I looked forward to it, yet I dreaded it.

I heard a hyena pacing through camp.

When Dick's snores got nasally, they sounded like a wounded animal. I would have kicked his leg if we had not been sleeping on separate cots. When Dick's snoring went silent, so did the hyena. Hyenas are normally raucous. When this drooling scavenger shut its mouth, it made me nervous. I heard the soft crunch of a leaf lightly stepped on. I heard a sound that a proper lady blowing her nose in church might make. I sat in bed and stared into a black void. Every sound seemed to come from the foot of the bed. I felt for the flashlight that I always left beside the bed. Found it. I clicked it on. The room was empty.

Could I hear the hyena breathing just a few inches from the wall? Or was it Dick? I hated not knowing and shined the light on my husband's face. He rolled away from it. The bed creaked. Something scurried away. It sounded bigger than a rodent. If it was the hyena, I hoped it stayed gone. I did find sleep that night—just not much.

"I thought when we left Nebraska we were leaving the wind behind."

"I guess it followed you," Cotton said at breakfast. "It's not usually this bad and it usually doesn't last long."

"I bet somebody in Nebraska said that once."

"At least the tsetse flies won't be driving you crazy," Cotton said.

"I think they'll find a way."

"It's a good day to check leopard baits."

We had hung two baits the previous day a thirty-minute drive from each other. Both had rotting sable flesh dripping scent from high in horizontal branches of erythrina trees. Leopards had visited them both.

"This one has the bigger paw," Cotton said while studying tracks around the second bait tree. "We will build a blind there and you will blast him tonight when he comes to feed." Cotton was looking at me.

"I think Dick needs to take this leopard. With the way I've been shooting, I'm afraid I'll wound him."

"Nonsense," Cotton said. "I've seen you shoot leopard."

"This one's yours," Dick said.

It was no use arguing with two stubborn men. "I guess I can try."

"That's the spirit. After we build the blind, we'll go look for a hartebeest."

We found one soon enough. And I promptly wounded him. What a mess. We tracked for an hour, finding tiny splotches of blood every five to ten minutes. My stomach churned like a mixer.

"There he is. Shoot him."

"I don't see him."

"Behind that bush. Shoot him."

I missed. *Please, just take my hunting license away.* It was as if I had never fired a rifle before. We all go through ruts, but this was ridiculous. Maybe I'd lost it. Maybe I never had it.

After another hour without finding another spot of blood, three more bull hartebeest joined ours. When they split up, we didn't know which to follow.

"If he was limping or dragging his foot, we could follow him."

I was barely listening. I wanted to cry.

"That bull is not hit hard. He is going to be fine. We never found good blood and he never acted properly hit. It's okay Mary. It was just a flesh wound."

"I am not shooting a leopard," I said.

"We'll go to the range and put a couple of holes in the paper—make sure the scope didn't get knocked off zero."

"I'm still not shooting a leopard." If I had been alone, I would have cried. The thought of wounding a hartebeest was bad enough. A dangerous cat was too much to ponder. I couldn't do it. Yet, I wanted to. Maybe I needed to visit a shrink.

Joan was back and forth from her quarters to the kitchen. She bustled to the laundry area. She swept floors. She picked flowers. She did not stop.

"She's trying to keep busy," I said to Dick.

"Yeah."

"She's trying to keep busy because she's nervous."

"About what?" Dick was reading a paperback.

"About me shooting a leopard."

"Shouldn't you be the nervous one?"

"I am." If he would have looked up from his book, he could have seen what I was talking about. "You remember Cotton was mauled by a leopard."

"He doesn't seem nervous." Dick glanced up from his book long enough to see Cotton resting in the shade.

"You're impossible."

"What did I say?"

I sighed as I sat down with my journal. Joan had reason to be nervous. I couldn't stop shaking. How was I supposed to shoot straight confronted with a leopard? "I really think you should sit in the blind tonight," I said.

"We already decided you were going to go first."

"You and Cotton decided. I need to be shooting better if I'm going to shoot a leopard."

"You were dead-on at the range after we moved your scope a couple of clicks. It was the scope, not you."

"I don't know about that. And I certainly don't know about shooting a leopard. Don't you need to be confident to shoot a leopard?"

"Just pretend it's a paper target."

"I wish it were that easy."

I saw Joan pacing when she couldn't find anything to do. Half her worry had to be due to my horrific shooting. If I wounded the leopard and Cotton had to go in after it, I would be a mess. If it mauled him, I would never forgive myself. I kept telling myself to think positive, to be confident. I kept trying to think about the target shooting and how easy it had been, how sure I was with every shot. All I really thought about were sharp fangs and claws lunging for Cotton's scalp.

When the time came to head for the leopard blind, I kept my misgivings to myself. If the leopard came, I would make a decision. If it weren't perfect, if I didn't feel comfortable or confident, I would not shoot. Simple as that.

Ninety-nine percent of the time spent in a leopard blind is boring. You stare out the shooting hole and anticipate the cat's appearance three hours before dark. Your professional hunter is either sleeping or reading. If there were a chance that a leopard was going to show up to feed that early, Cotton would have been watching for him.

I read for a while, but even with a soft blanket to sit on, the blind was uncomfortable. The leopard rarely shows up. There are, however, moments when your heartbeat increases and your stomach reminds you how much you crave that fearful expectation of a predator's visit.

Silence set in at dusk and Cotton leaned toward the shooting hole. Did he hear something? Or was it just prime time? Not knowing heightened my senses. I felt the air tickle the hairs on the back of my hand. I heard the breeze rustle a leaf in the erythrina tree where we hung the bait. I saw fading light dancing with shadows. I smelled the earthy scents of dirt and fresh-cut branches on the blind walls. The taste of nervous excitement dried my tongue. At any moment, a leopard could show.

Watching a slab of meat rot in the dying sun usually wasn't interesting, but the possibility—the hope—that a leopard may soon arrive kept me focused. Soon darkness invaded the day completely. The leopard never showed. Was I disappointed? A little. But without failure, the significance of success is lost.

"We'll come back in the morning. Try to catch him on the bait at first light."

I drifted in and out of sleep during the drive to camp. In some ways, relief allowed me to relax. I hadn't wounded a leopard. The fact I hadn't seen one was only a detail.

The following morning, Dick joined us in the cramped blind. In pitch darkness, I heard every sound and attached all kinds of danger to them. Any soft rustle sounded like the leopard sneaking around. Every crack of a branch was an elephant that might stomp right over our teensy blind. Strange birdcalls sounded more like horror-film creatures. The close, quiet sounds were the most disconcerting. The leopard could see in darkness—if he wanted to teach us a lesson for spying on him, we would be nearly helpless.

The sound of tearing and ripping and gnawing pushed aside every other noise. Something was in the tree. Something with teeth sharp enough to rip the flesh of a sable. I reached for my rifle. I heard myself breathing. Was I being too loud? Of course I was. Anything I could hear, the leopard could surely hear. I hoped it was too hungry to care.

I stared to the spot in the blind where I believed the shooting hole should be. One hand held the rifle, but I didn't move it. If I bumped something in the darkness, the leopard might not stick around. My right leg began to shake from a combination of adrenalin and a painful position. I heard the leopard feeding. Nobody moved. It seemed dawn would never break.

"I don't know if it's a leopard." Cotton's whisper was so light I had to think about what he said before deciphering it.

What else could it be?

Black crept to gray and the tree's outline went from a dark area to a definitive shape. I saw the hunk of sable. No leopard. I scanned the tree branches and the ground below—nothing. I was certain I still heard it chewing on flesh. I stared at the bait until my eyes went blurry. At one point, it seemed to move, but with the dull light, I couldn't be sure.

"I think it's a serval," Cotton whispered. "If you can get a shot take it. The leopard is not coming."

If I can get a shot? I couldn't even see it. The tearing flesh began to sound more like nibbling, more like the sound a badger would make while eating a rabbit than the imagined sound of a heavy tom leopard.

We waited another half hour. All I saw of the serval was its tawny, spotted tail before it scampered away.

"We'll look for hartebeest on the way to check the other bait. If a leopard has hit it, we will sit there tonight; otherwise, we leave for Fort Ikoma tomorrow."

We had taken three total animals at Rungwa, not counting the hartebeest I wounded. That was a low number for a Tanzania safari, but we understood the game well enough to understand the odds were normally in the animal's favor. It wouldn't be much fun if they weren't.

A lioness had carried the second bait away. Later in the day, Dick had a chance at a roan, but it ran before he could get a shot. That was it. We finished the day with a fillet of sable and rice pilaf before heading to the campfire for an after-dinner Amarula—a fitting drink to end a stay at any African camp.

Dick fell asleep before he could pull up the covers. I read for a few minutes and, for the first time in a while, fell asleep without a struggle. Wounded and charging leopards left my dreams alone that night. Maybe it was because Cotton forgot to tell me they had plenty of leopards at Fort Ikoma.

"Everything is so green," I said to Cotton as I stared out the window of the six-person charter plane.

"Yes, Fort Ikoma has been abnormally wet this year."

I wondered what that might do for hunting.

Most of the camp staff waited for us at the end of the airstrip. Peter, Masenga, and Joel were there. It was good to see them.

The Fort Ikoma camp was a paradise. Overlooking a trickling river with tall, far-spreading acacias lining both sides and a comfortable dining room under a thatched roof provided a breathtaking view. Cool air from the river tickled the edges of camp and prevented the midday heat from weighing us down. Like a timid child wanting to join a game, our secluded tent almost hid in the shadows of the glossy green leaves of massive fig trees. Double-shaded with a thatch roof, the tent had just enough amenities to keep us comfortable. Two double beds with two tables each, a private flush toilet and shower adjoining with hot and cold water, and the constant calls of starlings, swallows, and wagtails treated us to a peaceful retreat at any time of day.

"Should we get right to it," Cotton said after we had settled in.

"I'm ready if you are," Dick said to me.

I think Cotton wanted to boost my confidence. "We need leopard bait and camp meat, Mary. How about you and I find a couple impala?"

"Sounds good to me." In the short time since we had left camp, we had seen enough impala to feed ten camps for a year. Impala was just what I needed.

After two one-shot kills, Cotton was satisfied. So was I.

The only game animals outnumbering impala were wildebeest and zebra.

"The migration has started," Cotton said. As long as the grass stays green and moist, the zebras and wildebeest will stick around. That means we should find some fat lions living off the buffet."

The mention of lions lit Dick's eyes like diamonds. If I had a mirror, I would have probably seen horror in mine. Not only did they want me to shoot a leopard—an animal which had nearly ripped Cotton's scalp from his head—but also another big cat that can kill a person with one swat of its paw or one bite at the back of the neck.

"I'm not going to shoot a lion," I said.

"Why not?" Cotton stared at me as if I had told him I never liked him. "You have a license for one."

"Not the way I'm shooting."

"You just hammered those two impala."

"How many hunters have been killed or even mauled by an impala?"

"I'm sure there have been one or two—those horns are sharp."

Dick laughed.

I rolled my eyes.

"They think they're so funny," Joan said.

"I'm glad they can amuse themselves. One less thing for us to worry about."

That night, the lions mocked me with their roaring. It started in the distance, but as darkness settled in, they came creeping closer. The roars deepened and rose in volume. It was as if they were telling us they were coming. Camp was quiet and dark. They would roar, wait ten minutes to lull me near the edge of sleep, and then curl each tiny hair on my neck by piercing the night with another arrogant call. Baboons started screaming right outside our tent. The lions were moving in—I knew it.

"Since you're so caught up with lion fever, I think we should go find one this morning," Cotton said at breakfast. "We'll leave the camp kitties alone though. They provide a nice ambience, don't you think?"

"I think you're making fun of me."

"I'd never do that."

"Now, Cotton," Joan said. "Be nice."

We never found a lion that morning. I think I was secretly grateful—or maybe it was just relief. Either way, my emotions dueled. I wanted to shoot a lion. I did. I had done it before; I could do it again.

There is something about hunting dangerous game that brings out deep instincts and amplifies hunting's emotional rollercoaster. Dangerous game adds an element that demands you be at your best.

That's why I felt relief. I did not believe I was at my best. Without that confidence, I shouldn't have been hunting anything dangerous.

Dick shot a Thomson's gazelle for camp meat and an impala for leopard bait. Just after loading the impala, a light rain started. It felt like the world was whispering. Is there any smell fresher than a light rain? It seemed even more so in the Tanzania bush, as if cleaning the land. Even the herds of wildebeest and zebra competing with the raindrops in number seemed to pause, understanding the new feeling that a sprinkle brings to the savannah. It was a moment when only beauty existed. It was a moment I wanted to keep forever.

POACHERS: DICK

"Did you hear the lions last night?" Cotton asked Mary.

"Why do you insist on teasing me?"

"Who said I was teasing you?" Cotton acted shocked. "Why would you say such a thing?"

"Because you think I hear lions that aren't there."

"Believe me, these lions were close last night," he said. "How come I get the feeling I'm the one being teased now."

"I didn't hear them." Mary looked to Joan for support.

"There were lions last night, Mary. I'm surprised you didn't hear them. They roared and roared. You must have been sleeping well. Good for you. You needed a good night's rest."

"Did you hear them, Dick? I doubt it. You could sleep through a train wreck."

"I wondered why you weren't harassing me about them coming into camp," I said. "Somebody must have snuck a sleeping pill into your drink last night."

"Don't look at me," Cotton said. "Although, I have had a few clients I wouldn't mind putting to sleep during the day." Cotton gulped down the last of his tea. "When you're ready, we'll go."

We took just enough time to finish our tea and toast.

"This has been a productive area for us—especially for lion. Haven't hunted it yet this year, but it is always worth the drive."

By the time we arrived, the morning sun had burned away the night chill. We had to shed a few layers. We only saw a warthog and a few antelope—all female or young males. Without prey, there would be no lions.

In some ways, it felt like we had been punched in the gut. In other ways, it was just another day hunting. Sometimes you spend hours, days, weeks, or even years pursuing an elusive lion or mountain nyala and then other times a big, old kudu bull strolls across the road fifty yards from camp. You take the opportunities you get and are thankful for the time spent in the field.

"What? Where?" Cotton glanced toward Peter, then followed his pointing finger. Three men were running toward the tree line several hundred yards in the distance.

Masenga slammed his foot on the gas pedal and we lurched forward. The game guard, Japhary, was screaming and holding his rifle in the air. I gripped onto the railing beside the high seat. Mary gripped onto me. We bounced and jarred on the grassy plain as we sped toward three shirtless natives racing for the trees.

Cotton held the railing as he focused on the running men. Japhary continued to scream and wave the rifle over his head with one hand.

"Oh my God," Mary said.

"They must be poachers." I had to yell for her to hear me.

She gave me a dirty, *I don't want to chase poachers*, look.

I shrugged. What else could I do? Every man in the truck depended upon wildlife for his livelihood. Poachers were a direct assault upon that livelihood. Who was I to stop them from protecting their future? Mary understood this too—she just didn't want to be chasing them. I couldn't blame her.

The three men were great sprinters, but they were no match for the Land Cruiser. I don't know why they didn't run in three different directions. Safety of the herd I guess. When they realized they couldn't outrun the truck, they held up their hands in defeat.

Japhary leapt from the truck and yelled in their faces. He forced them to sit on the ground with their hands behind their backs and struck each of them across the face with the back of his hand.

Masenga and Peter tied their hands while the game scout screamed at them. None of them lifted their eyes from the ground.

"What are they going to do?" Mary asked.

"We will take all their snares, knives, bows, and poison arrows—at least they do not appear to have any automatic weapons. We also need to find out where their camp is and where they have planted more snares. This could take some time. Please accept my apologies, but we cannot just let this go."

"Do what you need to do?" I said.

"What do you do to them after you find everything?" Mary asked.

"If we were closer to town, we'd take them to the authorities. As it is, I must defer to the game guard. He is the law out here. He will decide."

Japhary's initial punishment involved a lot of shouting and slapping. Mary winced a few times, but none of the three was seriously injured. I had the feeling the game scout held back because of our presence.

When Japhary finished his interrogation, the three poachers piled into the back of the vehicle. After picking up a few small arrows, the game scout was the last to climb in. He kept his automatic weapon pointed at the prisoners.

Masenga drove slowly, retracing our tracks, stopping every now and again to retrieve a knife or snare that one of the poachers had dropped during the chase. Soon, he turned into the trees, following directions relayed from one of the prisoners. Every five or ten minutes, we stopped to retrieve a set snare.

The fourth snare had a young male hartebeest trapped by the hind leg. It was so weak it could not lift its head. With its eyes glazed over, it seemed resigned to its fate. Cotton grabbed the nearest rifle, chambered a round and shot the hartebeest through the heart. Peter and Masenga gutted it and threw it in back with the prisoners. I think we all wanted a turn slapping them. We refrained.

We drove through heavy brush to a small, temporary campsite. Drying meat hung from makeshift poles. Other meat cooled beneath the shadow of leafy branches placed as an umbrella. Three small stick huts, each barely large enough for a single man, formed a half-circle around a recently burned fire. A cache of weapons and snares were piled beside one of the huts. A heap of horns and hides beside another.

We gathered the horns, hides, and meat. It dropped the back of the Land Cruiser a few inches. Then Peter and Masenga shoved all the weapons into one of the huts. They stuffed dry grass into each of them and lit everything on fire. We confiscated or destroyed a few weeks' worth of poaching. The three prisoners reacted without emotion. They sat in the back of the truck, their eyes and heads lowered into a submissive posture.

"That will set them back a while," Cotton said. "Might not prevent further poaching, but it will take these three a while to get back into business."

"They can get everything they need to continue right here in the bush," I said.

Cotton shrugged. "That's true. A few game guards have been known to take them out, shoot them, and leave them for the hyenas. There are others, as corrupt as some politicians, who barely give poaching lip service and then look the other way when someone hands them a bribe under the table."

"What will happen to them?" Mary motioned toward the poachers.

"I don't know. If Japhary decides to take them back to town on his own, there is a chance that the authorities will just let them go. If he decides to punish them here, it could get ugly. I don't think that would be a good idea in front of clients—even unrefined folks such as you."

"I'll take that as a compliment."

"I wouldn't mean it any other way."

Cotton walked back to the vehicle and began a discussion with the game scout. After a few minutes, he called everyone back to the truck.

"We're going for a drive," Cotton said.

We rumbled through a game-less desolate expanse of land with only a few trees dotting the landscape as far as we could see. No antelope, no warthogs, no birds, not even many bugs. Two hours later, we stopped.

Japhary screamed at the prisoners and kicked them from the Land Cruiser. He jumped out, screamed at them again, kicked them again, and untied them. Then he climbed back in and we drove away.

"You're just going to let them go?"

"Japhary says the local law enforcement is dishonest. This will keep them from poaching longer than if they were turned in."

Japhary leaned forward. "I say I kill if I catch again. You see they run like scared dog when they see Japhary." He pointed at his chest.

"How long do you think it will keep them from poaching?"

"I'd guess a month," Cotton said.

The image of three shirtless poachers, in cutoff shorts, hiking across the savannah almost seemed cheerful. Then I thought about spending the night out there. Most predators hunted in darkness. Even though the afternoon heat toyed with the century mark, sunset brought frigid air. It would be a cold night.

They got off easy. Their practices indiscriminately decimate wildlife populations. Putting them out of commission for a month wasn't long enough. A few cold nights in the bush wouldn't make them change their ways.

We stopped to check a leopard bait a few hundred yards from the river's edge. Hit. Pugmarks indicated a big tom. The possibility of a spotted cat allowed us to re-focus.

Cotton started barking orders. "Refresh the bait with some of this meat. Build the blind here. Big enough for three people. Mary, you're coming with us."

"I'm not shooting."

"We'll see. Peter, make sure the bait branch is visible from the blind. Dick and Mary, you can relax. We will be here for a few minutes."

Sitting in a leopard blind is a test of mental stress. Compound it with many days in leopard blinds and it is a test of mental fortitude. Silent minutes waiting, without movement, for a hungry beast renowned for its stealth and killing power tickles the line between adrenalin and fear. As the minutes are swallowed by hours, eclectic strings of questions circle the edge of your thoughts.

At first, the questions are harmless and revolve around your immediate situation—hunting. Will the leopard come? Will I be ready if it does? Then, you think about other animals you have hunted or are not hunting because you are waiting for a leopard to revisit a rotting carcass. There are few opportunities to sit quietly during our busy lives. If the kind of silence you encounter in a leopard blind lasts for long stretches of time, deep reflection comes to you even if you are not searching for it. You think about choices you've made—choices you failed to make. How the invincibility of youth is no longer even a faded memory. You wonder if you have given your children the guidance to succeed.

If you're lucky, a leopard will interrupt your thoughts before you start to find answers. In the dark, confined space of a leopard blind, your mind wrestles with your faults above your virtues. That kind of reflection, even subconsciously, leads down a depressing path. Nobody wants to go there. You learn a lot about yourself in a leopard blind—some of it you wish you never knew.

We headed back to camp slightly disappointed that we hadn't seen a leopard, yet glad for the opportunity to hunt one. When we arrived, Joan was finishing preparations for Cotton's birthday dinner. She had arranged a big pot of flowers, covered the table with a tablecloth, place mats and matching napkins, swept the tent floor twice, re-fixed her hair, and smiled for her husband. She was beaming.

For dinner, the cook prepared Topi enchiladas, chalupas, bean soup, salad, and angel food cake with lemon icing—Cotton's favorite. We toasted our host with Amarula right before the entire staff paraded around the table singing "Happy

Birthday, Dear Bwána." After ten verses, they cheered and clapped for five minutes. Joan wrapped her arms around Cotton and kissed him.

"Today is Nancy's birthday," Mary said the next morning.

Nancy, our oldest daughter, had a heart that could hold the world. She had nothing but love for anyone and asked only love in return. I hoped her birthday was happy.

Sometimes, our hunting expeditions took us to places time never cared to visit. Places so far removed from the mundane worries that the rest of us agonize over each day. Places so far from a city that the footprint of human civilization does not exist.

Other times, our hunting expeditions took us to places within driving distance of a Catholic church. When they did, we went to Mass. The small church in Mugumu was packed, but a kind woman moved to allow Mary, Joan, Hillary, and I to sit together. We heard a harmony of voices so divine that we felt closer to heaven. Though he was not Catholic, Cotton had donated the organ to the church—another small way to give something back to a community who had given him so much.

After Mass, we drove back to camp, had a noon breakfast and took a nap. We needed our rest—we didn't want to fall asleep in the leopard blind.

We sat in the blind without talking and without moving, hoping to catch a glimpse of Africa's spotted ghost. There was a sense he was out there, stalking in the deepening shadows. Like a phantom, he refused to show himself. Silence and darkness.

On our way to check lion baits the next morning, Cotton had Masenga stop the truck. "A lioness." He pointed.

She struggled to lift her head to look back at us. Her body was half in the shade of an umbrella acacia.

"She's been mauled. Look at those wounds," Cotton said.

"She can barely move," Mary said. "It's horrible. Was it another lion?"

"Most likely a male going after her cubs. They probably didn't make it."

"It's so sad," Mary said.

"These things happen every day, usually without an audience."

Quiet ruled the next few minutes. Driving away, I couldn't see into my colleagues' heads, but the pitiful image of that bloodied lioness, with her eyes full of defeat and her once taut, confident muscles drooping, had left its imprint. One of nature's proudest predators losing heart is a picture that stays with you.

Forty-five minutes later, Cotton finally broke the silence. "More lions."

When you see a healthy, wild lion, it affects you in a way few animals can. A lion moves like a champion heavyweight boxer entering a room. He owns the place. Nobody in the room is better than he is. His shoulder muscles roll and bulge with each step. His smooth movements border on arrogance. The lion is tougher than you are. You know it and he knows it. The female lion is no different and, in many cases, more self-assured than her male counterpart. She will often stare directly into your eyes long enough to let you know she considers you beneath her.

Five females and three cubs lazed beside what remained of three small wildebeest kills. The largest lioness stood when we stopped. She stared at us, her mouth slightly open, lightly panting. The others ignored us.

"I do not expect the bait to be touched," Cotton said. "The pride male probably ate his fill and moved into the grass. If they were interested in the bait, they wouldn't have killed those wildebeest. It was likely a hunting lesson for the cubs."

Sure enough, the soft earth around the bait tree was free of tracks. We spent the next two hours driving and checking two different leopard baits. Same result—nothing.

"I think there's too much game," I said. "They don't need the baits."

"You may be right," Cotton said. "Hunting is too easy. Most of the baits haven't even attracted hyenas. All we can do is keep at it. These are good areas and there are many cats around. We just need to find one that isn't much of a hunter."

"Yeah, they exist."

"They usually starve to death before we get a chance to hunt them."

During the long drive to camp, we spotted wildebeest, kudu, and hartebeest before Masenga slammed on the brakes. We lunged forward. After a quick recovery, we scanned the horizon. Four eland—a dust cloud building behind their running hooves.

"That's a huge bull. Get your rifle ready, Dick. I want to see what they do."

They slowed, but like most eland, didn't stop moving.

"We must hurry to catch them at the trees," Hillary said.

Masenga sped down the road a few miles before cranking the wheel and vaulting us into four-foot grass. By the time he stopped, I could hardly move my white fingers from their grip on the roll bar. I didn't see any eland.

"There," Hillary pointed.

As big as eland are, they should be easy to see. But their dirty cream color blends with the landscape. Luckily, eland don't stand around much. Nomadic in nature, they seem as if they are on an endless trek to nowhere. When they moved, I saw them.

"If we hurry, we can get to the brush beside that baobab tree over there."

We made it without the eland spotting us, but they had moved close to a line of thick thorn trees. As I set up, they sped into a trot for no particular reason.

"If you're going to shoot, it better be now."

Hurrying the shot, I hit the bull low. He didn't go down, but it slowed him enough that I was able to put another bullet in his neck. He was dead by the time we walked up to him.

"If a lion or leopard had hit a bait, we might not have found him," Mary said.

"I guess we're as opportunistic as any predator."

"You got that right," Cotton said. "I'll take a big warthog I can see over a two-hour-old buffalo track any day."

After lunch, Cotton came to our tent while I was reading and Mary was writing in her journal. "One of the trucks will be leaving for Arusha Friday morning. If it's possible, could you send some of your luggage with that truck? It will be waiting for you when you arrive on Saturday."

I looked to Mary.

"That will be fine," she said. "Thanks for giving me plenty of time to pack."

"I helped unload all those bags. I figured you needed more than fifteen minutes."

"It's Monday already," I said. "She'll be frantic fifteen minutes before the truck leaves, even though she'll start as soon as you're gone."

"Maybe you'd like to pack?"

Cotton put up his hands. "I'm staying out of this one." He backed away and disappeared to his own tent.

"I better get started packing," Mary said after he was gone.

My judgment fought the urge to say something. I fell asleep reading a book. Mary woke me a few minutes before it was time to head out. With all her packing, she didn't have time for a nap.

"Since nothing fed on the baits, I think we'll go find Mary an eland this afternoon. If we're lucky, we'll run into a lion."

Tanzania was one of the few countries where lions did well inside and outside protected areas. Tanzania's lion policy provided an economic incentive for local people to protect the cats. When hunters came for lion, everyone benefited, even if a lion was not harvested. Without those benefits, the lion was, at best, competition, at worst, a man-eater. Lions not only killed game, but cattle as well—a significant loss to a Maasai. If it weren't for hunters bringing in much-needed money, that lion would be worth more to the tribe dead than alive. Just look at Kenya. Before the hunting ban went into effect in the seventies, wildlife thrived throughout the country. Today, it only thrives in parks.

"Kenya's painted as a shining example of wildlife conservation."

"It's a lie," Cotton said. "Their parks are magnificent, but beyond the park borders, game has disappeared. There is no reason not to kill it. They eat it; they sell it; they poison it when it eats their crops. Kenya's total ban on hunting should be a shining example on how to wipe out wildlife."

"So Tanzania's got it right then?"

"Better than most countries."

The United States model was hard to beat. Lots of people and lots of wildlife—not an easy combination. Tanzania had made mistakes—some policy, some practice—like shooting young lions or pushing the quota limits past the edge of sustainability. But when it came to rational wildlife management, Tanzania did it better than most African countries

At some point during most safaris, conversation always touches on hunting as a conservation tool. Few people hunt to conserve wildlife—they conserve wildlife because they love to hunt. And few hunters can imagine a world without its vast array of incredible creatures. Mary and I could not. The view from a mountaintop; the whisper of a hidden creek; the smell of a Cape buffalo hidden in the grass— those are the things that stay with a man, that reconnect him to his inner predator. If we did not hunt, it would be like denying who we were.

So, when Hillary pointed out an eland bull marching through a heat mirage, I wasn't surprised to see that hunter's look of intensity, focus, and excitement on my wife's face.

Cotton studied the bull's horns. "He's a good bull. Get your rifle and follow me."

I stayed in the truck with Masenga and Hillary, while Mary, Cotton, Peter, and Japhary worked their way to a thick line of thorn bushes. The eland stopped to stare in their direction. Its muscles tightened and it broke into a run. A shot. The bull increased its speed. Its loose skin flowed over heavy shoulders and the line of its back never seemed to undulate even when it broke into a sprint. That perfect combination of size and grace could only be found in nature.

Mary and the others followed it into the brush. I expected them to reappear at any moment. After an hour, I asked Hillary what he thought happened.

"They must track the bull. Check for blood."

"Do you think she hit it?"

Hillary turned his palms up. "I do not know. It did not appear so."

The minutes crawled by. The sun began to sear my skin. I dug through the small kit Mary packed everyday, knowing I probably messed up her entire system. I also knew she would get after me for being sunburned. Tube of bug spray, bottle of water, bag of wet wipes, everything but sunscreen. Where was Mary?

By the time they came back, I had forgotten about the sunscreen.

I stood to meet them at the vehicle.

Nobody offered information, so I asked. "What happened?"

Cotton glanced Mary's way.

"I missed," she said.

We drove away from camp early the next morning. The bush telegraph had reported a lion sighting the night before. Somebody told somebody who told somebody who Masenga knew that it was a big male.

"Half the time, the bush telegraph is right, so it's worth checking out," Cotton said.

"What about the other half?"

"Usually it's half right. Some of these fellas out here think any male is big. There's probably a lion; it might just be a youngster. It's worth a check."

A salmon sunrise spread across the savannah and revealed a landscape dotted with thin white thorn acacias and a calm zebra herd. The chill air biting through our layers of clothes would soon give way to a pulsing heat. Every few minutes we peeled off another layer.

A herd of wildebeest bucked and ran off in their hammer-like gait as soon as they saw us. A never-ending flock of quelea formed a river in the sky. Game was plentiful—too plentiful.

Peter thought he saw something at the edge of a dry streambed.

"What was it?" Cotton asked.

"*Simba.*"

"Male?"

Peter shook his head. "Female."

"Do you think she saw us?" Cotton asked.

"Yes, but no scared. She find place to hide where she can watch."

Cotton pressed his lips together and rubbed his forehead. "There could be a male. We've lost the element of surprise, but the ground is good for tracking."

Cotton wasn't looking at anyone as he spoke softly. It was more like he was think-ing out loud. "It doesn't matter if we walk over there or drive, they'll run off before we get there. At least if we drive, we might catch them moving—see if they're worth tracking." He looked at me. "I think we'll speed to the creek bed. We can make a plan if there's a male." He waved the driver forward. "Drive toward the river, Masenga. Normal speed."

Masenga started out slow.

"Faster. Drive a bit faster."

Two lionesses snuck around a bend in the creek. They weren't running, but we had obviously disturbed them.

"Let's check for male tracks," Cotton said. "Should be easy to find. The ground is soft." Cotton brought his .458. "Never pays to be careless with the big cats."

Hillary and Peter pointed out the first set of tracks. "Female," they said.

Searching an expanding circle, we found one other female track and noth-ing else.

"We had to look," Cotton said. "You never know."

"Bwana." Peter waved Cotton over. We followed.

"That's why the lions are here." Cotton pointed to a snare, the ground stained crimson around it. A quick search found the remains of a mostly devoured zebra. Japhary ripped the snare from the tree before storming back to the Land Cruiser.

"It's bad this year," Cotton said. "There's always a poacher or two around, but they're usually rare in the hunting concessions. They must have decimated the populations elsewhere."

"Bwana, come." Peter and Hillary were studying the ground.

Sneakers. A single pair, backing up, then running.

"Must have come to check the snare this morning and discovered the lions had checked it first. When was he here?" Cotton hollered to Peter, who had followed the tracks another fifteen yards.

Peter held up three fingers.

"Just a few hours ago. What do you say we hunt in that direction?"

"Wouldn't be doing our part if we just walked away," I said.

"What if he's armed or not alone?" Mary asked.

"If you don't want to do this, I'm not going to force you," Cotton said.

"It's okay. As long as we're careful."

"You know I'm always careful. I tell you what. I won't even fall asleep in the car today. Now, Dick on the other hand…"

"You guys are not near as funny as you think you are."

"That's just a rumor. We're much funnier than you think we are."

"That's not what I said."

"So you do think we're funny."

"This is pointless. Maybe you *should* take a nap."

"If you insist."

Japhary was more alert than usual. He often helped spot animals, but it was with more of a "going through the motions" attitude than the neck-stretching and shadow-searching he did now. He took his job as game guard seriously.

Peter pointed out a herd of wildebeest and four hartebeest bulls. We were checking them for a big male when Japhary shushed us. He had his hand up and his ear pointed out the back. He told Masenga to shut off the truck. Masenga looked to Cotton, who nodded.

Sweat bees buzzed in my ears—nothing else. Peter and the game guard began talking, pointing, and nodding. Cotton let them finish then asked, "What is it?"

"Animal is cry," Peter said pointing. "Much weak. Is dead soon."

"Lions?"

Peter shook his head.

"It's probably caught in a snare," Cotton said. "The poacher could be close. If he heard the truck, he's probably hiding. I think we'll drive over there. He might try to run when the truck approaches."

Peter jumped out and ran in front of the vehicle, watching the ground and jumping over small bushes. Japhary held his assault rifle in one hand and held onto the rail with the other. We just held on.

After a hundred yards, Japhary pointed to a zebra carcass under a tree. He started yelling when the poacher jumped from behind a small thorn bush and sprinted away. Peter ran after him. Masenga hit the gas and passed Peter easily. Japhary yelled. Cotton seemed calm. He kept looking in other directions—apparently for accomplices. I did the same. Neither of us saw anyone else.

The unarmed poacher stopped and waved his arms above his head. When Japhary pointed the gun at him, he fell to his knees, dropped his head, held out his hands, and begged. Japhary screamed at him.

The poacher was just a hair over five and a half feet. He was lean and had boyish features. And he clearly thought Japhary was going to shoot him.

Even after running the entire distance, Peter was not breathing heavily. He moved shoulder-to-shoulder with Cotton.

"Ask him where his friends are."

Peter began interrogating him as if he were a war criminal.

"He say he is alone. He say he find his camp burned and his friends gone."

"Tell him to show us where his snares are."

A threat from Japhary prompted the poacher to stand up and march toward the evidence of his crime.

He led us to six snares, two of which had dead zebras.

"Look at her leg," Mary said.

In the struggle to free herself, the zebra had ripped the skin and muscle down to the bone.

"How long do you think it took her to die?"

"Days. She had to starve to death."

The other zebra had been caught around the neck and most likely died within a few hours.

"What a shame."

"It's a crime," I said.

"It's a sin." Mary said.

"What now?" I asked Cotton. "What do we do with this one?" I wondered if his punishment would mirror the others.

"Maybe we should shoot him." I thought he was joking, but he wasn't smiling. Mary looked horrified.

"What do you think, Mary?" Cotton asked her. "Should we shoot him? We won't kill him; just shoot him in the ankle."

Mary glanced my way, her eyes wide.

By now, I knew he was joking and tipped off my wife with a sideways glance.

"You are horrible, Cotton."

"I believe Japhary will want to take this guy in. I don't want to waste two hours driving him to nowhere. I'll volunteer one of the skinners to take him so Japhary can stay."

"Will it do any good? Turning him in?"

"Depends. Probably not. Poacher kingpins have deep pockets. Bribes and back-room deals in the city are responsible for the deaths of uncountable animals. We might get lucky. A few upstanding, honest officers and judges can't be bought. And Tanzania is less corrupt than many African countries. Most likely, we can expect the same result as driving him a week's walk into the bush. It will put him out of poaching for a while, but he'll be back at it soon enough."

"That's a shame," Mary said.

"These guys are most likely outsiders who didn't know it was a hunting conces-sion. If the wrong game guard or villager caught them, it could have turned out much worse. They'll be back to poaching, but it won't be here."

We checked baits that afternoon—nothing had fed. We saw a few lionesses. If there were males around, they stayed hidden. We didn't get back to camp until ten. After a quick bite, we lumbered to the tent. I was asleep before Mary finished brushing her teeth.

Mary was standing at the mirror when I awoke.

"I guess the leopard decided to leave us alone," I said. She gave me one of her looks. I smiled on the inside.

"It wasn't just the leopard," she said. "Lions started in around midnight."

"Were they close?"

"They kept moving closer. There was no way I was going to get any sleep after that."

"Hello." It was the same unassuming voice calling from outside the tent every morning—our wake-up call.

"*Asante*," Mary said. "Thank you."

After a filling breakfast of eland liver and eggs, we drove off in search of lion once again. With only two hunting days remaining, the optimism supply was down to a few drops at the bottom of the barrel. The end of our hunt stared us in the face. We wished for just one extra day.

We found plenty of lionesses, but the males had us outsmarted. They didn't visit baits, they refused to reveal themselves, and the tracks they left were always a day old.

Just as the sun convinced me I was tired, a buffalo herd appeared on the horizon.

"Must be between three or four hundred," Cotton said. "Has to be a good bull. Let's try to move closer and glass them."

It was an open savannah, only a few flattop acacias and Egyptian thorn trees to use for cover. With that many eyes, they probably had us pinpointed anyway. To "move closer" we simply drove straight toward them. At three hundred yards out, half of them turned to face us. We stopped. Every binocular in the vehicle rose to hopeful eyes. A few minutes of silence followed.

"Mostly cows," Cotton said. "A few young bulls, but not what we're looking for. We'll just keep looking at them a while. A big bull can get lost in a herd this size."

More silence.

"Let's see if we can't get them to separate," Cotton finally said.

Driving right for them again, the first wall of buffalo rocked their heads before turning to run. We lost them in a rising dust cloud. Within a few moments, we could not see where we were going. Then, I saw a dark mass through the haze. They were close—if one turned to take us head on, it would be one heck of an impact. I braced myself.

After fifty more yards, I realized we were inside the herd, with buffalo breaking away from us in three directions. It would take hours for them to regroup. Masenga turned to the right, hoping to put some distance between the two factions before allowing the dust to settle.

We didn't follow them much further before Cotton called an end to it. The group behind us rumbled into the dust. The smaller group, which we were following, stopped. They turned to face us, their heavy gazes those of creatures reaching the end of their patience.

"Look at that bull," Cotton said.

Standing in front of the herd with his nose in the air, a heavy-bossed bull glared at us. I met his eyes. If he was afraid, it did not show. He snorted and raked his horns to the side before thundering off with what remained of his herd.

"Dick," Cotton said. "You need to shoot that bull."

I raised my thumb.

"We'll give them time to calm down, then we'll track them. I don't think they'll go far. It's hot." Cotton looked at the sun.

Umbrella trees dot the Tanzania savannah as if God placed them there specifically so creatures, two-footed or four, could find refuge from the oppressive sun.

I'm not sure what the others did while we sat under that acacia for forty-five minutes, but I slept, waking only when Cotton said it was time to go. We drove to where we had last seen the buffalo. Other than a few solitary trees, there was not much cover. We were in for a long hike.

A novice could follow the layered hoof prints on the soft dirt, but Peter would focus in on the bull's tracks and make sure we followed him even if he broke from the herd.

An hour into our hike, the savannah began to transform into wooded grassland.

"Peter says they are heading for the river," Cotton said. "It will give us more cover. As long as the wind doesn't shift and they do not cross the water, we should be on them shortly."

One hundred yards further Peter stopped to point. A small group was lazing in the shade of a tamarind tree. No sign of the old bull. We glassed from behind a thorn bush. If we had to move to a different vantage point, we'd have to retreat to do it. There were more trees and bushes than in the grassland, but they were sparse enough that we would be exposed in any direction besides back. At least the buffalo were calm. If the bull was lying down, we wouldn't have a good shot.

"There he is," Cotton said. "Set up the sticks."

Peter spread the homemade tripod in front of me. I settled in behind the scope.

"He's to the left of those three cows beside the big tree." Cotton was whispering. "Do you see him?"

It was impossible to miss a big old bull among a bunch of cows like that. "I got him."

"No shot. If he takes a step forward and you can see the shoulder, let him have it."

Two minutes seemed like two hours with the rifle propped in shooting sticks, the sun baking the back of my neck, and my muscles begging to shift positions. The bull's head didn't move. His tail didn't twitch. His muscles didn't spasm. Even the cows lying in the grass shook their heads to ward of flies. Two roughhousing younger bulls finally pushed into his backside. He took the perfect step forward.

"Take him now."

When the bullet struck, the bull kicked his foreleg up and turned to follow the herd. We sprinted after them, stopping after a few yards. Allowing his herd to rumble off, the mortally wounded bull turned. He didn't plan on going out without taking us down first.

I raised the rifle. The bull stumbled forward and fell.

"Shoot him again," Cotton said.

Since he was on the ground and quartering toward us, I shot him high in the front of his shoulder—too high.

The bull sprung to his feet. With blood spraying from his nostrils, he came at us. He was sixty yards away.

My next shot hit him in the head and turned him back into a tangle of thick bushes—a place we did not want to follow him.

"Let's backtrack to that tree over there," Cotton said. "Hopefully we'll hear a death bellow while we get a drink of water."

My mouth was dry.

"You hit him well with your first shot. Trouble with buffalo is they don't know when they're dead. Sometimes they need a few more reminders. Make sure your gun is loaded with a full magazine."

Cotton never took his eyes from the thick bush. "Have some water and we'll make a plan," he said.

Cotton talked quietly with Hillary, Peter, and Masenga while Mary and I shared a bottle of water. Nobody wanted to walk into that dark, shadowy bush without hearing a death bellow. It would be like walking into an ambush. We had no choice.

"Stay right beside me. If you see him, shoot him."

As we approached the tangle of thorns and shadows, the world held its breath. A bird didn't flutter; a cloud didn't shift.

The bushes spread for at least thirty feet in every direction. He could be anywhere. I saw a mix of bright and dark blood staining the ground. He was close.

"There he is. Shoot." Cotton was not whispering.

The bull tried to rise to his feet—he didn't have the strength, but the fire in his eyes was that of a warrior unwilling to give up. I took my time and fired another bullet into his heart. He rolled over and groaned, struggling toward us with his dying breath. What character.

Skinning and deboning a cape buffalo is a serious undertaking. Working with homemade *pangas* that they sharpened with other *pangas*, Peter and Masenga set to work. Peter's first incision sliced through the hide like a surgeon's scalpel. Each man carved, cut, and pulled until they had removed the full-body skin. Cutting the meat was quick, but messy. In less than an hour, the only parts of the buffalo remaining were a gut pile and a skeleton. Even those would be gone soon. The sky filled with circling vultures. As we loaded the meat into the truck, many of the birds perched in nearby trees to wait, staring at us like they were uninvited wedding guests looking to raid the buffet. As we drove away, the massive birds closed in like piranhas. Within moments, we were unable to see anything but swarming vultures bickering over scraps of intestine and leftover hunks of meat.

We covered the meat in the truck with palm-like fronds that Masenga cut from an unseen tree.

"Do we need to take the meat back to camp now," Mary asked.

"It should be fine until lunch. You'd be surprised how cool it stays under those leaves. When we stop, feel under there—it's almost cold." Cotton's half smile alone was usually enough to satisfy most inquiries. "We still have a couple good hours of hunting before lunch. We'll work our way toward camp. The meat will be fine, I promise. We'll make shish-kabob appetizers tonight and I'll let you test them before dinner."

Thirty minutes later, Hillary pointed to the west. "Eland."

Masenga stopped the truck and Cotton's binoculars went straight to his eyes. With a heat mirage rising from the dry ground, it almost looked as if the eland were walking into a different dimension. They marched along, their heads bobbing to the beat of their hooves.

"Let's go, Mary. There are two good bulls in there. I think we can get a shot at one of them."

Without cover between the eland and our position, Cotton's plan was simple and obvious. Walk right at them.

Too smart for that, the eland sped up to a trot shortly after Mary and Cotton left the vehicle. Mary set up to shoot.

I thought I saw the bull on the right lift his shoulders at the shot. Then the herd charged off.

"They are heading to the river," Hillary said.

The river was the concession boundary. Going after the bull there would require permission and paperwork, possibly many days worth.

One bull was falling behind the herd. He veered away, his course parallel with the river. He stopped behind a bush and looked over his shoulder. Mary set up for another shot.

She fired just as the eland started running again. The bull crashed to the ground, its shoulder shattered. A finishing bullet from Mary's 7mm ended its life. Her first bullet had passed through one lung, but the bull's adrenalin almost carried him to the river.

The meat and hide of Africa's largest antelope combined with those from a fifteen-hundred-pound Cape buffalo were all the Land Cruiser could take. The back bumper nearly dragged on the ground. It would feed the entire staff and their families for weeks.

That afternoon, we checked baits and looked for lions or their tracks. We saw eland marching; we saw zebras and wildebeest milling about; we saw hartebeest running wild; we saw elephants eating from high branches; we saw a pack of hyenas terrorizing a young impala ram. We did not see lions.

Mary fell asleep before I did. I think her fine shooting on the moving eland relieved some of the pressure she had been putting on herself. Sleep usually came easy for me, but that night, as I listened to a leopard sawing in the darkness, I thought about a Cape buffalo bull that had never known what it meant to give up. Throughout history, people have projected human traits onto animals. That night I understood why. Some animals like lions, elephants, bears, elk—and buffalo— often surprise us with their loyalty, gentleness, strength, royalty—and courage. When we see these honorable traits in animals, hope remains that we may one day possess them ourselves.

I would like to say we found a last-day lion—we didn't. We followed another buffalo herd but called off the stalk when we determined the best bull was too young. For a buffalo to be a fine trophy, it needed a hard, heavy boss. That only came with age.

Our last full day was hot and quiet. We checked lion baits, watched hornbills bob through the air, dozed off occasionally, and slapped away hoards of tsetse flies.

"I hate them," Mary said after one stung her back.

I knew better. I knew she would miss them when we were gone. Africa had a way of absorbing itself into your heart, leaving you with an empty feeling—a thirst quenched only by a return to her embrace. Tanzania is Africa. Fields of plains game by day, hunting cats prowling by night, and hippo-and-crocodile-infested water where elephants congregate. When people imagine Africa, they probably see a picture much like Tanzania.

I know Mary will miss the tsetse flies because, as much as I hated them myself, they were proof we were in wild Africa. We would gladly endure one of the most annoying insects in the world just to check one more lion bait.

PART III
JUST HUNTING
1995

GETTING STARTED: MARY

During an African safari, the sheer numbers, variety, and beauty of the avian life enhance the experience and sharpen the senses. Birds provide each day with harmony and grace. A day without Africa's birds would feel less alive—I could not imagine it. Dick and I grew up wingshooting. Why couldn't we integrate that part of our hunting life with the big-game hunting that had consumed much of our later years? Also, it would offer a nice touch to add more authenticity to the African dioramas for our future retail showrooms.

We visited Cotton one day and asked if he could handle a safari during which we could hunt birds as well as big game.

"Birds? You mean guineas and francolin and such?"

"We mean everything."

"I guess if you can get the licenses, we can get you the birds. Tanzania's a bird paradise. Actually sounds like fun. Just think of how much we'll learn. I'm sure I'll discover I'm not as smart as I think I am."

"I don't think that will ever happen."

"Mary? I thought we were friends."

"We are. I just know you better than you know yourself."

We'd had the time slot booked with Cotton for a few years. All we had to do was tweak the hunt's focus.

"We've already confirmed that we can get licenses from both the U.S. and Tanzania. The U.S. wants to see Tanzania's list first and then adjust it," Dick said.

"You still want to hunt lion and leopard?"

"Of course," Dick said.

"By the way," I said, "we're planning to bring a bird taxidermist with us to make sure all the skinning jobs are done correctly."

"I was wondering how my skinners were going to handle this job. Who's the taxidermist?"

"Stefan Savides. He's the best bird taxidermist we've ever seen. More of an artist than anything else."

"An artist, huh?" Cotton said. "If nothing else this should be an interesting hunt."

In Arusha, Stefan, Dick, and I met a family of Portuguese hunters who would be joining us at Cotton's Fort Ikoma camp. They were clients of a freelance professional hunter we knew well.

As usual, our friend, Mike Taylor, picked us up at the airport. It was good to see him. The familiar drive to the Impala hotel included the usual crevices, cracks, potholes, and craters.

"They're planning to start repairs on the road this month," Mike said.

"That's what you said last year," I said.

"One of these years, I will be right. It is the law of averages."

Mike helped unload the car and accompanied us to the front desk of the hotel.

"I am sorry sir, but we are full." The concierge appeared genuinely apologetic, but it didn't do Stefan any good.

"I have a reservation confirmation," Stefan said.

"Yes, I am sorry, but we have no more rooms. There is nothing I can do." The short, round man held his palms up.

It turned out that a government official had booked an entire floor. Stefan wasn't getting a room, reservation confirmation or not.

"There is a hotel next door," Mike said. "They should have a room."

"Is it a nice place?" I asked.

Mike half-shrugged. I felt sorry for Stefan.

"If they don't have anything, come back here. You can stay in our room," I said.

"I've stayed in lots of dumps before—I'm comfortable there."

"A dump in Africa is a lot different than a dump in San Diego," Dick said.

"It'll be fine. Meet you here for breakfast?"

"How about eight o'clock?" Dick said.

"Will you join us, Mike?" I asked.

"It would be my pleasure."

"See you in the morning."

Cotton and Hillary Dafi showed up for breakfast right at eight o'clock. "How's the list look?" Cotton asked. "They try to get you to bribe them for permission to shoot a bunch of endangered birds?"

"Here," Dick said, handing Cotton the list. "The U. S. removed a few—said we couldn't bring them back because they couldn't verify their status."

"Probably the most abundant birds on the list." Cotton unfolded and studied the document. "This is some list. I don't even know what some of these birds are. Many of them I've only seen from a distance or in pictures. Like I said—this is going to be an interesting hunt. Where's your artist?"

"He had to stay in another hotel. They sold his room to a government official or something."

Cotton laughed. "Government official could mean lots of things."

"What do you mean?" I asked.

"Could be some guests trashed the room last night or something else entirely. Maybe the manager's using it to push drugs—doesn't really matter. People always accept the government-official excuse. They get blamed for a great deal, much of it deserved, some of it not."

Cotton always had this confident, matter-of-fact style. Even when he didn't have an answer, he told you so with authority and you knew that was the last word on it. With his compact, solid build and his bulldog attitude, he was a man who people listened to. He got things done when others ran into obstacles. I am glad he was our friend.

"Did you have any trouble with the scatter-gun? Custom officials can be touchy about shotguns. They don't see them often and they look dangerous—especially pump actions."

"We sailed through. They checked our paperwork and glanced at the guns, but let us through without a hassle."

"Good. We're going to have a challenge getting close to some of these birds. The natives often kill what they can for food, but guineas are easier than hornbills. There'll be a lot of trial and error—hunting techniques do not exist for many of these birds. On a brighter note, we already have a few baits hanging from the clients who just left."

"Will Joan be joining us?" I asked.

"She's sorry she couldn't make it this year. That's one less woman to pick on me."

"What do you know about the Portuguese family?"

"I've never met them."

"We met them yesterday. They seem affable. It's a husband and wife with their son. He appears to be in his thirties."

"I think Lance, the other PH, has hunted with them before—he says they are good people."

The small charter airplane landed on a dirt runway with a two-room, flat-roofed building for an airport. Inside, a heavy, stone-faced woman stood behind a bar and stared at us.

"Would you like a drink while we load the Land Cruisers?" Cotton asked.

"Do they have bottled water?" I asked.

Cotton looked to the woman. "Still water. Two." He held up two fingers.

The woman pulled two short glasses from under the bar.

"No glass, please," I said, waving them off. There was a time when they were probably clear—not anymore.

She stared at me as if I had rejected her child for a beauty contest and then she held up the bottle with a questioning look. It was a 2.5-liter heavy glass container.

I said yes.

She shrugged and handed it over. *Whatever the crazy American woman wants.*

That bottle lasted three days, but I would be damned if I was going to drink from those filthy glasses.

The three-hour drive to the Fort Ikoma camp was along a mostly flat, dirt trail. It was smooth for a trail road and after an hour, we started to encounter game. With the migration in full swing, massive herds of wildebeest, zebra, and Thomson's gazelle spread across the plains, the constant motion like flowing rivers of hooves, horns, and stripes. We were back in Africa—in some ways, we were home.

At camp, a group of familiar faces gathered to greet us. I had to dry my eyes. We had come to know many of these fine people during our previous visits. I remembered wondering if I would ever see them again. Much can happen in Africa over the course of a year or two—the short life expectancy alone strains the odds of reuniting with people who are so much more than familiar faces.

Bariki and Joel, the mess waiters, smiled when they hurried to shake my hand. "Welcome, Mama. It is good you are here."

John and Vincent, the chefs, did the same—I looked forward to their cooking again. My intention of losing weight on safari was nothing but a dream with these two in charge of the food.

Kidago, the water boy and all-around camp helper, had the biggest smile. He was so happy and friendly and good-natured—I hadn't realized how much I missed that smile of his.

The driver, Masenga, and the three trackers, Old Peter, Young Peter, and Maisai, were gracious and professional with their greetings—genuine to the core.

I didn't recognize any of the skinners and a few faces were missing. I decided not to ask. The reasons they were not there could be private and maybe even painful.

"You are hungry, yes?" John asked.

Lunch was a good idea, but I wanted to unpack first.

"How about forty-five minutes?" Cotton said.

"Half an hour is enough."

"Okay, thirty minutes."

"What have you prepared?" I asked

"Eland," John said

Knowing John and Vincent, there would be an assortment of sides, but if I had to pick one kind of wild game meat that I missed most from Africa it was eland. This was turning out to be a great day—and we still had the afternoon for hunting.

"If we're going to dent this list, we better get started," Cotton said after lunch.

Stefan knew the first day might be his last chance to join us on the hunt. After that, we planned to keep him busy with birds to skin. He jumped at the chance.

Fields were aflame across the savannah. The tall, dry grass under a cloudless sky burned quickly and within days green shoots of new grass began coloring the scorched ground. The migrating herds lingered on these patches of green earth, gobbling down the rich nutrients for the long trek ahead. This migration of beasts is one of nature's great spectacles. Driven by the need to find fresh grass and water, this mass of bodies moves north for four months, during which countless numbers perish from exhaustion, thirst, predators, and drowning while they cross the Mara River.

Along with the wildebeest, zebras, and Thomson's gazelles, we encountered dik-dik, waterbuck, baboons, Grant's gazelles, ostriches, vervet monkeys, and impala—all on the first afternoon. With a congregation of prey animals like that, opportunistic predators were surely waiting in the shadows.

"How about we start with something traditional?" Cotton said, pointing to a line of brush. "A group of guineas just ran into those bushes. Let's get this bird hunt started."

Several guineas burst into the air—one crumpled from a load of lead. Dick's second blast missed. The lumbering birds landed in an open field and kicked dust from their feet as they ran for safety. Dick and Cotton returned to the vehicle laughing and carrying the helmeted guinea fowl by the neck. Bigger and slower than a pheasant, guineas are dark with white spots and have a bald blue and red head. Their dark tender meat falls off the bone.

Just before they reached the truck, Hillary spotted a crested crane walking behind a patch of tall grass.

"I saw them on the list," Cotton said. "They are one of the most magnificent birds in Africa. Let's see if we can sneak up on it."

A few moments later, Old Peter ran over and retrieved the downed bird. Before the day was over, Dick added a secretary bird and a sand grouse to the collection. Cotton wanted the guinea for us. The two Peters took the other birds. I saw them sharing the day's kill with Japhary while Kidago begged for a taste—I did not see them give in to his pleas. By the end of the hunt, they would all have their fill of birds and maybe even find a new favorite for the cooking pot.

Dinner conversation revolved around crested cranes and kori bustards and king fishers and how best to hunt the many different birds on the list.

The Portuguese family, Nuno, Alexandra, and their son, Lee, returned shortly after we crawled into bed. I thought I heard someone mention lion, but when a hunter brought a lion to camp, there was always a celebration, with honking horns, singing, and dancing.

I awoke at three in the morning to hyenas laughing, baboons barking, a leopard sawing, crickets chirping, frogs croaking, and lions roaring. I was a little nervous, but comfortable and happy. While I listened to the concert, it hit me. I was in Tanzania with good friends and good hunting. What else could I ask for?

LION LOOP: DICK

"We'll take the lion loop this morning," Cotton said. "Check some baits, maybe shoot a Tommy for leopard. It feels like a good day to hunt a lion."

"Are there bad days to hunt lions?" I asked.

"Maybe the day your daughter is getting married. Other than that I can't think of one."

"We have four daughters—so I guess there are four bad days to hunt lions."

After shooting a Thomson's gazelle, we went to check on a lion bait that had been hung the night before.

"The migration may keep them from hitting the baits, but there are so many lions in the area right now, we could find a fresh track or stumble into one."

"What about buffalo?" I said, pointing to the same herd Old Peter was pointing to.

They were so far in the distance that they looked like a big shadow moving across the horizon. Every back in the truck straightened. Buffalo tend to do that. The sight of buffalo holds the promise of adventure; the possibility of a long day tracking under a hot sun; the chance to face one of the world's great beasts; the scent of danger. Buffalo hunting has never been confused with boredom.

It looked like a herd of about fifty—not huge, but too big to be a bachelor herd. A small group could be a herd of dagga boys—ultimately what you look for when hunting buffalo. You still check every herd—dagga boys aren't always alone and any buffalo with a hard, well-developed boss and at least nine years of tough living behind it is a good buffalo. This herd had a couple of wide-horned bulls, but they had soft bosses. We moved on. Maybe someday, when they'd had time to grow old and cranky, we would meet them again. I looked forward to it.

"Lion." That one word from Hillary refocused our adrenalin.

It was a lone female keeping a close eye on the buffalo, most likely waiting for one of the young to move away from the herd. Lions are social cats—a female hunting alone would be rare. We glassed every clump of grass and every shadow. Lions have the ability to disappear in the sparsest cover.

We spotted two more females focused on the buffalo. Then, fifty yards behind them, an old male stood at the edge of long grass.

"That's the one."

Once we stepped down from the Land Cruiser, we could no longer see any of the lions over the brush.

"I'm not sure I like this," Mary said. "If he gets into that tall grass after the shot, it will be too dangerous."

"I'll make sure Dick shoots straight," Cotton said.

"How?"

Cotton placed his hand on my shoulder and looked me in the eye. "Shoot straight, Dick."

"You two are not funny. This is serious."

Cotton and I were not taking anything lightly, but laughter eases tension. By the time we walked away, we were focused.

With both Peters leading, we hiked in a big half-circle to keep cover between the lions and us. We had only seen three females, but knew there were probably more in the area—the last thing we wanted to do was stroll into one. Using the brush for cover, we slid into position less than one hundred yards from the lion. He was staring at us.

I rested the forestock into the shooting sticks. The lion looked from us to the grass and then began an unhurried walk toward it.

"You must shoot him before he gets into the grass."

I hurried. I shouldn't have. Too far back. The lion spun, attacking whatever it was that just bit it. Holding steady on the next shot, I put the big cat down with a .375 bullet through its heart.

"Hold on him." None of us had moved yet.

A lioness growled and bared her teeth. The other two had disappeared. When the irritated female took a few quick steps in our direction, I shifted the rifle toward her.

Cotton had his rifle up as well, but must have sensed my movement. "Stay on the male," he said.

I concentrated on the male's chest and tried to block out the female's angry growls. I heard fast, heavy steps. She was coming. It took all I had to keep myself from shifting focus to the female. I heard her stop. One more snarl, then silence.

When she disappeared into the tall grass, we relaxed. We waited for another half an hour before approaching the male. Holding our guns on him, we slowly walked the final few feet, uncomfortably aware of the fact a lioness might be hiding in the grass.

We stared at the huge beast for a moment—some of us from reverence, some just trying to figure out how we were going to load it into the Land Cruiser. Our first attempt involved Masegna, Old Peter, and Maisai jumping into the back to pull on a leg and the tail while the rest of us pushed and pulled from the ground. We never got its hindquarters over the high tailgate. Logically, we tried the head next—not a chance. By then, we were laughing too hard for frustration, but were balancing on that precipice.

Cotton grabbed a long rope from under the seat. Tying one end to the lion's back legs, we wrapped it around the roll bar in front of the high seats and then tied the other end to the base of the only close tree. It had a six-inch diameter. Would it hold up to the tension of a five-hundred-pound beast? We were about to find out.

Masenga inched the vehicle forward while the others guided the lion's hindquarters over the tailgate. You could hear the rope stretching and something creaking. I couldn't tell if it was the Land Cruiser stressed from the weight or the tree screaming that it was about to snap. Mary and I moved a safe distance to one side.

The roll bar, the rope, and the tree held. By ten in the morning on the second day we were headed back to camp with a cat that had eluded our focused efforts during our previous visit. Hunting has the ability to humble men and women who are champions of their industries. It can also embolden the meek and give them the confidence they need to face other challenges in their lives. Hunting the Big Five adds another dimension.

Two miles from camp, Masenga began honking the horn. Old Peter and the others started singing. More voices joined in as camp came into view. Every staff member danced and sang around us as we drove to the skinning shed. When Masenga parked in the shade, Peter and the boys pulled me from the truck and led me to a green chair. Then four of them hoisted me to their shoulders and carried me around camp, dancing and singing. When they finally put me down, each of them waited to shake my hand. They said "good job," "good lion," and "good shot." I said thank you. Then I asked Old Peter why we had so much trouble loading the lion when I weighed just as much and only four of them could pick me up.

He laughed and shook his head. "No, no," he said bringing over a tape measure. He held it up to me and then to the lion. "Lion very much big. Think it just eat hippo too—ugh." He held his hands out by his stomach.

Exhaustion replaced adrenaline. Mary and I walked to the tent where I fell asleep immediately. Two hours later Mary woke me. "You snored the entire time," she said.

"I guess that means you didn't sleep."

"I did a little. Mostly I caught up in my journal and tried to get my curling iron to work. I guess I won't be able to look good this entire trip."

"You look good now."

"My hair's flat and dry."

I had learned not to argue about it.

"Congratulations on your lion," she said and gave me a kiss. "He's beautiful."

"It's your turn."

"I hope I don't wound one. You know how dangerous it can get."

"You won't," I said.

"I hope not."

"You worry too much."

"You don't worry enough."

"There's no reason to worry if you don't wound one."

"That's easy for you to say," she said. "You've already got one in the skinning shed."

We took it easy the rest of the day, shooting a few more birds off the list. Just hunting and having fun.

We waited on the Portuguese family for dinner. It was our first chance to sit down and talk with them. Nuno, Alexandra, and Lee had hung baits all day. Their eyes were heavy. Nuno had many questions about the lion and throughout the meal always managed to shift the conversation back to the hunt.

Cotton and I retold the story so many times we had the exaggerations memorized. I wondered if Nuno would retell his story as often as he wanted to hear ours. I hoped it turned out to be a good story.

A breeze whispered through the trees that night. Behind that, the voices of hyenas and baboons. It was an enjoyable way to fall asleep.

"We're going to a big waterhole where we can have our fill of birds," Cotton said.

"How long is the drive?" Mary asked.

"About an hour."

"Maybe I can get some sleep," she said.

Mary drifted off once or twice during the drive, but never for long. The bumpy trail roads and open-air seats of the Land Cruiser prevented real rest. Had she been sleeping, she may have missed the cheetah. The fastest of all land predators, the cheetah can reach speeds up to seventy miles per hour and, within three hundred yards, can outsprint any prey animal.

"There is an ongoing debate here in Africa about whether the cheetah is more of a dog or a cat," Cotton said. "Their call is more like a bark than a roar and they have feet like a dog's with non-retractable claws. They are also the only cat to hunt almost entirely during the day."

"That is if you believe they are cats," I said.

"You have a point. What do you think, Mary?"

"I think they are beautiful."

"Well put."

We watched the cheetah for fifteen minutes hoping we might catch it during a hunt, but it was in a lazy mood.

Dry, yellow grass and gray trees and bushes painted the savannah in a constant hue that at first glance appeared desolate. There was more to it than its initial appearance, but when contrasted against the vibrant colors at the waterhole, the differences were distinct. No matter how many wildebeest and zebra swarmed the savannah, it seemed almost uninhabited when compared to the party at the water.

Water sustains life. In a place like Tanzania, where water was hard to come by, they became great gathering places. Trees grew tall and strong. New grass shot from the ground like green fire and animals of every size came to drink, eat, and hunt. Birds arrived as if it was the last water source on earth.

"I have used that line of trees to sneak up to this waterhole," Cotton said. "Always lots of birds. We should be able to take our pick. Then we can sit and let them come to us."

A few birds scattered from the trees and two duikers darted from behind bushes as we hiked toward the water. The closer we approached the more birds we encountered.

For the next two hours, we sat in the tall grass and blasted at birds as they flew overhead. We spent most of the morning laughing and admiring birds up close that we had observed from a distance for years.

Any time we arrived in camp with a pile of birds, most of the staff gathered around the vehicle to admire the colorful fowl and to argue over who got what. Cotton always picked the guinea fowl, doves, and francolin for us. After that, it went down the staff pecking order: trackers-skinners-drivers-cooks-watchmen-cleaning/laundry crew-waiter-water boy. The game guard, though not official staff, seemed to rank somewhere around the driver/cook section of the hunting camp ladder. They had all earned their position on the staff and locals considered Cotton's hunting camp the best place for employment in the area. Working for hunters made you "rich."

Driving into camp with birds was also one of the few times we actually saw Stefan. We brought him along to make sure the birds were skinned properly. Boy did he work. He started after breakfast and if we brought in birds for lunch, he worked until after dark, sometimes missing dinner. His "working" trip to Africa was just that. When we did get to spend some time with him, we enjoyed his company. Stefan was a great taxidermist and a good man. Cotton called him "interesting." I thought "strange bird" seemed more fitting, considering his chosen profession and lanky physique.

The Portuguese family arrived as we sat down for lunch. Apparently, Nuno had wounded a lion that they could not immediately locate. His professional hunter came back for Cotton's assistance. Grabbing a hunk of gazelle roast and a slice of bread, Cotton and both Peters left to help sort it out.

Alexandra and her son stayed in camp to have lunch. She was visibly shaken.

"Cotton is a very good PH," Mary said to her.

She nodded before changing the subject by asking about our children.

"That's why I'm afraid to shoot the big cats," Mary said once we were in our tent. "If you wound one, it puts too many people at risk. Joan would be pulling her hair out if she were here."

The next three hours in camp were quiet. Tension filled the hot air as we waited to hear the rumble of the Land Cruiser grinding down the trail road. The normal chatter from the staff quarters and the kitchen was gone; the birds seemed to have disappeared; even the water in the nearby river felt hushed. The silence added to the growing apprehension. Would they find the lion? Would they come back safe?

Alexandra and Lee busied themselves walking back and forth from their tent to the kitchen, retrieving water and snacks, taking walks down by the river, and strolling around camp—anything to keep their minds from the *what-ifs*. I wanted to tell them that worrying did no good, but Mary always seemed offended when I told her that. So I read a book and listened as the air grew still and the river whispered.

When they finally came back, there was a collective urge to run to the vehicle for an update. They weren't smiling and they weren't bloody.

The son was the first to the Land Cruiser. He peeked into the back without saying anything.

"We saw him once," the father said. "But we were unable to shoot. We did not find blood. I must have missed."

Later, Cotton told us that he was sure it had been a miss as well. When they found the lion, it seemed healthy. The other PH also told him that the only person in the truck who insisted the father had hit it was the father himself. It took two hours of following a bloodless track and then spotting a healthy lion for him to admit it. Nobody likes to admit a miss. It was better to be safe and make a thorough check. Cotton was glad that they saw the lion and were able to ascertain its health.

"There was no blood, he appeared to be walking normally, and every one of us saw a healthy lion."

"I'm just glad it wasn't wounded," Mary said.

So many zebras dotted the savannah that all we had to do was pick out a stallion and we would be done. Right. Like most truly wild animals, zebras rarely allow you to walk into shooting range. Since the first humans walked barefoot across those plains, they hunted big-game animals such as zebras. Over time, they developed longer-range weapons and became more efficient at hunting. Like all prey, zebras learned a healthy fear of this super-predator.

We struck out way too many times, but the sheer numbers tipped the scale in our favor and we eventually caught one off guard.

The zebra provided enough meat to bait a number of trees. We spent the next day hanging and dragging meat in likely looking areas. It's long, dirty, boring work, but one of the only ways to hunt leopard in Tanzania. Its effectiveness depends on many factors, but when a leopard scrambles up a tree just before dusk and stares into the distance with those mesmerizing yellow eyes, all the laborious and monotonous hours fit into that moment as a memory well worth the effort.

When we left the last freshly baited tree, Cotton said, "If we walk the edge of a nearby waterhole, we should find some sand grouse."

We shot ten and drove back to camp like kids who had been set free to explore nature in the most natural way possible—as a part of it.

Over the next few days, we checked and hung lion and leopard baits, Mary shot a topi and a magnificent Thomson's gazelle, we ate a disturbing amount of food, we shot some of the most amazing birds we had ever seen and missed even more. We managed to laugh every day and often forgot that our lives, well-lived by some standards, had been filled with so many years that we were closer to death than birth. We were surrounded by death everyday, but somehow felt more alive than we ever thought possible. Africa gives you that like no other place on earth. We loved her for it.

HUNTERS WATCHING HUNTERS: MARY

"Are there any fields not on fire? I don't know how much more of this smoke I can take," I said. It seemed as if hell was battling for control of Africa.

"I can feel ash in my lungs and my vision has started to blur."

"I admit it. We're a country of pyromaniacs."

The apparent madness of destruction was not madness at all, but a way to invigorate life. Fire occurred naturally in grass that dry, but professional hunters sometimes gave Mother Nature a nudge. After a field burned, new grass replaced the old quickly. Previously yellow fields turned from black to green in a matter of days. Without fire, the migrating game would walk by, taking most of the lions with them. The new grass held them a few more days and helped sustain them for the remainder of their trek.

Like most mornings, we went to complete the lion loop, checking baits with the hope a cat had fed. Like most mornings, the first bait was untouched. We were staring up at meat darkening by the hour. With that kind of smell, every predator within fifty miles should have been coming to investigate. With nothing more than a few hyena tracks, we decided to move to the next bait—maybe shoot a bird or two along the way.

A whistle stopped us.

"Looks like Peter has found something," Cotton said.

Until that moment, I thought Young Peter was with us at the base of the tree. Either he was a sneaky fellow or my perception skills needed practice.

When we caught up with him, he pointed out four sets of lion tracks.

"Females," Hillary said.

"Come, come." Young Peter waved us to follow him. Thirty yards further, he pointed to another track—much larger than the others. "They go to river," Peter said. "No like *nyama*."

Cotton said, "Let's drive to the river and see what we find."

The trees gradually became more abundant as we approached the Grumeti River. By the time we stopped next to the bank, everything was green and thick with leaves and heavy grass.

"There." Hillary pointed. "On the other side. Female."

She gave us an annoyed look before trotting into the grass.

"We know there is a male with her. We'll go shoot a wildebeest and hang some fresh meat. This may be your cat, Mary."

The idea of shooting another lion with Cotton both terrified and excited me. It was like that when I hunted any of the Big Five. I wanted to do it. I knew I could. Part of me needed to. There were many reasons why. There were also many reasons I did not want to. The fear that I may wound a dangerous animal was right at the top. Killing one of those magnificent creatures was also emotionally draining. The highs and lows and the grinder that so many of your emotions had to pass through was a feeling like nothing on earth. But it comes at a price. You must kill a beautiful beast. A beast you admire, respect, and love. It was part of being a human hunter—the hardest part. Maybe that was why we, in the Western world, had walled ourselves out of nature—we had become too sensitive to face the truth. When you hunt a great beast, such as a lion, it stays with you forever.

Wildebeest were even more plentiful than zebras. They were also more skittish. Any hint of danger had them jerking their heads and kicking dust into the air. But wildebeest sometimes offered a quick window when they stopped to look back. Sometimes they did so while still in range. A good bull did just that and I shot him.

An animal doesn't get labeled as "crazy" if it acts predictably. Most animals would drop within a few yards after being hit like that. This bull acted as if I had hit him with a pellet rifle, not a 7mm. He ran until he was nearly out of sight. Then he looked back, standing there as if I had not shot him at all. We watched him through our binoculars, afraid of how far he might run if we pushed him. He glanced forward, stumbled two steps to his right and fell over. His back legs and tail flung into the air once—then stillness.

Hurrying back to the river, Cotton searched for a good tree to hang the bait. The Peters quickly attached it to the tree with a chain, suspending it high enough so hyenas could not reach it but lions could. Then they dragged the stomach and intestines around in a wide crisscrossing pattern, leaving a blood and scent trail a blind cat could follow.

"Here kitty, kitty," I said.

Hillary got a kick out of that—he kept repeating it and laughing the entire morning.

"They should feed tonight," Cotton said. "We will come back first thing in the morning to check. If they did, we'll be sitting in a blind tomorrow evening. I know how much fun you have sitting in a blind."

"I'll sit anywhere you like, for as long as you say, as long as I have a good rest to make a perfect shot."

We spent the rest of the morning hunting birds. At one point, Dick shot a vulture that fell with its wings spread into an umbrella acacia. Young Peter zipped up his blue jumpsuit, put on Cotton's leather gloves, and covered his head with a stocking cap. When we were hanging leopard baits, I saw how easily he climbed a much taller albizia tree as if he were using a ladder. Thorns were the problem now. Only fifteen feet in the air, this tree was no match for Peter. The branches however, grew close together and were covered in an impenetrable wall of needle-like thorns—a slight touch often produced blood. He climbed as far as the thorns allowed, but the vulture was still out of reach. He asked for the shooting sticks. With those, he could move the bird, but getting it through the thorns proved more difficult. For fifteen minutes, he prodded the lifeless feathered form closer to the edge of the tree. It should have fallen off, but like the talons of a raptor, the tree held on. When Peter could no longer touch the bird with the stick, he climbed down.

Balancing on the highest point of the Land Cruiser, Hillary used the shooting sticks to knock the bird to the ground.

"No more shooting above acacias," Cotton said.

Even with all the new scratches and punctures in his suit, Young Peter was smiling. He was always smiling.

We talked about starting fires, shooting birds, and lion hunting while we ate kori bustard sandwiches for lunch. I knew the guinea fowl and sand grouse and dove would be great, but I did not expect the kori bustard to taste so delicious. It had a similar taste and texture to turkey. Africa always found ways to surprise us.

The scorched earth turned the natural oven of the day into a broiler. We tried not to breathe in the smoke and ash and pinched our eyes shut. The lone solace was the lack of tsetse flies stinging and pestering us. You would think hell's minions would bask in blackness and smoke.

Often those burned areas stopped at a wall of tall, dry grass. Why the fire chose that line to die out I could only guess, but it was almost as if hoards of those irritating flies were waiting for us. Within moments, there were swats, slaps, shoos, and stings throughout the Land Cruiser. We could not drive fast enough to escape.

"Look at that wildebeest," Cotton said. "It's injured."

As we drove closer, it tried to run, but didn't make it far.

"It will not live through the night," Hillary said.

"It might not make it through the next hour," Cotton said. "Look over there."

A mother cheetah and her two nearly grown cubs stood watching a wildebeest herd walk by in the distance.

"As soon as they see it, it's done for. A young wounded wildebeest is perfect practice for cheetahs of that age. We should stay and watch—people wait lifetimes to see a kill."

We drove a short distance, turned, and waited. The cheetahs studied the marching wildebeest, searching for an opportunity to strike. They kept their profiles low to the ground but didn't move. The wounded wildebeest was in no hurry to give away its position.

After half an hour, the wildebeest herd had mostly marched away and the cheetahs had relaxed. Masenga fired up the engine and drove the vehicle between the cheetahs and the disappearing herd. The three cats stood erect and stared at us as if we were standing in front of a television set during the best part of a movie. When they finally decided to move, it only took a moment for them to notice the wounded wildebeest.

The mother cheetah charged toward the wildebeest. When it didn't run, she slowed, circling in an attempt to avoid its horns. The two younger cats held back and watched.

Unwilling to go without a fight, the wildebeest swung its horns at the cheetah. She easily avoided them and after four failed attempts, managed, the fifth time, to jump onto the animal's back. She reached her mouth around to the front of its neck and clamped down. It struggled only a moment before giving in to its inevitable fate.

The cheetah strolled over to join her cubs. They watched us, apparently unwilling to feed with spectators. We waited with the video camera rolling, but they did not budge.

"If lions or hyenas catch the scent, they may not get to feed at all. We'll leave them be," Cotton said. "Cheetahs have a hard enough time as it is. They are always being chased away from their kills."

The three cats stared, waiting for us to leave them in peace. Behind them, a line of misty mountains overlooked a river of tall trees like a barrier separating two worlds. When we drove away, I wished them good hunting. In response, they did what cheetahs do—they trotted over to the kill and began to feed.

That night after the hyena and baboons and lions gave way to the sounds of the river, chatter built from the staff quarters. After fifteen minutes, the racket had grown. Two voices stood out above the rest. They must have been much closer. They were not speaking English and seemed to care little that others might be sleeping, or trying to sleep. I had no idea how Dick could snore through all that.

"Hey!" It was Cotton's angry, tired voice. "Shut it down."

The chatter died down briefly, but picked back up, this time only the two close voices—the staff quarters were silent.

"I said keep it down." Again, from within Cotton's tent.

It was as if they hadn't even heard him.

"What the hell is going on out there?" The tent unzipped. "I've got clients trying to sleep here."

I heard him yelling for a few moments catching only a few words and phrases— "I don't care" or "quiet" or "sleep."

I don't know what he said to them, but it did the job. I didn't hear another peep all night.

Cotton was all smiles while we drove the tedious rounds checking lion and leopard baits. After three leopard baits—nothing. After one lion bait—a hit. From the look of the tracks, it was a single lion, medium-sized paw, most likely a male.

I breathed sparsely as we searched the area around the putrid bait for tracks and hair. A long mane hair would verify a male; a short hair would verify nothing. We found a single short hair.

"We can sit in a blind tonight if you want, but I would hate to waste our time on a young male or a female. Sitting in blinds is more uncomfortable than it sounds. Especially considering we'd still have to build one."

"Why don't we just check it again in the morning?" Dick said.

"I think that's the best option."

"Bwana Cotton. We must speak." Hillary pulled Cotton back to the vehicle. That's where I wanted to go, away from the stench, but I didn't want to interrupt their conversation. I tried not to gag.

Finally, Cotton waved us over. I let out the big breath that I had been holding.

"I assume you heard me yelling last night."

I nodded. "I don't think Dick did."

"It turns out the head of Tanzania's police was here talking to Japhary." Cotton pointed at the game guard walking beside Old Peter. "Hillary thinks I should get back to camp and iron things out before he leaves for Arusha. I think he's right. It was dark and I was tired, but I shouldn't let myself get carried away. I know this man. He is a good man, but if he wanted to, he could make my life hell. I hope I did not offend him."

Cotton settled in behind the wheel. Hillary took Cotton's normal spot and Masenga tried to get comfortable in back with the two Peters and Japhary. Though Old Peter and Young Peter were always smiling, hard working, and almost too polite, it was obvious they considered every other native in camp beneath them. They held the most prestigious job in a hunting camp. They were trackers. When Masenga hopped in the back, he sat in the corner by the tailgate. The two Peters stood proudly behind the high seats, unwilling to sit down while on the job that they had earned, disinclined to squander the respect they deserved.

The police chief was still in camp. Cotton led him to the kitchen where they could talk in private. Half an hour later, they came to our tent.

"I am Adam," the police chief said shaking our hands with both of his. "I am very happy to meet you. You come all the way from America. I would much like to see America some day. What do you think of Tanzania? It is beautiful, yes? My friend, Cotton, says this is your magazine." He held up a Cabela's catalog. "You are very famous."

"Would you like a catalog or a hat?" I asked.

"Yes. I would like that very much."

Slipping back into the tent, I grabbed three catalogs and two hats. A simple gesture like a small gift was still customary all over the world. If it was genuine, it could go a long way toward building or sustaining relationships.

"I hope your stay in my country is filled with much happiness. The hunting is good, yes?"

"Outstanding," Dick said.

"Very good. I am happy. If you ever come back to Tanzania, you can come to me for anything you need. Thank you." He held up the catalogs. "Thank you," he said again and lifted the hat from his head. He turned back twice to wave and smile as he walked to his car.

"He seemed like a nice man," I said.

"He is," Cotton said. "Some of these high official types get full of themselves and try to flash their power and strong-arm you into a bribe or something. He is one of the good ones. Probably won't last. The good ones rarely do."

That afternoon, we stalked the river's edge hoping for two things. One—to find kingfishers. Two—to avoid hippos. Cotton had left the big gun in the Land Cruiser. So, the entire time, I was a nervous wit, jumping at every rustle in the undergrowth.

Hippos wounded from fighting like to hole up in secluded places to recover. Few animals have the truculence of a wounded hippo on land. A big bull might run you down just for disturbing an afternoon slumber. If you are in between him and the water, he might run over you to get to the river. I wished Cotton had brought the big rifle.

When I missed a pygmy kingfisher, not once, but twice, I wondered if my concern for our safety had my focus otherwise preoccupied.

I did manage to bring Stefan a pygmy kingfisher. We also bagged two crowned plovers on the way back to camp—just enough to keep "the bird man" busy until dinner. Stefan seemed at ease in almost any situation. He made no excuses for who he was and made instant connections with most of the staff.

"Sorry I am late for dinner," Cotton said, sitting down after we had already finished a bowl of soup. "Dominic is ill with malaria. His fever is one hundred five." Dominic was one of the cleaning crew.

As always, I ate too much. The heavy spaghetti would help me sleep soundly for once. Cotton had finished his meal before I was halfway through with mine and he promptly excused himself to go check on Dominic. He came back a few minutes later.

"The fever is back up. I'm going to drive him to the hospital."

"Is there anything we can do," I asked.

"No. Thank you though, Mary. I'll see you in the morning. We'll leave at the usual time."

I don't know how Cotton was able to get any sleep that night, but he met us for breakfast at six and didn't yawn once. I was watching.

Early mornings were monotonous. We drove the lion loop with a few leopard detours. We inspected every leopard bait—nothing fed. We checked every lion bait—not a track.

After that, we drove around, searching for lions or their fresh tracks and gladly sidetracked ourselves to hunt birds. And when the sun got hot—it always got hot—we slumped heavily in our seats and rumbled back to camp.

In the evenings, around a crackling fire, we talked and laughed and even argued some. It was there, sitting under a starry sky with hyenas and lions and hippos calling from the darkness, that we understood just how important those moments were. The friendships we formed and the memories we created would remain a part of us forever and would help shape the years yet to come.

Over the next few days, the birds came in flocks. We shot ducks, plovers, vultures, cranes, geese, francolins, kingfishers, hornbills, and many other winged prey that kept Stefan up until morning's early hours. I shot a wildebeest for bait and camp meat or *nyama*. I took out its heart with one shot. My confidence swelled.

If not for the incessant itching from being chewed raw by tsetse flies, those days would have been the most relaxed and, in some ways, the most enjoyable of the hunt. The flies, however, felt it was their evil duty to remind me that Africa had a dark balance. Pain, hardship, and death were as much a part of the continent as joy, beauty, and life. For every mesmerizing sunset, there was a dying waterhole. For every smiling child, there was an adult, not yet thirty, but considered elderly because of shortened life spans. For every peaceful moment, there was a tsetse fly waiting to drink your blood.

The final day at the Fort Ikoma camp started out with a chill. At least that's what Cotton called it. I was freezing and I had a migraine and an upset stomach. Taking some Tylenol and Pepto-Bismol, I put three layers of clothes on and snuggled next to Dick as we drove the lion loop. By the afternoon, I was complaining to myself about the heat and the tsetse flies. When we ambushed a flock of guineas, I forgot about any pain or discomfort.

We drove to camp early in order to pack our bags for the Rungwa camp. I wasn't disappointed we didn't find a lion or leopard—we would concentrate on them in Rungwa, but an uneasy feeling came over me. Dick was nodding off—I don't know how on those bumpy trails. Both Peters were smiling, as was Hillary. And Cotton was staring quietly ahead, his thoughts apparently somewhere else. As we pulled into camp, the staff was busy preparing for our departure on top of their regular tasks. I looked at their faces. Each of them smiled and waved as we passed by. My eyes began to well up. I said a silent prayer and asked God to watch over them. I hoped they would remember me. I would never forget them.

HUNTING BUDDIES: DICK

Growing up, I hunted mostly with my brothers, Jim and Jerry, and anyone else willing to put up with a restless kid who couldn't get enough of the outdoors. The polio epidemic of the 1940s and 50s shackled me in leg braces and often left me feeling like a prisoner in my own home. After regaining strength in my muscles, you could not keep me indoors. Jim and I spent all our free time roaming the Nebraska prairie in search of adventure. Jackrabbits were our main prey, but back then, we weren't too choosy. Anything we could bring home to eat was a trophy, whether it swam, jumped, crawled, slithered, or flew. Our success rate must have hovered around five percent, but we were never freer than while hunting and fishing. There was a time when I believed we would spend the rest of our lives right there on the prairie outside Chappell, Nebraska, hunting mule deer and grouse everyday until it was too hot to do anything else but go fishing or swimming. For us, Tom Sawyer and Huck Finn were just ordinary boys doing the things we all did—or at least tried to do. We believed our youth would last forever.

Somewhere along the line, we allowed reality to get in the way of our aspirations. There was no distinct cut-off point where you forgot you were a kid and suddenly found yourself aspiring to be grown up. Time slowly replaces your youthful pleasures with things far less enjoyable and, eventually, you forget how fun playing in the dirt really was. Some of us, though, are lucky enough to remember a few things. I still find wonder, awe, and unrivaled enjoyment when I am stalking one of the earth's magnificent beasts—I just switched hunting partners. I guess some part of the woman I love forgot to grow up as well.

So, when we arrived at the Rungwa camp and Mary hurried to unpack, I knew why. It was early afternoon, plenty of time left in the day for hunting—the kids in us were ready to explore.

I shot an impala for leopard bait and asked Peter to cut out the liver before hanging it in a nearby tree. Taking one end of a rope, Peter pulled off his shoes and climbed the tree as if he had spikes on his feet and hands. Hillary tied the other end to the impala and we all watched as Peter hoisted it up, securing it so that it hung from the wide limb. Then, cutting off nearby leaves, he hid the bait from nosy vultures circling above. Anywhere else, an antelope hanging in a tree might seem out of place. In Africa, it is common for leopards to keep their meals high and dry.

When I was young, I envisioned hunting lions and tigers and rhinoceros, but I did not envision Africa. At least if I did, I allowed my imagination to gloss over it. Even after many visits, it still amazed me like no other place I had ever been.

Hanging leopard baits can take all afternoon—leaving little time for hunting. That day we finished with enough daylight so that we would have time for a stalk if we encountered a good trophy.

When Peter pointed out a kudu hiding its horns in the branches of an acacia, we decided it deserved a closer look.

"He had big bases," Cotton said as we weaved through the brush. "If his horns are as long as I think they are, he'll be a fine trophy."

The bull was standing in the open when we found him. "Shoot that bull," Cotton said.

A few moments later, we were walking toward a lifeless kudu. Cotton pointed out the horn's ivory tips and Peter wrapped his hands around their bases. Mary gave me a hug.

By the time we loaded the kudu into the truck, it was dark. Of all the so-called common plains game, the kudu is the most sought-after by traveling hunters. With black horns that spiral into the air, it is anything but common. These horns may be what first draw you to pursue the kudu as a trophy, but the hunter's desire to harvest one comes from a deeper respect for its worthiness as prey. It is called the gray ghost because of its ability to disappear. A big bull will stand perfectly still in the shadow of a thorn tree while you pass by. Even seasoned hunters look through these antelope as if they were more air than flesh and bone.

Kudu may be common throughout much of southern and east Africa, but easy to hunt—sorry. Even if you luck into one, as I did on that occasion, you more often come away with a fleeting glance than you do with a big bull in the back of the Land Cruiser.

Mary proved as much the following day.

It was the type of day that added fifty pounds to your weight. Without a breeze for relief, the sun seared our skin. Just driving around hanging baits felt as if we had been hiking all day. Days like that are not so bad if you are seeing game, but most animals are too smart to be out in that kind of heat. The only creatures silly enough to endure that discomfort are also willing to spend hard-earned money to do so. Sometimes, it is a wonder our species put a man on the moon.

Once again, late in the day, Peter noticed three female kudus standing in the shade.

"I want to glass the shadows," Cotton said lifting his binoculars.

The cows stared at us while we scanned the surrounding trees and bushes.

I was thinking we should move on when Cotton said, "There." Three kudu bulls lumbered across an open field with their horns tilted back. The cows were right behind them.

"*Ume*. Big," Peter said. He held his hands wide apart.

"That kudu in the front is bigger than Dick's," Cotton said. "Get your rifle, Mary."

Peter followed the tracks easily enough. A five-hundred-pound animal running across loose, dry dirt offers a distinct trail. Six of them created a road.

As easy as they were to follow, they were difficult to catch. They had stopped running twenty yards into the trees, but continued weaving through the forest as if they knew we were on their tails. With a gentle breeze blowing in our faces, it was doubtful they smelled us. Four humans stomping through the bush, however, do not sound like anything a kudu would want to wait for. As quietly as we tried to walk, as much as we tried to mimic Peter's soft steps, the kudu's big ears heard everything. After an hour, Peter stopped, pointed at the ground, and waved his hand toward the mostly dry riverbed.

"They've gone into the next hunting block," Cotton said. "They must know you are a crack shot."

"Are you being sarcastic?" Mary asked.

"Do I strike you has someone who even knows what sarcasm is?"

"As a matter of fact—"

"We best be getting back to the truck," Cotton cut her off. "It's getting awfully hot."

"That's what I thought," Mary said. "You can dish it out, but you can't take it."

"I can take it all right. I just don't want to right now. It's too hot."

"You know we love you, Cotton, but sometimes you're as impossible as Dick."

"Once again, I have no idea what I did," I said.

"You know. Maybe not right this moment, but you know."

"So now I'm in trouble for something I may or may not have done or may do in the future. I'll never understand how this works."

"At least she's focused on you now, my friend," Cotton said.

The following morning, we checked lion baits. The first one had been hit. There were three separate sets of tracks, one much larger than the other two.

"This could be your lion, Mary," Cotton said. "Are you ready?"

"You know I'm never ready for the dangerous animals."

"I know that's what you like to say, but you've never had any problems when the time comes. I'll tell you what. Let's shoot an impala for camp meat and leopard bait. It will be good practice."

"I don't like wounding impalas either," Mary said.

"You won't."

She didn't. She hit one perfectly and missed the next. I wished she had missed the first one instead.

"I'm worried about the lion tonight," she said after lunch. "I have no confidence. I'd never forgive myself if something happened because of my poor shooting. I don't know if Joan could ever forgive me either."

"You're worrying about things that will not happen. I know you can do it. You know you can do it. So, just do it."

As if anything I said could stop her worrying. Until it was over, she was going to badger herself. I understood the nervousness. Everybody wants to perform well, especially if poor performance means a creature suffers—or worse. But clinging to negatives rarely allows you to move forward.

"Just concentrate on small steps," I said. "Getting comfortable in the blind, finding a small target on the lion, squeezing the trigger—the rest will take care of itself."

"I'll try," she said. "It would just be easier if I wasn't shooting so badly."

Lions were at the bait when we arrived. Three of them. Two young females and one big, old female that looked as if her days were coming to an end. Her swagger had given way to a slow, drooping gait. Once a proud hunter and provider for her pride, she seemed resigned to the fact that she would probably eat last at a fresh kill.

There was no male.

I couldn't tell if Mary felt relief or disappointment.

"I guess I won't be wounding a lion tonight," she said.

"Or any other night," Cotton said. "You will shoot perfectly—I know you will."

"I just need to convince myself of that."

"Let's find something that will help to convince you. Perhaps a kudu or a roan. Maybe we'll even run into a big lion. That would be great."

"Maybe if I can hit a kudu, I'll feel better about the lion. I obviously wasn't supposed to shoot a lion tonight." She glanced to the sky. "Somebody must not think I'm ready."

We hadn't gone far before a small herd of sable galloped across the trail. A big bull led the charge. No antelope is more regal than a bull sable. Shiny black coat highlighted with distinct white facial markings, a thick mane of hair running down a muscular neck and a pair of scimitar-shaped horns that curve back like Native American war bonnets. The sable is one of the great trophies in all of Africa. They back up all that beauty and majesty with an unrivaled toughness among antelope. I've seen sable take shot after shot before finally hitting the ground and then, with their last ounce of strength, turn to fight with an admirable display of spirit. All wild creatures deserve respect—the sable demands it.

I doubted we would catch up to them. The momentum from their sprint across the trail road would probably push them at least one hundred yards. But you do not pass up opportunities in Africa. If you have a chance at a good sable, you take it.

It took us twenty minutes to find the herd. By then, they had staked out shady spots to escape the rising heat. One of the cows stared in our direction with that frightened and focused look many prey animals have when they sense danger. The bull was standing off to the right, his foreleg illuminated by a patch of light. The sun painted a bulls-eye on my target.

Cotton reached out to take the shooting sticks from Peter. Moving slowly, he opened them up two feet in front of my position. The moment did not need words. We could see the cow. We understood how quickly it could go from a perfect shooting situation to a stampede. I lowered the forestock onto the shooting sticks. When I looked through the scope, I found the bull. He was staring in our direction. I only had a moment before I would be left aiming at a small dust cloud. I touched the trigger just enough. I heard the bullet hit. The bull ran off with the cows as if I had missed.

We found him piled up fifty yards into the bush. When he saw us approaching, he kicked to regain his feet and raked his horns toward us. We shifted quickly into a better position and I shot again. Then it was over.

"Look where your first bullet hit." Cotton poked his finger into the entry wound. "It couldn't have been more perfect. It's amazing he didn't just drop."

It was a testament to the power and brute strength of a beast as tough as Africa itself.

Throughout the rest of the afternoon, we spotted fourteen lions, four of them males—none of them old enough. With that many big cats in the area, it was only a matter of time.

"Last-chance kudu?" Cotton pointed toward a bull standing tall on a distant slope.

"How much time do we have?"

"Not long. We better move."

Mary climbed from the truck. I handed her the rifle and let her go with Cotton.

Sunsets around the world can move you in ways few events can. A Tanzania sunset, surrounded by a wild Africa, brings out feral emotions you have never experienced. Masenga sat behind the driver's seat, but I watched the sunset alone. I wondered how anyone could question his or her faith at such a moment. That kind of natural beauty strengthened mine.

As God put the finishing touches on His latest masterpiece, I heard a rifle shot. Mary had found her kudu. A few moments later, I heard another shot, and another. One shot usually meant a kill or a clean miss. Two shots could mean she had to give him one more in order to ease any suffering. Three shots, unless with an animal like buffalo, usually meant the first shot had not been optimal.

Dusk brought a layer of cold air to the dying day. I slipped on my jacket. With each passing minute, the feeling that she was still searching for a wounded animal grew. I didn't like that feeling. My wife could shoot well, but she sometimes allowed one misplaced bullet to get into her head and rattle her. When one bad experience spirals confidence, it can take a long time to repair. Mary made up for her precarious shooting self-assurance with a determination that bordered on reckless. When hunting, she pushed herself beyond what most men would. If she needed to climb ten thousand feet to find a mountain nyala in Ethiopia, she would do so without complaint—even when the pain would hold most people back.

When they finally returned, I could not read their faces. All I saw was fatigue. I waited. Mary handed me her unloaded rifle and began to climb up.

"What happened?" I asked.

"Mary shot a fine kudu bull. We field dressed it, but need to get it loaded before the hyenas discover an easy meal."

When Mary settled in beside me she said, "I broke his front leg. It was horrible."

"It was a tough shot. You missed by an inch or two." Cotton said. "The bull was quartering away in heavy brush. She had a small window to shoot through and an unsteady rest. She did fine. You did fine."

"I wounded him. I wasn't one hundred percent comfortable with the shot and I took it anyway. It's my fault."

"Don't be so hard on yourself," Cotton said. "It happens to everybody."

"That doesn't make me feel better."

We drove to camp in relative silence. I wished her experience had been better, but was happy she got her kudu. Finding a big, mature bull that had a wary nature was tough with any species, but kudu were often a bit more cautious than other horned creatures. I knew hunters who had been to kudu-rich countries multiple times only to come away without a trophy bull. Mary got hers, and for that, I was pleased.

Returning to hunting camp after a long day often seems to take forever. Whether hiking down a mountain trail after stalking elk all day, or driving forty minutes along a bumpy track that barely passes for a trail road in Tanzania, you are so ready to relax beside a warm fire that you begin to count the minutes. Each step seems harder and each mile bumpier.

That night, it wasn't so bad. It had been a long day. Mary was a little down. But as we sat in silence rumbling down a trail that had become familiar, I realized how lucky I was. Surrounded every day by lions, buffalo, kudu, elephants, and all of Africa's creatures was enough. But to share it with my favorite hunting partner, to have my best friend sitting beside me—it was as if God had made the world just for me and, just to make it a little better, sprinkled a blessing over our slice of paradise. I did not pretend to deserve it, but I would always appreciate it.

CAT LADY: MARY

"Do you know what I did with my sweater?" Dick asked.

"Is it not in your bag?"

"I didn't look."

"Did you look anywhere?"

My husband shrugged.

He needed it that morning. I had bundled up in a long-sleeve shirt and a sweater and I was still cold. "Here it is," I said. "It was in your bag."

"Thanks."

I didn't answer him; I just gave him a look.

"I want to check the leopard bait first," Cotton said. "I have a good feeling today. If nothing has fed, we'll check the lion baits and see what we can find."

"Pretty much the same thing we do most days."

"If you can come up with a less tedious way to hunt lions or leopards, I'm all ears. Until then, let's go check some baits." Cotton stood and clapped his hands as if he was overly excited about the prospect.

In all my years of hunting, I had learned you should trust your feelings. You should at least explore them. When a professional hunter, with many years of experience, says he has a feeling, you should take notice. Checking baits was rarely exciting. Even if something had fed, you spent an hour or two building a blind and later sat in that blind for many more hours hoping the cat would return. Big cats come to a bait while you are in the blind about ten percent of the time—if you are lucky. But if you spend enough time checking baits and sitting in blinds, you will get your cat.

When we discovered the leopard bait had gone untouched, our optimism slid down a slope like it was on snow skis. It was in Cotton's eyes. It was in his slowed step. It was apparent in his silence. He had been sure a leopard would feed. It's never fun to question your gut. But what do you do when the hunting gods change the wind on you? You make a new plan or move on.

A rising sun joined us on the forty-five minute drive to the first lion bait. Before we arrived, Dick and I had each removed our sweaters. Dick even nodded off once. Game was sparse and the idea of inspecting rotting meat didn't fire up the senses. I think we all allowed ourselves to lull into complacency. When Peter told Cotton to stop the truck long before we could see the bait tree, I began scanning for roan or some other plains game. Peter jumped from the Land Cruiser and began studying the ground.

"*Simba*," he said. He joined his two middle fingers and his thumbs to form a big circle, showing it to us while he raised his eyebrows. Translation—big *simba*. The tracks were fresh and they were heading toward the bait.

Cotton tapped Masenga's shoulder.

He killed the engine and sat back in his seat.

Cotton then motioned for us to climb down and for me to bring my rifle. I didn't hesitate and I didn't protest. I may have been afraid to shoot a lion, but I still wanted to shoot one. At that moment, adrenaline trumped fear. Unwilling to miss the action, Dick climbed down as well. Of all the animals I had hunted, lions were the only ones that stared at me as if I were beneath them. It felt like they were looking for fear. I am sure they smelled it on me.

We followed Peter down the trail road for fifty yards before he veered left into the thorny brush. Fifty yards more, we slowed our steps and crouched. Stopping behind a clumped row of thin trees, Peter pointed toward the bait tree. Lying in the grass under the shade, a lioness stared into the day with three maturing cubs lazing beside her. I did not see a male. Apparently, Cotton didn't either. He scanned the area, checking every shadow and every slightly discolored patch of grass. He was sure the male was close. We all were.

Peter tapped Cotton's shoulder and whispered into his ear as he pointed past the tree. I searched with and then without my binoculars. I saw nothing but slightly swaying five-foot grass. Dick shrugged his shoulders. He didn't see it either. After another five minutes, Cotton leaned over and whispered in my ear.

"I can see the male, but only the back half of him. It might be immature. We could wait for him to move, but lions can sit for hours. I want to get a better look at him. Follow right behind me. Stay close and walk right in my footsteps." He motioned for everybody else to stay put and snatched the shooting sticks from Peter. I didn't care for shooting from the sticks, but it was better than off-hand. If I couldn't get steady, I wouldn't shoot.

Each step took at least ten seconds as we worked our way toward a row of bushes. Cotton watched the lioness more than the lion and I watched Cotton, paying extra close attention to his steps. He carried the shooting sticks in one hand and his big .450 in the other. My .375 seemed to be made from cement. My legs trembled with my weight until I could shift it with another step. When Cotton stopped, I stood directly behind him. From there, I could stand up straight and still be hidden. By then, a combination of fear, fatigue, and anticipation had my heart playing drums. My hands were shaking. If I couldn't calm down, I would never be able to shoot.

Cotton set up the shooting sticks. "Get him in your scope as if you were going to shoot," he whispered. "But do not shoot unless I tell you. I still can't see his face."

The lion was quartering away slightly. I found the shoulder through the scope and lined up the crosshairs. A small clump of grass obstructed the view of his head. I didn't expect him to move. He had not so much as twitched his tail. Then, as if he could hear my thoughts, he stood, turned his head, and looked in our direction. He was beautiful. I was terrified.

"Shoot him."

I heard myself breathing.

"Find your spot and squeeze."

I focused on the spot, forcing myself to look away from his eyes. I took a deep breath. My chest burned. My heart tried to pound its way out. It was a small target, but I did not think about that. I just thought about focusing on a single crease. I let the next moments go. I hardly remember them. The part of me that rarely gets used in day-to-day life took over.

When the bullet struck the lion, his muscles tensed and he jolted. Then he started to walk away as if the bullet had merely annoyed him.

"Again. Shoot him again."

It took me a moment to find him in the scope. When I did, I fired without hesitation. I expected a severe reaction this time, but it was not much different from the first shot. He walked a few more steps and then toppled over—dead.

"Reload."

I dropped two bullets before I was able to fill the magazine. My hands were out of control. How I stayed calm for that second shot, I will never know. I prayed the lion would not get up. No way I could shoot straight again. He did not move. Thank God.

The other lions had disappeared—hopefully miles away.

My first shot had been low and too far back. My second shot was perfect. Instincts can sometimes save you from yourself.

It took a while to sink in. It was after the singing and dancing and being carried around on the chair. It was after the celebration had drifted back into the normal hubbub of camp work. It was sitting quietly around a fire that danced like a glowing ghost to the primal rhythms of a place that has no real sense of time. I shot a lion. Me. A girl from Casper, Wyoming, whose mother sacrificed so much just to feed her children. That girl's life was so long ago, her home so distant, that this place, this Dark Continent, full of life and death, full of mystery, felt more like home. In that moment, I understood clearly who I was, who I had always been.

"Did you hear those strange sounds last night?" I asked.

"I didn't hear anything," Dick said.

"Of course you didn't, you were snoring before I crawled into bed."

"What did they sound like?" Cotton asked. He took a sip of his morning tea.

"It was kind of a grunting and rattling noise."

Hillary held up his hand and quickly finished his bite of toast. "I think what you heard was porcupine."

"It sounded more like a Sasquatch."

"I do not know this Sasquatch."

"It's like an ape-man," Cotton said. "It's a legendary American monster. I'm not sure if Africa has a version—most places do."

"Africa has many legends of monsters. We also have many real beasts we must live with every day. People, however, fear what they do not know."

"It's like that everywhere," Dick said.

The first leopard bait we checked that morning had a big-maned lion resting under the tree. He wasn't ready to allow anything to steal the meal that he could not reach. It was good to see another old lion even if we were done hunting them. For one, lions are always exciting to see. More importantly, it provided more evidence that lion numbers in the area were high enough that the limited quotas would have no negative effect on the population.

We drove around all morning checking leopard baits—nothing fed. Without a leopard blind to build and no big hartebeest or roan sightings, we headed in for an early lunch. It was hot anyway.

The waiters served impala stew over rice around the table. They placed a plate of French toast in front of me. A joke? Nobody was laughing. French toast was not my first choice for lunch—I would much rather have had impala stew over rice.

"Did you ask for that?" Dick said.

"No, they just brought it."

"I guess Waziri wanted to make you something special."

Not wanting to offend Waziri, I ate the French toast as well as a bowl of salad. I had a bite of Dick's stew. It was delicious. The French toast was soggy.

The next morning we found the same old lion sitting under the same, untouched, rotting bait. Only the most fearless or hungry leopard would risk feeding there. We sat and admired the lion's patience—it was more refined than our own—before moving on to the next bait tree.

There, we found what we were looking for—a gnawed-on slab of impala meat, massive claw marks on the tree, and fresh tracks. The leopard hadn't fed much. It should be back.

Time to build a blind. No matter how often you see it, it is always interesting. Two, maybe three, men who have never known anything other than the African bush, use only items from the immediate surroundings and, in a matter of minutes, fashion a solid, temporary, and highly functional structure. Old Peter, Masenga, and Young Peter used one tool—a *panga*—and cut down a pile of branches and a heap of grass. Then, they peeled bark from a nearby tree to tie it all together. When they finished, I could not push the grass blind over. If I had not seen them build it, I would look over it as if it were a natural part of the landscape. Those men survived in the bush because they had to. It is what they had always done. It is what their fathers and grandfathers did. What they saw as an easy, everyday task, I found fascinating.

"We have one more bait to check. It's far enough away that another tom might hit it. If that's the case, you'll be sitting in two different blinds tonight. Wouldn't that be something if you both shot your leopard on the same night?" Cotton had regained that confident, cheerful air about him. Shooting two leopards in one night was nearly unheard of. Cotton believed it was possible.

I did not know how I felt about sitting in a leopard blind without Dick. A leopard blind can be a scary place—dark, stuffy, intensely quiet. Most of the time, it is boring. You can do nothing but sit—no talking, no moving, no making noise of any kind. You can only stare at meat hanging in a tree for so long. But when your professional hunter tells you the leopard might investigate the blind, that it might look right into the shooting hole and that whatever you do, don't look it in the eyes, you can't help but get anxious every time a twig snaps. If I had to sit in a leopard blind without my husband, I would. I just did not want to very much.

On the way to the last bait, I saw a roan slip into the trees. Apparently, nobody else saw it—that was rare.

"I would still like to shoot a roan," I said.

Cotton said, "Okay."

"What about that one back there?" Maybe he wasn't any good and everyone else knew that with a quick glance. He looked bigger than any other I had seen.

Cotton tapped Masenga's shoulder, signaling for him to stop. When our PH saw the roan, he said, "Stop. Stop." We rolled a few more yards before coming to rest.

Until that point, every roan we encountered was running like there was a pack of wild dogs chasing it. This one kept his head down and walked slowly near thorn bushes and small trees thick with leaves. He had not given us a glance. Maybe he was going deaf and blind. He looked old. Old animals do not last long in the African bush. It would be fine with me if he did not see, hear, or smell us. Sneaking up to any wild animal, no matter the circumstances, is always exhilarating. If it is not, you either are dead or might as well be.

After a ten-minute stalk, we closed the distance to seventy-five yards—close enough for a six-hundred-pound animal.

While the trackers loaded the heavy brute into the back of the Land Cruiser, they pointed at the bullet hole and nodded approvingly. It made me feel better about shooting a leopard.

The second leopard bait had been untouched.

"Before lunch, I want to sight in the rifles," Cotton said. "You can never be too careful with leopards."

My .375 turned out to be two clicks low and one click right—not much, but now it was spot on. With leopard hunting, every fraction of an inch counts. I didn't want to take any chances and Cotton knew first-hand how quickly a leopard hunt could turn deadly—a leopard mauling is not something you want to experience a second time.

For lunch, the waiters passed out salads to everyone, including me. Then they brought the main course—kudu steak. I love kudu. Waziri himself delivered my plate last—it was not a kudu steak. "My treat for you." He beamed a big genuine smile.

I looked down at the plate and returned his smile as best as I could. I didn't make eye contact. It was a single boiled egg, covered in dough and deep-fried—beside it a small pile of carrots.

"Very good, Mama," he said. "Enjoy." He bowed and returned to the kitchen.

"What's that?" Dick asked.

"I think it's an egg."

"Would you like some of my steak?"

"Just a bite. This will be fine."

"You're going to eat it?"

"I guess Waziri thinks I don't like game meat."

I saw Dick talking to Cotton later. Waziri never cooked me anything special after that. I hoped he was not offended. He was a fine cook and it was nice he put forth the extra effort for me—I just did not care for his specials. I wanted to eat the animals we hunted.

Cotton, Dick, and I were in the leopard blind three hours before sunset. We read while we waited. A variety of birds called softly back and forth as if they were at some avian meeting. I heard go-away birds, hornbills, guinea fowl, hawks, and, as dusk approached, a lonely owl. It had a different call than any owl I had ever heard—a kind of quick *putting* sound.

When it was too dark to read, we put down our books and waited. Every once in a while, a baboon screeched from behind us. Other than that, it was quiet until right before dark. Then, it was as if the baboons had gathered for a massive battle. Screaming and screeching and hooting and growling.

Cotton leaned in so his lips almost touched my ears and whispered almost inaudibly. "The leopard is coming."

My eyes turned into baseballs. Was I ready to shoot a leopard? Would he get there before it was too dark to shoot? Did my leg really hurt that bad? My leg had felt fine before—now it was battling my nerves for attention. It would be too dark in less than five minutes

The baboons screamed and moved closer. The cat pushed them toward our position. Then a single loud screech cut off abruptly. The rest of the baboons went quiet. We were left listening to a slight ruffle of dry leaves dying on nearby trees. I felt the darkness closing in. It was like being in a windowless room with the door creeping shut.

"He killed a baboon," Cotton said. "He will not come tonight. It is too dark to shoot anyway."

We rolled into camp late, dirty, and tired—mentally exhausted. The excitement that a leopard had fed, the fear and self-doubt all day, the inability to communicate with people a few feet away, the silence taking my mind places I wished it would not go. The leopard was coming. The leopard was not coming. Darkness. Silence.

I should have fallen asleep as fast as Dick. A nearby lion bickering with a hyena prevented that. The lion sounded angry. He sounded hungry. Maybe he would eat the hyena and shut them both up.

I enjoyed the sounds of Africa—there was nothing like a lion roar or a hippo grunt, but I like to be able to see when I hear them. Everything sounds closer in the dark. I felt the vibrations in the lion's voice. When the hyena hollered back, it was as if they were taunting me. The big, mean bully everyone was afraid of and his annoying sidekick laughing at my fear.

I heard a distress call. I could not tell what it was, but it came from the same area where the lion had been roaring. I am sure he made a kill. I did not hear the lion or the hyena the rest of the night. Lying in bed, I thought about the next day—our last full day. As much as they frightened me—and they did frighten me—I knew I would miss the night sounds. I would miss the lion roars and hyena laughs. I would miss the sound of elephants snapping branches in nearby sausage trees. I would miss the strange cry of the bush baby. I would miss that unnerving sound of a leopard sawing as it patrolled the creek bed. I would always be able to hear them if I closed my eyes, but it was not the same. In the darkness of Africa's night, it felt different.

Our last full day in Tanzania started the way most of our days started since we had moved to the Rungwa camp—checking baits.

As we approached the first tree, a leopard sprung from its branches and darted into the brush. I only caught a glimpse of it, but excited chatter gushed from Cotton, Hillary, Old Peter, and Young Peter. I heard the word *ndume* more than once.

"What does *ndume* mean?" I asked.

"It was a male," Cotton said. "A big tom. We need to get some fresh bait in the tree. Peter and the boys will start building a blind while we go shoot an impala. You need to shoot that leopard. First, you need to shoot an impala. Think you can do that?"

"If I can't shoot an impala, I sure as heck better not try to shoot a leopard."

We found a small herd in short order.

"We'll just move into position and you can pick one out and shoot it. It doesn't matter if it's a male or female. Just take your time, pick your spot and bring home the meat."

The impala decided not to cooperate. Every time we tried to set up, they charged away. After the third episode, Cotton said, "The nice thing about impala is that there are plenty of them and they are easy to find. Let's let these be for now."

"I hope that wasn't the kiss of death."

For a while, I thought it was. We drove around for an hour looking for impala. Normally, we could not drive ten minutes without a herd running across the trail or grazing in a nearby field. When we needed one, they disappeared. Murphy's Law, I guess.

Eventually, I shot one and we hurried to hang it in the tree. By then, the boys had built the blind and it was time for lunch.

After Waziri served us *all* roan steaks for lunch, Dick took a nap. He fell asleep easily—as always. Too jumpy to sleep, I wrote in my journal, read a few chapters in the adventure novel I was working on, and said my prayers. The last thing I wanted to do before hunting leopard was to forget to say my prayers.

Another night in a leopard blind. Part of me could not wait. Part of me wanted to hide under the cot in the tent.

We were in the blind by four that afternoon. I had periodically been glancing out the shooting hole and was losing faith that the leopard would show before dark. I did not like it when they came after dark. It made me feel exposed and defenseless. Like the cat could see me, but I could not see it. I did not like that feeling.

At six o'clock, my muscles went tight. I heard a leopard sawing. It was just once and not for long, but I was sure I heard it. For the next twenty minutes, I stared out the shooting hole, waiting for the leopard I knew was coming. During that time, I saw nothing move and I heard nothing except a light breeze crinkling leaves. Maybe it had been my imagination. I glanced to the two men beside me. Dick was still reading his book. There was not near enough light in the blind anymore for that. Cotton was staring through his peephole. I watched him for a few moments. With a resolved focus, he rarely blinked. He thought a leopard was coming as well.

I watched Cotton for another minute, wondering if he intended to give me a signal. His stare never wavered. I gazed back through the hole—still nothing. My eyes burned and, though the air had cooled, I started to sweat. I rubbed my eyes with my thumb and finger and looked away. When I glanced back, a big tom leopard stood staring up at the meat. He had a beautiful coat with large rosettes and a muscled neck. His collar of rosettes under his neck ran bold and distinct on lighter, nearly white fur. He stood perfectly still, staring at what appeared to be a free meal. Even unmoving, I could sense his power.

Part of me wanted to grab my husband and holler, "Look at the leopard, Dick. Isn't it awesome?" Part of me wanted to shove my rifle barrel out the hole before it was too late. And part of me, the part winning, just wanted to sit and enjoy the rare moment.

With his mouth slightly open, his pink tongue resting on his ivory teeth, he turned his head slowly and stared with his haunting yellow eyes right at us. *Don't make eye contact.* Cotton had told us that more than once. Yet, the leopard's eyes were mesmerizing, like forbidden jewels in an Egyptian tomb. Behind those eyes, a calculating and fierce predator studied a structure that, only a day before, had not been there. My head kept telling my eyes to look away, but they did not listen. They were locked in the leopard's spell.

The tom climbed the tree, reaching the branch in two graceful bounds, his claws audibly scratching the bark. Once in the branch, standing above the bait, he turned to face us again. From there, he stared. This time his gaze was more than curious. It was piercing, menacing. He knew something was wrong and he knew whatever it was, it had something to do with the squared patch of grass that had sprouted stiff and heavy overnight. It felt as if he dared me to move. I rolled my fingers into a fist in an attempt to quell the trembling.

The leopard stared at us for nearly five minutes. Then, without so much as a glance at the bait, he climbed higher into the tree.

"Get ready," Cotton whispered.

I inched the rifle barrel out the shooting hole and tried to find the spotted cat through my scope. I found the bait. *Need to look higher.* I found leaves and branches. Had he climbed down the tree? No, I was certain he had gone up. I was moving only slightly, but it does not take much to tip off a leopard. A predator both capable of catching a mouse and taking down a waterbuck should have no problem pinpointing the clumsy movements of a human being. He was up there. I needed to find him before he found me.

What had been an empty branch a second before now had a leopard perched atop it looking down at the bait. He was standing broadside.

"Shoot him now." Cotton's whisper was no longer reserved and soft. It was forceful through clenched teeth.

Pick a single spot on the shoulder and fire. One spot. Squeeze the trigger. Aim. Squeeze.

The leopard's body whipped from the branch, but the claws from one paw gripped the wood. He dangled there for a moment, swinging gently like a pod from a sausage tree.

Then, the cat's limp body dropped, hitting the ground with a hollow thud.

"Yes!"

"Great shot!"

Excitement was always the first of many emotions when one of the Big Five went down. It was nothing like the way it looked on television. Relief, for so many reasons, that had built up finally blows like an erupting volcano. You could not hold it in if you wanted to. The tears and the sadness, they would come later.

At that moment, we cheered. If you are part of it—a true part of it—it is impossible not to.

That initial elation never lasts. Verification that the beast is done prevents it. We moved in cautiously and focused. I prayed the touch of Cotton's rifle barrel induced no reaction. Our leopard did not move. We hugged and shook hands. Then, though it happened without a word, reverence for a magnificent animal made us stop to stare. We stared for a long time.

The celebration re-ignited as we entered camp. The staff swarmed around the Land Cruiser singing and dancing. They carried me through the camp on the chair. One by one, they came to shake my hands and tell me "Good shot, Mama," or "Very good, Mama." They each posed for pictures from two cameras and were grateful when we handed them Polaroids. In some parts of East Africa, a few people still believe cameras steal their souls and only allow a picture if you pay them money—some souls are worth more than others I guess. If they believed it in Rungwa, it did not show—or they enjoyed being able to carry their souls around on a piece of glossy paper.

The celebration lasted well into the night. After dinner, the staff joined us around the campfire for more dancing and singing. Stephan joined in with the dancing and showed them a few moves they had probably never seen before. I know we had not. Stephan deserved a little party time. He had been working so hard on the backlog of birds we had from the Fort Ikoma camp. We danced and sang until the staff returned to their own quarters. I heard them late into the night. They deserved the party too.

After the staff left us at the fire, we sat quietly for a few moments and soaked in the night. Orange embers floated into a dark sky filled with so many stars that I felt small. Beyond the soft crackle of the fire, hyenas and lions bickered in the distance. Under them, the soothing melody of running water from the creek seemed to whisper that, for this moment, in this place, all was right with the world. I said an extra prayer of thanks that night. I thanked God for creating me and allowing me to see how His touch had given us all we needed. He would never reveal all its mysteries. Some people would search them out. Some would ignore them and others, like those of us around that campfire, would enjoy them. And if they remained mysterious—that was just fine with us.

PART IV
IF ONLY WE HAD KNOWN
1997

SECOND-CHANCE
LEOPARD: DICK

Hunting often fast-tracks friendships when personalities gel. Too often, those relationships are full of huge gaps of time when you have little contact until your next expedition. During the previous five years, we had spent a good deal of time with Cotton and Joan. We hunted with Cotton three times over that period—this would be our fourth. We had dinner with them occasionally in Denver, and they often joined us for our annual fondue party in Vail. Cotton was more of a hunting buddy than a guide. We were comfortable with Cotton and he was comfortable with us. We had hunted birds, plains game, and dangerous game together and we had never been let down.

Our plans to open more retail stores had many of our big cats earmarked for new Cabela's showrooms. Our own trophy room would not be complete without lions and leopards. Nobody hunted lions and leopards like Cotton. His success—and our success with him—spoke for itself. It was time to go back.

We met Cotton and Hillary in Arusha and took a charter plane to Rungwa. It was as if we had never left. Familiar faces greeted us: Bariki and Joel, the mess waiters; Old Peter and Young Peter, two of the best trackers in all of Tanzania; Maisai, the assistant tracker; Masenga, the driver; young Kidago, the water boy. They were all smiling. Peter's English had improved vastly. Our Swahili had improved by a word or two. They said, "Welcome." We said, "*Asante sana.*"

"It's good to be back," I said.

"It's good to have you back, my friend." Cotton gripped my shoulder.

I stood outside a tent I knew others had used, but that I considered ours. I always felt different when I was in Africa. Was it because any slight breeze was noticeable? Was it because I never knew what the day would bring? Or was it because I felt closer to creation, closer to understanding what it meant to be alive? It was all of that and more. I had missed the African sun. It was good to see her again. Later, she would set and the horizon would glow like fire and a lion would roar. After that, I would fall asleep happy.

Ten minutes from camp, we spotted a bachelor herd of buffalo on an open plain. They turned to stare at us as we moved away from the Cruiser. The five of them formed a half-circle and took a few steps toward us, more curious than anything else. The air beneath their bellies filled with dust. The lead bull lifted his head and glared down his nose as if he were aiming.

We had walked straight toward them. Normally, you had to be extra cautious stalking buffalo. You had to be careful to keep the wind in your favor, to be quiet, to move only when all eyes were facing away. This group of old *dagga boys*, however, carried themselves with a certain arrogance, like a small band of elite soldiers. They had lived long enough to survive lion attacks and drought. They had lived long enough to stare down death. Together, they must have felt indestructible. Nothing messed with a crew like that and they knew it.

The bull on the left stood with its nose toward the ground showing off his heavy boss. He knew how to use it. He took a step forward, his hulking body moving next to that of the lead bull. Together, they formed a thick wall of muscle, horn, and tenacity.

"I don't have a shot," Mary said.

"If he lifts his head, I want you to shoot him low in the center of the chest."

I saw Mary give Cotton a questioning look, but he was concentrating on the buffalo. I knew what she was thinking. The full frontal shot was risky. Slightly off to the right or left and you miss everything, leaving yourself with a wounded and enraged Cape buffalo. It doesn't get more dangerous than that.

Mary settled back in behind the scope. We waited. How much patience did a buffalo have? How much did we have? How long could it hold that position? What about Mary?

A bull from the back moved around the edge. When it muscled beside the shooter, Mary's bull lifted its head.

"Take him."

Nothing.

"Whenever you're ready."

Never one to rush a shot, Mary waited until she was completely comfortable.

The echo of the bullet's deep impact hung in the air like the building dust cloud behind the fleeing *dagga boys*.

Old Peter grabbed the shooting sticks from under Mary's forestock and hurried after the buffalo. We followed.

It was easy to stay with them across that open plain. Just watch the dust cloud. They headed for an area where thin trees grew close together. Visibility would drop to less than fifty yards in any direction. Before they reached them, the wounded bull stopped. The others stopped with him. They all turned to face us.

Blood ran from the bull's nose like water. His head was turned toward us, but his body was broadside.

"Shoot him again."

This time Mary didn't hesitate. She dropped the gun into the shooting sticks and squeezed. The bulls lumbered into the young trees. Then silence.

Old Peter pointed out blood every few steps. What began as a multitude of tracks became a single track here and there along with splatterings of blood on dead leaves. We moved five yards at a time, checking the tracks and then stopping to glass. Buffalo were known for doubling back for an ambush. A few steps then glass, always looking in every direction and listening to the silence for any indication we were closing in.

When we found him, he stood alone facing some unknown object to the east. Just before Mary hit him with another round, he turned toward us, his eyes going quickly from recognition to rage. The impact of Mary's bullet staggered him. He regained his footing briefly and then fell. Moving closer, Mary shot him twice more before it was over.

"It's a fine buffalo," Cotton said.

"I had to shoot him five times."

"That has more to do with the buffalo than your shooting." Cotton handed her a bottle of water. "When the boys finish cutting it up, I'll show you the bullet holes in the heart and lungs."

Old Peter, Young Peter, Masenga, and the game guard all pitched in to field dress, skin, and quarter the buffalo. It took an hour. When Young Peter pulled out the heart and lungs, Cotton had him bring them over.

"Where did the Mama shoot?"

Young Peter held up the heart first and put his finger through a hole on one side. "Here," he said. Next, he pointed to another hole in the lower right lung. "And here."

"Both of those were fatal shots. Many have said it before, but it is true—buffalo are the only animals that will kill you after they're dead. This old bull was dead after the first shot; he just didn't know it."

We spent the next two hours hanging buffalo meat for lion baits. We saved the best cuts of meat for ourselves and for the camp staff. At each tree, we spent fifteen minutes dragging a scent for the lions to discover. I had never seen anything go to waste in Africa. Even if a lion or leopard did not feed, you dropped the meat and it was gone within hours. Tanzania was full of opportunistic carnivores. They hunted when they needed, but would take any meal they could find.

A female leopard fed on one bait, hyenas had fed on one of the lion baits, and what appeared to be a large leopard fed on the final bait. Too late to build a blind before dark, we would check it again in the morning. If the cat returned, then we would build a blind. We refreshed six of ten baits before heading for camp. On the way back, Mary shot a Lichtenstein's hartebeest. We placed it in the back and took it to camp to have it skinned and deboned. You could almost see the staff salivating when we brought it in.

Cotton seemed deep in thought. Other than some small talk, it was a quiet breakfast. The silence continued throughout the morning. We would drive to a tree and check the bait. Cotton, Hillary, and both Peters would hold a brief discussion and then we would drive to the next bait.

"We need to shoot an impala for bait," Cotton said stepping away from the truck.

We slipped along a brush line until piercing the one hundred yard mark on an impala ram. One shot later, he was in the truck. Peter did not gut him until we reached the bait tree. He made an extra effort to splatter blood as far as possible. Then, as if he had a leopard's claws, he scrambled up the tree with a rope. Young Peter tied the other end to the impala. Within a few minutes, Old Peter had it hoisted up and secured to a sturdy branch. He threw a few leaf-covered branches over it to hide it from vultures and shinnied back down.

"Good spot," he said. "Bwana shoot leopard here."

"No," Hillary said. "Bwana will shoot his leopard tonight. The leopard will come to the zebra bait."

"What do you think, Cotton?" Mary asked.

"There's a good chance the leopard will come again tonight. The rest is up to Dick."

"So if anything goes wrong, you can pass blame." I had never seen Cotton pass blame before.

Pointing his finger back and forth between himself and me, he said, "At least we understand each other."

When we pulled up to the last bait tree, Peter and Hillary jumped from the Cruiser and ran to it. They looked up into the tree, put their hands on their foreheads, and carried on about something.

"What's going on?"

"Can you see the bait up there? Does it look any different than yesterday?"

"It's pulled up on the branch," Mary said. "It's not hanging anymore."

"That's the entire back half of a zebra. No small leopard did that. You ready to sit in a blind tonight?"

"What did I say?" Hillary and Peter were walking back toward the vehicle. "What did I say? I said Bwana Dick will shoot his leopard tonight. Right here." Hillary pointed into the tree. "It is a big *chui*. You will kill your leopard tonight."

Old Peter started singing softly as they built the blind inside a nearby thorn bush. Within a few moments, Young Peter and Masenga joined in, all of them in perfect rhythm and harmony as if they practiced that song for hours each night. I could not understand the words, but it filled the dry air with a celebratory tune. For the first time all morning, Cotton smirked. A leopard lurked nearby. When it returned to finish its meal, we would be waiting.

Listening to the smooth melody, we watched the men work, but did not really see them working. It was as if their song allowed us to see beyond the brush and the trees and the useless worries littering our lives. We felt the purity of a more simple time. A time when schedules and deadlines did not exist, when song and dance echoed through the night because a successful hunt was truly a cause for celebration. They sang now only because it was the natural thing to do. I envied them in that moment.

Somewhere in our need to structure our lives, we lose the ability to burst into spontaneous song. Children around the world do it to a certain age, but some cultures hold on to it into adulthood. I had been so far removed from it that I could no longer understand it. But I could appreciate it. Having been witness to the building of many leopard blinds, that one was the most enjoyable I could remember—and all I did was listen.

On our way back to the blind later that afternoon, Hillary tapped my shoulder and raised his thumb into the air. Old Peter and Young Peter shared a freshly rolled cigarette. Mary chewed on her lower lip. And Cotton looked focused. I tried to picture the tree, the bait, and the branch. From which direction would the leopard approach? Where would it climb the tree? Would it feed immediately? Would it stand broadside? I ran through a number of scenarios. I came to one certain conclusion—learned from hunting numerous cats, from reading, and from picking the brains of professional hunters who knew more about the spotted cats than the volumes written about them—leopards were unpredictable.

Once in a leopard blind, you are alone. Even with your good friend and professional hunter, even with your wife sitting so close your legs are touching, you are alone. I had developed a love/hate relationship with leopard blinds. It was not the fear I hated; I used that to keep me focused. Nor was it the monotony of staring at an empty tree. What I hated was the silence—it was exhausting. When strung out over several days, it prevented you from thinking straight. In a leopard blind, you could begin to understand the horrors of solitary confinement.

That night, we only waited two hours for the leopard to show. Like a specter, he appeared without sound or warning. Leopards are more like ghosts than any animal I had ever hunted. They stalk in the night with silence and purpose and just when they confuse you into believing they do not exist, they give you a brief glimpse—just enough to make you question it.

This leopard stood only a moment before flashing up the tree. He gave me an opening while he inspected the bait. At the shot, he leapt from the tree. I heard the bullet hit a branch. We heard him coughing in the brush as he circled to the right side of the tree. Then, from the thorns, we saw a flash as he charged the blind, growling with fire in his eyes. He turned after a few yards. Then he was gone. For a long time after that, it was quiet.

I have missed more often than I care to admit, but when it comes to leopard or any dangerous game, your first shot has to count. People get hurt when it does not. I was sitting in a blind with a good rest and a leopard silhouetted on a branch less than thirty yards away. There was no excuse.

The next morning we found four baits had been chewed on—two leopards and two lions.

"Both lions look big," Cotton said. "The tracks indicate males and the long hairs we found on the trees suggest big males. One leopard is big; the other is a female. What do you want to do?"

"I want another crack at leopard."

"That's what I thought you'd say." Cotton slapped my shoulder.

The leopard had fed on a bait hung at one far end of Cotton's massive area. We found the half-eaten impala carcass at the edge of a deep *korongo* with a rocky slope. A tangle of evergreens and thorn bushes surrounded the big fig tree where

Teri Wolff

These two lions were reluctant to walk away from their recent kill.

Teri Wolff

Waiting for leftovers.

A typical lion machan.

Dinner.

Maasai tribesmen eyeballing the outsiders.

This young lion thought it was a leopard.

Maasai children outside their stick-and-mud home.

Despite her fears, Mary got her leopard.

Time to hang another leopard bait.

Blinds are made from nearby resources.

This character might be responsible for the hyena's reputation.

Teri Wolff

Cari's first zebra hunt was emotional.

These buffalo deserved a closer look.

Only on a luxury safari do you get your own truck ladder.

You spend lots of time in a Land Cruiser—not as comfortable as it looks.

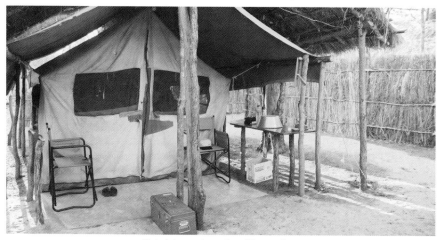

Primitive and comfortable—perfect.

The dining chalet at Hillary's camp.

Teri Wolff

The kitchen stove.

The camp laundramat.

Taking a break.

The end-of-day gathering place.

Dick and a fine Cape buffalo.

Two hearts, one passion.

the bait hung. One of the tree's branches extended horizontally for fifteen yards before reaching up to join the rest of the gnarly gray mass of wood and tiny leaves. Using their sharpened *pangas*, Old Peter and Young Peter chopped out a section of thorns and began building another blind. When they finished, we drove an hour and a half back to camp for lunch.

The missed shot from the day before poked at my brain. How had I missed? It had felt right. I could still picture the spots through my scope. I had picked a specific rosette, held my breath and squeezed. I could not remember a branch or twig that might have deflected the shot. I told myself to let it go. I told myself everybody missed. Then I told myself, never again. Not with leopard. I could have wounded it. That was unacceptable. I didn't deserve a second chance, but if I got the opportunity, I would not miss. I checked the scope and tacked a few bullseyes at targets to bolster my confidence.

The odds of everything coming together on a leopard hunt are slim. I had a chance on the second day and blew it. In three days, we'd had four leopards feeding at different baits. I would take those numbers any time. I had been on twenty-one day leopard hunts when the spotted cats refused every piece of meat we offered. It was a testament to the number of big cats in Cotton's area. Leopards were probably the most miscounted big-game animal in Africa. Their numbers were usually underestimated, but when you have multiple leopards feeding nightly, those miscalculations were leading to overpopulation. I was glad for the opportunities, but long-term predator overpopulation never leads to satisfactory outcomes—not for leopards or for people.

Masenga dropped us off a mile from the blind. We hiked the rest of the way, taking our time and keeping conversation and noise to a minimum. By the time we ducked into the blind, sweat dripped from my nose. I could smell myself; a leopard would catch the scent five miles away. If the wind changed or the leopard decided to circle the area before committing, we would be busted.

Settling in behind the shooting hole, I took a few minutes to get comfortable with the position and study the branch that the leopard had to step onto if it wanted to feed. The shot path was clear. If I missed again, I had no excuse.

I stared through the small shooting hole and watched the dark shadows under the thorns. He could have been staring back at me. I would not know. Even if he moved in that tangle of shade, leaves, and barbed branches, I would not have seen him. Hope had a way of holding on. So I waited and watched as the sun and shadows played tricks with me. Was that dark spot there before? Did it move? Were those eyes looking at me? Was that a rosette?

I was certain I saw the leopard crouched low beside a large tree root. The longer I studied it, the more I convinced myself it had to be a leopard. I was sure I saw a tail snake to one side. I wanted to look through the scope; I wanted to point it out to Cotton. It was too risky.

Ten minutes passed—it did not move. Twenty—maybe a twitch. Forty-five—it was still there. Leopards were patient, but this was beyond impressive. I felt a cool breeze rise from the *korongo*. Staring into the unchanging scene, my eyes began to blur. I had to look away. I peeked at Cotton—he stared through his own observation gap. I glanced at Mary—she had given up on the book she had been reading. I reached for my rifle, finding comfort in its cool reliability. My crossed legs were falling asleep. I picked up a small twig and rolled it in my fingers, then let it fall to the ground. The tiny click might as well have been a gunshot. Neither Mary nor Cotton seemed to notice.

When I peered back through the shooting hole, a leopard stood at the base of the tree. He was looking up. The form I thought was a leopard a few minutes before was still there, still unmoving. It no longer looked like a leopard.

The tom took his time climbing the tree. He looked up to study the bait while we stared at him. He glanced to his left and then watched the shadows ahead of him for five minutes. He studied the bait again. His hunger prodded him to climb; his caution warned him to hold steady; his patience allowed it.

While the leopard focused on the meat, I inched my rifle barrel toward the shooting hole. When he looked in our direction, I had to hold it in mid-air. My muscles started shaking from the strain. I did not take my eyes off the leopard. He did not alter his yellow stare. The leopard went from staring at me to standing above the bait in a blink. I heard a click as his claws raked the tree. A moment later, he stood on the branch above the meat staring in my direction. I still could not move.

When the spotted cat reached down with one paw to claw at the hanging slab of muscle, I moved the barrel through the hole. He was hanging half off the branch. No shot. We waited. A cool breeze swept through the shooting holes. The leopard growled. Like a quick-moving spider, a tingle ran under my skin.

A moment like that pumps the blood like nothing else. Except for maybe the next moment. That instant when you touch the trigger, when you begin to apply pressure, when you know the ultimate predator before you finally made a mistake. Like all predators, I planned to take advantage of that mistake.

A hollow thud echoed down the *korongo* when the leopard hit the ground. He never moved. When that happens, especially with leopard, you don't know whether to cheer, cry, or keep shooting. I kept my crosshairs on the pile of spots. If they moved, I would shoot again. I sat with a mixture of disbelief and readiness while the world analyzed whether it was safe to move. Birds finally tested the quiet with a few soft calls.

My second-chance leopard. I shared the moment of triumph and sorrow with my wife and my friend. We did not yell or shed tears, at least not outwardly. Instead, we approached the fallen beast with cautious reverence. Once we verified death, we silently saluted him for all he was—beautiful, powerful, cunning, and a masterful hunter.

The boys would celebrate later with song and dance and the customary parading of the successful hunter. When the evening rested to the soft glow of a campfire, we would give one last toast, to each other, to the leopard, to Africa.

SECOND-CHANCE LION: MARY

"Shoot it in the shoulder. Right between a black stripe and a white stripe. Take your time. Squeeze the—"

The rifle went off right in middle of Cotton's calm whispering.

"Good shot. Shoot again." Cotton was no longer whispering.

After the second shot, the zebra charged toward nearby *miombo* woodland. If not for the unmistakable sound of a bullet striking a big animal, I might have thought I missed.

"Shoot again. No wait. Too far. Let's give him a minute."

Cotton was looking through binoculars, following the still running creature as it neared the wooded edge. "Looks like we might have to track him," he said.

We started out jogging, but when Old Peter found the track, we slowed to a quick walk, following it like wild dogs on a fresh scent. The zebra was just inside the tree line, facing away from us. Without slowing down further, we circled until I had a quartering away shot.

Breathing heavily, I took a minute to steady the crosshairs.

"Whenever you're ready. Right in the shoulder." Cotton's soothing whisper always helped.

This time, the zebra kicked his back legs and ran a few more yards. He didn't fall. I wanted to cry.

"Again."

I fired for the fourth time. The zebra fell. Tears blurred my vision as we approached it. Two of the four shots were in the kill zone. The other two were gut shots—the worst. I had no idea which bullet hit first, second, third, or last. All I knew was that the zebra was dead and two of my shots had hit him in the stomach. I held my head down.

"Two of your shots were perfect," Cotton said. "Zebras are just tough."

"I think lions are safe with me behind the trigger."

"We can shoot some paper targets, but you know the problem with those?"

"What's that?"

"They always hold still for the next shot."

In some ways, I enjoy lion *machans* better than leopard blinds. In some ways, I hate them more. They are usually roomier and often more comfortable. I have sat in *machans* with mattresses lining the floor. I have never been comfortable in a leopard blind. Leopards are sneakier than lions, slipping in like serial killers with soft growls that resonate like an ice pick touching the back of your neck. Lions approach a bait like gang members itching for a rumble. They are coming to take the food and they do not care who knows it. Most creatures give way, sometimes running for safety when a pride shows up, almost like an old Western where mothers shuffle their children inside and close the windows and storeowners lock up shop. At least with lions, you usually know when they have arrived.

The problem with lions was they were not afraid of me—ever. When lions came to a bait, they stared at the blind with those penetrating eyes that had the ability to bore into my heart and measure my conviction. I hate it when a lion stares at me. It is worse when one swaggers toward the *machan* with its mouth open just enough that I can see yellow-stained teeth. The lion could kill me so easily if it wanted to. We both knew it. Somehow, the rifle never gave me comfort when it came to lions.

We shot a few targets—the .375 was spot on. That helped a little.

As we ducked into the blind, I questioned myself. Was I ready to shoot a lion? I had shot lions before, but my confidence always waned during the hours leading up to the moment. Did I need to shoot another lion? Would I regret it if I did not even try? What if I gut-shot it like I did that poor zebra?

I settled in behind a half-read paperback and prepared for a long afternoon. Sitting in a hot *machan* waiting for lions slows time. Ten minutes feels like thirty. If it was ninety degrees, it felt like one-hundred-ten. If your paperback weighed an ounce, it felt like five pounds. Sit and wait. Muscles stiffen and pain creeps like a snake.

As discouraging as it sometimes feels, you never truly lose hope. If you are still in the blind and you can still see the bait, there is always a chance a lion will show. As the minutes crawl by, that hope can change. At first, you dream of an old lion with a heavy, luxurious mane, standing broadside, falling to a single, well-placed shot. After an hour, you start hoping for a good representative male lion—one that is at least five years old and has a full mane. As dusk approaches, you just want to see a lion—you do not even need to shoot. You do not even care if it is a male. You just want to see a lion. You want proof you had not just wasted three hours of an expensive, time-constrained hunt.

I heard a loud crunching sound. My head snapped up from the book. It was still early, but lions were hungry when they were hungry. I peeked out the shooting hole. Hyenas. I counted four. Their long jaws and mouths dripped with slobber as they jostled for position on a zebra hindquarter hanging low from a tree. They could just reach the lower quarter of the bait and each time they clamped down with those powerful jaws, the cracking of bone and muscle gave me chills.

It seemed like a lot of work for the hyenas to reach up for a small hunk of meat, but they stayed until sunset and continued to fight for scraps. From our positions, we could not see the sunset. It cast a soft, pink glow around the hyenas. They began laughing and yipping and carrying on. A few moments before dark, we found out why. We could only see silhouettes, but the lions had arrived.

Back and forth bickering continued into darkness. With lions roaring and growling and hyenas bawling back, the deafening sound hammered around us. I felt surrounded by the hungry predators. At times, it felt like they were right outside the blind. Then it stopped. We waited for a few minutes. Cotton clicked on his flashlight. Four sets of eyes stared back. One of them belonged to a full-maned male. He stared at us as if we were interrupting a deep thought—a mixture of irritation and curiosity. I am not sure I liked where he might take either one of those.

We kept our eyes on them; they watched us. Within ten minutes, Masenga arrived with the Land Cruiser. The lions lumbered off a few yards, but a quick flashlight scan into the brush made those steady eyes glow. I could only see their eyes reflecting in the light, but a lion watching me was an uncomfortable feeling.

"Five minutes earlier and we would have had him," Cotton said on the way back to camp. "Hunting is a game of inches and seconds."

It was early in the hunt and, according to Cotton, cats had been readily coming to baits. Lion and leopard hunting was hit and miss, even in an area as well-managed as Cotton's.

That night, after listening to Cotton and Dick tell mostly true stories, I listened to Tanzania until Dick started snoring. Closing my eyes, I heard more strange sounds in ten minutes than I could ever remember. Rustles, creaks, snaps, grumbles, growls, chits, whistles, yaps, grunts, howls, roars, mews, clicks, scrapes, rasps, cries, screams, chirps, splashes, scratches, peeps, snorts, saws, gurgles, stomps, crashes, and hisses. I don't recall silence.

In the morning, I listened again. I had to concentrate to hear past the bustle of the morning camp rituals, but below the generator, voices, clanks, slams, and footsteps, there were whistles, chirps, whispers, peeps, caws, tweets, and squeaks. The morning sounded more vibrant and less menacing.

When Kidago came to our tent and said, "Good morning," I had already been awake for twenty minutes. Those two words from that unassuming, heavily accented voice meant a new day was upon us. A new hunt with unknown opportunities and risks. Anything could happen.

It began with a buffalo herd. We saw them in the distance, found their hundreds of tracks that had pounded the ground flatter than it already was, and followed them for two hours. At one point, it appeared as if we might get a shot, but the bull we wanted lost himself in the herd. When they headed for the river, we abandoned the trail.

We had invested two hours—not too much. Six hours on a track was common. Even if you never see your quarry, you retain hope. You have to. Hunting requires it. One hundred missed opportunities would have you questioning your love of the pursuit if not for the one encounter that made it all worthwhile. It does not matter if the hunt ends with a well-placed shot on a Cape buffalo or if you find yourself face-to-face with a broken-tusked elephant bull you have tracked for days. You are not going to shoot, but when he shakes his head and rumbles forward a few steps, you think about it. That, or run like hell. Either way, it is an unforgettable experience you will never find sitting at home watching a wildlife channel. You are not a mere spectator; you are a participant. There is nothing like it.

Hiking back to the vehicle, we encountered oribi, duiker, impala, reedbuck, giraffes, dik-diks, warthogs, and zebras. Dick stalked and shot one of the zebra stallions. By the time we loaded it, everyone was hungry.

Before heading back to camp, we stopped to check one last bait. Hit. Leopard. By the look of the tracks, a big male.

"Looks like you're under the gun again tonight, Mary," Cotton said, while the boys replenished the bait with some of Dick's zebra.

It felt like razors scratching my stomach. Now I had all afternoon to think about the leopard. To think about errant shots and slashing claws; about bandages wrapped around Cotton's head from the time a wounded leopard attacked him; about all the work that goes into hunting the solitary cat; about the last time I shot a leopard when everything went perfect. I prayed it would go well. That I would shoot straight and the leopard would die quickly. I said two *Our Fathers* and a dozen *Hail Marys*. In some ways, sitting in camp waiting is worse than sitting in a dark, cold blind waiting. Part of me wanted to get it over with. Then again, there was this crazy part of me that wanted a drawn-out experience. That part was never as loud as the worrywart always pestering my thoughts.

We settled into the blind at four. We read, with intermittent glances through the shooting holes, until six. By then, the dull light made our eyes work too hard. If the leopard was going to come, it had better come soon. We waited. Staring and listening. I prayed some more and wondered if anyone else heard my lips moving.

A rustle shot me to attention. I heard it again. Too noisy for a leopard. It had to be something else, didn't it? I stared hard in the direction I thought it came from. It sounded like something small and quick. Probably a mouse.

As dusk crept in, I started to give up on the leopard. It allowed my stomach to relax. I could not wound a leopard that did not show. Then, right before it was too dark to shoot, I heard another sound—something soft, quiet, and sneaky. That was no mouse. My stomach began looking for a way out.

The coming night squeezed the gray from the air until blackness ruled. A low, barely audible growl from somewhere nearby crinkled my skin. All I wanted to hear now was the sound of the approaching Land Cruiser. In darkness, the leopard held the advantages. He could see; we could not. I wished Cotton would turn on his flashlight. At least we would be able to see if Africa's spotted cat was stalking us. For a few horrific moments, there was nothing—besides the perceived thumping of my heart and the sound of air passing through my nose.

When the leopard's claws scraped, I almost screamed. But it was climbing the tree—hopefully the bait tree and not the tree beside our roofless blind. Not the tree with a large branch hanging over the top of us—a branch from which an irritated leopard could pounce on three unsuspecting hunters. I looked up. All I saw was black. It felt like we were being watched. As I stared into nothing, the leopard started to feed. The gnawing, crunching, flesh-ripping sounds should have been disturbing. I was relieved to hear them. Cotton finally clicked on his flashlight.

Yellow eyes burned toward us. Below them, bloodstained teeth glimmered in the torchlight. When a big cat stares, you do not see it as much as you feel it. You feel it in your chest—it creeps down from your throat and eats its way to your belly. A leopard's stare is made to instill fear, to induce hesitation. It worked on me every time.

One moment this tom was picking at my soul, the next I was staring at an empty branch.

That night I curled up in blankets and listened to the lions and hyenas fighting over something—probably a kill or territory—and I wondered what the leopard thought of all that noise.

Checking baits along lion loop the next morning, we discovered one had been fed on. Judging by the tracks and the long hairs in the tree bark, there was one male and at least five females.

"Looks like another night in a *machan*," Cotton said.

"I can't wait."

"A little discomfort makes for a better hunt," Cotton said. "The more pain, the more memorable."

"I think I'll remember just fine if a big male comes right after we sit down."

"Yes, but if we had hung only one bait and this was our first night, would it be as rewarding?"

"Make that happen and I'll let you know."

"If you keep coming back, it might eventually happen. For now, you might have to settle for a sixth-day lion."

"I didn't expect so many chances," I said.

"Lions and leopards have been feeding well the entire month. We can always count on the leopard population. But we must be careful with the lions. They are more susceptible to population declines. We will not use the entire quota if I think they could use a break."

"It seems like there's plenty this year."

"This has been a good year. God willing, nothing will go wrong during the off-season. How about an impala before lunch, Dick?" Cotton raised his binoculars. "Looks like a good ram."

Through a gap in the brush line and across the other side of an open field, we could see a small herd of grazing impala.

"A short walk around the other side of that baobab and we should be in a good position."

For the first five minutes, we strolled along as if it were a Sunday afternoon in the park. I felt lost without Peter leading us. Most professional hunters relied on their trackers, not only for tracking, but also for finding their way around the bush. Most clients relied on their professional hunters for safety and trophy judgment. Native trackers like Peter were vital to a successful safari. When it came to finding game, they did most of the work. When it came to field-dressing game, they did most of the work. When it came to hanging bait and building blinds, they did most of the work. Their knowledge of the land and the ways of the animals would be written down as legend in any western country. Men like Peter were rare. We often mention trackers as if every native-born man in any African country had an innate ability to follow game. Even in Africa, it was a special talent refined from years of learning and hard work. Some of the best seemed to have a sixth sense, but without the hard work and the lifetime surviving in the bush, it would not develop properly. Could anyone track as well as Peter? Maybe. But that's like saying anyone could play basketball like Michael Jordan or paint as well as Leonardo da Vinci. Usually, a combination of talent and hard work separate the exceptional from the common. I felt lost without Peter, not because we were lost, but because with him we could not get lost.

When we could see the other side of the massive baobab tree, we stepped lighter, concentrating on where we placed each foot. One broken stick could alert the herd. The stalk had started on a whim. Dick had shot plenty of impala; they were not high on his list of desired animals to hunt. Yet, when it looked as if we might get a shot, instinct took over. It was beside the point that Dick did not *need* another impala ram. At that moment, the only thing that mattered was moving close enough to shoot that one.

Remaining inside the brush line fifty yards from the baobab, we caught sight of a few females standing at attention.

"Get ready," Cotton whispered.

Dick worked the bolt on his rifle slowly, feeding a bullet into the chamber. Every tiny click, every smooth scrape of metal on metal echoed in the still, hot air. None of the females glanced at us. Their focus was directed elsewhere. A tawny blur flashed by to the far side of the herd immediately followed by another. The second flash stopped briefly. It was the ram, his tongue hanging while he breathed heavily. He was chasing a hot female.

Dick stabilized his rifle between the branch and trunk of a thin tree. Before he could squeeze the trigger, the ram charged off again. This time the other females followed at an easy pace.

"Let's go," Cotton hurried after them. We followed.

After fifteen steps, Cotton stopped. We almost ran into him.

Twenty yards away, a panting female impala had skidded to a stop. She stared at us for an instant before charging off to join the other females. The ram was oblivious to why she changed directions. With his tongue still hanging and a goofy look on his face, he ran within ten yards of us without looking in our direction.

Dick stepped to the side and lifted his rifle. We waited. If the ram stopped, Dick might get a shot. With the females heading for Kenya, we would have to be lucky. They never stopped. Neither did the ram.

We watched them disappear. Then we started laughing. The first giggle soon transformed into a full-blown guffaw. I don't think any of us were sure why we were laughing so hard, but it was a good laugh—the kind that made your stomach muscles ache.

Lunch felt quiet. Cotton and Dick talked politics and hunting, but I could not involve myself in the conversation. I heard them, but I was not listening. Lions consumed my thoughts. How could they be so nonchalant about it? Didn't they realize that, just a few hours from now, we would be sitting in a tight-quartered blind fifty yards from a stinking bait, waiting for one of the earth's most impressive predators to show up? I am surprised they were not talking about man-eaters. They probably wanted to, but felt it would not be tactful. Typical.

I was thinking about man-eaters. There were the famous man-eating lions like the Tsavo pair, but they did not worry me. I was more concerned with the unreported man-eating events—most of them undocumented. Even if you only counted the documented cases, the Tsavo lions were amateurs compared to many of the predators that had turned to human flesh. Despite all that, I knew lion attacks were rare. I knew it, but it did not make me feel better. Images of your own blood dripping from a lion's canines are never fully suppressed by mere facts.

After all my trips to Africa, I was still afraid of lions. Most of all, I was afraid that I would wound one. The only thing worse than wounding an animal was wounding a dangerous animal. Not only have you caused the beast extra suffering, but you have put others in danger. Dangerous animals that are wounded would rather face their attackers than flee. It almost feels like revenge. If a lion can pounce on an unsuspecting ungulate with all its refined senses, what chance would a citified human have? I didn't know why I put myself through it. I could not help it. A hunter hunts. And I did not intend to give up hunting yet.

So, while the boys debated the role of the federal government, I mostly ignored them. I tried to picture the lion in my crosshairs; tried to envision the perfect shot placement; tried to see the lion go down instantly. If that could happen, I would be a happy hunter.

We had been in the blind for half an hour when the lions started calling. Unlike the leopard from the previous evening, the lions announced their arrival. It was their territory and if anything else was near their dinner, it had better make way. They strutted in like gunslingers, confident and willing to fight. They stood around the meat for a moment, some of them inspecting it, some of them checking out the slightly out-of-place, recently sprouted, thick patch of grass in the shadows, and some of them stood guard as if expecting a scavenger to try to sneak in for a scrap.

The five females tore into the meat, growling and ripping at the carcass, snapping at each other, occasionally chasing subordinates away from the "free" meal. The male stayed inside the brush and watched the females bicker. We could see his face, but that was about it. How long could he sit there and watch the lionesses gorge themselves?

He looked our way as if he knew we were hiding in the grass. His stare was more of a *you had better not bother me* than an *I'm hungry but worried* stare.

I shivered.

When the lion turned his hard, yellow eyes back toward the bait, Cotton tapped my knee. He motioned for me to prepare.

I eased the .375 barrel through the shooting hole. Looking through the scope,

I saw the beast's face more clearly. He had a short, heavy nose with a white beard and a black chest. I could not see how far back the mane went, but it was full under his neck and below his ears. Even half-hidden in the shadows and brush, he was noble. When he moved, even slightly, it was with an unmistakable arrogance. He knew he was in charge. When he stood, my breath stopped.

The male towered above the females. When he began a slow approach toward them, they all paused. As he closed the distance, the nearest females hurried to grab another scrap before retreating from his path. He growled and snapped at a slow-to-move lioness. She snapped back, but without conviction.

The big male gripped his claws into the meat and stared back at the females he had chased away. The lionesses on the opposite side ignored him and continued feeding. From the side of his mouth, he began to gnaw on the bottom half of the zebra carcass. He did not hurry to eat all he could as the females had. He took his time, confident they would not try to take what was rightfully his.

His position had him quartering toward me and a female blocked half his body. No shot. If he did not move soon, daylight would creep into dusk. We waited until the light softened to a dull gray. Two of the lionesses decided their stomachs overruled their bravery and slipped in for another bite. Instead of going around to the other side, they tried to sneak in right next to the big guy. He was on top of one of them in a burst of speed. She was on her back submissively, but with her teeth bare. When he let her go, he was facing us head on.

I put one right in his chest.

He ripped at the air with his claw before stumbling backward off the edge of the *korongo*. The lionesses glanced around before rumbling off a short distance. Only twenty-five yards from the bait, they looked back before disappearing into the *korongo* one by one.

It was quiet then. Nobody said "nice shot" or "congratulations" or asked how the shot felt. There were too many unknowns at the moment. We sat and listened as darkness extended its predatory rule over Tanzania. When the lionesses started growling and snarling, I almost jumped in Dick's lap.

"It's best if we wait for the truck," Cotton finally said. "Too dangerous to approach the *korongo* at the moment."

Fine with me. Those females sounded angry—and if the male was only wounded—I did not even want to think about that.

I did what I always do in such a situation; I prayed. I prayed for the lion to be dead. I prayed for the truck to arrive soon. I prayed for the females to leave. I prayed nobody would get hurt. I prayed until we walked up to the edge of the *korongo* and searched for the lion with flashlights. Cotton held the butt of his big rifle tight on his shoulder. I said one last quick prayer.

The dead lion had rolled a few feet down the ravine before coming to a rest against heavy brush. We backed the Land Cruiser until the rear wheels hugged the edge. From there, we only had to move the lion three or four feet up the hill. It sounded so simple. Reluctant to jump out of the truck, Old Peter and the others insisted Cotton cover them with his rifle. Dick and I kept our flashlights searching the darkness for the lionesses.

It took forty-five minutes to move that lion those few feet. Twice, a nearby female growled. Both times, Old Peter, Young Peter, Masenga, and Maisai leapt into truck and hid behind Cotton. After a minute or two of silence, they would laugh at each other and get back to work. Four men moving five-hundred pounds of limp, dead weight a few feet uphill is more difficult than it sounds. Inch by inch they moved him up the hill, lodging large branches below him to prevent a further roll and eventually pulled, pushed, and shifted the lion into the back of the truck.

As late as it was, I thought the usual celebration after a lion kill would be subdued. I was wrong.

The music carried far into the starry night, rising into a harmonious blend of voices and drums like a cool breeze from a quiet riverbed. They carried me around camp in the chair and set me beside the fire. The dancing and singing pushed deep into the night. We drank and laughed and partied until after midnight. It was a celebration of a beast we admired. The lion was regal, bold, fierce, strong, confident, and beautiful. It was also a celebration of a place with an ancient beat and undiscovered mysteries—a place which embraced life and death in all their brutal realities. On our first visit to Africa, I discovered a part of myself that I did not know existed. Each subsequent visit, I rediscovered myself, always finding new surprises that added shape to who I was. Finally, it was a celebration of people. Of people like Cotton, whose dedication helped define an industry and whose genuine personality helped define a friendship. Of people like Hillary, whose zest and eagerness to master his craft ensured a successful future. Of people like Old Peter and Young Peter, whose quiet determination and natural skills led us to more game than we ever could have hoped for. Of people like Masenga, Bariki, and Kidago, whose embrace of life under less than ideal conditions should be an inspiration to us all.

Many years later, thinking of that night, I remembered joy. I hoped the others who were there with me remembered it the same way.

OPPORTUNITY: DICK

A heavy heat hammered the back of my neck as we drove from bait tree to bait tree, hoping the next would show evidence that a predator had visited during the night. It became a disheartening routine. We would drive and drive, only occasionally spotting a distant wildebeest or impala seeking refuge from the sun under a shade tree. We would unload at each bait, inspect an untouched quarter of a zebra or wildebeest or hartebeest, search the surrounding area for nearby tracks, and pile back into the truck to do it all over again at the next bait at least half an hour away. The sun seemed to follow us with a tracking beam and the tsetse flies, with their ability to bite through armor, struck at the most inopportune times, like when we were trying to climb down from the truck or taking a drink of water. There was no action, no respite from the sun, and no mercy from the flies. Camp was a welcome sight.

"What are these?" I asked Mary back in the tent. She had smartly opted to forego the morning hunt.

"Joel and Bariki gave them to us. Aren't they great?" She picked up one of two handmade baskets. "Look how tight these are. And they gave us this too." She reached for a hollowed-out yellowish gourd. "I almost cried when they brought them over. It was so sweet. Did anything feed?"

"The tsetse flies got their fill of my blood."

"I despise those creatures. I think they despise me too. I always seem to get the worst of it."

"Not today."

"If I had come, they would have ignored you."

"You're not staying in camp again."

With no reason to sit in a blind that evening, we just hunted for whatever felt right at the moment. Roan, eland, impala, hartebeest, and warthog each gave us reason for a close look, but we passed on them all. Mary took a fine zebra stallion that would help replenish baits and we gave serious thought to an impressive bull sable. However, we had recently booked a trip to Zimbabwe, where we would have the opportunity to hunt some of the best sable in Africa. It was a good bull, but not outstanding. We decided to take our chances in Zim.

"You snored right through the lions and hyenas again last night," Mary said. "I don't know which is worse, you or them."

"Even if they come into camp," Cotton said, "Dick's snoring will scare them off."

"Or call them in."

We checked the three closest baits—no hits. We added fresh zebra meat and moved on. I dozed on and off during the long drive to the further baits. Masenga was driving so fast, we could not hope to see much anyway. He held the steering wheel with both hands and leaned forward until his chin almost touched his wrists.

When Masenga slammed on the brakes, Old Peter had to grab my shoulders to prevent me from flying over the hood. What was happening? Oh yeah, lions, leopards, tsetse flies—Tanzania. Cotton was studying something through his binoculars. I stretched my neck in an attempt to see. Someone said, "Male."

Male what? Where? Cotton and the others were staring into the distance. There, what's that?

Just as I discovered them sitting together beside a wall of long grass, Cotton said, "Do you see the lions under the tree there."

I nodded.

"The male is on the left, behind that green bush."

I saw a cat standing there, but could not tell if it was a good male. "I see him."

"We need to get closer."

Cotton had Masenga drive the truck away from the lions until we were out of sight. Then Old Peter and Young Peter led us on foot back toward our quarry. We went into sneak mode after five minutes. We spotted one of the females ten minutes after that. She was lying on her side, the bright sun reflecting off her light-colored belly. We were close enough to see her stomach rise and fall with each breath. I saw what I thought was the same bush, but I did not see anything resembling a lion. Had he moved?

I was staring at the bush when Young Peter tapped my shoulder and pointed to Old Peter and Cotton, who, in a crouched position, had moved ten paces. Finding a balance between a sneak and a hurry, I started forward. I caught up the next time they stopped. The dusty air fought against my lungs. I had to concentrate to find a normal rhythm to my breathing. Every breath felt loud. New sweat stung my forehead. The rifle felt damp under my clammy hands. I still had not seen the male.

For the next five steps, we were too exposed. A lioness was going to spot us and alert the entire pride. If that happened, we would be done. But we needed those five steps. Without them, there was no shot. He was standing behind a different bush, thorns and small leaves blurring his outline. If we could get through a gap in the cover unnoticed, I would have a shooting lane. From there, Cotton and I went alone.

Could we be this lucky? Could we stalk our lion at mid-morning without having to sit and wait in a cramped, stuffy blind? Four more steps. Three. Two. Wait. Do not move. A lioness stared in our direction, her chin up, her muscles tight. My leg began to shake. It was my right leg—my bad knee straining under pressure. Cats are patient. They have the ability to study a situation longer than many humans do. My knee was not going to hold out. Sweat poured off my nose. My leg felt like a slinky under my weight.

The lioness finally rested her head on her paws, giving us our window. We took our last two steps and set up beside a fig tree.

There he was. Lion—worldwide symbol of power, strength, and royalty. One look at this stately beast and it was easy to see why. A luxurious mane rippled in the breeze. Lean, well-developed muscle bulged under his tawny skin. His confident gaze seemed to hold the power to command the wind. Everything about this predator was regal. An indifferent yawn revealed a mouth that haunts nightmares. The lion's noble beauty was matched only by his savage power. This was a creature that preferred to kill buffalo, prey that fights back. I respected the lion for many reasons. In that moment, they were all justified.

Like the lion, I was a hunter. He made no apologies about it. Neither would I. But I would honor him and I would celebrate everything he was. His existence provided so much for me.

I held my breath. My forefinger touched the trigger. A bead of sweat rolled over my temple. I applied pressure.

At the impact, the lion twirled, roared, and retreated into the brush, toward a nearby *korongo*. Cotton and I stared into the thorns for a few silent minutes. When I looked away, Old Peter was standing beside Cotton.

"Where are the females?" Cotton asked.

"They go." Peter waved his hand. "Bwana make good shot. Lion dead in *korongo*."

"Did you see him go down?" I asked.

"Not see into *korongo*. He go in, then die."

"Peter has a way of knowing these things. Don't you, old friend?" Cotton shook Peter's hand.

Our tracker then extended his hand to me. "Good shot," he said. "Good lion."

Young Peter shook my hand next and then every smile disappeared as we prepared for the follow up. No matter how sure Old Peter was that the lion died in the *korongo*, we had all seen enough *dead* animals spring to their feet at inopportune moments to know going in after a lion warranted extreme caution. During our slow walk toward the *korongo*, I glanced to my left multiple times. Peter said the females had retreated, but like *dead* beasts, lions, in general, were unpredictable. It felt like they were watching us.

We slipped by the bush he had been standing beside. I glanced at his tracks. A few yards further, we found bright red blood—lots of it. I began to feel confident we would find the lion just as Old Peter said we would. The sight of blood intensified the reality. My fingers tightened around the rifle; my heart hit my chest as if it was a punching bag. The leaves and plant debris crunching under our feet sounded like fireworks. As we drew closer to the edge of the *korongo*, I seemed to form tunnel vision, my eyes focusing on a single opening in the brushy draw. If I were a wounded lion, that was the path I would have taken.

With my mind set on that spot, I hesitated when we turned to the right. Initially, I had a hard time taking my eyes off that opening, but Old Peter knew his trade better than most. I trusted him more than I trusted my gut. A quick glance to the ground verified we were still on an easy-to-follow blood trail.

Sometimes it is dangerous to let your mind lead you in one direction without evidence. Other times, it can save your life. That time, it would not have mattered. We found the lion as dead as Old Peter predicted, following the blood trail twenty yards down the slope and then fifteen yards back up. He died just below that opening of the brushy draw. He had doubled back in an attempt to ambush his attackers—a tactic wounded buffalo often used.

"Good thing you hit him well. Could have turned hairy in a hurry."

Two to three minutes from camp, the boys in back started singing the familiar cat celebration song. As we rumbled closer to camp, many voices joined those from the truck as if they had been singing the same tune all along. A dancing staff, waving their arms, smiling and singing, met us as we pulled in. They formed a circle around the Land Cruiser and danced with us toward the skinning shed.

Knowing we still had the afternoon to hunt, the mid-day celebration was more subdued than those started in the evening. One moment, we were dancing, singing, and congratulating ourselves; the next, we were sitting at the dining table eating salad while the rest of the staff went back to their duties as if they had never stopped.

"What have you got there, Hillary?"

"A little joke for my friend, Masenga." Hillary carried half a sandwich on a plate and called for Masenga to join us. He turned and put his finger to his mouth in a *don't give up the joke* gesture. "It is a very hot pepper."

Cotton leaned in. "These two are always playing pranks on each other. Masenga never fails to fall for it."

When Masenga arrived, Hillary spoke in English so that we could understand. "I have made you a special treat, because you drive so well to get the *Bwana* and the Mama their lions."

Masenga bowed to us. I smiled at him. Mary turned away, unwilling to be part of the joke, but not giving it away either. Masenga began to leave with the sandwich.

"Please, sit to eat," Hillary said.

Masenga smiled and sat next to Cotton. He took one bite, a pleased grin on his face. Chewing it up, his grin faded until his eyes popped and the bite came back out onto the plate. He was sweating, chugging water, and wiping his tongue with his fingers. Hillary was almost on the ground with laughter. Cotton chuckled, obviously having seen this kind of stunt many times.

"You guys are horrible," Mary said. "Look at him, he's burning up." She offered Masenga her water and a piece of bread, which he chugged and devoured. Once his mouth had cooled, he laughed and pointed at Hillary with a *you'll get yours* look on his face.

"He thinks he can play a joke on me. I am too smart for that," Hillary said after Masenga had left. "He will try today. But it is too early. I will see it coming."

"Please tell me you wouldn't do this in front of all your clients," Mary said.

"Only those who would appreciate the joke or those who would take the greatest offense to it," Cotton said. "With you and Dick, I think we have both."

"I feel sorry for him."

"You want us to be ourselves, don't you?" Cotton said.

We had become so comfortable with each other that we would know if they were trying to put on a show. Cotton was more than a professional hunter or guide. Cotton was our friend—one of my favorite hunting buddies.

"Only one cat left," Cotton said. He looked toward Mary. "You ready to shoot a leopard?"

"I'm terrified I'll wound him."

Within fifteen minutes of leaving camp, we had encountered a high number of game animals.

"The *Bwana* next to us is burning much of his land," Hillary said, pointing toward rising smoke on the horizon.

"The fellow who runs the adjoining concession has been burning everything like he's a pyromaniac," Cotton said. "Seems like he's burned his entire block. It's pushing the animals over here. It's good for us now, but when the new grass starts to shoot up, his place is going to pull game from all over. Must have an important client coming."

"Is that a good strategy," Mary asked.

"It could be. I'm sure it's worked for him in the past—I've seen him do it before. It's a gamble and it deemphasizes his other clients, but we all have to burn. We try to do it in sections here, so as not to disturb the animals too much. It has always worked for us."

"*Mbogo*," Peter said, tapping Cotton's shoulder.

"Stop, stop."

We jerked to a halt and began glassing a herd of more than one hundred buffalo on a wide-open savannah.

"There's an old bull on the right. I don't know how we're going to get close enough. There's no cover and I don't think they'll let us walk right up to them. We could take our chances and spend all afternoon trying to cat and mouse them or we could move on and try to find something else. What do you want to do?"

That was always a tough one. By the end of the day, you usually second-guessed your choice whatever it may have been. Normally, it was better to pursue the animal you could see as opposed to one you may never encounter. Then again, I hated to lose an entire afternoon chasing a herd we had little chance of catching up to. A lone bull—for sure. A big herd—maybe.

"Is he a world record?"

"He's a very good bull," Cotton said. "Not great, but very good. Old and heavy with deep curls."

"What would you do?"

"If I had never shot a buffalo, I would try."

"I've shot plenty of buffalo. Let's see what else we can find." I loved buffalo hunting, but with the odds stacked against us, why not see what other opportunities the day would offer. We were in a place where hunting four different species in a single day was common. It was one of the few places in the world where you could walk away from a trophy bull and feel confident you would get another chance before your time was up.

Africa has a way of humbling even the most confident hunters.

For the rest of the long, hot, fruitless day, I thought about that old bull, wondering how close they would have let us approach. We would never know. I told myself to forget about it, but a small tic in the back of my mind refused to let it go.

So, when I fell to sleep that night, I was not surprised to see a big buffalo bull staring me in the eyes before turning to walk into the blackness. I did not follow him in my dream either.

"That hyena was pretty scary last night, wasn't it?" Mary said the next morning.

"What hyena?"

She lowered her head and gave me a stern look. "You know what I'm talking about."

"No, I don't."

"I woke you up at eleven. You hit the side of the tent to scare it away."

"Oh."

"You don't remember?"

"Not really."

"I swear, a train could come through the tent and you wouldn't hear it."

"I'm sure it wasn't as close as you think."

"It brushed against the tent. How much closer could it get?"

Before we left for breakfast, I walked around the tent. "I can't find any tracks."

"Of course you can't. You can see where Kidago swept the dust already."

"I'm sure he did that last night."

"Then where are our footprints?"

I shrugged. I was not going to win the argument.

"You know I'm right," she said.

I shrugged again and we strolled toward the mess tent.

We spent the day searching for buffalo or their tracks. We found neither. That hard-to-get bull from the day before would have been a welcome sight. Sable, giraffe, oribi, reedbuck, zebra, and hartebeest were in good supply. The only sign of buffalo we found was a day-old track at an almost dry waterhole.

After a light lunch of salad and watermelon, we happened across a small herd of hartebeest.

"We need some camp meat, Dick. What do you say?"

"I could use a little action."

It should have been an easy stalk. Hug the tree line; slip into range; blast him in the shoulder. One hour and two miles later, I was ready to retreat. That herd was skittish. The slightest change in wind direction or the softest crunch of dry leaves sent them racing away. At one point, we stopped two hundred fifty yards from them. I told Cotton, "This is close enough. I can make this shot." As my finger slid toward the trigger, a single warthog scampered in their direction. They bolted as if a lion were chasing them.

We finally caught a break. For reasons only a hartebeest could understand—or possibly a wildebeest—they turned around and sprinted toward us. I stayed on the bull the entire time. When they stopped, one hundred yards out, I fired. They wheeled together, but the bull only made it six or seven steps before stumbling sideways and tipping over.

We spent the afternoon hunting buffalo. We found old sign, dry air, and a hot sun. By dusk, I was ready for a cool drink, a warm shower, and a hot meal. After indulging in all three, I walked hand-in-hand with my wife to our tent. It had been a day with only one real opportunity and we took advantage of it.

Staring up at a dark sky full of constellations mostly foreign in our home state of Nebraska, I thought about the kids. Africa had become a part of who we were. It had influenced us in ways we would never fully understand. If we could share Africa with our children, we could share a piece of ourselves. I wondered if it would touch them in the same way it did us. I hoped so.

RECONNECT: MARY

"It's such a difficult area to track buffalo," Cotton said as we approached what he called Buffalo Basin. "Too many rocks. These guys are good enough to track here, but it's just a slow process. It's also close to the river. We can only hunt on this side and they cross over whenever we pressure them. It's best to drive around the edge and try a stalk once you spot a good bull."

"Or find them somewhere else."

"We take eighty percent of our buffalo from Buffalo Basin. You have to go where the buffalo are."

We spotted a herd of around fifty shortly after that. They were plodding across the horizon like a caravan of tired pioneers.

"I'd like you to take that bull in the back," Cotton said to Dick.

We drove fast to put some distance between us and them, jumped out of the truck, and stumbled over soccer-sized rocks for fifteen minutes to position ourselves for an ambush. Old Peter could have covered the same amount of ground in half the time. He was always subtle about waiting for us and even pretended to be tired himself, bless his heart. As we descended one small hill, the rocks gave way to heavy brush. It would provide perfect cover to sneak into range of the buffalo if they had continued in the same direction.

They had. When the lead cow stepped past us, I just knew she would smell us. She was so close—only a few yards. We were sitting in the shadow of a heavy thorn bush. I was shaking. If they did smell us, they could stomp us into the ground. She lumbered by, her head swaying back and forth slightly. Behind her, more cows, calves, and a few small bulls hammered by. Then, as if one of us had jumped and screamed, the entire herd stampeded away, leaving only dust and a musty aroma hanging in the air.

We were after them like a Labrador behind a wounded pheasant. Following them into the open exposed us. If there had been any question about what they had smelled, a quick glance back would confirm the danger.

When the buffalo turned back, it was not to check to see if they were being pursued; it was to confront the pursuers. They formed a black wall that felt like a dare. Dick set up for a shot. He fired. We watched a moving dust cloud as it rolled toward the horizon.

"They're heading for the river."

"Did I miss?"

"I think so. It did not look or sound like he was hit. I never saw him falling behind the herd. Let's take it slow. Look for blood and tracks. Maybe they won't cross the river if we don't push them."

When the ground was not covered in rocks, I could have followed the pounded earth without help, but in most places, it was as if a thousand dump trucks had picked that spot to dispose of their extra rocks. Had we not seen them run off, I doubt even Old Peter could have tracked them. After an hour, Dick and I had each slipped numerous times and my feet and ankles burned with pain. We had not found a spot of blood.

"What if they cross the river?" I asked.

"Gone. Even if we find blood, we cannot cross after him. The manager there is over-protective of his area. Maybe they haven't crossed yet." Cotton's last statement was said without conviction.

It did little for hope.

At that time of year, the river was shallow and narrow. We found where the buffalo had entered the water. They had never stopped running. We never found blood. On the long, hot trek back to the Land Cruiser, we tried to convince ourselves that Dick had missed. It was better than believing the alternative—a wounded buffalo suffering across the river. With no proof either way, I prayed that he had missed.

"I want to check the leopard bait just a few miles to the west. After that, we can hunt our way back for lunch."

Our discouraged mood shifted at the bait tree. A leopard had fed. By the look of the pugmarks, it was a good male. While building the blind, Young Peter sliced his thigh when chopping grass with his razor-sharp *panga*. It left a deep, long wound. Blood flowed down his leg and dripped into a pool beside his foot. He tried to keep working, but Cotton would not have it. As we rushed back to camp, Young Peter forced a painful smile to stay on his face. His eyes claimed worry, but he insisted he was fine.

Young Peter did not join us for the leopard hunt, but Cotton assured us he was doing well. "Took a few stitches and it will be sore tomorrow. At least he didn't sever an artery. I heard you shooting before lunch. Everything sighted in okay?"

"Mary should be able to hit a dime at one hundred yards after the way she was shooting."

"Plenty of room for error. The leopard's spots at the shoulder are the size of half-dollars. Just aim for one of those spots."

I was reading a paperback when the leopard announced his arrival with a burst of sawing. A bushbuck barked. The leopard did not have to hunt for food tonight. Every creature in the bush could scream at him for all he cared.

I nearly dropped my book. The pages flapped in my shaking hands and I had to think consciously about each of the next steps: *Close the book. Slowly place it on the ground behind you. Touch the rifle. Compose yourself.* I hoped the leopard took his time—I would never hit him in the state I was in. We had over an hour before dark. Plenty of time to settle down.

We knew he was coming. We were watching for him. One second the space was empty, the next, it was full of spots. I would never understand how they did that. I would never tire of the marvel.

The leopard hid the entire front half of his body behind the tree. He stood there, unmoving, for ten minutes. If you stare at the spots long enough, they begin to blend and you have to look away to refocus. I was afraid to look away. What if I took my eyes off him and he stepped into the open? I did not want to miss that.

Cotton tapped my knee.

I slowly turned my head to look at him.

He motioned for me to breathe in.

I wasn't breathing? By their mere presence, leopards could make you do strange things. I concentrated on my breathing and my nerves began to calm. Through hand gestures and lip-reading, Cotton told me to get ready. I took my time pushing the rifle barrel through the shooting hole. I looked through the scope for my first up-close glance at the leopard's coat—at least the part I could see. It was beautiful.

The leopard's tail moved slightly. Other than that, he was as patient as a rock. Why didn't he just climb the tree and start eating? He had to be hungry or he would not be there. After forty minutes, sweat was dripping from my nose and my arms were trembling from holding the rifle. I kept stealing glances at Cotton for guidance. He never took his eyes from his peephole.

When the big cat finally moved, he sprung up the tree in two quick bounds. He crouched low in the crook of the tree and stared in our direction. I tried not to look into those yellow eyes. He watched us from that position for another fifteen minutes. I could feel night scraping at the muted light. Then, he was on the limb with the bait. He pulled it up, laid down on it, and gave us another heavy stare. He may have been nervous, but he looked confident and angry to me. Five minutes later, he stood and began to feed.

I looked to Cotton one last time. He was looking back at me, pointing at his chest. I did not like chest shots, especially on dangerous game. I put the cross-hairs in the middle of the leopard's chest and picked a single spot. The longer I held it there, the more I believed I could make the shot. All I had to do was squeeze the trigger.

The tom looked up, his face and teeth were stained crimson. His upper lip twitched.

I thought I might have heard a whisper. "Shoot." Tension rose in the darkening quiet. Then I heard it repeatedly: *Shoot. Shoot. Shoot.* It was in my head now, prodding me to finish the hunt. *Shoot. Shoot. Shoot.* My hands were sweating, but steady. *Shoot.* Would I make that shot? Would I miss? *Shoot.*

When I gave in, it did not feel like a conscious decision. I had decided to shoot. I knew I did, but I did not remember that thought process. I did not even remember squeezing the trigger. When the bullet struck, the leopard gave us three coughing bursts and then leapt from the tree. There was a rustling. Then, save the pounding in my chest, quiet.

The kind of silence that follows a shot at a leopard is hard to define. At that moment, you are so focused, so in tune, you can hear a leaf fall. You know you can. But a leaf never falls. Nothing moves; nothing makes a sound. When it does, it is like an explosion. Whether a whisper from your companion or a grunt from the leopard, it almost hurts your ears. Wild emotions you rarely tap into threaten to burst. I wanted to scream, cry, laugh. I prayed.

The leopard grunted. My heart plopped into the acid in my stomach. Tears welled in my eyes. If it was not dead and was still around, it had to be wounded.

Cotton stared through the blind until the Land Cruiser was nearly on top of us. By now, twilight's ghostly shadows had given way to darkness. Not only was the leopard wounded somewhere out there in the tall grass, it was too dark to see it. I felt queasy.

"I think it would be best if you stayed here," Cotton whispered when the truck stopped outside the blind.

I protested. I had fired the weapon. I had squeezed the trigger. I had wounded the leopard.

"If it was not dark, I could let you go. Your safety is my responsibility. This time, I must insist. Besides, this is the perfect opportunity for Hillary to test himself." Cotton actually smiled.

Was I shaking that badly? Cotton rarely asked me to stay behind. I trusted his judgment, but whatever happened next was on me. I bore the responsibility. If someone were mauled, it would be my fault. How could I live with that?

Cotton and Hillary walked into the blackness with their firearms: a .375 rifle for Cotton, a pump-action, twelve-gauge shotgun for Hillary. Cotton would have preferred the shotgun, but this was a learning opportunity for Hillary. He was almost finished with his apprenticeship and facing a wounded leopard would reveal much about everything he had learned over the years. It would be a true test of his readiness.

They moved at the speed of melting ice. Cotton and Hillary had their firearms to their shoulders, the rest of the crew were scanning the ground with flashlights. Soon, Dick and I were alone, staring at their backs. Then at darkness.

The leopard started grunting. He grunted and growled and sawed for five minutes. *Just follow the sound. Was it between them and us? Did they even hear it?* What had I done?

When the blast of the shotgun crashed through the night, I nearly jumped on Dick's back. I could not pray fast enough.

What happened? Was everyone okay? Had the leopard charged? Why was there no screaming, happy or otherwise? *Please God, please.*

"Can you hear anything, Dick?"

"Not since the shot."

"What do you think that means?"

"Maybe they're checking out the leopard."

"I hope so." I would not be able to endure anything else.

When they ambled back to the blind, they were all smiling. Thank God.

"Well?" I said to Cotton.

"You hit him so well he couldn't charge. He was not happy and would have taken us out if he had the strength. Hillary here did a fine job of finishing him with the shotgun." Cotton put his hand on Hillary's back like a proud coach.

"How far did he go?"

"Less than fifteen yards."

"Really? You were gone so long and we couldn't see you."

"The bush is thick and tall."

"If I hit him so well, why wasn't he dead?" Leopards did not share the same tough-to-bring-down reputation as Cape buffalo and lions.

"You hit him perfect. Come have a look." Cotton led us to the downed cat where Old Peter lifted the leopard's head and placed his finger in the entry hole.

"I wouldn't have shot him anyplace different," Cotton continued. "The angle must have been strange. Look here." Cotton instructed Peter to turn the cat over. "Somehow, the bullet exited from his belly even though you were shooting up into the tree. When we found him, he was growling and grunting. He tried to lunge toward us, but Hillary put an end to that. When he was growling and we couldn't see him, it was kind of hairy. We knew we had to be right on top of him, but the grass was so thick. He could have sprung at us from a few feet."

"I'm just glad everyone is safe."

"Was there ever any doubt?"

"I don't think I want to answer that."

"You probably shouldn't." Cotton winked and we all climbed into the Land Cruiser.

Driving back to camp, thinking about the traditional celebration waiting for us, I kept stealing glances at the world's most beautiful cat. More than any animal I know, the leopard retains its dignity and grace even in death. Though I hid it well, I cried. I had killed a magnificent creature. I love animals. I love them for their beauty, power, grace, resilience, stealth, incredible senses, and their instincts. Animals have provided me with so much joy, so much adventure, and so many memories. How could I kill animals that I loved? It is all of those very qualities that I respect which pushed me to participate in their world—a world that never apologized for its will to survive. I love animals. I love to hunt them. And I will not apologize for shedding a tear when I kill one.

The celebration lasted deep into the night. We had taken our last big cat. It had been a good hunt with good people. We took a moment to recognize those truths around a rhythmic fire. We drank. We danced. We sang. We laughed. Underneath all that, there was a quiet girl who had grown up in Wyoming. She never dreamed how different the world would be from her childhood home. As she explored that world and met its people, she grew to realize how much they all had in common.

The animals, the people, and the places I had been—all of them allowed me to reconnect with a girl from Wyoming who saw the world through fresh, awe-filled eyes.

"We'll go back to Buffalo Basin again today; see if we can't find that bull we missed yesterday," Cotton said during morning tea.

We found one buffalo all day. It was a young female. She had died trying to give birth the night before. Neither she, nor the calf survived. By the time we found her, vultures had already started to feast.

"Hyenas and lions won't be far behind," Cotton said. "By this time tomorrow, there will only be a few bones left. It's amazing how efficient African scavengers are."

"If you don't eat, you die."

"Africa understands the meaning to that statement," Cotton said.

We went back the next morning—our last at Rungwa—to test Cotton's prediction. Some of the hide had not been eaten or carried away, but other than that, all that was left were bones and a bloodstained ground covered with vulture and hyena tracks. We looked for buffalo, but our hearts were not into it. We would be leaving after lunch to hunt the swamp-dwelling sitatunga in northern Tanzania. I was looking forward to hunting that unique antelope, but I was sad to leave Rungwa. Only Cotton and Hillary would join us. I had come to trust Old Peter completely when it came to finding and tracking game and keeping us from getting lost. I would miss him. I would miss them all. Young Peter, Masenga, Maisai, Michael, Bariki, Isadori, John, Zwai, and young Kidago, whose constant smile never let me forget how fortunate I was. He found great joy in life. We could learn a lot from him.

When we left camp, the entire staff gathered around the Land Cruiser. They waved and smiled. I cried. There was a real chance we would never see them again. I was sure we would hunt with Cotton again. But when? Two years? Three? By then, anything could happen—especially in Africa. I missed them the moment we drove away and I felt a little empty during the flight to our next camp.

The charter plane ride to Moyowoshi was bumpy and hot. If I were prone to motion sickness, I would have been holding the vomit bag ten minutes into the flight.

"I've never been to this camp." Cotton had to yell in order for us to hear him over the engine. "I've been told they have good sitatunga. The sitatunga, however, is a sneaky antelope. Hunters spend weeks looking and never see one."

"Do you hunt from *makoros*?"

"Not here. They have *machans* built into the swamp and, supposedly, the antelope have become accustomed to them. We will see. If worse comes to worse, we can hunt duiker and suni at Mount Meru."

Henry, a local guide, met us at the airstrip in a Land Cruiser that looked as if it had been around since World War II. Henry literally had parts fastened together with wire and duct tape. It was in need of new shocks, but ran well and carried us safely to camp. As bumpy as the ride was and as much as I worried we would break down—especially when the door fell off—the fact that it ran as well as it did was a testament to Land Cruiser's early engineers and manufacturers.

Henry was tall, well fed, and tanned like a surfer. He was friendly and talkative, but in fifteen minutes had not mentioned sitatunga or hunting. I figured he had to talk about those things all the time and needed a reprieve. We were there to hunt sitatunga, however, so I finally brought it up.

"How has the hunting been?"

"Sorry?"

"The hunting. Has it been good?"

"I wish I could say it has, but this has been a difficult season."

"How difficult?" Cotton said.

"We have taken only two bulls this year and one of them was young."

Cotton, Dick, and I gave each other that *what are we in for* look. Hunting should never be a guaranteed endeavor, but nobody likes to hear a negative report right before they hit the field or, in our case, the swamp.

The camp had no generator and the tents were as old as the Land Cruiser. Their heavy canvas walls seemed to absorb the area's extreme humidity. We decided to spend as much time outside of them as we could. At night, the sheets stuck to our skin and made sleep all but impossible. Of course, Dick snored within minutes of lying down.

The hunting area was a two-hour drive from camp and then another thirty minutes in a *makoro* to the *machans*. They had built the *machans* on ten-foot stilts right on the water where we could look over the reeds and try to catch the world's most aquatic antelope sneaking through the shallows.

Suspended above water, sitting in eager silence, we watched as a black sky went from a deep blue to a soft gray. When the gray transformed like a slow dream to a pale pink and then to a golden sunrise, it felt like God giving us a personal hello.

A splash refocused our attention. Was it a sitatunga? Probably just a bird. Maybe a crocodile or nearby hippo. It could be a sitatunga and that possibility had us leaning forward searching the reeds like a bear studying the river right before the salmon run. It was out there somewhere, this mystery of the swamp, this unbelievable antelope that is more at home neck-deep in water than on land. The breeze flowed through the tall reeds and we listened to their whispers, hoping to tap into the ancient secrets that place would only reveal subtly and over a great deal of time. With our limited time, we needed the antelope to make a mistake. In a wild place like that, whether you are a bug, a sitatunga, or a human, mistakes got you killed. Places such as those do not suffer fools—I did not expect it to be easy.

Twenty minutes later, we had no idea what had made the splash and we never heard another. Two hours later, the whispers from the reeds began to feel like heckles.

For lunch, Henry pulled out a bag of peanut butter sandwiches.

"It is not much, I know. We have not had a hunter in camp for more than a week. If you would not mind too much, we would be grateful if you would shoot an impala for camp meat."

"I don't think we're going to see any impala way out here," Dick said.

"Not here. On the way back to camp, we will find one. I will have to clear it with the game guard, but he is a decent chap. It is only two hundred dollars for a female."

I looked to Dick for a reaction. They wanted us to shoot camp meat and then pay for it to boot? Smelled a little fishy to me, but fresh game meat sounded more appetizing than peanut butter sandwiches.

Dick must have been thinking the same thing. "Do you not have impala on quota?"

"Of course we do. Why do you ask?"

"I was just wondering why we needed permission from the game guard."

"This would be on top of the trophy quota. We are allowed a second quota for females of certain species for camp meat and culling. It is a courtesy to the game guard to ask his permission."

"If we find one, I'll shoot it."

Cotton visited us at our tent after a dinner of fresh impala liver. "I do appreciate the fresh meat, but I'm not sure you should have to pay for it."

"Some people would pay two hundred dollars for a fresh impala steak and not get the enjoyment of hunting it. Besides, that impala will feed some of the camp staff as well. Think of it as an anti-poaching donation."

"I just wanted to say something. This fellow probably gets paid to shoot a few females anyway. I just hate to see you pay him for no reason."

"There are other reasons. I don't feel it's worth making a big deal out of. Thanks though. I appreciate your concern."

"Concern? I just figured if you're going to give away two hundred bucks, it might as well be to me." Cotton had a way of making uncomfortable situations easy.

"What do you think of the sitatunga hunting?" I asked.

"I think if we have another day like today, we should fly back to Arusha and hunt duiker and suni."

"The swamp is beautiful though, isn't it?" I said. "Of course, there is air-conditioning in Arusha." We would protest moving on to Arusha more if Dick had not just shot a sitatunga in Botswana earlier in the year and if we were not heading for the Bangwela swamps in Zambia for sitatunga in a few weeks. Bangwela offered high odds on good representatives of the species. We would give it one more day and then take our chances in Zambia. It had been an enjoyable hunt. I did not want to end it with four days of sitting in a sweatbox waiting for a ghost.

"It sounded like a coyote eating a rabbit," I told Dick, Cotton, and Henry.

"Probably a jackal caught something," Henry said. "It sometimes feels like we are overrun with those little scavengers. Them and hyena. But a hyena would have been louder. They eat like an uninvited in-law. The jackal is much more polite."

"Whatever it was, it feasted right outside our tent. Why do they always do that to me?"

"You're the only one who will stay awake and listen to them," Cotton said.

I am sure he thought he was funny.

By noon, we were sweating and glancing only occasionally into the whispering reeds. We decided to call the plane. It picked us up at four that afternoon and by seven, we were in Arusha checking in at an air-conditioned hotel. When I am hunting, I usually do not mind the heat or cold or whatever. But, after a long, hot, and sticky hunt, the cool manufactured air feels like a touch of heaven.

"Cotton says you go loony when you hunt for suni," Hillary said. He twirled his finger beside his head.

Hillary would become a fine professional hunter. He and I would hunt together these last two days while Cotton and Dick hunted in another area to cover as much ground as possible.

"We will walk the edge of the thorns for suni. When they run across, you shoot."

"I'll try."

"You will shoot well."

It must have been standard PH procedure to stretch the truth to their poor shooting clients. Maybe they understood better than I did that my problem was confidence. One bad shot and I let it tumble. I needed to work on that.

Suni hunting reminded me of rabbit hunting. Walking along a brush line, searching the tangle, waiting for movement you are never ready for. You think you are, constantly reminding yourself to stay alert. You hear and feel the dry leaves and crisp twigs crunch and snap under your boots. You hardly notice the weight of the gun as it presses against your sweating palms.

When the first suni darted from cover and Hillary said "Shoot," I had thought I might have seen what appeared to be a flash—like the shadow of a bird zipping by overhead. I saw the third one more clearly as it raced from left-to-right. It planted all four feet, made a quick right angle turn, and disappeared into heavy cover.

"I need a shotgun," I said. "If they don't stop, I'll never hit them with this." I raised my scoped 7mm.

"They stop, but it is quick." Hillary snapped his fingers. "You need to shoot when they stop. You will shoot very well."

I still wished I had a shotgun.

"We will go to shoot a duiker. They do not run so much. It will be good practice for suni."

I did not fare much better with the Harvey's duiker. I missed the only one we encountered. Hillary failed to comment on my *good* shooting.

After striking out with duiker, we headed back to the same suni spot, planning to give it one more try. I am glad we did. We had not walked more than fifty yards before a pair of suni zipped past us, disappearing under a nearby bush. Hillary ducked to look under the bush.

"Come. Shoot." He pulled on my sleeve.

Dropping straight into a sitting positing, I anchored my elbows on my knees, found the suni through the scope, aimed for the middle of the dainty antelope, and fired. It fell in a heap.

"Good shot." Hillary popped to his feet and ran toward the six-foot bush. Ducking into it, he snagged his shirt on a branch of thorns. He yanked it free and half-disappeared into the tangle. When he emerged, he was holding a male suni by the hind legs, a wide grin on his face.

I could have been ten again, hunting jackrabbits with my brother, Jim, in the Wyoming fields. There was no difference between that young girl from yesteryear and the smiling grandmother waiting to touch the warm prey in her hands. It was a moment without time. Though I would never be that girl again, I remembered what all young hunters know instinctively and what I hoped they never lost. I remembered the pure, unadulterated enjoyment of the hunt. It is a state of wonder you rarely feel after a certain age. As we grow older, we allow cynicism and ego to cloud our memories, to suppress our awe. I wanted to ask that girl where she had been hiding, but before I got a chance, she melted away like a Tanzanian sunset.

We met Dick's group at a little waterhole pounded rough around the edges by small antelope. Old mud, baked hard and gray from the sun's unyielding heat, told the story of a waterhole that was, not long ago, much larger. Would there be anything left in a month? Not without rain.

We skinned my suni and Dick's duiker there.

While the boys were finishing the dirty part of hunting, I noticed something glimmering under a bush. Curiosity forced me to have a closer look. As I walked toward the shiny object, it occurred to me that it was the only item out of place in that serene setting. That is why it caught my attention. Reaching Arusha required only a short drive, but I did not expect to find a Coke can beside the only waterhole for miles. That small, seemingly insignificant piece of aluminum almost ruined the day. I could not allow it. I picked it up, walked it to the Land Cruiser, threw it in back, and tried to forget it.

I had been in remote areas all over the world, wild places populated with animals and people. You would never find a can in the deep bush. Even if some careless western hunter dropped one, when a local villager discovered it, he or she would find some use for it. Waste was an unknown concept in some places. It was sad to see how quickly we, as humans, could forget that. I wished I were less wasteful. Something else I needed to work on.

The following day—our last—Dick shot a suni near the same place I shot mine, but it was on the way back to the hotel, tired, hungry, and ready for a shower that we stopped to enjoy one last gift from Africa. Set against the soft glow of a pinkish sunset, a leopard sat proudly at the base of a wide, dark tree. The fading light was like a thin veil floating above the stealthy tom. He stared at us, his tongue lightly panting over his bottom teeth.

"Look up into the tree," Cotton said softly.

Like a bad joke, a recently built *machan* rested empty, twelve feet above this elusive, big cat. He tolerated our presence only a whisper longer. Then, in one smooth movement, he was gone, nothing more than a passing breeze.

We left Tanzania the next morning.

Cotton died of a heart attack a few years later. Tanzania would never be the same.

PART V
FOREVER
2002

WELCOME HOME: MARY

After Cotton died, we did not think we would ever go back to Tanzania. How could we? For us, Cotton and Tanzania were inseparable. Tanzania, however, does not lend itself to being ignored. Like with an old friend, you are drawn to rekindle a neglected relationship.

We wanted to share Tanzania with some of our children. They would never know Cotton the way we knew him—in the field—but they could see and begin to know the place that shaped a significant portion of his and our lives. We decided to take two of our daughters, Teri and Cari, and their husbands, Dan and Bill. Though we could not hunt with our beloved Cotton, we could hunt with Hillary Dafi. He had urged us to visit his camp for some time, but we kept putting it off. We chose Argentina, Australia, Spain, Mongolia, Mexico, Cameroon, Zambia, Zimbabwe, and South Africa.

Maybe we were afraid of what it would be like without Cotton. Maybe we had too many other places we wanted to explore. Maybe time just got away from us as it always does. Maybe we just were not ready.

Watching our daughters' eager faces washed away my hesitation. They may never know what it was like to hunt with Cotton—I was sorry for that—but they were about to experience something I could never experience again. They were going to see Tanzania for the first time. They were going to gaze upon a hazy Mount Kilimanjaro. They were going to hear the lions and hyenas bicker under a sky full of more stars than they had ever seen. They were going to walk on ground where few humans had ever been. They were going to meet people who lived life like there was no tomorrow because reality required it. And maybe, if they opened themselves, Tanzania might do to them what it did to us.

"Sorry, sir, can you step back through," the security guard said to our son-in-law, Bill, when the metal detector went off. "Please remove your belt and watch.

Do you have anything in your pockets?"

Bill removed his watch, belt, and a handful of change. He walked back through, a beep and red light informing him that he had failed again.

"Please step over here, sir." The security guard had Bill lift his shirt while he waved his electronic wand all around Bill's body. "Please pull your pockets out so I can see them," the security guard said when the wand went off.

Fifteen minutes later, with Bill nearly down to his boxer shorts, the guard found a new wand and Bill was allowed to join us on the other side of security.

"No terrorist is going to get by that guy, that's for sure."

Our flights took us from Denver through Chicago, Frankfurt and Cairo, then to Addis Ababa, Ethiopia, where we would spend one night before flying on to Arusha.

Our good friends and two of Ethiopia's best professional hunters, Nassos and Jason Russos, met us in Addis Ababa and drove us to our hotel, where we had dinner and drinks while we talked about old times, current events, and future plans.

The following morning, they accompanied us to the airport.

The sights and sounds outside the vehicle windows transfixed our daughters. Outdoor markets lined the streets. Among the rush of people, shepherds walked herds of goats toward the market. Under the drone of the vehicle were the sounds of Addis Ababa, including *baaing* goats and chattering voices.

"What's the language?" Cari asked.

"There are around eighty different languages spoken in Ethiopia, with Oromo and Amharic the most widely used," Jason said.

As we weaved through traffic a New Yorker would consider abhorrent, I realized how organized our road system was in the United Sates. I felt like a wildebeest during the migration trying to jostle its way past slower-paced animals. With three unmarked lanes, it was every driver for himself and anything went. Half the time I was terrified; the other half I was bored from not moving. When we finally made it to the airport, the kids could not believe the droves of people. Dick and I just smiled.

"It's the Ethiopia way," Jason said. "Whenever somebody goes on a trip, all their family and friends come to the airport to wish them a safe journey. Of all these people, maybe ten percent are flying today."

"If everybody wasn't smiling, I'd be worried it was an angry mob," Cari said.

"We may have to push our way through, but it should be relatively painless."

After saying goodbye to Nassos and Jason, we hurried to security to wait for an hour and a half. We had to get through security before we could even check in. At the check-in counter, the agent looked over all of our tickets and passports before weighing our bags—as always they were too heavy. After another thirty minutes waiting, the young, cordial agent pushed all our papers back to us and said, "I am very sorry." He pointed at our tickets. "Your flight was changed. It leave one hour ago."

"It's not supposed to leave for two hours."

"I am sorry. It was changed."

"What are we supposed to do now?"

"Please, you wait here." He disappeared into a single, olive-green door behind the counter. The color matched his stiff uniform. He returned five minutes later, accompanied by a tall, slender man wearing a much more important-looking uniform. The tall man's eyes were calm, almost bored. He sighed when his subordinate explained the situation to him in a language we could not understand—probably Oromo or Amharic. The tall man stared at the screen for a few moments, and then walked back through the door without a word. The first man put his hands together as if in prayer. "I am very sorry," he said. "Please wait."

When the tall man returned, he brought four other people with him. Three of them crowded around one computer and two of them around another. The last agent, a young woman with a serious, unchanging expression, read aloud from a single sheet of paper. After five minutes, the first young man said something and pointed to his computer screen. All six of them crowded around to have a look. After they agreed with one another, he finally spoke to us. "I am happy to find you a flight."

"When?"

"Tomorrow, one-thirty. You are reserved. Thank you."

The tall man nodded at us, before disappearing into the back with the others.

"There's nothing we can do to change it," Teri said as we started venting our frustration. "Maybe there's a reason we needed to stay one more night and we just don't know it yet."

"We'd better call Nassos and Jason. See if they can pick us back up," Dick said.

"We could get a taxi."

"Let's call Nassos first."

"Taxis are run like bus services," Jason said when he picked us up. "Each driver has a zone he cannot leave. When you reach the end of his area, you have to find another taxi and you usually have to share with many people—as many as can squeeze into the vehicle. You were smart to call."

Our adventure had started. Another enjoyable evening with Nassos and Jason made the delay more than bearable. Teri especially appreciated the extra time. She and Dan were working hard to get their new greenhouse up and running and the hotel had a beautiful garden to explore.

We met the kids in the hotel lobby the next morning.

"Did you hear the chanting and screaming last night?" Cari asked.

"You mean the lions?" Teri said.

"I didn't hear any lions," Cari said. "It sounded like somebody chanting through a bullhorn. Then a woman screaming. It kept me up all night. It sounded like some horrible sacrificial ceremony."

"All we heard were lions," Teri said. "I thought I was crazy at first, but Dan woke up and heard them too."

"I think you're all crazy," Dick said. "We didn't hear anything."

"Let's go ask the concierge," Cari said to Teri.

They returned ten minutes later.

"What did they tell you?" I asked.

"The first gal we talked to thought we were crazy. She said, 'No way, not here.' Then we went down to the reception desk and they said there was a graduation or wedding—I couldn't understand which—and that might be what I heard. They had no explanation for the lions."

Teri and Dan remained adamant they had heard lions. They asked Jason when he arrived.

"There is a place in town called Lion Park. They have around twenty lions. It is about five miles away, but a lion's roar can carry great distances."

"See Dad, we weren't crazy."

"That is yet to be determined," Dick said.

Ethiopia was one of our favorite places. We loved the Russoses. We loved the people. We loved the wildlife. The unintended layover ended up being too short.

We actually made our next flight. When we last flew on Ethiopian Air, the plane had been sticky with grime and a thick stench of body odor and garbage hung in the air. This plane was clean, comfortable, and odor-free. After a brief stop in Cairo, we landed in Arusha.

We were back. Tanzania. Awaiting us were open savannahs, riverine forests, beautiful people, musical languages, lion, leopard, elephant, hippo, zebra, kudu, wildebeest, tsetse flies, brush fires, campfires, baobab trees, acacias, too many birds to count, and an intense feeling of homecoming. The hot, dry air caressed my face as I stepped away from the airplane. I could not stop myself from smiling.

Mount Kilimanjaro rose over the region as if protecting it like an ancient tribal god. The kids could not keep their eyes away from it. Nobody could. With its bottom half shrouded in a soft cloud and its flat crown of snow, it stood as an endless reminder of God's powerful hand.

Hillary and our good friend, Mike Taylor, were there to meet us.

"It has been too long," Mike said.

"Five years," Dick said.

"Yes, five years is much too long."

We agreed.

The last time we saw Mike's daughters, they were sweet little children, playing simple games and singing innocent songs. Now they were beautiful young women and still the pride of the family.

On the way to the Dik Dik Hotel, Teri and Cari were glued to the windows again. Their interest in the people, the culture, and the landscape gave me comfort. The experience would cause them to reflect upon the way they saw the world. The road to the Dik Dik Hotel was lined with pedestrians, mostly women and children. Many of the children tended to goats, cattle, and chickens. Nearly all the women carried heavy loads on their heads—baskets, blankets, straw, sticks, pots, and anything else that needed hauling. Some of the more talented women had loads stacked over six-feet high.

After twenty minutes, we turned down a winding dirt road protected by large banana trees and other lush vegetation. It was like driving through a leafy tunnel. Teri was pointing to and identifying many of the trees and bushes, and asking questions about those she did not recognize. She and Mike, a first-rate guide, who could name all the plants and trees by their common and scientific names, hit it off right away. He gave her two flora field guides for the hunt. Afterwards, he gave us a tour of the hotel's garden. Teri would have stayed out there for hours with Mike had darkness not got in the way.

Hillary was late joining us for dinner. "I am very sorry. My wife's mother died two days ago and I had to finish with the arrangements."

I guess Teri was right. There had been another reason why we missed our flight.

During dinner, after toasting Teri and Dan on their anniversary, Cari pelted Mike with questions, mostly revolving around tribal history, culture, and language. She spent much of the meal writing down and learning pronunciation of Swahili. Our first day in Tanzania and our girls had embraced its gifts, seeing them all with fresh eyes and open hearts. I could not wait for them to experience the bush.

A dozen smiling men loaded three Land Cruisers with our gear after we landed on a dirt airstrip. The biggest smiles came from familiar faces—faces that I had feared, on more than one occasion, I would never see again. They gathered around us for hugs and handshakes. Masenga was first to greet us. He said *"Jambo, Mama. Jambo, Bwana."* Then Bariki, who used to be Dick's favorite dining-tent butler and bartender, but was now a tracker. Even Durani was there. He had been our driver when we hunted with Cotton in the early years. It was good to see him again. Then wise and gentle Peter—Old Peter—smiled and gave me a long, soft embrace. *"Jambo,* Mama," he said. "Welcome home."

I could not hold back the tears after that. Dear Peter had been Cotton's most trusted tracker. His age made him a rare man in Tanzania, where life expectancy had just recently reached forty-four years. He had beat more odds than most people could imagine.

"I have moved camp," Hillary said as he led us to one of the Land Cruisers. "The old spot was very hot. The new camp is close to the river with much shade."

Hillary had built the new camp in much the same way Cotton had built the old. "I learned from best," he said.

Reed walls with matching gates surrounded the camp to give visitors a sense of comfort. Though sturdy, they would not keep any animal out of the camp. Human activity, for the most part, did that. If an elephant or leopard wanted in, six-foot reeds, no matter how tightly secured, were not going to keep them out. Well-worn pathways led from each thatched-roof tent to the campfire where cocktails and conversation opened up after a hard day of hunting. Each tent had two single beds, a counter with two washbasins, a small green table with one box of tissues and a bottle of water, and a reed-walled shower attached at the back zipper of the tent. The two fifty-gallon oil drums with hoses suspended above the shower were filled with hot and cold water each evening for washing up. A generator provided electricity in the morning and evening. Hillary had built a fine camp.

After a delicious oribi filet with mixed vegetables and potatoes, we headed for the range. Dick and I shot our rifles twice each. They were spot on. We said good luck to the kids and joined Hillary, Peter, and Masenga for a pleasant drive to re-acclimate ourselves to Rungwa. Peter was right—I was home.

We spent that afternoon driving, talking, and half-heartedly looking for game. Dick shot a zebra for bait, but I mostly just took in the sights, sounds, and smells. Baobabs and sausage trees, zebras and giraffes, dust and burning grass, hippo grunts and go-away bird chants. It was a sensory overload. Even when we hung baits, a normally dirty, stinky, monotonous job, I smiled. It was all part of our return to Tanzania.

I thought about the girls and their husbands. How were they doing? Had they shot anything? Did they feel the way I felt? Were the tsetse flies devouring them? I had never been a fan of tsetse flies, but Tanzania would not be the same without them. The girls needed to know what a sting felt like—I just hoped the flies would not relentlessly attack them the way they always did me.

By the time we finished hanging the second bait, it was too dark to continue. We headed back to camp for our first night—our first fireside conversation. I wanted to hear the kids' stories. I wanted to see the looks on their faces. I wanted to share a toast with them. This was no ordinary return to Tanzania. Two of our children were there—they were experiencing, first-hand, why their parents felt compelled to return so often. I wanted Africa to touch them in the same way it had touched us. Then, they would know more about us than we could ever share in any other way.

As we pulled into camp, I saw their silhouettes standing beside a dancing fire, its sparks floating into the darkness. I did not run to join them, but I wanted to. I smiled as I approached. They all smiled back.

"How'd you do?" Teri asked.

Never mind how we did. How did you do? "Your father shot a zebra. How about you? How was your first day?"

"Nothing like I thought it would be," Cari said.

"What do you mean?"

"I guess I imagined it would be like you see on television. Open fields with animals walking around everywhere. Lions and elephants and giraffes and zebras as far as you can see."

"You might find that some place like Ngoro Ngoro Crater, but areas like that are rare," Dick said. "Even areas like this are rare. The variety and volume of game here is unrivaled in much of Africa."

"I'm not complaining," Cari said. "In many ways, this is better. You have to work for your animals."

"What did you see," I asked.

"Mostly duikers and zebras today."

"What about your group," I asked Teri and Dan.

"It started out slow for us too," Teri said. "But then we saw some oribi, steenbok, giraffe, zebra, vultures, and another bird, a hamerkop."

"They are such a neat bird," I said. "Did anybody else shoot anything?"

"I shot a steenbok," Dan said.

"Alex told us that you sometimes see a male alone, but never a female," Teri said. "And that if you shoot a male that is with a female, she will quickly join with another male. Tell them what happened after the steenbok," she said to Dan.

"We hadn't gone more than half a mile when Alex and our tracker, Raphael, started freaking out. I was digging in my bag for a pair of sunglasses when they started saying, '*Simba! Simba! Simba!*' Of course, eagle-eye Teri saw him before I did."

"He was so beautiful," she said. "Huge, with an awesome mane." She held her hands wide on either side of her head.

"I saw him just before he slipped into a draw; I think Alex called it a *korongo*. Anyway, the second he disappeared, Alex said we needed to shoot a zebra for bait. It took us an hour to find a zebra, an hour to stalk it, and another hour to get it skinned, gutted and into the truck. Then we took it back to a tree near where we had seen the lion, hung part of it, and dragged the guts all over to create a strong scent."

"It was gross," Teri said to Cari and me.

The men laughed at us. Typical.

"We had only driven a few hundred yards when Raphael said, 'Look, he is here.' I didn't see him right away, so Raphael grabbed my ear and pointed my face in the right direction. I never had a rush like that. I'll never forget the way the lion looked at me without fear in his eyes. He ran less than fifty yards before stopping behind a thorn bush. Alex and I hurried to get into position, but the best we could do was a head-on shot through the bush. All I could focus on were his huge yellow eyes. They were almost hypnotic."

You could see Dan searching for the right words to convey what he felt as he looked into the lion's eyes. I wanted to tell him there were no words.

"Alex said to pull the trigger whenever I felt safe with the shot. Just as my finger was heading for the trigger, Alex tapped my shoulder and said. 'Do not take the shot unless you are absolutely sure.' I didn't take the shot. I didn't take the *simba* when I had a chance."

"You made the right choice," Teri said.

"I know, but sometimes you never get a second chance."

"Sounds like you had a great day," I said.

"Yeah, we had a good day. My God," he said quietly. "I hope we have a good day tomorrow."

I hoped so too.

I looked into the darkening sky. There was one star out—the first star—Ben's star. I said a silent prayer for Joan. Then I thanked Cotton for introducing us to this place. I believed he was still there, with his half-crooked smile and his soft patient voice to settle my nerves when I needed it most.

It was good to be home.

FIRST-TIME TEARS: CARI

"I wish we could call the kids," I said to Bill. "I miss them."

"I do to, but there aren't any phones out here."

"I just want to hear their voices." Bill and I would have similar conversations almost every day. Brady was three years old and Trinity only nine months. Even though I knew it would be hard to leave them for such an extended journey, I was still a wreck. Only the constant wonders of Africa periodically took my thoughts from the girls.

"There's nothing you can do about it here," Bill said. "You need to try to enjoy yourself."

Sitting around camp and lying awake in bed were always hard. Watching giraffes or tracking buffalo refocused me to the moment I was in, instead of those I had left at home.

Mom and Dad had warned us the mornings would be cold, but I was unprepared for that kind of chill. It seeped through my tank top, my long-sleeve shirt, my heavy sweater, and my pullover wind jacket. It penetrated my gloves as if they were not even there. My legs felt bare. I did not know what the temperature was; I just knew it was cold. We left camp at six in the morning; by nine I had shed most of my layers and had to remind myself not to complain about the heat.

I was the only client in camp who had never been hunting. My parents had traveled the world following the tracks of game animals. Bill and Dan had hunted birds, small game, and deer all their lives. Teri had joined my parents on a hunt in Zambia a few years before. This was my first time. I did not know what to expect. In many ways, I did not think it would be so hard—especially in Africa, where I was led to believe I would be surrounded by beasts as far as I could see. How I was led to believe that, I am not sure. Nature shows were influential. The stories and pictures my parents and other family members brought home added to the myth. Just like on the nature programs, they left out all the driving around, the long hikes, the impossible-to-see-through tall grass, the dense forests, the thick brush, and the long stretches when it felt like there was not an animal left on the continent. The animals were not captive; they were not tame; they were not acclimated to human presence. If I had known the challenges and beauty intertwined with the hunt, I might have insisted on being a part of it much earlier.

"Stop," Bariki, our main tracker, said from the back. When the truck stopped, he and Earnest, another tracker, jumped out to inspect the road. Durani, the driver, joined them a moment later. Gamshard, our professional hunter, stayed with us and Mkulu, the game guard, barely looked up from his spot in the back corner of the Land Cruiser.

"What is it," I asked.

"*Nyati* track," Gam said. "Buffalo."

Bill's back straightened. He had heard about buffalo hunting from some of my brothers and was looking forward to adding a story of his own.

"We must wait to see if the tracks are fresh," Gam said.

Bariki, Earnest, and Durani walked away from the road, never once pulling their gaze from the ground. After they had moved fifty yards, Gam said, "Come, we will go."

Bill grabbed his rifle and we hurried to catch up with the trackers. Mkulu slid out of the truck to follow behind us. Forty minutes later, Bariki leaned over to look at a pile of buffalo dung. He scrapped it with his shoe. I wondered if he planned to clean it off before he climbed back into the truck. He and Gam spoke in Swahili for a few moments and then Gam turned to us.

"*Nyati* are many hours ahead. We will go back."

On our hike back to the vehicle, I saw something move to our right. "Oh my God, there's a leopard," I said way too loudly.

"*Chui, chui.* Good."

A leopard at midday? Unheard of.

"Shoot, Bill. Shoot."

The leopard was one hundred yards out and dropping into a ravine. I had never seen an animal move like that—almost as if it were floating. Bill snapped the gun to his shoulder. The leopard walked up the opposite side of the *korongo* and stopped halfway behind a wide acacia.

"Shoot," Gam said softly. "Shoot."

I heard the shot and thought I saw the leopard run, but Gam and the others started cheering and clapping right after Bill fired.

Gam told Durani to run back to retrieve the vehicle while we moved in. When we closed the distance to around thirty yards, I saw its tail move. I wondered if it was just nerves or if it was still alive. Its chest tightened as it struggled for air. Its paws scraped the ground weakly. He forced a heavy growl from his throat.

I started bawling.

I had never seen an animal shot and killed. Sure, Dad, Mom, and my brothers brought home plenty of dead animals, but they did not kill them in front of me. I had no idea what it felt like.

Bill said, "I'm going to put him out of his misery."

I jumped at the shot. Tears ran down my face as Gam and the others congratulated my husband. It was a beautiful animal—one of the most beautiful I had ever seen. And now it was dead. Logically, I understood it—knew the role hunting played in not only conservation, but in feeding the will of the predator in us all. Emotionally, it was hard. A moment ago, this spotted creature, with its unmatched combination of power and grace, was a living, breathing entity. Now, because of us, it was lifeless. There was no getting around that fact.

While the others smiled and found a certain pride in the moment, I cried. Under the tears and sorrow and brutal reality, I felt something else. There was some pride, I guess, maybe even joy, and part of me wanted to celebrate with the others. I had so many conflicting emotions in that one moment. That was what separated us from other predators—we felt remorse and joy at the same time, and filtered through the emotions with evolved intelligence to understand their meanings. Before that moment, I thought I could be a hunter. After all, my brothers were; my mother was; why couldn't I be? Watching an animal die gave me pause. Could I do it? Could I actually shoot a living creature? If I was willing to eat something or use it in some other way, shouldn't I be willing to kill it myself?

I thought about it over the next hour while Gam talked with Bill about shooting a zebra for lion bait. I had not really been listening to them until I heard Bill mention my name.

"I think Cari wants to take a zebra."

Gam glanced in my direction. In that quick look, I saw skepticism. I had wanted to shoot a zebra. But that was before I saw the leopard die. Did I still want to shoot one?

"Zebra is a good animal to start," Gam said. "We will find an easy one."

We found a herd with a good stallion. If I did not try, I would never know. I would always question myself if I passed the opportunity to hunt while on a hunting safari in Tanzania.

I focused on what I had to do during the short stalk. Just like on the range. Breathe, hold, squeeze. But this was not a paper target. It was a beautiful creature, full of life and an instinct to survive. Breathe, hold, squeeze.

The crosshairs jumped in tandem with my nerves.

"I can't get steady," I said softly.

"Take your time; shoot when you are ready," Gam said.

The zebras started to run.

"Wait. Do not shoot."

We hurried after them, setting up just in time to see them move away again. We followed them. This on-again, off-again routine did not help my unease. We set up at two hundred yards out. My breath trembled.

"Wait until you are ready," Gam said.

Would I ever be ready?

I squeezed. The zebra jumped, took a step, and tipped over. I cried.

"Good shot."

Part of me felt like smiling, but when I looked at the zebra, I saw movement. Oh, please no. What had I done?

It got worse as we closed the distance. His back legs kicked and struggled, his head raked on the ground; strange guttural sounds blew from his nostrils. But it was his eyes, his big, brown, beautiful eyes—so full of fear. This zebra, the first animal I had ever shot, stared at me with a look that pierced through my eyes and burrowed in to wrestle with my soul.

The shot, my shot, had been too low.

"You must shoot again."

It was so hard. He was looking at me. He was struggling to live. Tears were running down my face like the blood running down his legs. I had to finish it. I wiped my eyes, but tears blurred my vision. I hit him well with the second shot. It was not enough. His back legs were not as strong, but still kicking. His head now flopped to the ground, resigned to his fate.

"Again."

I could not, yet I had to. I needed to end its pain.

The next shot finished it. The zebra stallion was dead.

My hands went limp and I let Gam take the rifle from me. The vehicle pulled up behind us. Bariki and the others went to admire the animal. I went to sit down. I went to cry.

"If you ever get to the point where it doesn't bother you, it's time to quit hunting," Bill said.

Did everyone feel that way? Were those emotions part of hunting? According to my husband, who had been hunting all his life and who held his emotion in better than I did, they were. I did not know if that was something I could handle.

Gam stayed with me in the vehicle and let me cry for ten minutes. When I finally started to calm down, he said, "Do you wish for a picture?"

I tried to smile through the tears while they took photos, but I was not successful.

On the way back to camp, Bariki tapped me on the shoulder. "You sing, yes?"

"Yes," I said.

"I teach song of cat. It is good song. It is happy song."

"I would like that," I said.

"*Twende pamoja chinja mnyama na Cari. Twende pamoja chinja mnyama na Cari.*"

"That was my name."

"Yes, you do good hunt. Song for you."

"Can I hear it again?"

This time Earnest, Durani, and Mkulu joined in. "*Twende pamoja chinja mnyama na Cari. Twende pamoja chinja mnyama na Cari.*"

I did not know its literal meaning, but I loved it.

A few minutes from camp, we stopped to decorate the vehicle in branches. Bariki cut extra branches for the rest of us to wave. When we started moving again, they began singing again, this time ending with Bill's name. Their harmony was perfect. I hesitated to add my own voice, but I could not help myself. It was a celebration. The hunter had returned with his prey. We sang an ancient song, passed down through generations of hunters. We did not have to know the words to understand the meaning.

Most of the camp staff rushed to greet us. Skinners, cooks, waiters, and water boys joined in the chorus. They cheered and jumped on the moving truck, smiling, clapping, and singing. Coaxing Bill from the vehicle, they had him sit in one of the campfire chairs. Then, four or five men hoisted him into the air and carried him around, never once missing a note in the hunter's victory song.

Everyone took a turn to congratulate Bill. Then many of them moved on to me. When Teri and Dan asked me about the hunt, tears ran down my face. Through sniffles and sobs, I told them what happened.

"I'm not sure if I'll ever try it again," I said. "I don't know if I can."

"It's hard for everybody," Teri said. "I haven't hunted much, but I've been hunting with Mom and I've seen it in her eyes. And Dan says it bothers him too."

"If it didn't bother you, I'd think there was something wrong with you," Dan said.

"I still don't know if I can do it again."

"That's okay," Teri said. "Whatever you decide is fine. Everyone understands."

Maybe they did; maybe they did not. It did not seem as if they did. There were so many smiles and so much laughter and cheery banter. I felt alone in my sorrow and remorse.

"Did you guys get anything?" I asked.

"We checked our lion bait the first thing," Teri said. "It was hit, so we spent the morning building a blind. We'll go back later to sit and wait for him."

We talked about the leopard and the lion until Teri and Dan left for the blind. Though on my mind, the zebra didn't come up in discussion again until Mom and Dad returned to camp.

"Let us play a joke on your mother and father, yes?" Gam said after I woke from a short, much-needed nap.

"What kind of joke?"

"We will not tell them Bill shot a leopard. We will hide it under the zebra. Do you want us to play a joke?"

"Sure, we can play a joke on them."

It would have been a good joke had someone from camp not earlier radioed that Bill had shot a leopard in the middle of the day without baiting—it was a rare event.

When my parents asked about the zebra and leopard, I cried.

"I wish it wouldn't have been your first animal," Mom said. "Don't let this turn you against hunting. You don't have to quit. Those feelings are natural."

"I'm not against hunting," I said. "I just don't know if I can do it again."

Mom nodded. "I hope you can try, but if you don't, it's okay."

While we waited for Teri and Dan to return from their lion hunt, we probed Mom and Dad about the jackal, the zebra, and the hyena my father had shot during the day. Mom offered more details than Dad did, but their beaming faces told me all I needed to know. I understood why they loved Africa. I was not sure if I understood why they loved hunting yet, but over the next few weeks, I hoped to find out.

We heard the low, steady hum of a well-used Land Cruiser a few minutes before Teri and Dan returned to camp.

"I don't hear any singing," Mom said.

"No lion," Dad said.

"A lion and a leopard in the same day might be asking too much."

We waited for them to join us beside the fire.

"No lion, huh?"

Teri glanced at Dan.

"I missed," he said.

We waited for further explanation.

"It wasn't a good situation," Teri said. "It was almost dark, we were crammed into a small *machan*, and the lion was quartered."

"At least it was a clean miss," Dad said. "Nobody wants a wounded lion on their hands."

"It was kind of tense," Teri said. "It was almost dark and I felt like we were rushed."

"I shouldn't have taken the shot," Dan said. "But Dick is right. At least I missed."

"What was it like?" I asked Teri.

"Other than being too cramped, it was neat. They had built the *machan* twenty-five feet into a tree and put together a ladder for easy access. There was a small waterhole not too far away, which brought plenty of wildlife past us. We watched a nervous buffalo herd come for a drink. I think they knew the lions were close—I'd never seen buffalo act that jumpy before. I kept falling asleep. I think the jet lag is starting to set in."

"How long before the lions came?"

"It was funny. I haven't even told you yet, Dan. But I kept hearing this low-toned growling that I thought might be a wild creature. It sounded close, but it was so quiet. I kept looking out the shooting hole and trying to look behind me. Then I figured out it was Alex's stomach rumbling. I'm glad I didn't ask him what it was. It was uncomfortable and hard to stay quiet and still, especially with all these tsetse fly bites on my ankles—they were the only things keeping me awake until the lions showed up. Then it was so fast, I didn't even get to see them. I didn't want to move when Dan was trying to shoot."

"I missed," Dan said. "What can I say?"

"Even though everyone thought he had missed, we searched for blood for hours. In the dark, in the long grass. I was terrified. Oh, I can hardly take it." Teri sat down to remove her shoes and socks. "It feels like thousands of tiny ants are gnawing on my ankles."

Her ankles were swollen to the size of pineapples and were covered with red and purple splotches. "That's from tsetse flies?" I asked.

"They've been gnawing on her all day," Dan said.

"I wonder if you're having an allergic reaction," Mom said.

"We've got some hydrocortisone if you want to try it," I said.

"Thanks," Teri said. "I feel so tired."

"You'd better eat something," Mom said. "Then go straight to bed."

"I plan to."

Bill and I were the last to retire that evening. I guess the adrenaline of a novice hunter's first kill and Bill's first dangerous game animal took time to wear off.

That and the fact we had stayed in camp for much of the afternoon when everyone else was out hunting hard. Lying in bed, staring into the dark, I heard a hyena giggle, or whatever sound it was that hyenas made. I tried not to think about the leopard or the zebra. I tried not to think about my role in their deaths. I fell asleep thinking about it.

"Happy Birthday," I said to Bill when the wake-up call came in the form of an innocent, young, native voice saying, "Good morning." If we did not answer right away, he'd call again, slightly louder. "Good morning."

"We will look for buffalo today," Gam said as Bill and I ate over-easy eggs for breakfast.

Finding buffalo was more difficult than it sounded. We found a few old tracks, but nothing fresh enough to follow. With some of the meat from my zebra, we baited for lion and decided to stop near a waterhole for lunch.

"Come, look here," Bariki said as we finished our sandwiches.

We followed him to a nearby field of seven-foot grass. He walked into a small opening and waved for us to follow him.

As we stepped into the labyrinth of lightly swaying blades, I noticed a faint scent in the air. I could not quite place it. It smelled dirty, almost musty, with a hint of livestock. Though not strong enough to be offensive, it was unpleasant. A few more yards in and the field opened to a wide area where most of the grass had been flattened.

"*Nyati*," Bariki waved his hand around the area before bending over to pick up a pile of buffalo dung. "*Nyati*," he said again.

That is what the smell was—buffalo—or, at least, what they left behind.

"Looks like a big herd," Bill said.

"Yes, many. They here just in morning."

There was no telling how far they had traveled since the morning, and trying to follow tracks seven-to-eight-hours old usually turned out to be a fool's errand.

"Why does this grass have so much green left in it, while so much of the other grass is brown and easy to burn," I asked Gam as we loaded back into the vehicle.

"This is the winter season. Most grass is good for burning. Some grass near the water is not good for burning. When the water goes dry, the grass goes dry. *Nyati* use the grass to hide. It is tall and thick. *Nyati* are not easy to see if grass is not burned."

"What about the trees?" I asked.

"Fire does not burn the trees. They have much moisture inside."

"I didn't know that."

"Fire and smoke are very good in Tanzania. When we collect honey, we use smoke to push bees; then we steal the honey."

Bumping along an uneven trail road littered with rocks and dips and elephant footprints from the rainy season, I thought about the girls. They were in my thoughts most of the time, but when game was scarce, the sun was ramming us with heat, and the tsetse flies were hungry, it made me homesick. Trinity was probably running all over the place by now—she took three steps the day we left.

The only thing worse than the relentless, blood-sucking vermin known as tsetse flies was the pain of being away from my girls. There were times when I just wanted to go home, when I did not care if I spent another minute in Tanzania.

Tanzania had a way of reminding you that some places were deserving of your attention. And if you gave it to her, she would reward you with a discovery, or, in some cases, a rediscovery of yourself.

"*Nyati.*" Bariki was pointing at a dark mass huddled below a single acacia so far in the distance that I questioned how he could tell they were buffalo. How did he know they were not wildebeest? They looked more like wildebeest to me. Even through my binoculars, I could not make out anything but a black mass of animals. The tree seemed to give them some scale, but not enough for me to distinguish between buffalo or wildebeest.

"We must go by foot from here," Gam said. "We must be quiet."

With six of us traipsing through the brush, it sounded more like a herd of elephants than a stealthy pack of lions. Bariki and Earnest led. Gam, Bill, and I followed close behind. Mkulu mostly hung back and kept to himself—I never heard him walking. I really only heard Bill and me. Bariki and Earnest moved like a breeze. Gam occasionally rustled dry leaves with his shoe, but it was like a whisper compared to the snapping twigs, scraping dirt, and snagging clothing that shattered any resemblance of silence while Bill and I clogged along. I tried to follow exactly in Gam's light footsteps, but my years of pounding on cement and asphalt with total disregard for stealth fought with me the entire time.

At one hundred fifty yards, Bill and Gam broke away from the group to move the last few yards by themselves. Watching from behind a small thorn bush, I leaned over and steadied my hands just above my knees. They moved slowly, Bill following only a few inches behind Gam. They would take one or two steps and then stop in mid-stride, holding until Gam was certain none of the many eyes were following them. A small insect fluttered around my eyes, easily dodging my attempts to swat it away. As if it were some sort of dare, the bug kept buzzing, trying to annoy me as much as my brothers did when we were younger. I wanted to kill that insect.

When Bill finally set his rifle on the shooting sticks, I braced for the blast. I waited. Gam leaned in close to Bill's ear while he focused through the scope. Why didn't he shoot? Then, as if a lion had popped up from the grass, the herd charged away, leaving only a settling dust cloud behind them.

Bariki and Earnest started toward Bill and Gam. Mkulu waited for me to follow them before putting his hands in his pockets and strolling behind.

"The wind changed. They caught our scent."

"So what now?"

"Now we track," Gam said. "There is a good bull." Gamshard held his hands wide on either side of his head. "Bill must shoot this buffalo."

"What are we waiting for?" I asked.

Gam laughed. "Is she this bossy at home?"

"No," Bill said. "It's much worse at home."

Everybody laughed. I gave Bill my best *you're going to get it* look.

Up and down rocky hills, through dry riverbeds, under heavy thorn bushes, we tracked and we tracked, never seeming to gain ground. They had to stop and rest at some point, didn't they? I needed to.

We pressed on, following heavy sign I could see on soft ground and almost no sign, at least that I could see, over the rocks and through the valleys. There were long stretches, lasting twenty to thirty minutes, when I wondered if we were walking just to walk. I did not see any tracks. Then we would stumble from a hardened hill to a dry water hole and find the ground stamped with fresh buffalo tracks and dotted with steaming dung. We had to be closing in on them.

After two more hours under the relentless sun, Gam stopped and looked into the sky. "We must go back." He looked at us for reaction. "It is late. We will not find the buffalo before dark. The wind is keeping us in the buffalo's nose."

I was hot, exhausted, thirsty. All the adrenaline from the expectation that we would find the buffalo evaporated faster than my sweat did in that dry heat. Walking another two hours back to the truck seemed impossible. Walking back up the last hill seemed improbable. I didn't have a choice.

For the next half hour, I trudged, with my head down, in a weary trance, pushing the next step from a stubborn refusal to quit. All I wanted was to slump into that uncomfortable high bench on the Land Cruiser. Glancing at my watch almost caused me to collapse. How could it have only been thirty minutes? Did we really have another hour and a half? I wanted to whimper.

I glanced up and peered around Gam. Was that the truck? Only a few hundred yards further? If any strength had remained in my legs, I might have run. The sight of the Land Cruiser and the thought of a drink of water gave me a final surge of energy. A few hundred yards—no problem.

That evening at dinner, we heard about the buffalo Mom shot. She had to shoot him four times, even though each of her shots hit its mark. I was not sure about hunting something you had to shoot four times. Hillary and Dad praised her two off-hand shots from seventy-five yards, saying they could not have done better themselves.

When Teri appeared from her tent, we could see that she was not doing well. Her fever had not let up and her ankles looked like something out of a Stephen King novel. Massively swelled with oozing bites that looked like blisters, her ankles had turned an ugly mix of maroon, deep purple, and black.

"I think you must stay in camp to heal," Hillary said. "If you do not rest, you will not feel better for a long time. I must insist that you to stay in camp for one or two days."

"I hate it, but I know you're right."

"Joel will take good care of you."

A few minutes later, the entire camp staff marched around the table clapping and singing Happy Birthday to Bill. We ate and drank and laughed until Dad started nodding off at the table.

"I think it's time for us to go to bed," Mom said. "Come on, Dick, you're falling asleep."

"I'm just resting."

"It's time for bed."

The rest of us were right behind them.

"Happy Birthday, Cari," Bill said the next morning. He had awoken before me and was waiting for me to get ready.

Within an hour of leaving camp, we ran across a herd of zebra.

"You need a zebra," Gam said to Bill. "And we need bait for lion and leopard."

I felt exposed during the stalk. Unlike some of the other herds we had seen, this bunch used no trees for cover.

Had we been a pack of lions, they might have allowed us to breech the two hundred yards they insisted on keeping between us. Every time we tried, one of the females rocked her head back and kicked her legs, and the herd would run. After the third time that happened, Gam stopped us at the impassable two-hundred-yard mark.

"We must shoot now." He put his binoculars to his eyes.

Using the shooting sticks, Bill peered at the zebras through his scope. A few minutes passed. Nobody said a word.

Finally, he looked up from the scope. Seeing us staring at him, he said, "Which one do you want me to shoot?"

"On the left. It is a good male. Shoot when you are ready."

He fired. The zebra fell. I did not cry.

I expected to when we moved in—especially if it was still alive.

It wasn't. Thank goodness.

Durani met us with the Land Cruiser and after loading the entire zebra, we headed for a nearby waterhole. Along the way, Bill and Gam made a short stalk and a good shot on a female oribi for camp meat. The little creature looked almost cute and helpless, and it looked dead. I almost cried. I was not getting used to the killing, but I was beginning to understand it better. Hunting in Tanzania revealed to me how sheltered I had been from life's realities. My actions, even the simple and necessary act of eating, did not come without consequences.

I found it interesting when Bariki, Earnest, and Durani skinned the zebra, but it was hard to watch. They cut, pulled, and sliced, exposing blood and muscle. The smell, though unpleasant, was neither strong nor unbearable. I turned away before they ripped open the belly to release its entrails.

Mkulu had disappeared. Right when I was going to ask Gam where Mkulu had gone, our unsmiling game guard emerged from the woodland carrying an armful of branches. He spent the next few minutes building a campfire. Once burning to his satisfaction, he called to Durani who cut a few slices of zebra meat and carried it over. Then Mkulu cut a pile of meat from the oribi's haunch.

The odor changed. Instead of that stale scent I would forever associate with death, a crisp aroma of wood-fire cooked steak floated toward us. Hunger tapped at my stomach and I hoped they would offer me a piece of the fresh kill. I wanted to taste the exotic, local fare cooked over an open fire.

There was no contest between the meats. I would eat oribi for every meal. I would eat zebra only if I had to. Any meat not slated for baiting or meals went directly to the camp staff and their families—nothing was wasted. I was beginning to toy with the idea of hunting again. At least I was no longer ruling it out completely.

That night we ate penne pasta with oribi—delectable. Dad got his buffalo, Mom said her sandwich for lunch tasted like it had been rolled in dirt, Dan shot a dik-dik and an oribi, and Teri stayed in camp—she was feeling better.

"Raphael said, 'The jackal was going to go home to tell all his friends the white guy can't shoot so don't worry about him.'" Dan was finishing a story of a missed shot on a jackal, when Alex and Gam excused themselves again. I had an idea what they were up to.

When Joel, carrying another cake, led a second singing procession into the dining tent, we were not surprised. They sang the song from Bill's leopard kill. I joined in. I could not help myself. I love to sing and to sing with such talented voices in a remote camp in Tanzania was an opportunity I could not pass.

They sang and danced around the table four times before placing the cake before me. "*Asante sana*," I said. "Thank you very much."

Joel smiled and bowed slightly.

"Could you please pass me some napkins, Bill?" I glanced around and mentally counted the faces. I would have to cut the slices thin. "I want everyone to have some," I said to Joel.

He told the men to stick around for some cake. I saw some of them lick their lips. The cake did not last long, but the party did. We sang and danced some more—at my request—and then everyone said "*Lala salama*," which meant "good night," or more precisely, "sleep in peace."

The fire quickly became my favorite spot in camp. I never knew how much it would mean to me or how much I would miss it in the years that followed. But around the fire with millions of stars listening to our conversations, I discovered hunting was so much more than tracking, stalking, spotting, and shooting animals. It was all of those things, but after a day in the bush, when you are tired and hungry, you see the flames dancing like an ancient Maasai ritual and you are drawn. Weariness drifts into the night like ashes floating above the flames. Around the fire, you see faces of people you love like you have never seen them before—glowing in every sense of the word. Stories are told with more life and openness. Something about the soft light makes you feel secure and alive.

That night, I sat in one of the canvas chairs and leaned back to look at the stars. I had never seen so many. The more I stared, the more I thought about mortality and the everyday things that give life its deepest meanings. I understood, finally, why my parents loved Africa. I understood a hunting camp was a special place and a campfire had few equals when it came to camaraderie.

I stared at the stars and believed I wanted to be a part of it. It was there, on the night of my birthday, I decided I wanted to try to be a hunter. It was sad and it was hard, but it was good.

ON HUNTING CATS: DICK

Cat hunting is a long, monotonous process. It starts out by hanging meat in a likely looking tree, driving a long distance to another likely looking tree and hanging more meat. Then, after you have hung enough meat in enough trees far enough away from each other, you start to check them. Morning after morning, day after day, mile after bumpy mile. You drive to each bait; check to see if it has been gnawed on; check for tracks; and move on to the next bait. Every once in a while, a slab of meat gets chewed on. You check the tracks and claw marks on the trees—if it is a lion, you look for long mane hairs to make sure you are dealing with a male. Most often, you find hyena tracks or smallish lion and leopard tracks. Sometimes you move the bait; sometimes you leave it, hoping a male will join with the females the next evening.

An entire hunt can go on like this without a single large male cat coming to feed. Most often, one will feed and you will spend a couple of hours building a blind or *machan* to sit in late that afternoon. Then, you sit for hours, unable to move, unable to talk, and wait. If a cat does come—it usually does not—you have to ensure it is an old cat. If not, you start the process over again.

I have never been disappointed hunting cats in Africa. I have come away empty-handed many times, pushed to the limits of mental and physical exhaustion, but disappointed—never.

Lions and leopards like to surprise you. They challenge you with their unpredictability and though you may not shoot one, you will come away with an experience like nothing on earth.

We had been hanging and checking lion and leopard baits for four days. Rarely do you get lucky early on a cat hunt. Unless, of course, your name is Bill and you find a leopard in the middle of the day. I had been to Africa more than thirty times and I had never found a leopard like that—not when I was hunting them.

We had allowed ourselves to drift into a lull. The anticipation that a cat might have fed faded each time we checked an untouched bait. Hope remained at some level, but after four days of nothing, we suppressed that hope with a layer of pessimism. If unchecked, negativity can twist you into a cat-hunting cynic and that is no fun for anybody. You have to hold on to hope—without it, there is no point.

"I think we should move this bait to the next *korongo*," Hillary said. "It has water. Maybe the lion will come for drink as well as a meal."

Moving bait is always a risky decision. You have already created a heavy, fresh scent. You can never get the same odor with two-day-old meat. Young Peter zipped up the tree, unlatched the chain they used to hang the bait, and let the meat drop.

We drove for fifteen minutes before stopping beside a running creek. The heavy vegetation, water, and shadows cooled the ravine by ten degrees. The mid-morning sun penetrated in small, sharp rays like light shining through bullet holes in a windowless room. It felt more like a great spot for leopard than lion. Hillary and Peter had hunted far more cats than I had—I trusted their judgment. We hiked around the area for thirty minutes studying possible bait trees with a suitable area to build a *machan* or blind nearby.

When Hillary found the tree he wanted, he called for Peter to bring the meat. It looked like a fever tree, but the bark did not seem yellow enough.

"It's some sort of acacia," Mary said. "I bet Teri would know."

"And if she didn't, she could look it up in her book."

Hillary moved closer as we talked. "It is what you call a flood thorn tree. It only grows by water."

Several branches fanned from low on the trunk, reaching ten feet high before spreading into a canopy of leaves and thorns. The brush was thick and dark behind the tree before descending into the shallow *korongo*. Heavy bushes and smaller trees formed a half-circle on either side. Away from the water, the ground opened to a few small bushes until reaching a small grove of big, heavy-trunked trees where we would build a *machan* if a lion fell into the temptation of an easy meal.

With the bait re-hung and noon approaching, Hillary suggested we check one last leopard bait on our way in for lunch. We were familiar with the bait—we checked it every day. The dusty ground surrounding the tree allowed us to make a wide circle looking for tracks without getting out of the vehicle. Most days, we drove around the tree at a speed too fast for me to see tracks on the ground.

"*Polepole*," Peter said. "*Polepole*."

The truck slowed.

"*Simama*."

Masenga stopped the Land Cruiser. Both Peters jumped from the back. They walked with their eyes to the ground toward the tree.

"Back, back," Hillary said, instructing Masenga to back up in tandem with our two trackers.

Old Peter and Young Peter were standing under the tree discussing the tracks on the ground when we rolled up to them. I stretched out my neck trying to see the size of the tracks.

"Whoa!"

A quick growl shot down from above and a small leopard sprang from the tree directly overhead. The trackers reeled back. Mary shrieked as it hit the ground not more than three feet from Old Peter before disappearing into the nearby brush.

Everybody's eyes were wide. It could have jumped into the back of the Land Cruiser. It could have mauled the trackers at any point. Within moments, everyone was laughing nervously. It had been a small cat—a female or a young male. None of us had expected it to be there at midday; once again, the leopard proved it was anything but predictable.

"That was scary," Mary said.

"I thought it was kind of fun."

"Yeah, real fun when someone gets mauled."

"Oh no, Mama," Hillary said. "The leopard was frightened. Did you see how it ran away? It did not want to attack. It wanted to get away fast."

"Could you tell if it was a male or female?"

"No, it was gone too fast." Hillary spoke with Old Peter for a moment. "Peter says it was a young female. He was close enough to get a good look under legs."

Peter pretended to pull an imaginary cat's tail up and look under it.

"I think I'd like to ride in the front with Masenga on our way back to camp," Mary said. "The tsetses are horrible today. I'm being eaten alive."

"Yes. You must sit in the front. It is not good to have flies bite you all over."

I wished I had a picture of the look on Old Peter's face when that leopard leapt from the tree. Peter was nimble for his age—he even out-jumped his much younger colleague, Young Peter.

"I had a nice conversation with Masenga today," Mary said.

"About what?"

"About our families mostly. Did you know that he has three wives and nine kids?"

"Did you tell him we had nine kids as well?"

"He thought that was amazing. I believe he thought it was odd that I bore all nine myself."

"Different culture, I guess."

"I'd say. He is such a nice man though. It's a shame we never truly get to know many of the people over here."

"Sometimes we do."

"It's never enough. Most of these men have interesting stories, if we just had time to hear them."

"Cari and Bill are back," Dick said.

"Do you think they got something?"

"Let's go find out."

We met them at the skinning shed. They were unloading a Cape buffalo.

"He's gorgeous," Mary said.

Cari was not crying.

Teri joined us a moment later. "Congratulations on your buffalo," she said.

"Thanks," Bill said. "Have you heard from Dan today?"

"He was in a few minutes ago to drop off a hartebeest. They're skinning it now."

"So how was your first buffalo?" Mary asked.

"Unbelievable," Bill said. "We found his tracks around nine this morning. They were fresh and he was alone. It was the perfect situation."

"It was kind of gross when Bariki stuck his finger in the poop to see how warm it was," Cari said. "You know he shook your hand later," she said to Bill.

"By that point, I didn't care. Anyway, we tracked him for almost two hours before we thought we might have lost the trail."

"I didn't know we'd be gone that long. I didn't take a hat or anything."

"What did you think of the trackers?"

"At first it was easy for me to follow the tracks," Cari said. "Then we went through some tall grass and then some thick trees with lots of undergrowth. I kept looking for tracks, but rarely saw any after we left the open fields."

"We were starting to split up in a wide circle to look for tracks when he jumped up out of the trees right next to us and took off running," Bill said. "Scared the hell out of us."

"It was right there, as close as the truck." Cari pointed to the Land Cruiser. "I couldn't believe how loud it was. I thought he was going to charge over us. Gam said we needed to follow him as close as we could because a buffalo will not walk too far without stopping. We did for about twenty more minutes, before we lost the track."

"We spread out in a big circle again. Gam, Cari, and I got separated from the others by about three hundred yards, when Gam saw him through his binos and had us come over. He told Cari to stay behind a tree while he and I snuck thirty yards closer. He was looking right at us, kind of staring us down. I used Gam's shoulder for a rest and shot him in the chest. When he took off, he headed right toward Cari. That scared the crap out of me. I thought it might try to run her down. But after about fifteen yards, he turned left and ran straight away from us."

"I never even saw him run my way, so I wasn't too scared."

"Gam and I took off running as fast as we could, trying to keep up with the bull. It seemed like we ran forever. Somehow, Earnest had caught up with us, even though he started three hundred yards back. Of course, we lost the tracks again. It was hit and miss for a while. We'd find the tracks, lose the tracks, then find them again. We were trying to re-find the tracks when Earnest tapped Gam on the shoulder and pointed at the buffalo. It was standing broadside and went down at the next shot. I put one more into him for insurance. Then Gam and I snuck around him. We tapped him with the barrel and he didn't move. Then we poked him in the eye and he didn't blink. We were sure he was dead. Gam started to lift his horns to see where the first shot hit him, when the buffalo moved. Gam jumped about ten feet. I jumped twice as far. I was ready to shoot him again when Gam told me to wait. It was just nerves. It scared the hell out of us, but was funny after the fact." Bill started laughing.

"Tell them the really funny part," Cari said.

"If you think it was so funny, you should tell it."

Cari gave Bill one of those half-joking, *you had better watch it* looks.

"About ten minutes later, we were trying to roll him over for pictures and Bariki grabbed his tail and I grabbed his horns. We started to pull when this loud growling grunt came out of his mouth. I dropped the horns and jumped back about ten feet. I don't know if I thought he was coming back to life or what, but when you're holding a buffalo's horns and it growls at you, it's a little scary. Everybody was laughing at me, but I think I'd jump just as far if it happened again."

Hillary walked up from the mess tent. "Please clean up, have a drink by the fire, and we will eat when Dan returns." He smiled and bowed his head before spinning around to return to his tent.

"I guess we're done hunting for the day."

"Guess so."

"I'm going to go have a shower then," Mary said. "Congratulations on your buffalo again, Billy. He is beautiful."

After cleaning up, we found Bill, Cari, and Teri by the fire. Bill stood a little taller that day and drank each beer as if it were the last one in camp. Cari and Teri were trying to pry open a baobab seedpod.

"It's slimy," Cari said when it finally popped open.

"You think some of these trees and plants would grow in Nebraska?" Teri asked mostly to herself.

"Maybe in a controlled environment," I said. "Baobabs probably take hundreds of years to grow. You'd never see the results."

"Maybe even longer," Teri said. "They are one of the longest living trees on earth. It would be interesting to see a young one. Or how long they take to germinate. I asked Alex what a young one looked like. He said he didn't know, that he'd never seen a young one. Then, he asked around and none of the trackers or anyone else had either. It was as if it had never occurred to them to wonder about something like what a young baobab looks like. Too busy trying to survive I guess."

When Dan's group returned, they drove straight to the skinning shed. That usually meant he had found success. We hurried over. It was a sable. One of Africa's most striking antelope—impressive in every way.

"I wish I could have been there," Teri said.

After dinner that evening, as we sat around the campfire, Cari spoke softly.

"Is it true that Gam has an uncle who is an Al Qaeda member?" she asked Hillary.

"I do not know of this. But it is possible. Gam is from the north where terrorism has a strong network. You do not need to worry about Gamshard. He is no terrorist. He loves America. He has no control over his uncle. You do not control your uncle, do you?"

"It just shocks me. I could never see Gam involved in something like that."

"Gam is a very good man. Did he tell you about this uncle?"

"He was not proud of it. He said that his uncle gave funds to a very bad organization and that most people here are against terrorism."

"This is true. But much of Africa is always in some war. Not so true for Tanzania though. Tanzania, even with many different tribes, is a peaceful country."

Mary and I had traveled throughout Africa, much of it in places where the political scuffling and power grabs went mostly unnoticed. There were a few times when we ran into rebel groups or "military" roadblocks where kids in army greens searched our luggage. Even though we had guns and ammunition, they never seemed to find anything that interested them. In our limited experience, Africa rarely showed her ugly side. And she had a side so ugly most people turned away and pretended it did not exist. I hoped we would never have anything other than a peripheral encounter with Africa's darker alter ego. We were wholly content with the annoyance of tsetse flies and the rare possibility of a dangerous meeting with a member of the local wildlife as the most unpleasant experiences on a continent we loved.

We saw true poverty—people too poor to have running water let alone cars, televisions, and laptops. Yet their lack of material things rarely affected their contentedness. Most of the varied groups of people we had the pleasure to meet in Africa would not understand depression the way westerners do. Finding basic, everyday needs like food, water, and shelter consume too much of their time.

I hoped I never met Gam's uncle. My idea of Africa, though laced with a bit of delusional nostalgia, was still my Africa. A guy like Gam's uncle would only serve to chip away at my belief that there were places on earth that God wanted to keep just how they were.

We spent the next morning checking the same baits we checked every morning. We found evidence of what looked to be a lone male lion feeding on one bait and a possible male leopard on another. Neither track looked huge. We decided to hold off on building a blind or *machan* until we checked the remaining baits.

Hyenas had fed on the bait we placed near the *korongo* the day before. Peter raised it another foot to discourage the short-legged undertakers of Africa from stealing away with too much of our lion feed.

We had only driven five or ten minutes when Hillary told Masenga to stop.

"Look," he pointed. "*Nyati*. Buffalo."

We all grabbed our binoculars.

"Bull?" I said.

"Too far to see. But a lone buffalo is usually a bull. We will move closer." Using a stick, Hillary waved it in front of the windshield, giving Masenga the signal to go. He leaned down. "*Polepole*," he said. Slowly.

We inched forward.

With the same navigational stick, Hillary guided Masenga around two separate warthog dens lying hidden in three-foot grass.

Peter had a perplexed look on his face. He pulled his binoculars down, then back up, then down again. "No *nyati*," he said.

"No?"

"No."

Hillary stared through his binoculars, trying to steady them as Masenga rolled the Land Cruiser forward. "Yes. *Nyati*. There." Hillary pointed to the dark form under the shade of an acacia.

"*Mti*," Peter said.

"No *mti*. Nyati." Not nearly as convinced as Peter, Hillary told Masenga to stop.

We spent the next few minutes studying the unmoving object through our binoculars. I thought it looked like a buffalo.

"*Mti*," Peter said again.

"What does that mean, *mti*?" Mary asked.

"It means tree."

"Tree?" I said. "It's black and lying down. And it sure looks like it has horns to me."

"Black from fire," Peter said.

"What about the horns?" I asked.

"Not all black."

Still certain it was a buffalo, I shrugged.

"I think Peter is correct," Hillary said. "It looks like a tree now." He tapped the windshield with his stick and said, "Go. Go."

We drove right up to it—a half-burned log, the gray on one end posing as buffalo horns.

"Should I shoot it?" I asked.

"No, not big enough. We can do better."

Having checked every bait, we hunted our way back to camp. We spotted a few wildebeest and zebra, as well as one decent kudu that we would tell the kids about. We were nearly halfway back to camp when a voice from behind us said, "*Simba, simba.*"

Masenga nearly threw us over the hood when he slammed on the brakes.

A mature male lion glanced up from his slumber beneath an acacia. He regarded us with a bit of annoyance before popping to his feet and jogging toward the heavier brush. At nearly three hundred yards and only a few more seconds before he entered the brush, it seemed like a perfect opportunity to try out one of the predator calls I had brought along. I wanted to see how the local wildlife would react to a jackrabbit or cottontail squeal.

Snatching a jackrabbit call from my bag, I blew a quick series of screams. The lion stopped to look back at us, but did not linger. Though not known for the kind of stealth that leopards posses, lions can be like phantoms, disappearing into a patch of grass or a slight fold in the earth with one smooth movement as if gliding on a layer of air.

"That is a good bait tree," Hillary said pointing. "We can get the lion to come back and Mama can shoot it. I think this is our lion."

"I hope so," I said. "It was a good lion."

"Yes, very good."

On the way back to camp, Mary asked if we could stop to gather lucky beans for the girls. We passed a pod mahogany every day. Each pod contained a few brown and bright orange seeds the size of nickels that were locally said to bring good luck.

"We have twice the luck today," Hillary said as we walked toward the tree.

"What do you mean?"

"Look here. A dead porcupine. The quills are lucky like the beans."

We gathered quills while Peter knocked a seedpod from the tree. The ground below the tree was littered with opened pods without a seed in sight. Hornbills cracked them open to eat the arils and discarded the seeds. Any seed not devoured by rodents had a chance to germinate into new trees.

Mary found a few seeds and took two quills each and placed them on the ground outside each of the girl's tents.

"I'm not superstitious," she said. "But I hope it brings them luck."

"You don't think being in Tanzania is lucky enough?"

"I think we've been lucky."

When the kids came in, they met us by the fire. Bill had shot a hyena and a sable.

"I must have stepped in or stood on an ant pile today," Cari said.

"No."

"It was horrible. They were all over me. Thousands of them crawling and biting me. Gam told me to go behind a bush remove all my clothes, including my shoes and socks, and pick off the ants. You cannot imagine all the ants that were on my shoes. They had big pinchers and getting them off was next to impossible, especially on the skin. Bill and I spent forty minutes trying to flick and pluck them off—I was in tears. There was no way we were going to get them all off my clothes, so we doused them with bug spray. I smelled especially pleasant the rest of the day."

"Did it help with the tsetse flies?" Teri asked.

"I think it attracted them. They wouldn't leave me alone and didn't seem to be biting anyone else."

"Your sable is beautiful, Billy," Mary said.

"I almost shot it," Cari said.

"Why didn't you?"

"I couldn't find him through the scope."

"You still have one on license," I said. "You'll get one."

"I hope so."

As was often the case, Mary and I left for our tent before anyone else.

"Cari seems to be doing better," I said.

"I think she's beginning to understand it. I'm glad she hasn't rejected it wholesale. If she did, I could appreciate why. It's a difficult thing when an animal dies, especially at your own hand, but it's also a beautiful thing and I think that's what she's beginning to understand. I hope she decides to shoot, but if she doesn't, I will support her."

We climbed into the *machan* an hour before first light and waited. We waited to hear footsteps or rustling or, better yet, gnawing. Sitting in darkness, you often imagine noises or imagine your preferred quarry as the source of every little click. I did and I am sure Mary did. An hour and half later, we checked the bait—no gnawing, no claw marks, no tracks. Our perfectly placed bait, dripping with the scent of blood and reaching out to every scavenger within two miles had not enticed our king of beasts.

In Africa, new opportunities replace failed attempts. Sometimes they took days, sometimes, years, like the many Mary and I spent pursuing mountain nyala in

Ethiopia. But if you give them time and effort, they always appear.

Finding only hyena tracks at two of the eleven baits left me second-guessing the placements. It was something I rarely did. We hired professional hunters because they had knowledge and experience that we did not have—who was I to question that expertise? I did not live there. I did not hunt cats for a living. I did not spend years refining my cat-hunting skills. But sometimes, human nature gets the best of us and we question people we know are using their years of experience to enhance the few moments we were fortunate enough to spend in their country. I wanted to tell Hillary that this bait or that bait had not been sniffed by lions yet and it might be time to think about moving them.

As we were checking the twelfth and last bait, something happened that reminded me of my lack of expertise. I had shot a few big cats and hunted them almost every year for ten years. I knew more than the average person about hanging baits and building *machans* and reading a lion's behavior signals, but compared to Hillary, Peter, and the others, I knew next to nothing. It would be like trying to tell a politician how to lie.

Pulling up to the last bait—a leopard bait—I wondered: *What was the point?* It had not been touched before. We had not seen any tracks or any sign. We had to drive an extra thirty minutes away from camp just to get there. We would probably be having sandwiches on the truck again.

I usually like to get out and inspect the bait and help check for tracks. Sometimes, it took half an hour or longer. I decided to close my eyes for a quick nap. I heard some chatter over by the tree. Pessimism overshadowed a brief inclination to look up and I started to drift off.

Something touched my shoulder. Thinking I must have fallen into Mary, I scooted away. This time it came as a tapping, light but full of energy. Forcing myself to open my eyes, I saw Young Peter's smiling face. "Come, bait gone. Big *chui* hungry. Impala close. Bring rifle."

Bring rifle? *Chui?* Had they found a leopard?

I was fumbling with a handful of bullets when Hillary jogged over. "Stay. We will drive. It is too close to the bait to shoot. We do not want to disturb the leopard."

I relaxed back into the high chair as Hillary slipped behind the wheel. "We will go to find fresh bait," he said. "The boys will build the blind. We will come back to check tomorrow. I think then the leopard will return and the blind will be ready for us. He is a big leopard. The bait is gone."

Though only looking for an impala, we spooked a pair of bull kudu big enough that we had to pursue them. After thirty minutes trudging behind them, twice being grabbed by wait-a-bit thorns, we lost the track. After another thirty minutes, we had our impala and were cruising back to the tree. Peter and the boys had built a fine blind, as usual. It looked as uncomfortable as ever—four feet tall, five feet wide, and on uneven ground. A perfect leopard blind. I could not wait to use it.

"Will we sit in it tonight?" Mary asked.

"Not tonight. Leopard fed much already. His belly needs rest. If he comes back to check for food tonight, we will sit tomorrow. He will be hungry then. We will try for lion near camp tonight."

Hope had reclaimed its rightful spot at the forefront of my thoughts. Now, every bait had a chance, no matter how untouched it had been. Now, Hillary and Peter were genius cat hunters with a near legendary ability to outthink lions and leopards. Did I expect to encounter a lion at the same tree that had been untouched the previous night? Not really. But I had regained that guarded optimism that allowed each new day to begin with limitless possibilities.

That evening, the lion failed to show. No surprise.

We had not tracked anything that day, had not hiked much, but I could hardly keep my eyes open through dinner. I slept heavy that night, knowing we had eleven days remaining—knowing we would get another chance at the cats. We were in Tanzania after all, where new opportunities reinvented themselves by the day.

We never made it back to the leopard bait the next day. Every bait along the river road had been untouched, but when we checked baits at two different *korongos*, we found both devoured.

"Look here." Hillary pointed at a tuft of hair caught in the tree bark. The hairs were long and a few of them black. "This is a good lion. Big mane." Hillary held his hands out like a child describing a giant bluegill he had just caught. In some ways, Hillary was like a kid. He smiled like a kid, always finding joy in the simple everyday pleasures, such as a scorpion scampering across the dining table or an elephant blocking a road with uprooted trees.

"Guess we need to find some bait," I said. Finding bait meant hunting. After driving and checking baits for the last few hours, a stalk sounded refreshing.

"This area has many zebras." Hillary fired an imaginary rifle.

Once again, we left Peter, Masenga, Andres, and Gama to build a *machan* and clear a shooting path while we went to have fun.

Zebra hunting is often a game of extremes—it is either extremely easy or extremely hard. Usually a species of opportunity, you rarely set out specifically to hunt zebra. Besides some of the specialty species, the Big Five, kudu and eland, most common game species fit into the opportunity category. If you see a good one while hunting something else, you try for a stalk. If your stalk fails, no big deal. You'll get another chance. That was usually the case with zebra, but there were times when these striped beauties drove us mad. A zebra on an open *veldt* is often easy to see, but difficult to approach. A zebra in a *miombo* forest is like a chameleon. Like an optical illusion, you can look right through its stripes.

We needed to shoot a zebra quickly—a prime setup for a difficult hunt. The hunting gods, however, smiled on us that day. We found a herd with a stallion within a few minutes. They saw us and darted into the brush.

"They will not go far. They will relax in cover."

We found them easily enough. Or, I should say, Hillary found them. He pointed and said, "There."

I looked right through them. Then they moved. There they were—disappearing again into the trees.

"Let us move closer."

We did. I looked through them again. The zebras moved off again. This time, I kept my eyes on them and still almost lost them.

"The stallion is in front. Shoot when you can."

Unwilling to risk them moving off again, I touched the trigger when the cross-hairs settled inside a white stripe on the shoulder. The stallion rocked at the impact, kicking his back legs before running. One of the toughest common animals in Africa, zebras rarely go down easily. I have seen zebras take more lead than a Chinese-manufactured toy before dropping.

Blood-splattered leaves led us twenty yards to the heaped zebra. It looked as if he had toppled over in mid-stride. Leaving the carcass, we hurried back to the bait tree where we picked up the others to help with transport. Within minutes, the boys had secured their favorite cuts of meat and were hanging fresh bait.

"Just when I think I understand how you choose a tree to hang bait, you pick something that seems so out of place," Mary said to Hillary

Hanging the bait on a lonely tree two hundred yards from a waterhole would have seemed logical enough, if numerous thick-trunked trees suitable for hanging bait had not surrounded the same waterhole.

"Cotton always told me to think like a lion or a leopard. From this tree, a lion can keep watch for an invading hyena or other scavenger. He can protect his food and get water when he is thirsty. Many times, it is not possible to use a good tree like this. Many times, there is no good place for a *machan*. Here we have big tree to build a *machan*." Hillary pointed to a nearby baobab with a large flat area where the branches forked away from a gray trunk scarred by elephants.

To think like a lion, or better yet, a leopard—that would be something. Animals were creatures of habit just as people were. If you could get them into a pattern or slightly alter that pattern, you could capitalize on any mistakes. With cats, you find a tree you would like to use if you were a lion or leopard and then use an enticement to push them into a temporary pattern you can exploit. Sometimes it works, often it does not, but there are few proven ways to hunt creatures of the shadows. Creatures that move under the cloak of darkness.

Think, bait, wait.

In the end, it is the waiting that gets to you. Actually, it is the waiting in the blind that tests the limits of your mental endurance. At least when you are driving from bait to bait, day after day, mile after jarring mile, you have the distraction of open human communication. In a dark, stuffy blind, you have only the need of that same interaction. Spending night after silent night crammed in a blind, waiting for a creature that specializes in killing, taxes your thoughts. It is one of the reasons I love leopard hunting.

"Do you hear?" Hillary asked.

"What?"

"There is a vehicle coming. Must be Teri and Dan. Do you want to meet them at the road? We could have lunch before we sit in the *machan*."

"I would like that very much," Mary said.

"We must hurry." Hillary jumped behind the wheel and bounced and jerked the Land Cruiser over heavy grass and through thin thorn bushes. He even barreled over a few young trees that sprung up defiantly as they cleared the rear bumper. Mary and I had white-knuckle grips on the roll bar and bruises on our bouncing behinds by the time we reached the road.

Had we missed them?

Hillary cut the engine. For a few moments, all I heard were the echoing hum of the engine and memories of branches slapping my forearm as I tried to guard my face. It itched now as droplets of pinkish blood formed from irritating scratches.

We sat on the road, without talking, without moving, trying to hear over the wind's whisper, imagining the steady drum of an approaching vehicle beyond our own breath.

Hillary pointed down the road and smiled with his eyes.

I did not hear anything.

Hillary nodded.

Nothing but wind.

Then, less than a minute before the Land Cruiser drove into view, I finally heard it. Maybe sixty years of shooting without protection had something to do with that. I had never seen Hillary wear earmuffs or plugs and he was no adolescent. Being in tune with your environment makes up for many physical limitations. In our world, where background noise eats away our natural senses from the moment of birth, tuning into your environment takes work. For Hillary, it was essential to his profession.

"Did you find your lion this morning?" Teri asked.

"No, did you?"

"No."

"That makes the score zero to four—lions."

"We have time," Hillary said. "There are many baits, many *simba*, many *chui*. You should not worry."

"We'll see you tonight then," Mary said after a quick sable-steak sandwich.

"Hopefully, it'll be late and you'll be singing."

Mary crossed her fingers and held them in the air.

The *machan* had just enough room for three pygmy-sized people. At least it was level.

"I'm glad we're in the tree. I don't like ground blinds for lions," Mary said. "Lions are too curious."

It was common for lions to walk to the base of your tree and inspect the odd shape in its branches. For some reason, it felt safer if an animal, which usually refrains from climbing, would have to shinny up a tree to gnaw on your bones.

It was best if the shooter—Mary—sat on one side with a sturdy elbow rest. You should always find a comfortable shooting position long before a lion or leopard shows. By the time a cat closes in on the bait, you should be able to calm your nerves. With a solid rest, it should be target practice. In reality, it is rarely easy to shoot one of the Big Five. There is something about shooting an animal that can bite, claw, gore, or stomp you to death that overwhelms some people. Those animals have an air about them, a certain look in their eyes, in the way they bore into you, that is designed to instill fear. Whether it is the buffalo's *don't come any closer or you'll regret it* look, or the lion's arrogance, sizing you up as if you are beneath it, or the elephant's somber, gentle stare that can change without warning, all these beasts have the ability to make you question your mortality. I loved hunting dangerous game.

The tight *machan* took the stuffy air from outside and pushed it in around us. Our sweaty elbows tapped against one another as we sat reading or fighting sleep. The three of us, Hillary, Mary, and I, had spent enough time waiting for lions that we did not expect to see or hear anything until closer to dusk—still two hours distant.

A rustle or a snapping twig or no reason at all caused us to glance up through the holes to the fly-gathering bait. It looked the same. Back to the book. Heat and fatigue pulled my head toward my chest only to have a need to remain alert snap it back up. If the lion came, I wanted to see it. I just could not fight the silent monotony. Then a distant hyena call instigated a low grunt response from a lion. Though not close, it was not as far as the hyena. Hope pushed the heat and fatigue and doubt from our tight little blind as strongly as if the lion had been standing at the bait.

We waited. For a sound. A barking baboon? A scampering warthog? A chattering bird? Something. Anything.

We waited and we watched. We watched a slab of meat as it seemed to morph into a black glob. We watched the sun dip into the tree line like it was sinking in quicksand. We watched grayness become blackness.

There. The unmistakable sound of crunching bone. I tried to see through the black soup. Nothing. I did not even know if I was looking down. Another crunch. Was the lion out there? I heard Hillary moving, his elbow ramming mine. Then, finally, he clicked on a flashlight and shined it on the bait. Below the bait, at the base of the tree, sat a lonely hyena, gnawing on a two-foot bone steadied between its paws.

We watched it crunch away. It stared into the light once or twice, apathetic to the source, and continued eating for another few minutes. Then its ears perked and it stared into the darkness. Taking the bone with it, we watched as it skulked into the night. And then we watched headlights approach from a diesel-engine vehicle.

With Peter's help, we climbed down the wobbly branch steps and plopped into our well-worn seats high above the bed of the truck. We did not talk. Then, with only the rumbling of the Land Cruiser beneath us and the sound of cold air rushing by our ears, we drove three hours back to camp in darkness and silence.

Pulling in around midnight, my teeth were chattering and my gloved fingers numb.

"We will have dinner in fifteen minutes," Hillary said.

All I wanted was a warm bed. "Sounds good."

"Looks like the skinners are busy. Should we go have a look?" Mary asked.

All I wanted was to wash my hands and get something to eat. "Sounds like fun."

"Is that a lion? Oh, it is. It is a lion. Whose truck is that? Is that Cari and Billy's truck?"

"I think so," I said.

"Look how big its head is. That's a big lion. Not a huge mane, but a beautiful cat. Haven't Billy and Cari had a wonderful safari?"

We strolled hand-in-hand to our tent under the stars, under the clicks and squeaks of the night, under the memory of our own first safari and we squeezed our fingers together.

I washed my hands and sat on the bed while Mary cleaned up. I never made it to dinner. I vaguely remember her telling me to take off my shoes. Then I slept.

Cari and Bill were still talking about their lion the next morning. Your first lion was worth talking about. I took my first lion nearly fifteen years earlier and it still came up in conversation. I had images of it when Cari told me about the lion they shot the night before.

"When we saw that the tracks were as big as Gam's hand, we knew it was a big lion. There were female tracks as well—the male's were twice as big. There was nothing left of the bait except a few scraps clinging to the chain."

"You're lucky they came back."

"We got ready for a long wait in the blind, when a female snuck out of the grass to inspect the bait. It was funny. She stood on her back feet, sniffed the meat, slapped it with her paw and then walked back into the grass. Didn't we eat this yesterday? I could not see her after she went into the grass, but Gam could see her and the male. He told Bill it was a big, old male, but without a huge mane."

"It was a big lion, I'll tell you that," Mary said.

"When Bill shot, it started roaring and thrashing," Cari said. "When it stopped, Gam thought it was dead, but we decided to wait for the truck to show up anyway. Before the truck showed, we heard him grunting and roaring to our right, so we knew he was moving. Gam told me to wait at the blind while he, Bill, and the others went to have a look. They didn't find the lion at first. Then, I heard a shot and didn't know if they killed him or not." Cari took a sip of her drink. "They had."

When it comes to that point, it's all about putting the lion down quickly. The safety of the group and ending any suffering are the only priorities. The only thing worse than wounding an animal was wounding a dangerous animal.

"My shot ended up being a little too far forward," Bill said. "It went through one shoulder and came out the neck on the other side. Only one lung was hit. He was dead; he just didn't know it yet."

"I've seen animals live a long time with a hole in one lung."

"I'm just glad we found him as fast as we did."

"Congratulations," I said. "It's a fine lion." There was no such thing as a bad lion, but an old lion like that was well past prime breeding age, and with lions that was more important than mane size.

I fell asleep at breakfast. Hillary asked if we wanted to stay in camp and rest while he and Masenga checked baits. I don't think Mary wanted to, but I was feeling weak and needed the sleep. I went back to the tent and dozed the morning away.

"Do you want to eat lunch?" Mary woke me just after noon.

Hillary sat waiting for us at the dining table.

"Anything eating?" I asked him.

"No lion, but a big leopard jumped from the tree when we arrived. We hung more bait and will sit in the *machan* tonight. Maybe we interrupted the *chui's* meal and he will still be hungry."

"Only one way to find out," I said.

"Yes. We must sit in the *machan* and wait. When the leopard comes, you shoot. But do not miss. You miss and all of this work is for nothing." Hillary had a coy smile on his face.

"Have you already built the *machan*?" Mary asked.

"I sent Masenga with the others to build it while we eat and rest. We will leave at four."

I took a shower and then I slept until it was time to leave. Mary fixed her hair or something. I could not really tell for sure in my sleep.

Waiting in a hot, stuffy *machan* for a leopard is not that much different from waiting in a hot, stuffy *machan* for a lion. You cannot move. You cannot talk. You cannot cough. You cannot urinate—you never want to drink too much before sitting in a blind or *machan*.

With leopards, all of those requirements are more important. Lions will tolerate a little sound or slight movement. Leopards will patiently study your ambush site, sometimes for hours before showing themselves. If they feel anything is amiss, you will never see them. Most of the time, you never see them.

I know we were quiet for four hours that night. Nobody moved. Nobody talked. Nobody snored. Nobody coughed. Nobody urinated. Yet the leopard did not show. Maybe the sweat beads racing down the side of my head scared it off. Maybe it could hear the creaking in my aging joints. Maybe it just found something else to eat. All I knew for sure was the leopard did not show.

As the late nights of nothing grew in number, our drives back to camp became as silent as our time in the *machans*. We had worked so hard being quiet that we were too exhausted for conversation. Mary and I sometimes slept until a deep rut in the road jolted us or a low-hanging branch slapped us in the head. I lost my hat twice on the way back to camp that night. Even when we drove down into a sandy *korongo* and the tires buried themselves, we quietly went to work digging and dinking until both back tires found traction and rolled through the sand. Then we slumped back into our seats and stared at the headlights as they bounced in the darkness.

We rolled into camp again without fanfare. There was no singing or dancing. There was no leopard or lion.

COMMUNICATION: TERI

"We're getting a little frustrated with Alex," I said to my parents.

"Why's that?"

"Just a lot of little things. It's not really a big deal, we just thought we'd let you know." Dan and I had approached my parents outside their tent. Their professional hunter, Hillary, ran the camp. Maybe he needed to know about these things, maybe he did not. Mom and Dad were experienced clients. They had been hunting all over the world. They had been to Africa nearly thirty times. Maybe our concerns were unfounded. We did not know, but needed to talk to someone who might.

"We never know what's going on. Alex rarely fills us in, even when we ask specific questions."

"Have you said anything to him about this?" my dad asked.

"Not directly. We just keep asking questions, hoping he'll fill us in. Sometimes he does, sometimes he seems to ignore us. But that's not our main concern. We can figure out a lot just by paying attention."

"Tell them about the game guard," Dan said.

"There have been a couple of times where he has made it clear he would let us do something illegal if we paid him."

"Illegal? Like what?"

"That's one of the problems. We aren't one hundred percent sure on some of the laws. He's hard to understand, but I'm sure one time he was telling us that if we shot something we didn't like, he would turn his head for us to shoot another animal of the same species—as long as we paid him."

"Does he do this in front of Alex?"

"No, usually when Alex is checking a bait or something."

"Bribes are common practice over here. Sometimes a few extra dollars can get things done faster or get you better service, but that usually falls under tipping.

Even that can spin into something more sinister. If it doesn't feel right, it probably isn't."

"Today, when we left Teri in camp and told her we'd be back at lunch, I just figured we'd stay close. When it was almost noon, Alex told me we were too far from camp to go back and just to tell Teri that we had been on a track and couldn't get away from it."

"Basically, he told Dan to lie to me."

"I told him I'd tell her the truth. I never know how far from camp we are. Half the time we could be driving in circles and I wouldn't know it out here. It's hard to get your bearings. Especially when the sun is high."

"What do you think we should do?"

"I'd give it a couple of more days. I can talk to Hillary for you. I know you're reluctant to offend the guy who controls your safari, but you might want to tell Alex how you feel. These guys work for tips. He'll change things quickly if he's worried about getting paid."

"We didn't want to ruffle any feathers unless it was absolutely necessary. Thanks for talking with us."

As Dan and I walked back to our tent, I took his hand. "You're not leaving me in camp again tomorrow."

"Wouldn't dream of it. I know you probably wanted to get out of camp, but I'm okay with the fact we didn't go back out this evening. These seventeen-hour days are starting to take a toll. It was nice to sit back and relax for a change, hang out by the fire, drink a few beers, tell a few stories."

"I enjoy those things as well, but I've been in camp for three days. I'm ready to get back in the field."

I thought the camp was awesome, if not a little primitive, and I had a chance to get to know some of the staff better than if I had been hunting those three days. I felt a close bond with Joel, the headwaiter, especially. He spoke better English than most of the staff and was easy to talk to. Working in Hillary's camp during the six-month-long hunting season kept him from his two sons and one daughter for half the year. I do not know how he did it. I left for a few weeks and could hardly stand it. I guess you do what you have to. Joel was a good man.

Camp was made up of five green burlap wall tents, each covered by a grass canopy for extra shade. The staff slept in round huts made from mud, grass, and twigs. Hillary had placed his camp beside a mostly dry riverbed lined with seven-foot-high grass thicker than a wheat field and trees of every size and shape. Large rock outcroppings in the sandy river bottom looked almost like hippos. Every day, two men would walk down to a muddy looking spot and start digging. From these holes, they gathered water in buckets and filled fifty-gallon oil drums for showers, cooking, and washing clothing.

I was stuck in camp, but too restless to sleep much. Between fitful bouts of sleep, I strolled around with a young man named Christian and studied the plants and trees. He knew more about flora than anyone I had met before then. He knew how long it took seeds of each plant to germinate, which plants could survive with little water, which plants thrived with little sun. He told me about the whistling thorn tree's relationship with ants. He said the tree provides a home and food for the ants and they protect the tree from invading browsers. When a giraffe tries to eat the acacia's leaves, the ants will swarm and attack its tongue until they drive it away. My three days in camp with Christian were an education. This young man, with his fire for life and his knowledge of botany, would have a significant impact on the rest of my life. Those three days inflamed a passion for plants that I have had since I was a girl digging in the dirt beside my grandmother while she cultivated her garden. I was ready to get back into the field, but my time in camp was far from wasted.

"Is everything okay?" Hillary asked Dan at breakfast.

"I'm just tired."

"Are you sure?"

"Yes."

A few minutes later, we saw Hillary pull my father to the side. I kept glancing over at them as they talked quietly.

Alex walked in and said, "Good morning."

"Hello," I said without looking up from my French toast and sausage. The rest of breakfast was quiet. Gamshard and Cari talked a little, but I mostly hovered over my food until I was finished.

When we pulled away from camp, I stared at the trees and grass as they blurred past. The morning smelled wet, like a fresh rain.

"Today we check new baits," Alex said. "Gam has his *simba* and *chui*. We use his baits now. If no feeding, we go find buffalo."

"There are your mom and dad," Dan said, pointing ahead.

"Look like they wait to talk," Alex said.

We pulled beside them.

"There is a good roan past the black tree," Hillary said. "You should go look and see if you can find it."

"Where are you guys off too?" I asked.

"Going to check some baits," Dad said. "We're the Master Baiters."

Dan and I laughed. Mom looked horrified. I am not sure anybody else got it.

An eight-foot trunk of a tree burned black from a grass fire stood out like a lighthouse each day as we returned to camp. Whenever we saw the black tree trunk, we knew our three-hour drive was almost complete. The lone roan antelope bolted as soon as we rounded the bend. Its horns swept back near its shoulders, and its slightly stiff gait was a lesson in grace as it almost floated on the dust below its hooves.

"Is good bull. We track," Alex said.

We caught up to the roan once, but the wind changed and he spooked.

"Wind no good. We check baits."

Alex almost seemed to be going out of his way to talk to us.

Only one bait had been touched. A small leopard, probably a female, had barely nibbled on it. Her tracks revealed that she had paced around the tree many times before climbing up for a taste. And that is all she had. I couldn't blame her. The meat was turning black and smelled like a garbage dump. I gagged when the breeze blew just right. According to Alex, it was not quite rancid enough for the leopard. I knew some picky eaters, but this gal took it to a different level.

With the stench creeping toward the back of my throat, we headed for the truck. A warthog burst from a nearby bush like a rocket.

"*Gwasi, gwasi.*" Warthog. Rafael, our head tracker, was pointing. "Shoot, shoot."

Dan glanced at Alex while unslinging his rifle.

"Yes, good warthog. Shoot."

Dropping to one knee, Dan aimed. The warthog, running straight away, was not going to stop.

"Shoot in Texas," Alex said. "Shoot in Texas."

The boar had his tail pointed up, giving Dan a perfect bull's-eye target. He fired. The warthog rolled and slid on its side, stopping in a lifeless heap.

Raphael and Able cheered and clapped. Kevin, the assistant professional hunter, smiled at me. He was always looking at me. I moved closer to Dan who had reloaded and was keeping his aim on the warthog.

Dan had made a perfect Texas heart shot. The warthog had died almost instantly. Quick killing shots are the best. I did not want to go through the same experience Cari had.

Kevin asked if he could get a photo with the warthog and me. Strange as that seemed, I obliged. Other than me, Kevin probably did the least amount of work.

"I think he has a crush on you," Dan whispered in my ear, while Raphael and Able loaded the warthog into the back.

A dark energy seemed to surround Kevin. Maybe it was just me, but I stayed close to my husband when Kevin was around. Dan thought it was funny. Maybe it was. He was probably just being sweet. It just did not feel right to me and I tend to put a lot of trust in my feelings.

The tsetse flies bombarded the truck that afternoon. They stung my shoulder. They stung my back. They stung my arms. They stung my ankles. I slapped and shrieked and cursed.

Alex had Michael stop the truck.

"We get *tembo* dung to make burn. It drive tsetse away."

"Did he just say that we're going to burn elephant shit?"

"Yes, I believe he did. My mom told me that it works, but the smell can get as bad as the flies if you're not moving."

Rafael and Able gathered armfuls of elephant dung. I thought Kevin was doing the same, but when he walked back to the truck, he had a handful of small flowers. They looked like white dandelions. He handed them to me.

"What are they called?" I asked.

Kevin shrugged. "I give. You keep."

"Thank you." I placed them in my camera bag and snapped it shut. Dan chuckled. I gave him an elbow to the ribs.

Some tsetse flies managed to push through the smelly smoke and feast on my legs, but the smoke fought back the onslaught we had been experiencing. The stench was not nearly as vulgar as the leopard bait. I never gagged once.

Half an hour before sunset, Rafael spotted a herd of fifty buffalo marching across a muddy *dambo*. The lead buffalo were entering a *mopane* forest. A swath of thick grass ran in a line parallel to their path. If they stayed out of that, we would have a chance. I hated following buffalo late in the afternoon. You could end up following a wounded bull in the dark. Nobody wanted that.

Alex let Rafael lead, but prodded him to hurry. They led us into the grass. First Rafael, then Alex, then Dan, then me, and right behind me, Kevin. When I turned around, he had a dopey smile on his face. I did not turn around again.

We pushed through the grass for twenty-five yards before peeking out the other side. The buffalo were ambling from right to left, a few of them stopping to sample green shoots of grass.

"Bull there," Alex whispered, pointing with his eyes. "Gray on back. You see?"

"The grass is too tall. I need the sticks," Dan said.

He set up; his finger clicked the safety.

A grunt and a crash of hooves had everyone ducking and stumbling back. A straggling cow had scented us and alerted the entire herd.

Weaving quickly through the grass and trees, we caught up to them within a few minutes. They busted us again before we could relocate the bull and we called off the chase. By then, the sunless light had turned a gray-blue and the shadows had deepened to the color of black shoe polish. In the grass, it was like one big shadow. The truck was little more than a silhouette by the time we came through the grass into the *dambo*.

"I don't think I've ever seen so many stars." I snuggled up to Dan during the long drive to camp.

"No smog to cover it up," he said.

"There's not that much smog in Sidney."

"No, but there are usually more clouds."

"Have you ever seen this many stars on a clear night anywhere else?"

"If I have, I don't remember it."

Rafael, Able, and Kasano, the game guard, seemed excited about something. They kept up a lively chatter all the way back.

"I think my throat would be sore if I talked that much."

Dan did not say anything. He just held me tighter as we stared at the stars and listened to a rhythmic language. Buffalo or no buffalo, it was a good night.

"Good morning," Hillary said. He was alone in the mess tent. "Did you sleep well?"

"We did," I said. "How about you?"

"These lions and leopards keep me awake as I try to think of ways to outsmart them." Hillary tapped his temple. "They have caused us a great deal of stress on this hunt."

"Bill's done well," Dan said.

"Yes, the rest of us could use some of his luck."

"Are you getting worried?" I asked.

"We must keep baiting. There are many lions and leopards here. We also have many prey species for them to hunt. I think, maybe they are just being too picky. Now that Bill does not need as much luck, I think we will take some of it. Then, I may be able to sleep better."

Dan rubbed Bill's head as we finished breakfast—just in case.

Like most mornings, we drove around with a stinky zebra or smelly wildebeest hindquarter in the back and checked baits. The sooner we found one where a cat had been feeding, the sooner we could get that rising odor out of the truck.

"We have two leopard tracks," Alex said. "One small, one good. Need more bait. Check again."

"Are you going to use it all here?"

"No, not all."

"That's too bad."

Alex smiled, but I was unsure if he understood my sarcasm.

I had a difficult time keeping my eyes open as we rumbled toward the next bait tree. Then, someone said *jackal* and the vehicle jerked to a stop. My eyes popped open and I snapped my head back and forth.

"You're going to have to stand up," Dan said. "He's way over there under a lone umbrella acacia."

I found him through the binoculars. "I don't know how anybody saw that. He barely looks like a rock with the naked eye."

"You want to go after him?" Dan asked.

"No, I think we leave. Too close to bait. If lion feed, shot scare away."

Sure enough, when we set up to glass the bait from a distance, we found a single male lion standing beneath it.

It was a young male, probably banished from his pride within the last month. We watched until we were certain he was alone. Then we snuck in close for a photo op. His mostly non-existent mane hung under his neck like peach fuzz. He stood panting lightly below the suspended buffalo leg, his pink tongue lapping over an impressive set of teeth. Unaware of our presence, his yellow eyes revealed a young cat, confident, proud, and naïve. He almost looked tame. Had he seen us, his eyes would have revealed something else. I preferred this encounter.

Two hundred yards from the next bait, we found three female lions resting in the grass. As we drove past them, the big female growled and gave us a quick false charge. At the bait, we discovered the females had been feeding. There were no male tracks.

"We will put out last meat here. Hope for male to come. Male like to find female, yes."

"And I was just getting used to the smell."

As we were hanging the bait, we heard a truck approaching. It was my parents and Hillary.

"Did you see the lionesses?" I asked.

"No. Where were they?"

"You drove right past them just over there." I pointed.

"They're still there." Dan was looking through his binoculars.

"You must have been within a few feet of them."

"That just goes to show you how well they blend," Dad said.

"We saw you baiting the tree and did not expect to see lions," Hillary said. "I think we would see them if we were looking."

"What are you guys doing?" I asked.

"Looking for a zebra or wildebeest," Dad said. "The Master Baiters need more bait."

"We just saw a herd of zebras," Dan said.

"Where?" Hillary asked Alex.

A set of quick directions and they were gone.

At the next two baits, we found hyena tracks. Alex decided to raise each of the baits another foot.

We settled in for a quiet lunch under an acacia where the nearby brush and grass grew six feet high or more. The trackers had moved off to smoke and chew on *biltong* in a small patch of shade beside an impressively tall termite mound. Alex kept glancing at them as if he wished he could join them. An unsettling feeling rose from my gut and gnawed at my thoughts. I felt like I could hear something moving in the brush, but when I concentrated, it was only the breeze.

"What is it?" Dan asked.

"I don't know." I was whispering so Alex wouldn't hear. "I have this feeling that something's out there."

"I've been thinking the same thing," Dan said. "It's weird. Like I really want to go take a look."

"Exactly."

Ten minutes later, the crew piled into the Land Cruiser and we drove off.

"What are you doing?" I asked Dan as we rounded a corner.

"This happy little thorn is poking my toe." He was digging in a shoe he had just taken off.

"We're supposed to be looking for buffalo."

Dan stared out into the trees and grass. "What the hell is that?" he said.

I thought he was joking.

"*Simba*." I heard from behind us.

"It's a lion," I said.

One, two, three, four. The more we looked, the bigger the pride became. We saw one good male for sure. They had not seen us yet.

"Load gun," Alex said as we stepped away from the Land Cruiser.

Three young females scampered into the grass as we rounded a corner. I did not think they had seen us. While Alex and Raphael concentrated on the big male, I noticed more female lions as well as a number of cubs. One in the grass to our left; two beside a thorn bush to our right; four just ahead. Was that one behind that tree? They were everywhere. Alex had to see them, didn't he? I wanted to say something, but we were on a stalk, silence imperative.

When Dan set up to shoot with his .375, I tried to keep my eyes on some of the females. I had a strong feeling that something was not right, like someone was tugging on my shirt collar. Dan fired.

Hit, the lion walked toward the long grass. Dan shot again. The cat vanished into the silence.

We walked slowly toward where the lion had entered the grass. There—female. There—another female. Over there—female. Back there—female. We were surrounded. The six-foot grass was too thick. Visibility inside would be a foot or two at best.

"Too dangerous. We must wait. We get car, come back to wait."

We drove the truck up to the tall grass and tried to peer in from a higher vantage point. It was too thick.

A growl erupted from behind us. The sound of something running through the grass.

"*Hobe! Hobe!*" Go! Go!

Michael punched the gas just in time. Kevin almost flipped out the back, his legs shooting into the air as he tumbled. An angry lioness was gaining, her lips curling into a snarl, deep primal grunts reminding us of fear.

"*Haraka!*" Hurry!

Kevin, now sitting in the back, had a mixture of shock, fear, and relief on his face.

Finally, the lioness gave up. Maybe we'd put enough distance between her and her cubs.

"You should throw bait. Slow her down," Alex said.

Raphael laughed and shook his head. "No. No bait. Throw Kevin. Kevin bait."

"That not bad idea," Alex said. "We put bait nearby. Maybe wounded lion get hungry come for eat."

We jumped from the bed of the truck to tie a bait to a nearby tree.

"The zebra leg. It has rope. We tie quickly." Raphael cocked his head toward the lioness, now one hundred yards behind us. She had been joined by five other females. They walked toward us with a menacing gait—a rival gang defending their home turf from intruders. The male appeared behind them. He was favoring his right leg.

When we left the truck, Dan had grabbed his .30-06. "I think the scope on the .375 is off," he had said. "I know this one's dead on."

"Shoot."

Some of the females were growling lightly. They kept coming. Standing broadside to us, the male glared in our direction.

Dan fired.

The male dropped.

The females scattered—a little.

They quickly regrouped when a young male swaggered over to the male Dan had shot.

"Why don't they run off?"

"Many lions have courage from numbers. Shoot into air."

Some of the lions took notice.

"Shoot again."

This time they walked off, disappearing one by one into the long grass. The young male was the last to go. He glanced back at the old male one last time. Then he was gone.

I stared after him for a long time, stared into the hypnotic slow dance of the swaying grass, and wished I could read his thoughts. What was inside his head?

Did he find it beneath him to be giving way to other creatures? Did he see the old male's death as an opportunity or feel it as a loss? Or did he think nothing at all, his actions triggered by instinct alone?

Dan put one more bullet into the already dead lion. Silence followed by an echoing blast, then silence again. The second silence hung in the air like the final note of *Taps*.

I knelt down next to the majestic animal. I touched its head and said a prayer of thanks. Then I wiped tears from my eyes. They were tears of joy. They were tears of sadness. We all took turns hugging and congratulating Dan. Kasano wrapped his arms around him and would not let go. Alex later told us that Kasano was a new game guard and had never been on a lion hunt before. When Kasano finally let Dan go, he said, "*Asante sana.* Thank you. Thank you. Thank you."

We decorated the Land Cruiser with leaves and branches during the slow drive to camp. Just when the first grass-roofed hut was in view, the boys began the lion and leopard song.

"Is happy song. Happy hunters come back safe. Happy hunters kill great beast. Is happy song when time begin. Is happy song now."

Their melodious voices seemed to lift us into the air, allowing our emotions to soar like bateleur eagles, graceful, joyful, hopeful.

Joel led a procession of bodies as they ran down the road to great us. They raised their arms and jumped up and down. Cari, Bill, and Gamshard soon joined them. Cari joined in the chorus. Bill smiled knowingly. Dan stood a little taller. And I wiped away another tear.

Late that night, when Mom and Dad returned from another long stretch sitting in a *machan*, Dan and I told our story again.

"Good job," Dad said. He shook Dan's hand and then turned to walk away.

"I'm so happy for you. Isn't it great," Mom said. Her eyes were heavy. They both carried themselves as if they were stuck in a never-ending marathon.

"I hope they get their cats soon," I said to Dan.

"It's starting to wear them down."

"We haven't spent much time with them on this hunt. They're gone so early in the morning and don't get back until late. Dad looks tired and weak. I hope he's not overdoing it."

"You're dad doesn't know how to take it easy. It's not in him."

"I think he needs to learn."

"Ain't gonna happen."

I looked at the stars. They seemed to twinkle a little brighter that night. The generator hummed at the edge of camp. Laughing and soft voices rose from the staff quarters. Light smoke from the dying campfire wafted toward us. A quick breeze cooled the air just enough to give me goose bumps. As we strolled toward our tent, toward the end of a day I would never forget, I took my husband's hand and we looked up at the stars together.

NEVER FORGET: MARY

"I wish we could spend more time with the kids," I said.

"You want to give up on the cats?"

"I just hope we get them soon."

We both dozed on and off during the thirty-minute ride to the first bait. Dick even snored some. I hoped I didn't.

"The leopard fed again," Hillary said.

"Too bad he never shows until after dark. Even then, he tiptoes around waiting for us to skedaddle."

"He is a cautious cat," Hillary said. "I do not think this is the cat for us. I think we should take this bait to the lion tree. A lion is not as wary as a leopard."

At the tree, a single lioness guarded the meat as if the king had threatened her well-being if she were to fail. She dug her paws into the ground and growled as we approached. We yelled at her and waved our arms in the air. Hillary kept his rifle pointed in her direction. She took a few quick steps toward us and when we did not retreat, she trotted into the brush. Just before disappearing, she turned and snarled at us.

High in a gray, thick-limbed tree, the *machan* overlooked a small lake riddled with yellow water lilies. Giant pod mahogany and palm trees surrounded and shaded most of the lake. Lazing beneath their shadows, heavy green grasses provided food and cover for the grazers and browsers. In all my time in *machans*, I had never sat with a more picturesque backdrop.

Numerous bugs flew in and attacked us with kamikaze resolve and the sun hammered us with heat, but the surrounding peace helped me ignore them. If a lion showed, great. If one did not, I would be okay with that too. I could have waited in that spot all day—if we didn't have a dozen more lion and leopard baits to check.

Many of the baits had been hit, but nothing that would pull us from our initial plan. We hiked to a shady spot beside the river to have a picnic lunch while enjoying the boisterous company of a hippo pod. They splashed around, grunting and growling while we prepared our lunch. The hippos kept wary eyes on our actions.

As he often did, Peter appeared as if from under a thorn bush. He spoke quietly with Hillary as we munched on our cold sandwiches.

"Your rifle, Mary. There is a steenbok in a small clearing just there." Hillary pointed. "Peter says it is a good male. Bring your rifle; we will have a look."

I hammered it with a bullet in its boiler room. Peter jumped and cheered.

"Good shot, Mama." He raced into the clearing to retrieve our most recent kill. Carrying it by its back legs to the river, he skinned and deboned it. Within moments, he and the others were cooking the fresh meat over an open fire. Occasionally, the scent drifted into our shade. Our sandwiches now tasted bland.

Peter, though, bless his heart, offered us a leaf full of the steenbok's finest cuts. "You make very good shot, Mama. Meat is very good."

"*Asante sana.*"

"*Karibu.*"

The primordial allure of killing your food and eating it right there in the field made it extra tender. I asked if we could save some for the next day's sandwiches, but weighing in at only twenty-five pounds on the hoof, the steenbok meat was gone before I opened my mouth. The boys had devoured it within minutes.

Several lionesses hurried into the brush when we returned to the *machan*.

"It is better if they are not here," Hillary said. "If the boys are loud when they leave, the lions will believe we are all gone. But we will be in the tree waiting for them."

"What happened to the ladder?" With rope made from the bark of a nearby fig tree, Peter and the others had tied steps to two long straight sticks. It was mangled.

"An elephant must have found it offensive," Hillary said.

It took ten minutes to build another sturdy, twelve-step ladder so that Dick and I could climb safely into a *machan* twenty feet in the air.

We listened as the Land Cruiser putted into the thorns. For a few minutes, silence strangled the air. Nobody moved. Then, like a bell, giving the world permission to speak, a ground hornbill called in the distance. Its guttural roar-like call seemed to awaken every other bird and creature in the area. The chirps, squeaks, screams, ticks, rustles, caws, and tweets seemed to ricochet off one another.

I was staring toward the smooth lake, where most of the sounds seemed to emanate from, when Peter tapped my leg.

"*Simba,*" he whispered.

Already? I looked toward the bait much too quickly. A lioness. Once she made sure all was safe, she could call the rest of the pride—hopefully there was an old male nearby.

She ambled to the bait, studied it for a few moments, and then turned to walk toward our tree. She drifted closer. Her yellow, perfectly round eyes seemed to stare into mine, as if to warn me that she knew I was there and that she did not care for it. Once under my side of the *machan*, she stared up at me, those calculating eyes probing mine for a sign of weakness.

We did not move. We did not breathe.

After making sure I was convinced of my inferiority to her, she strutted behind us and melted into the brush. Quiet returned.

For the next two hours, I watched the grass and the thorns and the trees. Besides the occasional dove or kingfisher, nothing moved. At times, I thought I heard soft walking.

At dusk, six lionesses and a few cubs moved in as if they had just returned home from a hard day's work. The male must have stopped off for a drink. As the females took up strategic positions around the bait, we waited. As one of them started to gnaw on the bottom half of the hanging meat, we waited. As the cubs wrestled one another and tugged on an adult's ears, we waited. And as the gray light turned a dark blue under a full moon, we waited. When the male still did not show, we quit waiting.

The rising rumble in the distance signaled the Land Cruiser's return. Its approach did not seem to bother the lions.

"Lions rule the night," Hillary said, his voice just above a whisper. "They do not fear even the vehicle."

As they rolled in, I noticed the game guard standing in the back with his automatic rifle tight to his shoulder. He looked scared and prime to overreact. I hoped the lions did not show any aggression. Andrew held a big spotlight on two of the closest females. One of them stood up to face the new intruders. The game guard leaned into his rifle. The lioness growled, her bared incisors glimmering in the artificial light. Three more growls from the surrounding lionesses felt like a vice on the back of my neck. Then every one of them disappeared. Were they regrouping? Were they gone for good? They had not seemed frightened.

We hurried down the ladder and piled into the Land Cruiser. I was not at ease until I felt the night air cooling my face as we sped into the darkness.

Just as I was beginning to doze off, I heard someone say, "*Simba.*"

The truck jerked to a stop. Right there, in the middle of the road stood a big male, the rest of his pride lurking on either side of us.

"There are at least twenty," Hillary said.

"Look at him. He thinks the road belongs to him. It's like he expects us to turn and run."

It was stare-down. Who would flinch first? He was standing in our road. He was blocking our path to camp. He was not used to giving way. While we concentrated on him, the lionesses and cubs moved to our sides. A few of them were close enough that they could have jumped into the back with us. I wanted to start moving. Once they were behind us, they stopped and watched, their eyes reflecting the beams from our flashlights. My light jumped from one set of eyes to the next. I needed to know their positions. They seemed to be forming a plan. The male would move out of the way if we just drove toward him. I knew he would. I guess everybody else believed we were perfectly safe. Didn't they understand that Mama always knows best?

Other than the steady hum of the generator, camp was quiet when we pulled in just before midnight. Hungry and tired, we ate a quick bite and dragged ourselves down the dirt path toward our tent.

"You guys better sleep in tomorrow." Cari's voice called from the darkness. She and Teri met up with us at our tent.

"It's hard to shoot a leopard if he's gone before you get there."

"We're going to sleep until seven. You should as well."

"We could use a little extra rest, Dick. We keep falling asleep in the truck."

"Whatever you want to do."

"We'll tell Hillary," Teri said. "He's still in the dining tent."

I put my head on the pillow, closed my eyes, and then I heard an unassuming voice waking us. "Good morning. Good morning."

Was it seven already? I just fell asleep, didn't I? "Thank you." My feet flopped to the floor. "Wake up, Dick. It's time to get ready."

Dick grumbled and then said, "I'm up." He did not open his eyes.

I brushed my teeth and started working on my hair. "Are you going to get up, Dick?"

"I'm up. I told you that." This time, he rolled out of bed.

"We must go to the open savannah first. We need more bait." Hillary was staring at the riverbed and nibbling on a piece of toast.

"We are the Master Baiters."

"I wish I could be a Master Baiter like you," Teri said.

"You guys are horrible," I said. "I used to wash your mouth out with soap for that kind of thing."

"Dad started it."

"You know I've never cared who started it."

Dick dropped a zebra with one shot just after ten o'clock. We headed for the bait where we sat the previous evening.

Shortly before arriving, Hillary told Durani to stop the vehicle. "These lions have been too aggressive. It would be best if we all loaded up and had our rifles ready in case the females become cheeky. They may not be willing to give up their kill easily—even though they did not kill it."

We held our weapons at the edge of the vehicle and searched the nearby grass as we approached the bait tree. I tried to prepare myself for anything, tried to appear poised and ready for a quick charge. My palms sweat and my knee would not stop shaking. We never saw a lion.

Hillary joined us in the shade, while Peter, Andrew, and Durani replenished the bait. "There are signs of a big male. Many tracks and this." He held up a single hair. Heavy and black, it drooped over his index finger.

"Looks like one we might want to get a better look at."

"He has not fed yet. I found this hair on a thorn bush beside a trail. I think he will be hungry soon."

Hillary watched the boys hanging the zebra, but he did not seem to be paying attention. "I think maybe we will build a bigger *machan*. One we can sleep in. If the lions are here at first light, we will not disturb them with the car." Hillary seemed to be thinking aloud more than asking for our opinion.

I had slept in *machans* before. I preferred not to. They were usually uncomfortable; lions were loud at night, growling and roaring and fighting; and I was always afraid one of them might try to climb the tree. I needed sleep if I was going to shoot a dangerous animal. But if Hillary decided our best chance was to sleep in a tree, then I would sleep in a tree. Well, maybe I would not sleep.

"We need to check all the baits first," Hillary said. "And see if a better opportunity will find us."

A leopard had fed at the first bait we checked. Looked like a male. Female lions ate off the next bait. Females and cubs at the one after that. Another probable male leopard. A possible female leopard on the next.

We found three lionesses and three cubs guarding the final bait. From across a *korongo*, they watched our movements carefully.

"I want to check for a male. See if he left any tracks or hair."

Peter and Andrew hopped out to gather rocks. When they had their arms full, they came back to the truck. Standing close in case they had to throw themselves back in, they began lobbing golf ball-sized stones across the rocky *korongo*, yelling and waving their arms between tosses. After two or three stones ricocheted off boulders ten yards short of the lions, two of the females began growling. Finally, they rounded up the cubs and moved into the grass, snarling back at us the entire time.

We took our rifles across the *korongo* to search for signs of a male. Without spending any time checking nearby bush trails, we decided there was no male with them and retreated back to the vehicle. I was the first one in the truck. I knew those females were out there somewhere watching us.

"We will sit for leopard tonight," Hillary said. "The male lions are not showing themselves. If we give them a night free from our presence, maybe they will be braver."

For some reason, I did not think it was the lions that needed courage.

We sat in silence until after dark, waiting for a leopard. We might as well have been waiting for a ghost.

It was close to midnight again when we made it back to camp. Too late to see how the kids had done. Almost too late to eat. Dick was snoring before I pulled my socks off.

"Take your time for breakfast," Hillary said. "Peter, Gama, and I will go to check the close lion bait."

We were finished with breakfast and waiting when the truck returned. "The lions did not feed last night, but we found many tracks leading into the *korongo*. We will put up another bait further downstream."

"How many will that make in that *korongo*?"

Hillary counted quickly in his head. "Five spread out over many miles. The lions will come. If I were a lion, I would come."

So we spent the morning doing what we usually did—hanging and checking baits. The *korongo* was a riverbed trickling with water—it raged during the rainy season. Walking quietly was impossible. Dry, crunchy leaves covered the ground even with many brown, yellow, and orange leaves having yet to fall. Some of the trees were still lush and green. Below the trees, green bushes clung to the side of the *korongo*, sucking the moisture that remained underground. Surrounding them, small saplings sprouted feebly as if reaching for a small taste of the sun. A few clusters of white and yellow flowers found a way to bloom. The sun had not yet raised enough to warm the low air in the ravine. We could still see our breath. Within an hour, we would be sweating.

By the time we finished checking every bait, we found that one male leopard had fed, as well as one male lion where two cheeky lionesses growled at us and false-charged before allowing us to inspect the bait.

"I think it might be best if you each hunt from different *machans* tonight."

I did not care for the idea.

"Whatever you think helps our chances," Dick said.

"I suppose, if that's what you think is best." I would have rather stayed with Dick.

"You and I will sit for lion," Hillary said. "Dick will go with Peter and Gama to wait for leopard."

I was tired. Dick could hardly keep his eyes open. He looked like he had been riding a roller coaster for ten days straight and he hated roller coasters.

While Hillary, Dick, and I ate lunch, Peter, Andrew, Gama, and Durani chopped at the bases of saplings, branches, and grass and loaded the back of the Land Cruiser to the top of the bed.

"Are you going to finish your sandwich or boiled eggs?" I asked Dick.

He shook his head.

"Do you mind if I give them to the boys?"

The trackers usually brought *biltong* and hand-rolled cigarettes for lunch. We tried to supplement their meager lunches with some of our own. Peter always smiled graciously and bowed when I handed it over. "*Asante sana*. Thank you."

When they finished our leftovers, we drove to the leopard bait, where we built a quick blind for Dick, Peter, and Gama. We closed them up with big, leafy branches. Peter smiled and waved. Dick already had his nose in a book.

"Good luck," I hollered to him.

"Thanks, you too." His voice was muffled behind the grass and branches.

On the way to the lion *machan*, Hillary had Durani stop to cut down a wide acacia bush. It was leafless, gray, and bursting with thorns.

"What's that for?" I asked.

"We will put it at the bottom of the ladder to make sure one of those cheeky female lions does not try to climb into the *machan* with us."

That made me feel *so* much better about hunting without Dick.

When Durani closed us in, I felt cold and alone. Focused light filtered through the shooting holes and the dry air felt stuffy and constricting inside the blind. I tried to read, but I checked the bait so often I never finished a single page before one heavy, old female lion and one three-year-old cruised in for dinner.

The old gal gave us a distrustful stare and then they ate. For two hours, they took turns gnawing and tearing at the muscle of a kudu's foreleg. The crunching and ripping sounds slithered up the tree and crawled under my skin. Hillary seemed bored with them.

While one of them fed, the other watched the grass. I kept expecting a big male to claim the free meal. He never showed.

When the sun set and dusk's gray turned a hard blue, I began wishing for Durani to return with the Land Cruiser. The growling and grinding was bad enough when I could see the lions. In darkness, it dug like a corkscrew in the back of my neck.

Then it stopped. That was worse. I peered into blackness. I heard soft, pacing steps. My eyes probably shined like lighthouses to their excellent night vision. For all I knew, one of them was studying the best way to climb our tree to nibble on dessert.

I heard the click of Hillary's flashlight and searched the beam for hungry eyes. One of them was staring up at us from behind the bait tree. Her yellow eyes reflected the light and looked like glowing orbs or ghostly creatures suspended in the blackness. I could not see the other lion. *Please don't let her be under the tree.*

Hillary clicked the flashlight off. Wasn't he worried about the other lioness? The quiet tightened its grip around me, tricking me into believing I was being stalked.

When I first thought I heard the vehicle, I almost clapped my hands. When it didn't show, I felt abandoned. Why was it taking so long? Had something happened to Dick? Maybe he got his leopard. Even if he had, they should have been back by then. Where was that other lioness? What if she went to get the male? What if she could sense my fear? Why didn't Hillary turn the light back on? I would give him some fresh batteries back at camp if he were worried about that.

The next time I thought I heard the vehicle I tempered my expectations, while praying my ears did not deceive me. Then more silence. Maybe I wanted to hear it so badly that I subconsciously convinced myself the distant hum was more than a figment of my imagination.

No. Wait. There it was again. This time, I heard the distinct rattle of the diesel. I heard it coming closer. *Thank You, God.*

I did not hear the lions run off, but I was focused on the approaching vehicle. Peering through the shooting hole, I finally saw the headlights. Yippee!

"Did you see anything?" Dick asked as I climbed into my seat. It was nearly ten o'clock. We had a two hour drive back to camp.

"Females. What about you?"

"A couple of hyenas came by, but that was it."

Dick's head bobbed all the way back to camp. He went straight to bed. I had half of a bowl of soup before dragging my feet to the tent. Dick's booming snores and the distant roars of a lion couldn't even keep me awake.

"Teri and Dan leave already?" I asked Cari at breakfast.

"They wanted to get a jump on buffalo this morning."

"Hillary say you be back for lunch," Joel said. "Vincent make you something special. You no have lunch in camp much."

"That would be nice," I said.

"What time do you think you'll come in," Cari asked.

"I'd say about one."

At one thirty, we were still checking and hanging baits. We had so many hung now, it took us all morning just to check them. Our new meat came from a zebra Billy had shot the day before.

"I can't believe nothing fed last night."

"Lots of females and hyenas filled their bellies."

"We're running out of time."

"Still have five days."

"Doesn't seem like much. You think we'll sit anywhere tonight?"

"Where do you choose when you have so many options and nothing seems to be hungry?" Dick said.

"A night off would actually be nice. I'd like to visit with the kids around the fire for once."

"We'll see what Hillary has planned and go from there."

We stared into a land of tall, yellow grass undulating in the breeze. It stretched beyond our eyesight to a line of deep blue mountains coloring the horizon. Without a tree for shade, the heavy sun pushed down on our shoulders and the tsetse flies were on a mission: kill the humans; if that doesn't work, drive them mad. They attacked. I shrieked. They attacked. I slapped. They kept coming. Fly after fly, diving in and stinging with painful precision. They stung my arms. They stung my legs. They stung my back. They stung my ankles. I wanted to scream. Instead, I slapped and scratched and cooked under the midday sun. They must have liked their human flesh well done. Vile little creatures.

We managed to make it back to camp for lunch—at three o'clock. None of the kids had been in yet. We had chicken curry with rice, watermelon, and cucumber salad—we made sure to complement the chef. Cari and Billy showed up just as we were finishing.

"Shoot anything?"

"No. Bait anything?"

"We are the Master Baiters."

"That you are."

"I think we're going to take a break this afternoon. Nothing was feeding anyway."

"We're planning on doing the same. We've been hitting it hard and could use a rest."

"What about Teri and Dan?"

"Haven't seen them."

They pulled into camp just long enough to have a quick bite and rush back out. A leopard had fed. You do not waste opportunities like that.

"We salted up one of your leopard baits today," Cari said. "Gam said leopards love the salty flavor. He said that's why after they taste human flesh once, they always want it."

"Is that some old African legend?"

"That's what he said. I don't know."

"Maybe. Maybe they just figure out how slow and weak we are. I would guess it's much easier to kill a human than a sharp-horned hartebeest. Then again, maybe it's the salt. If it is, we may have found a new market for the Morton people."

"Gam says it will work," Cari said.

"It can't hurt," Dick said. "Nothing else is working."

We waited for Teri and Dan to return before eating supper. They strolled in at nine. No singing. At least they made it back before midnight.

"A big female came in," Teri said.

"What did you think?"

"I think all the waiting, the cramped space, and the boredom are all worth it when a leopard climbs into a tree next to you. What a rush. She was so beautiful, so sleek and elegant. But when you also know she is so dangerous, it makes it that much more intense."

"Did she come in quiet?"

"Before she showed up, a hyena came by. It made a lot of noise. The first we heard of the leopard was when her claws scraped on the tree as she climbed. That's when we knew she had arrived."

After dinner, we headed straight for the fire. The guys had finished all the beer a couple of days ago, but we still had some wine and amurula for a settling nightcap.

"So how's your luxury safari going, Cari?" Dan asked.

"Luxury safari?"

"You do realize you're the only one who stops for Coke breaks. The rest of us just pop one open if we're thirsty."

"I like to enjoy mine."

"What about the ladder?"

"What's wrong with the ladder?"

"Nothing. I just wish they'd make me a special ladder for climbing in and out of the truck."

"I'm sure they would if you asked. Don't even think about taking ours though."

"They're just teasing you, Cari," I said.

"I know."

"How many Coke stops do you make in a day anyway?" I asked.

"Et tu, Mother?"

We had an early morning tugging on the back of our collars, but nobody wanted the night to end. I know I didn't. Campfires are the desserts of the hunting day. You push through a hard day hunting, a great day hunting. You are tired and you have to get up early, but you always have enough time for a few minutes at the campfire. Sharing stories with an orange glimmer radiating from enthralled faces around you, feeling the cool air as it battles the penetrating heat, absorbing the smoky scent of slow-burning wood, and feeling safe under a dome of stars allows you to slip off to bed satisfied that the day had been lived well.

"We lost our game guard today," Teri said.

"Again?"

"While we were tracking buffalo. One minute he was right behind me, the next, we had to call off the hunt to find him. It's like having a five-year-old hunting in the bush with you. It's frustrating for everyone."

"At least he never loads that automatic rifle he carries," Dan said.

"What's the point of carrying it around?"

"I think it's for show. To make him feel like he has some authority. If he ever loaded it, I think I'd stay in camp."

"We get Coke breaks, a truck ladder, *and* a competent game guard," Cari said. "I'm beginning to see your point about our luxury safari."

"The mountains are beautiful." As we gained elevation, vegetation greened and the woods thickened.

"Cari and Billy said they saw klipspringer up here a few days ago. Seems thick for klipspringer."

"Maybe they were in a different area. Looks like a good spot for leopard."

"I had Peter hang two baits here last night," Hillary said. "We will check them. This is a good spot. It is difficult to hunt, but it has many leopards."

We found hyena tracks. No shortage of Africa's natural garbage disposal.

"Look over there," Hillary said. He pointed at a circling group of vultures. There had to be twenty in the air, many landing, and who knows how many already on the ground. "There has been a kill. We should have a look. Many lions have been shot on fresh kills."

We found a few vultures on the ground squabbling over scraps of an unknown creature. We drove right up. The birds flew a short distance and eyeballed us from the crooked limbs of nearby trees.

"Zebra," Peter said.

How could he tell that? All I saw were a few gnawed-on bones in a circle of bloodstained grass.

We searched the ground for tracks. Lots of lions—all females and cubs. Not one big male track. I also found a three-inch patch of skin—zebra skin.

"How long do you think it takes to devour a zebra like this?"

"Peter says they made this kill late last night."

As we drove away, some of the vultures swooped down to pick at the remaining bones.

Checking baits at the *korongo* proved just as fruitless. We had gone from cats feeding every night to nothing. Like they had all disappeared.

"I believe the full moon has them behaving strangely," Hillary said. "It is bright. They do not understand the difference between night and day."

Fourth bait—nothing. Oh well. Fifth bait—nothing. Had to be the moon. Sixth bait—nothing. At least we would get to spend another evening with the kids. Seventh bait—big male leopard.

"Look," Peter said. He pointed out the half-eaten bait, claw marks on the tree, and a paw print with the circumference of a big coffee mug. "Is very big. *Ume.*"

I could not imagine more invigorating words. Nothing like the prospect of a sharp-toothed, heavy clawed, spotted beast to get you excited about sitting in a dark, stuffy, uncomfortable blind.

We gathered sticks and branches and grass and piled them next to a bush heavy with thorns. Using the bush as a backdrop, Peter, Andrew, and Durani took the sticks and grass and wrapped them together. They built each wall individually and then Durani held them up as Peter and Andrew tied them together until they had essentially created a four-foot-tall, seven-foot-by-four-foot blind. They left the top open. The ground looked even enough and we would throw a blanket down. I was sure some rock or root or small stick would start jabbing me just as the leopard approached.

Dick peered into the blind. "Looks nice and uncomfortable."

"I guess the old bones will be creaking tonight."

"We will find some shade and eat lunch. Then we will rest until it is time to sit. Maybe tonight is our lucky night," Hillary said.

We had duiker sandwiches and rotten bananas, which I did not eat. I read two chapters of a novel, wrote in my journal, said my prayers, and unsuccessfully tried to sleep. Dick snored the entire time. Hillary seemed to be sleeping. The rest of the crew had walked off to have their lunch and had not returned. I was tired and hot and bored. Waiting to wait in a leopard blind was not much better than actually sitting in the blind. At least in the blind, there was a possibility for action. Unlike Dick and Hillary, I had a hard time falling asleep in one-hundred-degree heat while sitting on a bench seat. My neck hurt just looking at Dick, with his head all flopped over to the side. I watched a line of ants carry bits of food down a tree. I watched a hornbill bob through the air as if it were riding waves. I watched a dung beetle roll a small ball of dung three yards—it took him five minutes. I had a staring contest with a golf ball-sized spider with eight eyes—he won. I slapped fifty tsetse flies or the same fly fifty times. Underneath Dick's rattling snores, the background noise was a combination of tweets, chirps, squeaks, and squawks.

I lifted Dick's wrist to glance at his watch. We still had another hour before it would be time to go. I did not want to drink much before a five-hour stint in the blind. I took a drink of water anyway. Unable to sit still any longer, I went for a short walk, making sure to keep the vehicle in sight. I found lots of impala and zebra tracks. I gathered some seeds to give to Teri and picked a few yellow flowers that looked pretty, simply because I had nothing else to do.

By the time I strolled back to the Land Cruiser, Hillary and Dick were awake. A few minutes later, the rest of the crew showed up. They climbed into the bed of the truck without a word.

During the first ten minutes in the blind, I pulled a jabbing stick from under the blanket and dug up a pointy rock. After that, I found enough comfort to spend an hour reading. As the light softened, I stared out the shooting hole. I stared for as long as my eyes could take it, then I closed them and thought about what I needed to do if the leopard showed. I tried to imagine the leopard in the tree. I told myself to pick a single spot on its shoulder and squeeze. Then I stared back out the shooting hole.

The leopard never came.

I woke up just before we pulled into camp.

"I want you to sleep in tomorrow. I will go early to check baits along the *korongo*. Gamshard and your Cari have agreed to check the others. You need to rest. I believe we will be sitting for leopard or lion again tomorrow night. It will be late."

"It always is." We were too tired to argue. We were not the type to sit idle in camp, but without sleep, it was hard to function properly. You needed to be clear-headed and focused to shoot a dangerous creature like a big cat.

When Hillary and the crew returned late the following morning, they did not have the expected good news. One small leopard and packs of hyenas around the baits.

"I believe Gamshard will have better luck." Hillary was an eternal optimist.

It was our sixteenth day hunting. We could not give up, but our once-overflowing optimism waned with each passing hour. There were plenty of cats around. We had walked over their tracks. We had touched their claw marks with our fingers. We had replaced many devoured baits. They were there, just not when we were. I remember the first evening we sat in a *machan*. I felt like I'd had fifteen cups of strong coffee. Now, I struggled to keep my eyes open. Now the bait hanging in the tree was only a rotting slab of meat. It only vaguely represented the possibility of a sleek, powerful beast, standing broadside at the edge of dusk. I continued to cling to hope, but it was fading like the light during a fiery sunset.

We heard Cari's and Billy's vehicle pull in for lunch. Hillary beat them to the mess tent. "They have brought us good news."

"A leopard has fed?"

"No. Two leopards." Hillary held up two fingers.

I knew he would suggest that Dick and I hunt separately again. I knew it, but I still cringed when he did. I had nothing against hunting alone. And I enjoyed hunting with Hillary, but Dick was my partner, my hunting buddy. He gave my confidence the push it sometimes needed. He brought poise to my nervousness. Without Dick, I would never have traveled to Africa. Without Dick, I would have missed so much. I had to take the next step in my hunting life without the man whose mere presence gave me assurance.

Needing time to set up two blinds, we left right away. Cari and Billy wished us good luck. Teri and Dan were out hunting. At least we were able to see Cari for a moment.

I was into the final ten pages of the novel when it became too dark to see the words. I would have to wait to find out if the hero would save the day and get the girl. I peered through the shooting hole and found exactly what I expected. A darkening chunk of warthog hanging from a high limb. No leopard. No nothing. I sat and stared. I was not really looking at anything. I was just staring. There is not much else to do in a dark, confined space where the slightest movement could shatter your chances. I sat and stared, thinking about how much time I had spent sitting and staring; hoping a leopard, hungry enough or bold enough, would step onto a limb and silhouette itself. What if it did? How would I respond? Was I ready? I wished Dick were beside me. If the leopard did not come, what difference did it make?

I leaned close to the shooting hole, not to get a better look at that rotten meat, but to feel the cooling air. I closed my eyes and allowed it to tickle my cheeks. In the quiet, I reflected on how fortunate I had been my entire life. I grew up in a mountain community poor enough to experience the gratification of supplementing our food with meat we had to kill ourselves. I met a man who shared my faith and together we raised a family. That same man had ambitions that did not allow him to give up—he would not even know how. We started a tiny company with a shared love for the outdoors and a commitment to hard work. I was not poor anymore and the food I shot now, more often than not, supplemented the tables of other good people who were surrounded by a kind of poverty I had never known. I had hunted with, sang with, danced with, and cried with some of the most amazing people in the world.

I was unable to recall all the silent, uncomfortable hours that I spent in leopard or lion *machans*. It did not matter. Every minute had been worth it. If a leopard did not show in the few minutes remaining before dark, I would gather my gear and join my husband of forty-six years on another long ride back to camp. And that would be okay.

The scent of smoke hung lightly in the air. I looked as far to the right as I could. A soft glow was growing on the horizon. I did not think that could be good for leopard hunting. Then again, every animal on the savannah should be acclimated to a land afire.

Hillary tapped my thigh.

He was staring through his peephole still tapping my thigh. My gaze fell directly to the limb where the stinking bait hung. There was nothing there. I searched the limb from side to side and then down the trunk. There. At the base of the tree, staring up toward the inviting limb, stood an elegant creature. In the dim light, its rosettes were dark splotches against a sleek coat. Its shoulders rippled under its skin, its neck bulged with muscle, and its tail swayed slightly.

My hand took its time reaching for the rifle. Hillary was no longer tapping my thigh. I could not pull my eyes from the world's most beautiful big cat. I saw the dark collar of spots on its neck—a male. My fingers trembled. My chest rattled. My muscles tensed.

The leopard looked away from the bait, toward the fire. He glared toward the blind, his round eyes penetrating into the shooting hole. I closed my eyes. My breath burned as it scraped the walls of my lungs. When I opened my eyes, the leopard had his head cocked toward his rear, staring into the darkening shadows.

I started to move the rifle an inch toward me, then I touched the outside air with the barrel. I had to pull my gaze away to make room for the firearm. I hoped the leopard was not looking in our direction.

Hillary tapped my leg again.

I froze. I wanted to look, but I was afraid I might startle the leopard. Hillary's hand pressed on my leg. I tried not to move. It felt like I was having a minor seizure. When Hillary pulled his hand away, I risked a glance. The leopard was staring up at the bait. I moved the rifle further into the open. Pressing the butt against my shoulder, I settled in behind the scope. When I found the leopard, he was looking back as if he heard something. I could faintly hear the fire's soft warning.

I steadied the crosshairs on his shoulder. The angle was not good. Trying to take deep, soothing breaths, I waited.

Then I heard it. Shattering the silence like a rifle shot—a hyena cry. They would surely chase our cat away. I had to choose. Shoot now or risk allowing my only opportunity to slip into the night forever. My finger caressed the trigger guard. The angle was better. If I aimed slightly right, the bullet should travel through the kill zone. My eyes burned. I closed them. Shifting my weight, I relocated the leopard in the scope. The crosshairs moved an inch to the right. Then he was gone.

I remember my finger slipping from the trigger guard to the trigger. I remember finding the exact spot I wanted to shoot. I remember holding my breath. I do not remember him turning. I do not remember him running. I do not remember him slinking. One second, I was ready to squeeze; the next, I was staring at air.

The hyenas rumbled in a minute later. Four of them, slobber dripping from their mouths, horrid sounds gurgling from their throats. I almost shot one, but they never quit moving. They circled the tree, yipping and popping their jaws. They looked up and then hulked into the shadows.

Now that the leopard had gone and the hyenas had gone and it was dark, we allowed ourselves the simple pleasure of conversation.

"I do not believe he will go far." Hillary whispered. "He did not eat. He knows the hyenas could not eat... Wait. Listen. He is growling at the hyenas now. He will come back later. It would be best if we are no longer here."

As we waited for Dick, Peter, and Durani to show up with the Land Cruiser, I noticed we were almost surrounded by fire. It closed in on us from at least two directions. "The fire's getting closer."

"Gamshard's group has been relentless in their quest to burn the area. They are no longer worried about cats. They want to clear the ground for new growth and burn the grass so they can see the animals better."

"There's the leopard again."

"The hyenas are harassing him. It will give us time to leave."

Dick's crew arrived before the leopard. My husband did not have much to say. His leopard did not show. He listened to my story and then nodded off for the muscle-jarring, spine-snapping, slow ride to camp.

The kids were finishing dinner when we stumbled from the vehicle.

"We waited as long as we could, but finally got too hungry."

"We never make it back before ten," Dick said. "If you wait for us, you'll starve and then you won't get any sleep."

"You guys get anything?" I asked.

"Bill shot a buffalo, a hyena, and an impala."

"We're going to start calling your truck the meat wagon."

"Just lucky, I guess," Billy said.

The kids stayed up to share stories with us while we scarfed down fresh impala shish kabobs. I'm glad they did.

Hillary was the first to excuse himself.

It was one in the morning.

"Those impala kabobs were good last night," Teri said. "I think we need to shoot more impala."

"I love the liver," I said.

"Do you want that?" Hillary asked. "Vincent will make it right up for you."

"No, thank you."

"It is no trouble for him to make it. You must eat something. It will give you energy."

"That's okay. I'll have it another day."

I drank my cocoa and left for the tent to brush my teeth.

"Wait. Mama. Wait." Joel came running after me. "No you want to eat liver and onion?"

"Oh, has Vincent already fixed it?"

"Yes, Mama. Is good."

Joel pulled my seat out for me. My breakfast was on the table. Dick was finishing his usual bowl of cereal.

"If I don't quit eating so much, I'm going to get too fat for my clothes. The only exercise we're getting this trip is climbing in and out of the truck and the *machans*. Usually, we do some walking and tracking."

"The cats have a different plan."

"Yeah, to make me fat."

The liver was perfect. I ate it all.

The crew had loaded the back of the Land Cruiser with meat from Billy's buffalo and impala.

"We only have three more days to hunt. I'm not sure hanging more bait is going to help."

"You must have faith," Hillary said. "We will only hang meat where lions or leopards have fed. We want to give them extra incentive to return. The last day is no different from the first. Every day gives us the same chance. You will see. I believe we will find a leopard or lion feeding today."

I no longer expected to shoot a leopard. My best chance had been the night before.

We drove to one bait, checked it, drove to another, checked it, and drove to another. All morning long, we drove and checked. We replenished one bait that had been nibbled on. Then we checked the one where Dick had hunted the night before. There was not a scrap left.

Peter shinnied up the tree, scooted onto the limb, and waved the empty rope at us. Andrew threw him another rope and tied a new slab of meat on the other end. Peter pulled it up, retied it to the other rope, and left it dangling in the shadow of leaves as he shinnied back down to study the tracks.

"Good track," he said. "Hungry *chui*. Come back. Eat more." Peter shook Dick's hand. "Very good. We shoot tonight, yes?"

Dick shrugged. "Maybe."

"You shoot. I guide."

Peter sprang into the Land Cruiser. "One more." He held up his index finger. "One more. Mama shoot."

"Peter thinks we will find that another leopard has fed," Hillary said.

The last bait we checked had been fed on during the first few days of the hunt, but Hillary decided then that the tracks were not quite big enough. When we found the leopard had returned, I was not surprised when Hillary suggested that he and I sit for it. This late in the hunt, pickiness was no longer a luxury we could afford.

We climbed into the blind an hour earlier than usual. Hillary did not expect the leopard to show before dusk, but wanted every creature in the vicinity calm. He did not want anything to alert the leopard.

I had my novel finished within a few minutes. The hero did end up saving the day and getting the girl. Too bad the hunter could not get the leopard.

I closed the paperback and placed it in my bag. I began searching for a new book when I heard a faint humming. It grew louder. What was it? I glanced at Hillary. He looked up. The sky was black with bees—millions of bees. I had never seen anything like it. It was as if a dark cloud had covered the sun, only pinpricks of blue sky visible. And the faint hum had become a deafening buzz—almost a roar.

"Put your jacket on and cover your legs. You must cover your entire body or you will be stung. Your hood. Put on your hood."

They were not moving. They were suspended just above us, as if planning an attack. Had we disturbed a nearby hive? Maybe something else had. The way they hovered over us made me wonder if the crew built our blind right under a hive. I felt helpless. How would we escape if they attacked? I closed my hood over my head and cinched the strings tight. I put my gloves on and sat on my feet. Then I kept my head down and said my prayers. Before long, the buzzing died and I lifted my eyes. They were gone. Thank God.

I listened to the birds and insects and the slight crinkle of leaves shuddering in the wind. Every sound that was drowned out a moment ago seemed amplified. I pulled off my hood in order to hear them better and closed my eyes again. All was as it should be.

Then there was something else. Something both horrid and hopeful. It was one of the few warning sounds of an approaching leopard. Baboons and leopards are mortal enemies, so when a troop of baboons begins barking and screaming near a leopard bait, it often foreshadows the spotted cat's arrival. Baboon screams are like lizard claws running up the back of your neck. But when you are sitting in a leopard blind, they are welcome. Much better than bees.

It was early. Too early for leopard. Then again, the leopard is hungry when the leopard is hungry. He does not care about your schedule.

For a long time after that, silence dominated. With silence came questions. Had the leopard slipped away? Was it even there in the first place? Was it still approaching? Was it watching us?

I dared not move, even though my gut told me that there never was a leopard. Sometimes baboons just bark and scream. I dared not move, because even though my gut said one thing, my head reminded me that there was always a chance. That gave me hope. And hope is a powerful feeling.

During sunset, the baboons started up again, this time with an urgent persistence—this time they screamed of a leopard, their shrieks clearly full of hate and fear. This time the birds chirped and screeched fervently. This time, an abrupt silence signified the leopard's presence clearly. It was out there. Somewhere. Lurking in the shadows, testing the wind, surveying our trap. I told myself to hold still, to breathe quietly.

Hillary motioned for me to slide the rifle barrel through the shooting hole. Did he see the leopard? I did not.

My hands were clammy and sweat rolled beside my ear.

"The leopard is in the tree," I could barely make out Hillary's whispered words.

I peered through the scope. "I can't see him."

Hillary did not answer.

Where was it? The air was a darkening gray. I saw the bait. No leopard. I started shaking. I wanted to shout through my teeth. *Where is it?* I continued staring at the bait. Did it move? It did. The leopard was that dark spot above the bait. What camouflage. It had its back to us, but I could see it now. If it gave me an opening, I would be ready.

Finally, it stood, turned its head toward us, and exposed its shoulder. I fired.

I looked to Hillary for verification of a solid hit. I could barely see him in the dimming light.

"You shot it well, just perfect. It fell down, hit the ground, and did not go anywhere. It is lying behind the tree."

"Are you sure?"

"I'm sure."

"Good shot, Mama," Andrew said from beside Hillary. I could not see Andrew at all.

I was not sure.

We listened for ten minutes. Nothing. That was a good sign, wasn't it? Unless, of course, the leopard ran off immediately after I shot. It was now too dark to see the bait or the tree it was hanging in. Twilight in Tanzania only exists for a moment.

"I will turn on the light now," Hillary said softly.

I moved my head toward the shooting hole.

The flashlight's beam searched the ground around the tree. I didn't see anything. Not a tail; not a leg; not a spot.

Hillary and Andrew remained quiet. The light continued scanning under the brush and around the tree. I felt sick.

Hillary picked up his two-way radio and turned off the flashlight. Three times, he called for Masenga. No answer.

"You wait here, Mama. Andrew and I are going to the tree to see where your leopard fell."

"I think we should wait for the vehicle."

"Masenga did not answer. It may be a while. I just want to see."

"I don't think it's a good idea."

"Do not worry, Mama. You shot very well. We will be back in one moment." He checked the shotgun twice before moving toward the tree.

I snatched up the two-way radio and began calling for Masenga while I watched two men walk toward danger. I never heard a reply. *Please find the leopard dead.*

Please find the leopard dead. Lord, please let them find the leopard dead. Please keep them safe. I prayed the entire time they were out of the blind.

They returned after ten minutes. Hillary pulled his jacked tight to stave off the cold. Andrew did not look me in the eye.

"We did not find the leopard," Hillary said. "There is much blood below the tree. You hit him well, Mama. You will see. He did not go far. We will wait for the truck. Then we will go find him."

The fact that he wanted the extra eyes and firepower revealed his doubts.

Hillary finally received a reply on the radio. They were on their way. Dick's leopard never showed.

We did not talk while we waited. We listened instead. If the leopard was out there wounded, it might cough or otherwise give up its position. The sounds of the night were layered upon one another. You had to concentrate to hear many of the discrete whispers that blended to give the darkness its unique harmony. A few low-pitched birdcalls were accompanied by the squeaking, humming, and clicking of insects. Occasionally a strange howl or cry would rise above the underlying chorus. Many pitches and varying volumes of rustling grass and crackling leaves undulated throughout the exotic melody.

I thought I heard something walking softly, the way a leopard would move. Hillary never clicked on the flashlight to discredit or verify what I thought I heard.

After Dick's crew arrived, we slowly walked through the brush, searching with flashlights. Any shadow could lunge at us. My hands were shaking, my mind so focused I hardly noticed the men to my left and right. We took a step and stopped to search. Another step. Stop again. Despite the cold, I was sweating. What was that? Did something move? It was black. If the leopard charged, would we have time to react? Four more feet. Stop and listen. The shadows moved, waiting, like evil, murdering spirits to pounce on us. An hour and a half later, we quit.

"I am sorry, Mama," Hillary said. "But it is too dark to find blood. We must return in the morning and try to track the leopard. You shot him very well. I hope the hyenas do not find him before we do."

"I just hope we find him." I shuddered, partly from the frigid temperature, partly from a hollow, sinking pit in my stomach.

"Please, Mama, you should sit in the front. It is too cold to ride in the back."

For two hours, I rode in relative comfort while Dick and the others shivered in the back. I offered to switch with Dick at the halfway point, but he would not budge. Watching the headlights illuminate twenty yards of the winding trail road, I began to drift off. The darkness beside the lights moved like darting shadows. On more than one occasion, I thought I saw something scurry from the road, but it was always too quick to know for sure. Not even the engine's rough rumble or the jarring bumps of the road could keep me awake. Once or twice, my head whacked against the window and jolted me, but it never lasted. I could not keep my eyes open.

Despite Hillary's pleas that we eat some soup, Dick and I went to bed without supper.

I awoke during a dream for the first time in many nights, faint images of leopards prowling through thick, green brush, waiting to strike—waiting for revenge.

I had a hard time going back to sleep. My leopard was out there somewhere. He was dead or he was suffering. My stomach wiggled itself into my throat and I waited in the dark for the wake-up call.

A full moon and a sky of twinkling stars in the deep blue morning lit our walk to the vehicle. I stared at them during our drive back to the scene. I stared up at them and I prayed that we would find the leopard. My stomach continued to dissuade my hope.

A plate-sized splattering of blood stained the ground underneath the tree. It led toward a thick tangle of bushes. The moment we saw which direction the blood trail was going, I knew where the leopard was, or at least where it had been. We walked by it the night before, but it was too thick to inspect thoroughly in the darkness. The sharp-clawed cat might have been waiting in that dark layer of brush, still stewing over the wound I inflicted on it the night before. The blood trail was easy to follow in the morning light. Heavy splotches and drops splashed on the dry leaves and rocks under our feet. My stomach actually felt worse.

We moved in inches, each step deliberate and soft. The leopard was in the tangle somewhere. I felt it in the slow burn up and down my throat. It was too quiet—predator quiet. If the leopard came, it would come like lightning. React quickly or suffer a mauling. I would never forgive myself if something happened. My heart pleaded with me to pray, but my head would not allow it. I needed complete focus. More blood. It was leading us to the tangle. My grip tightened around my rifle. We took another step.

Fifty yards later, we found the leopard. It was dead.

Hillary said, "Yahoo!"

Peter clapped. "Good shot, Mama."

Andrew shook my hand. "Very good. Very good."

Dick smiled at me and I said another prayer, thanking God for the safe outcome.

When I knelt down to stroke its beautiful coat, the boys started to sing. They sang triumphantly. They sang reverently.

"I did not want to tell you, but I was worried when we started tracking," Hillary said. "There were fresh hyena tracks around the blood. We are lucky they did not get to the leopard before we did."

We moved the leopard to a nearby rock for photos and then had a drink of water while Peter and Andrew skinned it.

"Normally, we drive the cat back to the skinning shed," Hillary said. "We only have today and tomorrow left to hunt. We will skin it here and stay out all day. If we are lucky, Bwana Dick will shoot his leopard tonight. I think we are lucky." Hillary motioned toward my leopard.

In some ways, I felt relief more than anything else. We had spent nearly three weeks checking baits and sitting in blinds. I had finally taken one of the cats. I did not expect to find a lion. I did not even want to hunt for one until Dick took one of his cats.

I understood how my husband must have felt. He was happy for me; I knew that. I could see the pride in his eyes. But he was also tired. He had been sitting and baiting as long as I had. He just saw what success looked like. But for him, it was some distant goal that may never come to pass. If my small success could give him hope, he could find the endurance to finish the final two days and know, regardless of the outcome, that we gave it all we had in our pursuit of a beast with an unmatched combination of stealth, power, and instinct. Who could find disappointment in that?

"I want to rebuild Dick's blind if the leopard fed again last night," Hillary said.

"What's wrong with the old one?" Dick asked.

"I want to move it into the rocks. It is more hidden. The leopard may feel more comfortable feeding earlier if that other blind is no longer there to make him suspicious. There is a small opening in the rocks where heavy grass grows. We will make our blind to look like the same grass. I think this will work better. When we finish with that, it will be time for lunch."

The crew found a perfect nook in the rocks for the new blind. A wall of six-foot grass hid it well. I have no idea how Hillary even knew it was there. At seven feet across, it had plenty of room for the four of us who would be spending the evening there. Peter, Andrew, and Masenga chopped grass and used it to build the new blind.

When I saw Peter carrying pillows toward the blind, I wondered if Hillary planned to spend the night watching the bait. Didn't he know Dick snored like a lion? What leopard would stick around until first light listening to that? Wasn't he worried about the creepy bugs that come out at night? What about the snakes? What if the leopard knew about this little nook in the rocks? What if the leopard considered it his bed and came to investigate while we were sleeping? I did not think I brought warm enough clothes to spend the night out there. I wanted to ask Hillary about his plan, but he was busy giving orders and joking around with Dick. I waited until lunch.

"Our time is almost over. It is too far to drive back and forth in the night. It will be good, Mama. It doubles our chance of shooting a leopard. Peter says the leopard came shortly after they left last night. I think he may do so again tonight.

For the next few hours, my stomach turned like it had the night before.

Sitting in the stuffy blind, I tried to read and tried not to think about sleeping out there with five-inch bugs being hunted by five-foot snakes. I kept my gaze from the bait. If the leopard showed, I did not want to make it nervous with my googly eyes.

An hour later, I heard Hillary move. Then Dick gave me a nudge. I glanced at him. He pointed out the shooting hole.

I looked at the bait first—nothing there. Following the trunk down, I thought I saw something move to the right of the tree. My gaze shot to that direction. Its body mostly hidden by a leafy bush, a leopard stood staring up as if it were trying to figure out how an impala could have lost its back leg in a tree.

The leopard stood staring at that slab of meat for fifteen minutes. It glanced our way once. Then, as if using teleportation, it was up in the tree, standing over the bait, staring down at it. Fifteen seconds after that, it was dead on the ground. Dick does not need as much time as I do to prepare himself. He makes the decision to shoot, aims the rifle, and squeezes—nothing to it.

We gave the leopard a few minutes, watching it for movement. Dick had the crosshairs steady, his finger on the trigger. The big cat never moved.

We remained quiet for a few more minutes. It was like we could not believe it. After three weeks, with one day remaining, Dick and I both had our leopards. All those long, silent nights waiting for a ghost, alone with our thoughts, with our personal demons—they threatened to burst with relief at that moment. The unknown condition of the beast before us prevented it.

We approached slowly, two guns pointed and ready to fire. Hillary poked its back with his barrel. It did not move. We walked around to the head and he touched the cat's open eye with the same barrel—not a blink. Hillary raised his fist in the air and hollered. Peter and Andrew did a little dance, laughing and patting Dick on the back.

I cried. I could not help it.

None of us slept during the ride back to camp—not even Dick. Something indescribable fought the heavy exhaustion. When you hunt a specific animal to the point that it drains you physically and mentally, there are times when it feels pointless. Your muscles ache, you cannot think clearly, your eyes burn with a need for sleep. You start wishing only that the day will end and you can fall asleep, and maybe you can wake up with enough energy to try again in the morning. You never stay in camp, but you sometimes want to—it makes you feel like a quitter. Then on a day like every other day, it happens. Luck walks through the forest and climbs your tree.

We pulled into camp at ten thirty that night. The kids ran out to congratulate us. Peter and the crew hoisted Dick and I into chairs and carried us side by side to the fire. We danced and sang and drank. We held hands. We told stories. Just before midnight, Joel called us for dinner and we ate until we could not eat any more.

Later, on the way to the tent, we stopped at the dying campfire.

I took a moment to stare at Ben's star and I smiled a crooked little smile.

AFTERWORD

Two Hearts in Tanzania is a snapshot of memories that Dick and Mary Cabela have created during their world-wide pursuit of wild game. Of all we acquire during our brief moment on this untamable earth, it is the memories we create that we may be allowed to take with us. Some people live their lives by that possibility. Some of those people become legends.

There is a real chance that Dick and Mary will never visit Tanzania again. In some ways, they never left. It is as much a part of them as is their home. They lost something in that magical country they may never get back. That is okay. They took Tanzania with them as well. And it will stay with them forever.

When Cotton Gordon died, it was as if part of Tanzania died with him. He was so much more than a professional hunter. He was a friend. Dick and Mary continued their friendship with Joan, who courageously carried out her and Cotton's plans to hunt the world. I would love to read her story someday.

Like Tanzania, other countries have captured Dick and Mary's hearts. Countries like Cameroon, where they witnessed each of their five boys hunt Lord Derby's eland, and Ethiopia, where they chased mountain nyala across the heather-covered mountains four separate times and where Dick nearly lost his life. The list goes on: Zimbabwe, South Africa, Zambia, the South Pacific, Asia, South America, North America, and many more. Dick and Mary, and others like them, lose themselves in wild places. The hunting is important, but so are the relationships and culture and every creature from the tsetse fly to the elephant.

For Dick and Mary, hunting has always been more than stalking and shooting game. It has been a genuine way for them to connect to the feral part of themselves. It has been a glimpse into local cultures without the pomp and show of tourist traps. It has been the quiet conversation beside a warm fire at the end of a hard day. It has been developing lifelong friendships with people who make no apologies for who they are. For Dick and Mary Cabela, hunting is an integral part of what it means to be alive.

DAVID CABELA

2010

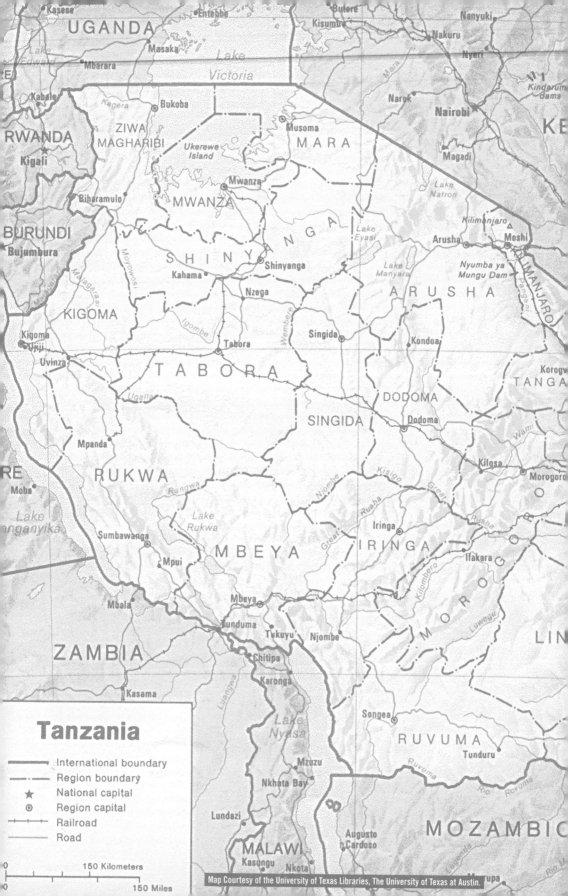

Tanzania

- —————— International boundary
- —·—·—· Region boundary
- ★ National capital
- ⊙ Region capital
- +++++ Railroad
- —————— Road

150 Kilometers

150 Miles